VOLUME THREE

bake
FROM SCRATCH™

ARTISAN RECIPES· FOR THE HOME BAKER

Brian Hart Hoffman

©83
PRESS™

83Press
1900 International Park Drive, Suite 50
Birmingham, Alabama 35243
www.83press.com

ISBN: 978-1-940772-59-2
Printed in China

VOLUME THREE

bake
FROM SCRATCH™

ARTISAN RECIPES
FOR THE HOME BAKER

BRIAN HART HOFFMAN

THE HOME BAKER IS A SPECIAL KIND OF INDIVIDUAL.

IN A WORLD OBSESSED WITH HIGH SPEED AND INSTANT GRATIFICATION, HOME BAKERS TAKE THE SLOW, MEASURED PATH TO PERFECTION. WE BAKE FROM SCRATCH.

The joys of baking are in the details: the warm scent of freshly grated nutmeg, the gratifying feeling of kneading dough by hand, and the gorgeous golden sheen of pastry just out of the oven and baked to flaky perfection. We call this long-form baking, and when done right, it stimulates every one of the senses.

With the third volume of our annual *Bake from Scratch* cookbook, bakers will find the ultimate resource for every kind of journey with dough and batter. Featuring over 600 recipes, visual tutorials, and straightforward techniques from our own test kitchen professionals as well as some of our favorite experienced bakers from around the world, it's the supreme source of baking knowledge.

Our collection of bread recipes runs the gamut from the simplest of quick breads to the most advanced of laminated doughs. We offer ways for you to recreate bakery-worthy croissants, French baguettes, and English muffins at home. For the holidays, you can try your hand at the yeasted, boozy stollen, a triumph of Old-World baking. And for those busy weeknights and low-key weekends, give our fuss-free scones, muffins, or banana bread loaves a go.

We have cakes, pies, cookies, and bars for every holiday and season, including the must-bake contemporary hits and all your favorite nostalgic classics. Find a cake for every occasion—from marble-swirled Bundts to sophisticated sheet cakes and an epic primer on classic birthday cake. In the dead heat of summer, keep it cool and creamy with our icebox pies and ice cream cakes. Once the leaves begin to change, bake our fall-ready pear and fig tarts. Come time for the holidays, we've got you covered with festive, flavorful recipes for all your cookie swaps, family feasts, and gifting needs. Just take your pick from an array of celebratory treats featuring buttery shortbread, new ways with gingerbread, bars that explore the height of decadence, and more.

These recipes go above and beyond clever flavor combinations and ingenious techniques. We created each recipe to be accessible to both the proficient and beginning baker. With helpful tips and clear, detailed instructions, we coach you every step of the way. Because our *Bake from Scratch* cookbook is about more than just the product–it's about the process. Dive in, and join us in celebrating the beloved craft, baking from scratch.

CAKES

LAYER
CAKES

Stack them up and show them off. Stuffed and covered with
buttercream, ice cream, ganache, and more, these layer
cakes will take any event from ordinary to sensational.

VIETNAMESE COFFEE CAKE

Makes 1 (8-inch) cake

We fell in love with Hummingbird High blogger Michelle Lopez's Vietnamese Iced Coffee Cake and made a black cocoa version of our own. Coffee has been elevating the flavor of classic chocolate cake for years. The winning pairing continues with this layer cake take on the sweet and strong Vietnamese Coffee. Black cocoa cake layers soaked in coffee are wrapped in a silky coat of sweetened condensed milk frosting.

1   cup (227 grams) unsalted butter, softened
1   cup (200 grams) granulated sugar
½   cup (110 grams) firmly packed dark brown sugar
3   large eggs (150 grams)
2   teaspoons (8 grams) vanilla extract
3   cups (375 grams) cake flour
½   cup (43 grams) black cocoa powder
1   teaspoon (5 grams) baking soda
1   teaspoon (3 grams) kosher salt
1   cup (240 grams) sour cream
½   cup (120 grams) boiling water
Vietnamese Coffee (recipe follows)
Vanilla Sweetened Condensed Milk Buttercream
     (recipe follows)
Chocolate Sweetened Condensed Milk Buttercream
     (recipe follows)

1. Preheat oven to 350°F (180°C). Butter and flour 3 (8-inch) round cake pans. Line bottom of pans with parchment paper; butter and flour pans again.
2. In the bowl of a stand mixer fitted with the paddle attachment, beat butter and sugars at medium speed until fluffy, 3 to 4 minutes, stopping to scrape sides of bowl. Add eggs, one at a time, beating well after each addition. Beat in vanilla.
3. In a medium bowl, sift together flour, black cocoa, baking soda, and salt. With mixer on low speed, gradually add flour mixture to butter mixture alternately with sour cream, beginning and ending with flour mixture, beating just until combined after each addition. Carefully add ½ cup (120 grams) boiling water; beat just until combined. Divide batter among prepared pans.
4. Bake until a wooden pick inserted in center comes out clean, 20 to 25 minutes. Let cool in pans for 10 minutes. Remove from pans, and let cool completely on wire racks.
5. Using a pastry brush, brush each cake layer with Vietnamese Coffee. Reserve ½ cup Vanilla Sweetened Condensed Milk Buttercream. Spread remaining Vanilla Sweetened Condensed Milk Buttercream between layers and on sides of cake. Dot sides of cake with ½ cup Chocolate Sweetened Condensed Milk Buttercream. Using a bench scraper, smear and smooth sides of cake. Decorate top of cake with remaining

½ cup Chocolate Sweetened Condensed Milk Buttercream and reserved ½ cup Vanilla Sweetened Condensed Milk Buttercream. Refrigerate until ready to serve. Let come to room temperature before serving.

VIETNAMESE COFFEE
Makes about 1 cup

3   tablespoons (18 grams) ground Vietnamese coffee*
¾   cup (180 grams) boiling water, divided
3   tablespoons (45 grams) sweetened condensed milk

1. In a drip coffee maker, place coffee grounds in a filter. Bloom coffee grounds by splashing with 1 tablespoon (15 grams) boiling water. Pour remaining boiling water in coffee maker; let coffee drip, about 5 minutes. (Alternatively, use a French press. Bloom coffee grounds by splashing with 1 tablespoon [15 grams] boiling water. Pour remaining boiling water in coffee maker; let stand for about 5 minutes before pressing down.) Once brewed, stir in condensed milk. Let cool before using.

We used Trung Nguyen Premium Blend, available at specialty food stores or online.

VANILLA SWEETENED CONDENSED MILK BUTTERCREAM
Makes about 4 cups

1   cup (227 grams) unsalted butter, softened
2   teaspoons (10 grams) Vietnamese Coffee (recipe precedes)
1   (14-ounce) can (396 grams) sweetened condensed milk
6   cups (720 grams) confectioners' sugar
½   teaspoon (1.5 grams) kosher salt

1. In the bowl of a stand mixer fitted with the paddle attachment, beat butter at medium speed until light and creamy, 6 to 7 minutes. Beat in Vietnamese Coffee. Add condensed milk in 4 additions, beating well after each addition. Beat in confectioners' sugar and salt. Reserve 1 cup for Chocolate Sweetened Condensed Milk Buttercream. Use immediately.

CHOCOLATE SWEETENED CONDENSED MILK BUTTERCREAM
Makes about 1 cup

1   cup Vanilla Sweetened Condensed Milk Buttercream
     (recipe precedes)
3   tablespoons (15 grams) black cocoa powder
2   tablespoons (30 grams) sweetened condensed milk

1. In a small bowl, stir together all ingredients using an offset spatula until combined. Use immediately.

PRO TIP
Vietnamese Coffee is a particularly strong brew, so not just any cup of joe will work in this recipe. If you can't find a Vietnamese brand, use a dark-roast coffee. The drip and French press methods of brewing ensure an extra-strong cup of coffee, so in this case, the way you brew also matters.

CLASSIC HUMMINGBIRD CAKE

Makes 1 (9-inch) cake

Bits of juicy pineapple and toasty pecan coalesce with sweet banana and warm notes of cinnamon, all blanketed in swoops of Cream Cheese Frosting. This hefty cake is far less diminutive than the bird it's named for. You don't cream the butter and sugar. (No stand mixer needed for the cake layers!) This method, along with the myriad of batter ingredients, lends a dense, crumbly texture that verges on half-cake, half-quick bread. It tastes even better the next day.

3⅓	cups (417 grams) all-purpose flour
1⅓	cups (267 grams) granulated sugar
1	teaspoon (2 grams) ground cinnamon
¾	teaspoon (3.75 grams) baking soda
½	teaspoon (1.5 grams) kosher salt
¼	teaspoon ground nutmeg
½	cup (57 grams) chopped pecans, toasted
1	cup (227 grams) mashed ripe banana
¾	cup (168 grams) canola oil
3	large eggs (150 grams), room temperature
1	teaspoon (4 grams) vanilla extract
1	cup (200 grams) finely chopped fresh pineapple

Cream Cheese Frosting (recipe follows)

1. Preheat oven to 350°F (180°C). Butter and flour 2 (9-inch) round cake pans. Line bottom of pans with parchment paper; butter and flour pans again.

2. In a large bowl, sift together flour, sugar, cinnamon, baking soda, salt, and nutmeg; stir in pecans. In a medium bowl, stir together banana, oil, eggs, and vanilla. Make a well in center of flour mixture; add banana mixture, stirring just until moistened. Fold in pineapple. Divide batter between prepared pans.

3. Bake until a wooden pick inserted in center comes out clean, 25 to 30 minutes. Let cool in pans for 10 minutes. Remove from pans, and let cool completely on wire racks. Spread Cream Cheese Frosting between layers and on top and sides of cake. Refrigerate for at least 1 hour before serving.

CREAM CHEESE FROSTING
Makes about 5½ cups

16	ounces (455 grams) cream cheese, softened
½	cup (113 grams) unsalted butter, softened
1	teaspoon (4 grams) vanilla extract
6½	cups (780 grams) confectioners' sugar

1. In the bowl of a stand mixer fitted with the paddle attachment, beat cream cheese and butter at medium speed until creamy, 3 to 4 minutes. Beat in vanilla. Gradually add confectioners' sugar, beating until smooth. Use immediately.

Photo by Stephen DeVries

APPLE SPICE CAKE WITH CINNAMON MASCARPONE FROSTING

Makes 1 (6-inch) cake

Recipe by Kelsey Siemens

Living on an apple farm means my family bakes with apples more than the average person. Pies and crisps are the usual suspects, with sauces, breads, and cakes popping up as well—but this Apple Spice Cake is something else. It's the epitome of cozy fall flavors, and the Cinnamon Mascarpone Frosting adds a bit of excitement without being overwhelmingly sweet.

¾ cup (170 grams) unsalted butter, softened
1½ cups (330 grams) firmly packed light brown sugar
3 large eggs (150 grams)
1 tablespoon (13 grams) vanilla extract
1¾ cups (219 grams) all-purpose flour
1 tablespoon (6 grams) ground cinnamon
1¼ teaspoons (6.25 grams) baking soda
1 teaspoon (2 grams) ground allspice
½ teaspoon (1 gram) ground ginger
⅛ teaspoon kosher salt
½ cup (120 grams) Greek yogurt
¾ cup (150 grams) shredded tart apple*
Cinnamon Mascarpone Frosting (recipe follows)
Garnish: ground cinnamon

1. Preheat oven to 350°F (180°C). Grease 3 (6-inch) round cake pans with butter. (See Note.)
2. In the bowl of a stand mixer fitted with the paddle attachment, beat butter and brown sugar at medium speed until fluffy, 3 to 4 minutes, stopping to scrape sides of bowl. Add eggs, one at a time, beating well after each addition. Beat in vanilla.
3. In a medium bowl, whisk together flour, cinnamon, baking soda, allspice, ginger, and salt. With mixer on low speed, gradually add half of flour mixture to butter mixture, beating just until combined. Beat in yogurt. Gradually add remaining flour mixture, beating just until combined. Gently stir in apple. Divide batter among prepared pans.
4. Bake until a wooden pick inserted in center comes out clean, 25 to 30 minutes. Let cool in pans for 5 to 10 minutes. Remove from pans, and let cool completely on wire racks.

5. Using a large serrated knife, carefully level each cake layer. Spread Cinnamon Mascarpone Frosting between layers. Using an offset spatula or butter knife, spread a thin crumb coat of Cinnamon Mascarpone Frosting on top and sides of cake. Refrigerate for 15 minutes. Spread remaining Cinnamon Mascarpone Frosting on top and sides of cake. Sprinkle with cinnamon, if desired.

*I use Elstar or Bramley apples. Granny Smith, Pink Lady, and Braeburn are also good choices.

Note: *You can also make this cake using 2 (8-inch) round cake pans.*

CINNAMON MASCARPONE FROSTING
Makes 4 cups

2 cups (480 grams) heavy whipping cream
1⅓ cups (283 grams) mascarpone cheese
¾ cup (150 grams) granulated sugar
2 teaspoons (4 grams) ground cinnamon

1. In the bowl of a stand mixer fitted with the paddle attachment, beat cream and mascarpone at medium-high speed until combined. Gradually add sugar and cinnamon, beating until smooth and stiff, about 3 minutes. Use immediately.

Photo by Kelsey Siemens

LONDON FOG CAKE

Makes 1 (8-inch) cake

Essentially an Earl Grey tea latte, the London Fog beverage was first dreamed up in Vancouver, British Columbia. For this cake version, we double down on the Earl Grey, featuring the light, bergamot-infused tea in both the rich cocoa cake and pillowy Swiss meringue buttercream. A final touch of salt from the caramel drizzle pushes this cake over the top to become a true showstopper. We adapted this cake from Tessa Huff's cookbook Layered, subbing in Earl Grey tea for the coffee in the cake, but otherwise sticking to the sweet original.

1   cup (200 grams) granulated sugar
1   cup (220 grams) firmly packed light brown sugar
⅓   cup (75 grams) canola oil
2   large eggs (100 grams)
1   large egg yolk (19 grams)
2   teaspoons (8 grams) vanilla extract
1   teaspoon (4 grams) almond extract
2½   cups (313 grams) all-purpose flour
1   cup (85 grams) unsweetened cocoa powder
2½   teaspoons (12.5 grams) baking powder
1   teaspoon (3 grams) kosher salt
¾   teaspoon (3.75 grams) baking soda
1½   cups (360 grams) whole milk
1   cup (240 grams) hot strong-brewed Earl Grey tea
Earl Grey Buttercream (recipe follows)
Salted Caramel Drizzle (recipe follows)
Garnish: flaked sea salt

1. Preheat oven to 350°F (180°C). Butter and flour 3 (8-inch) round cake pans. Line bottom of pans with parchment paper.
2. In a large bowl, stir together sugars and oil. Add eggs, egg yolk, and extracts, stirring to combine.
3. In a medium bowl, sift together flour, cocoa, baking powder, kosher salt, and baking soda. Gradually add flour mixture to sugar mixture alternately with milk, beginning and ending with flour mixture, stirring just until combined after each addition. Stir in hot tea just until combined. Divide batter among prepared pans.
4. Bake until a wooden pick inserted in center comes out clean, about 25 minutes. Let cool in pans for 10 minutes. Remove from pans, and let cool completely on wire racks. Spread Earl Grey Buttercream between layers and lightly on top and sides of cake. Refrigerate until set, 15 to 20 minutes. Pour Salted Caramel Drizzle over cake, letting it drip over edges. Garnish with sea salt, if desired.

EARL GREY BUTTERCREAM
Makes about 3 cups

2   cups (454 grams) unsalted butter, softened and divided
3   tablespoons plus 1 teaspoon (20 grams) loose Earl Grey tea
1   vanilla bean, split lengthwise, seeds scraped and reserved
5   large egg whites (150 grams)
1¼   cups (275 grams) firmly packed light brown sugar

1. In a small saucepan, bring 1 cup (227 grams) butter, loose tea, and vanilla bean and reserved seeds to a simmer over medium-low heat; simmer for 5 minutes. Remove from heat, and let steep for 5 minutes. Strain butter mixture through a fine-mesh sieve, discarding solids. Refrigerate until the consistency of softened butter, 20 to 30 minutes.
2. In the bowl of a stand mixer fitted with the whisk attachment, whisk together egg whites and brown sugar by hand. Place mixer bowl over a saucepan of simmering water. Cook, whisking occasionally, until mixture registers 155°F (68°C) to 160°F (71°C) on a candy thermometer. Carefully return bowl to stand mixer, and beat at high speed until medium-stiff peaks form, about 10 minutes. Switch to the paddle attachment.
3. With mixer on low speed, add tea-infused butter and remaining 1 cup (227 grams) butter, 2 tablespoons at a time, beating until combined. Increase mixer speed to medium-high, and beat until smooth, 3 to 5 minutes. Use immediately, or refrigerate in an airtight container for up to 3 days. Let come to room temperature before using.

SALTED CARAMEL DRIZZLE
Makes about 1¼ cups

¾   cup (150 grams) granulated sugar
2   tablespoons (42 grams) light corn syrup
2   tablespoons (30 grams) water
½   cup (120 grams) heavy whipping cream, room temperature
2   tablespoons (28 grams) unsalted butter, cubed and softened
1   teaspoon (3 grams) kosher salt
1   teaspoon (4 grams) vanilla extract

1. In a large skillet, heat sugar, corn syrup, and 2 tablespoons (30 grams) water over high heat. Cook, stirring occasionally, until golden amber colored; remove from heat. Slowly whisk in cream. Add butter, stirring until melted. Stir in salt and vanilla. Pour into a heatproof container, and let cool to room temperature. Use immediately, or refrigerate in an airtight container for up to 1 week.

MILK CHOCOLATE LAYER CAKE

Makes 1 (9-inch) cake

There's no shortage of chocolate cake recipes, but this two-layer beauty transcends comparison. A pure incarnation of rich milk chocolate flavor, our tender-crumbed cake is coated in a velvety milk chocolate ganache frosting and receives a pop of crunch and color from a sprinkle of crushed candy eggs. Trust us—this cake will have you melting.

¼   cup (57 grams) unsalted butter, softened
¾   cup (150 grams) granulated sugar
¼   cup (56 grams) untoasted sesame oil
2   large eggs (100 grams), room temperature
2½   cups (312 grams) cake flour
¼   cup (32 grams) dried nonfat milk
¼   cup (21 grams) unsweetened cocoa powder
1   teaspoon (3 grams) kosher salt
1   teaspoon (5 grams) baking soda
½   teaspoon (2.5 grams) baking powder
6   ounces (175 grams) 45% cacao milk chocolate, melted
1   cup (240 grams) whole buttermilk, room temperature and divided
1   teaspoon (4 grams) vanilla extract
½   teaspoon (2 grams) almond extract
Whipped Ganache Frosting (recipe follows)
Garnish: crushed candy-coated milk chocolate eggs*

1. Preheat oven to 350°F (180°C). Butter and flour 2 (9-inch) round cake pans.
2. In the bowl of a stand mixer fitted with the paddle attachment, beat butter, sugar, oil, and eggs at medium speed until well combined, about 2 minutes.
3. In a medium bowl, sift together flour, dried milk, cocoa, salt, baking soda, and baking powder. Add flour mixture, melted chocolate, ½ cup (120 grams) buttermilk, and extracts to butter mixture, beating until well combined. With mixer on low speed, add remaining ½ cup (120 grams) buttermilk, beating until combined. Divide batter between prepared pans.
4. Bake until a wooden pick inserted in center comes out clean, 20 to 25 minutes. Let cool in pans for 10 minutes. Remove from pans, and let cool completely on wire racks. Spread Whipped Ganache Frosting between layers and on top and sides of cake. Garnish with crushed chocolate eggs, if desired.

We used Cadbury Milk Chocolate Mini Eggs.

WHIPPED GANACHE FROSTING
Makes about 2¼ cups

12   ounces (340 grams) 45% cacao milk chocolate, chopped
1   teaspoon (4 grams) vanilla extract
½   teaspoon (1.5 grams) kosher salt
¾   cup (180 grams) heavy whipping cream

1. In a medium heatproof bowl, combine chocolate, vanilla, and salt.
2. In a small saucepan, heat cream over medium heat until just boiling. Pour hot cream over chocolate mixture; whisk until melted and smooth. Refrigerate for 1 hour.
3. Transfer chocolate mixture to the bowl of a stand mixer fitted with the whisk attachment. Beat at medium speed until light and fluffy, about 3 minutes. Use immediately.

Photo by Stephen DeVries

COCONUT PEACH CAKE

Makes 1 (9-inch) cake

Blending one traditional Southern classic, the cloud-like coconut cake, with blushing stone fruit, this triple-layer cake is an undeniable showstopper. A final coating of toasted coconut flakes brings a dash of color to the typically snowy-white appearance.

1½   cups (340 grams) unsalted butter, softened
2   cups (400 grams) granulated sugar
3   large eggs (150 grams), room temperature
3½   cups (437 grams) cake flour
1   teaspoon (5 grams) baking powder
1   teaspoon (5 grams) baking soda
½   teaspoon (1.5 grams) kosher salt
¾   cup (180 grams) coconut milk
½   cup (120 grams) whole buttermilk, room temperature
1½   teaspoons (6 grams) vanilla extract
Peach Simple Syrup (recipe follows)
American Buttercream (recipe follows)
1   cup (225 grams) sliced peeled fresh peaches (about 2 medium peaches)
Garnish: toasted coconut flakes

1. Preheat oven to 350°F (180°C). Butter and flour 3 (9-inch) round cake pans. Line bottom of pans with parchment paper; butter and flour pans again.
2. In the bowl of a stand mixer fitted with the paddle attachment, beat butter and sugar at medium speed until fluffy, 3 to 4 minutes, stopping to scrape sides of bowl. Add eggs, one at a time, beating well after each addition.
3. In a medium bowl, whisk together flour, baking powder, baking soda, and salt. In a small bowl, stir together coconut milk and buttermilk. With mixer on low speed, gradually add flour mixture to butter mixture alternately with coconut milk mixture, beginning and ending with flour mixture, beating just until combined after each addition. Beat in vanilla. Divide batter among prepared pans.
4. Bake until a wooden pick inserted in center comes out clean, about 30 minutes. Let cool in pans for 10 minutes. Remove from pans, and let cool completely on wire racks. Brush layers with Peach Simple Syrup.
5. Place 2 cups American Buttercream in a piping bag fitted with a medium round tip. Pipe a ½-inch-thick layer of buttercream around edge of one cake layer. Spread buttercream within border. Layer half of peaches in center, gently pressing into buttercream and ensuring border is higher than peaches. Repeat layers once. Top with remaining cake layer. Spread a thin layer of American Buttercream on top and sides of cake. Freeze for 30 minutes. Spread remaining American Buttercream on top and sides of cake. Press toasted coconut into sides of cake, if desired. Cover and refrigerate for up to 4 days.

Peach Simple Syrup
Makes about 1½ cups

½   cup (112.5 grams) sliced peeled fresh peaches (about 1 medium peach)
½   cup (100 grams) granulated sugar
½   cup (120 grams) water

1. In a medium saucepan, heat all ingredients over medium heat until sugar is dissolved. Remove from heat, and let cool. Using an immersion blender, blend until mixture is smooth. Refrigerate in an airtight container for up to 2 weeks.

American Buttercream
Makes about 6 cups

2½   cups (567 grams) unsalted butter, softened
3   pounds (1,365 grams) confectioners' sugar
1   cup (240 grams) heavy whipping cream
2   teaspoons (6 grams) kosher salt

1. In the bowl of a stand mixer fitted with the paddle attachment, beat butter at medium speed until creamy, 5 to 6 minutes. Reduce mixer speed to low. Gradually add confectioners' sugar, cream, and salt, beating until smooth. Use immediately.

GINGERBREAD LAYER CAKE WITH RUM FROSTING

Makes 1 (9-inch) cake

This simple cake has a very tender and moist crumb courtesy of a coffee-spiked cake batter. The batter will be loose due to the addition of coffee, but it'll bake up into neat, fluffy layers, so don't be concerned. The warm, boozy coat of Rum Frosting complements the hit of gingerbread spices found within.

1   cup (227 grams) unsalted butter, softened
2¼   cups (495 grams) firmly packed light brown sugar
3   large eggs (150 grams)
¾   cup (243 grams) unsulphured molasses
3¾   cups (469 grams) all-purpose flour
1   tablespoon (6 grams) ground ginger
1½   teaspoons (7.5 grams) baking powder
1½   teaspoons (3 grams) ground cinnamon
¾   teaspoon (2.25 grams) kosher salt
½   teaspoon (2.5 grams) baking soda
1½   cups (360 grams) hot coffee
Rum Frosting (recipe follows)
Garnish: red currants

1. Preheat oven to 350°F (180°C). Line 3 (9-inch) round cake pans with parchment paper; butter and flour edges of pans.
2. In the bowl of a stand mixer fitted with the paddle attachment, beat butter and brown sugar at medium speed until fluffy, 3 to 4 minutes, stopping to scrape sides of bowl. Add eggs, one at a time, beating well after each addition. Stir in molasses.
3. In a large bowl, whisk together flour, ginger, baking powder, cinnamon, salt, and baking soda. With mixer on low speed, gradually add flour mixture to butter mixture alternately with hot coffee, beginning and ending with flour mixture, beating just until combined after each addition. Divide batter among prepared pans.
4. Bake until a wooden pick inserted in center comes out clean, 30 to 33 minutes. Let cool in pans for 10 minutes. Remove from pans, and let cool completely on wire racks. Spread Rum Frosting between layers and on top and sides of cake. Garnish with red currants, if desired. Store at room temperature for up to 2 days, or refrigerate for up to 5 days.

RUM FROSTING
Makes 7 cups

1   cup (227 grams) unsalted butter, softened
10   cups (1,200 grams) confectioners' sugar, divided
6   tablespoons (90 grams) spiced rum
6   tablespoons (90 grams) whole milk
2   teaspoons (12 grams) vanilla bean paste

1. In the bowl of a stand mixer fitted with the paddle attachment, beat butter at medium speed until creamy. With mixer on low speed, gradually add 2 cups (240 grams) confectioners' sugar, beating until combined. Add rum, milk, and vanilla bean paste, beating until combined. Gradually add remaining 8 cups (960 grams) confectioners' sugar, beating until combined. Increase mixer speed to high, and beat for 1 minute. Use immediately.

LANE CAKE

Makes 1 (9-inch) cake

With cooked raisins, coconut, and pecans, this cake's traditional filling tends to be dark and overly sweet. To brighten the color and flavor, we used a combination of golden raisins and dried cherries instead of regular raisins. Brushing Bourbon Simple Syrup on the cake layers before frosting and adding a touch of bourbon to the frosting heightens the aromatic boozy flavor the cake is known for without overpowering it.

1	cup (227 grams) unsalted butter, softened
2¼	cups (450 grams) granulated sugar
1	teaspoon (4 grams) vanilla extract
½	teaspoon (2 grams) almond extract
3½	cups (437 grams) cake flour
1	tablespoon (15 grams) baking powder
¼	teaspoon kosher salt
1	cup (240 grams) whole buttermilk
8	large egg whites (240 grams)

Bourbon Simple Syrup (recipe follows)
Lane Cake Filling (recipe follows)
Lane Cake Frosting (recipe follows)

1. Preheat oven to 350°F (180°C). Butter and flour 3 (9-inch) round light-colored cake pans.

2. In the bowl of a stand mixer fitted with the paddle attachment, beat butter and sugar at medium speed until fluffy, 3 to 4 minutes, stopping to scrape sides of bowl. Beat in extracts.

3. In a medium bowl, whisk together flour, baking powder, and salt. With mixer on low speed, gradually add flour mixture to butter mixture alternately with buttermilk, beginning and ending with flour mixture, beating just until combined after each addition. Transfer batter to a large bowl; set aside.

4. Clean bowl of stand mixer. Using the whisk attachment, beat egg whites at high speed until stiff peaks form. Gently fold egg whites into batter in thirds. Divide batter among prepared pans.

5. Bake until a wooden pick inserted in center comes out clean, 18 to 20 minutes. Let cool in pans for 10 minutes. Remove from pans, and place on wire racks. While still slightly warm, brush each cake layer with Bourbon Simple Syrup twice. Let cool completely.

6. Spread warm Lane Cake Filling between layers, leaving a ¼-inch border. Wrap tightly in plastic wrap, and refrigerate for at least 6 hours or overnight.

7. Spread Lane Cake Frosting on top and sides of cake. Serve within 2 hours. Leftover cake can be stored in an airtight container at room temperature for up to 3 days.

BOURBON SIMPLE SYRUP

Makes about 1 cup

1	cup (200 grams) granulated sugar
½	cup (120 grams) water
½	cup (120 grams) bourbon

1. In a small saucepan, bring all ingredients to a boil over high heat. Reduce heat to low, and simmer for 10 minutes; remove from heat. Let cool completely. Refrigerate in an airtight container for up to 2 weeks.

LANE CAKE FILLING

Makes about 4 cups

1½	cups (170 grams) chopped pecans
½	cup (113 grams) unsalted butter
1¼	cups (250 grams) granulated sugar
8	large egg yolks (149 grams)
1	cup (60 grams) sweetened flaked coconut
½	cup (64 grams) golden raisins
½	cup (64 grams) chopped dried cherries
⅓	cup (80 grams) bourbon

1. In a medium saucepan, cook pecans and butter over medium heat until butter is melted. Stir in sugar until combined. Stir in egg yolks until well combined; cook, stirring occasionally, until mixture is very thick, 4 to 5 minutes. Remove from heat; stir in coconut, raisins, cherries, and bourbon. Let stand for 5 minutes. Use immediately.

LANE CAKE FROSTING

Makes about 5 cups

2	cups (400 grams) granulated sugar
½	cup (120 grams) water
¼	cup (60 grams) bourbon
6	large egg whites (180 grams)

1. In a medium saucepan, bring sugar, ½ cup (120 grams) water, and bourbon to a boil over high heat. Reduce heat to medium-high, and cook until a candy thermometer registers 248°F (120°C).

2. Meanwhile, in the bowl of a stand mixer fitted with the whisk attachment, beat egg whites at medium-high speed until stiff peaks form. With mixer running, pour hot sugar mixture into egg whites in a slow, steady stream, avoiding whisk. Beat until frosting cools to room temperature and has a spreadable consistency, about 10 minutes. Use immediately.

BAKED ALASKA

Makes 1 (9-inch) dessert

One of the most famous half-baked desserts, the Baked Alaska was actually created in New York. In 1867, the head chef at the illustrious Delmonico's restaurant designed a new cake to celebrate the United States' purchase of Alaska from the Russians. In our Neapolitan version, dramatic peaks of torched meringue encase a medley of chocolate, strawberry, and vanilla ice creams. For this recipe, you will have leftover ice cream of each flavor if you make the following recipes from scratch—lucky you.

Vanilla Sponge Cake (recipe follows)
3¾ cups (627 grams) Strawberry Ice Cream (recipe follows)
2 cups (456 grams) Vanilla Ice Cream (recipe follows)
1½ cups (342 grams) Chocolate Ice Cream (recipe follows)
Meringue (recipe follows)

1. Remove bowl or mold with Vanilla Sponge Cake from freezer; spread softened Strawberry Ice Cream into and up sides of cake layer. Cover with a piece of plastic wrap, pressing wrap directly onto surface. Use a slightly smaller bowl to help shape first ice cream layer. Freeze until firm, 1 to 2 hours.
2. Repeat procedure with Vanilla Ice Cream and Chocolate Ice Cream. Place round cake layer on top, and cover with plastic wrap. Freeze overnight.
3. Invert Baked Alaska onto a serving plate. Remove all plastic wrap, and cover with Meringue. Using a kitchen torch, brown Meringue. Serve immediately, or cover and freeze for up to 6 months. Remove from freezer 5 minutes before serving. Use a long chef's knife dipped in warm water to cut into wedges.

Note: *You can substitute high-quality ice cream for homemade ice cream. Leftover ice cream will keep in freezer for up to 4 months in an airtight plastic container.*

VANILLA SPONGE CAKE
Makes 1 (10x5-inch) cake and 1 (9-inch) cake

6 large eggs (300 grams), separated
1 cup (200 grams) superfine castor sugar, divided, plus more for sprinkling
1½ teaspoons (6 grams) vanilla extract
⅛ teaspoon cream of tartar
1½ cups (188 grams) all-purpose flour, sifted

1. Preheat oven to 375°F (190°C). Line a 10x5-inch jelly roll pan with parchment paper, letting excess extend over sides of pan. Line bottom of a 9-inch round cake pan with parchment paper.
2. In a large bowl, whisk together egg yolks and ¾ cup (150 grams) castor sugar until pale and thickened; whisk in vanilla.
3. In the bowl of a stand mixer fitted with the whisk attachment, beat egg whites and cream of tartar at high speed until soft peaks

form. Gradually add remaining ¼ cup (50 grams) castor sugar, beating until glossy stiff peaks form.
4. Fold half of flour into yolk mixture. Fold in one-fourth of egg whites. Fold in remaining flour; fold in remaining egg whites. Spread 2 cups (228 grams) batter in prepared round cake pan; spread remaining batter in prepared jelly roll pan.
5. Bake round cake layer for 10 minutes, and bake jelly roll layer for 15 minutes. Let round cake layer cool completely on a wire rack.
6. Line inside of 9-inch round bowl or mold with plastic wrap. Turn mold upside down on a work surface. Sprinkle a tea towel with castor sugar. Turn out warm jelly roll layer onto prepared towel. Top with another tea towel, and gently place over top of upside-down bowl to shape and let cool completely.
7. Remove top tea towel, and gently lift cake off of bowl. Invert lined bowl right-side up, and gently lower cake into bowl. Gently push cake down into bowl; trim edges, reserving scraps. Use scraps to fill in two sides that dip down into bowl; trim edges. Cover with plastic wrap, and freeze overnight.

STRAWBERRY ICE CREAM
Makes 5 cups

1 cup (25 grams) freeze-dried strawberries
½ cup (120 grams) water
½ cup (160 grams) strawberry preserves
Vanilla Ice Cream (recipe follows)

1. In the container of a blender, blend freeze-dried strawberries until they reach a powder consistency; remove from container. Place ½ cup (120 grams) water, preserves, and ⅓ cup (26 grams) strawberry powder in container, and blend until smooth. Prepare Vanilla Ice Cream as directed, adding strawberry mixture with cream mixture. Proceed as directed.

VANILLA ICE CREAM
Makes 5 cups

1¾ cups (420 grams) heavy whipping cream
1¼ cups (300 grams) whole milk
½ cup (170 grams) light corn syrup
½ cup (100 grams) granulated sugar, divided
1 tablespoon (18 grams) vanilla bean paste
¼ teaspoon kosher salt
6 large egg yolks (112 grams)

1. Line an 8- or 9-inch square metal cake pan with plastic wrap; place in freezer.
2. In a medium saucepan, combine cream, milk, corn syrup, ¼ cup (50 grams) sugar, vanilla bean paste, and salt. Heat over medium-high heat, stirring occasionally, until a candy thermometer registers 170°F (77°C). Remove from heat.
3. In a medium bowl, whisk together egg yolks and remaining ¼ cup

(50 grams) sugar. Add 1 cup hot cream mixture to egg mixture, whisking constantly. Add egg mixture to remaining hot cream mixture in pan, whisking to combine. Cook over medium-low heat until mixture is thickened and a candy thermometer registers 180°F (82°C), 7 to 10 minutes. Immediately pour custard into a large bowl, and let cool until no longer steaming, 10 to 20 minutes.

4. Transfer 1 cup mixture to a jar with a tight-fitting lid. Place remaining mixture in a large jar with a tight-fitting lid. Refrigerate large jar and freeze small jar for at least 6 hours or up to 24 hours.

5. Remove frozen base from freezer, and let stand at room temperature for 10 minutes. Scrape frozen base into a large bowl; add refrigerated base, and stir occasionally until frozen base is dissolved. Transfer mixture to an ice cream maker, and churn until soft serve consistency, about 20 minutes.

6. Transfer ice cream to prepared pan, and press plastic wrap directly onto surface. Freeze overnight. Remove from freezer, and let stand at room temperature for 10 minutes to soften.

Chocolate Ice Cream

Makes 5 cups

Vanilla Ice Cream (recipe precedes)
¾ cup (64 grams) unsweetened cocoa powder
½ cup (85 grams) chopped 62% cacao bittersweet chocolate

1. Prepare Vanilla Ice Cream as directed, adding cocoa with cream mixture. Once custard has cooked, add chopped chocolate, whisking to combine. Proceed as directed.

Meringue

Makes about 4 cups

1 cup plus 3 tablespoons (236 grams) granulated sugar, divided
⅓ cup (80 grams) water
3 large egg whites (90 grams)
⅛ teaspoon kosher salt

1. In a medium saucepan, heat 1 cup plus 1 tablespoon (212 grams) sugar and ⅓ cup (80 grams) water over high heat until a candy thermometer registers 240°F (116°C).

2. In the bowl of a stand mixer fitted with the whisk attachment, beat egg whites and salt at medium speed until foamy. Add remaining 2 tablespoons (24 grams) sugar, beating until combined. Increase mixer speed to high. Gradually add sugar syrup, beating until a stiff meringue forms, 4 to 5 minutes.

PRO TIP

Freezing our ice cream custard 6 hours before churning may seem like overkill, but trust us. Ensuring that your custard is extremely cold before going into the ice cream maker keeps ice crystals from forming and results in the creamiest, dreamiest ice cream texture.

PLAN IT OUT

Day 1: Make ice cream bases. Refrigerate and freeze for 6 hours. Churn. Freeze overnight.
Day 2: Make Vanilla Sponge Cake. Assemble Baked Alaska. Freeze overnight.
Day 3: Make and cover with Meringue. Serve.

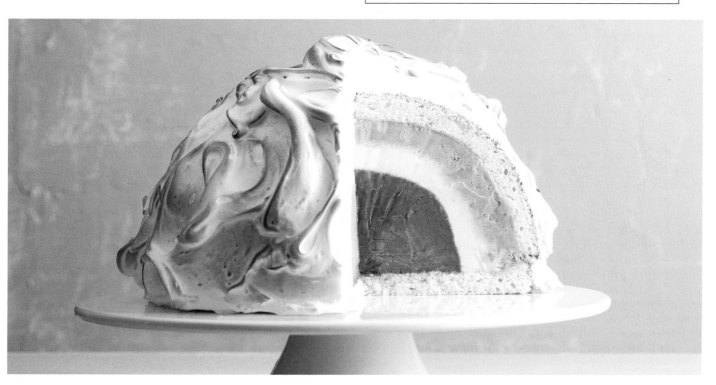

PLAN IT OUT
Day 1: Make Maraschino Cherry Ice Cream base. Freeze overnight.
Day 2: Churn ice cream. Freeze for at least 6 hours. Bake Confetti Cake. Assemble Confetti Ice Cream Cake. Freeze for at least 4 hours. Top with Sweetened Whipped Cream. Serve.

CONFETTI ICE CREAM CAKE

Makes 1 (9-inch) cake

This beauty was inspired by pastry chef Christina Tosi's funfetti Birthday Cake served at New York City's Momofuku Milk Bar. Maraschino cherries are for more than just topping a sundae. We flavor our Vanilla Ice Cream with the sweetened fruit because a cake this vibrant needs an ice cream that can keep up. Use your leftover Confetti Cake scraps for birthday cake milkshakes, or use your hands to shape into little balls for a streusel-like garnish to pile on top of the cake.

Confetti Cake (recipe follows)
5   cups (1,140 grams) Maraschino Cherry
      Ice Cream (recipe follows)
Sweetened Whipped Cream (recipe follows)
Garnish: colored sprinkles

1. Line a tall-sided 9-inch round springform pan with plastic wrap.
2. Gently place half-circle Confetti Cake layers in prepared pan. Remove Maraschino Cherry Ice Cream layer from freezer, and place on top of cake layer. Top with remaining Confetti Cake layer, and cover with plastic wrap. Freeze overnight.
3. Remove cake from pan, and remove plastic wrap. Top with Sweetened Whipped Cream. Garnish with sprinkles, if desired. Serve immediately, or wrap in plastic wrap, and freeze for up to 3 months. (If you plan on freezing, wait to top with Sweetened Whipped Cream until ready to serve.) Remove from freezer 5 minutes before serving. Use a long chef's knife dipped in warm water to cut into wedges.

CONFETTI CAKE

Makes 2 (9-inch) cake layers

1   cup (227 grams) unsalted butter, softened
2¼   cups (450 grams) granulated sugar
1   teaspoon (4 grams) vanilla extract
½   teaspoon (2 grams) almond extract
3½   cups (437 grams) cake flour
1   tablespoon (15 grams) baking powder
¼   teaspoon kosher salt
1   cup (240 grams) whole buttermilk
½   cup (83 grams) colored sprinkles*
8   large egg whites (240 grams)

1. Preheat oven to 350°F (180°C). Butter and flour a 16¼x11¼-inch half sheet pan**; line pan with parchment paper.
2. In the bowl of a stand mixer fitted with the paddle attachment, beat butter and sugar at medium speed until fluffy, 3 to 4 minutes, stopping to scrape sides of bowl. Beat in extracts.

3. In a medium bowl, whisk together flour, baking powder, and salt. With mixer on low speed, gradually add flour mixture to butter mixture alternately with buttermilk, beginning and ending with flour mixture, beating just until combined after each addition. Add sprinkles, beating just until combined. Transfer batter to a large bowl; set aside.
4. Clean bowl of stand mixer. Using the whisk attachment, beat egg whites at high speed until stiff peaks form. Gently fold egg whites into batter in thirds. Pour batter into prepared pan.
5. Bake until a wooden pick inserted in center comes out clean, 25 to 30 minutes, rotating pan halfway through baking. Let cool completely in pan.
6. Using a 9-inch parchment round as a guide, cut one cake layer from far right side of pan, avoiding edges of cake. Fold parchment circle in half, and cut two half-circle layers from far left side of pan. (The two half-circle layers will fit as the bottom layer in springform pan during assembly.)

We used Betty Crocker Rainbow Sprinkles. These sprinkles' colors don't bleed when stirred into the cake batter.

**We used Nordic Ware Baker's Half Sheet Pan, available on nordicware.com.*

MARASCHINO CHERRY ICE CREAM

Makes 5 cups

5   cups (1,140 grams) Vanilla Ice Cream (recipe on page 26)
1   cup (204 grams) chopped drained maraschino cherries
2   tablespoons (30 grams) maraschino cherry juice

1. Line a 9-inch round metal cake pan with plastic wrap; place in freezer.
2. Prepare Vanilla Ice Cream as directed, adding cherries and juice with cream mixture. Proceed as directed.

Note: *You can substitute high-quality ice cream for homemade ice cream. Leftover ice cream will keep in freezer for up to 4 months in an airtight plastic container.*

SWEETENED WHIPPED CREAM

Makes about 3 cups

1½   cups (360 grams) heavy whipping cream
½   cup (60 grams) confectioners' sugar

1. In the bowl of a stand mixer fitted with the whisk attachment, beat cream and confectioners' sugar at medium speed until stiff peaks form. Use immediately.

FROSÉ BOMBE GLACÉE

Makes 1 (9-inch) bombe

Frosé. All. Day. We made sorbet with your favorite rose-hued sipper and let it take center stage in our take on la bombe glacée, a classic frozen French dessert that resembles a cannonball (hence the name). We brush the Citrus Genoise layers in rosé once they're out of the oven, which not only strengthens the overall flavor but keeps them extra tender even when frozen.

Rosé Sorbet (recipe follows)
Citrus Genoise (recipe follows)
Chocolate Glaze (recipe follows)

1. Prepare Rosé Sorbet, and freeze overnight. Prepare Citrus Genoise. Place cake layer on top of sorbet layer in mold. Wrap in plastic wrap, and return to freezer for at least 6 hours.
2. Line a rimmed sheet pan with plastic wrap; top with a wire rack.
3. Invert frozen bombe onto wire rack, and remove plastic wrap. Using a serrated knife, trim cake edges so they are flush with edges of sorbet. Quickly pour warm Chocolate Glaze over bombe all at once. (Because of how quickly the glaze sets, it is crucial that you pour all the glaze on in one fluid motion.) Tap pan on counter a few times to ensure an even cover.
4. Using 2 large spatulas, transfer bombe to a serving plate. Serve immediately, or place on a cardboard round, and return to freezer uncovered. Remove from freezer 5 minutes before serving. Use a long chef's knife dipped in warm water to cut into wedges.

ROSÉ SORBET
Makes 4 cups

2¼   cups (540 grams) dry rosé, divided
¾   cup (180 grams) water
1   teaspoon (3 grams) low-sugar or no-sugar-needed fruit pectin
⅛   teaspoon kosher salt
3½   cups (550 grams) red seedless grapes
2   medium Bartlett pears (360 grams), chopped
½   cup (100 grams) granulated sugar
⅓   cup (113 grams) light corn syrup

1. In a small saucepan, boil 2 cups (480 grams) rosé over medium-high heat until reduced to ⅓ cup, 30 to 40 minutes. Pour into a small bowl; let cool.
2. In same saucepan, heat ¾ cup (180 grams) water, pectin, salt, and remaining ¼ cup (60 grams) rosé over medium-high

heat. Cook, stirring occasionally, until pectin is dissolved, about 5 minutes. Remove from heat, and let cool for 10 minutes.
3. Line a 9-inch round bowl* or mold with plastic wrap, and place in freezer.
4. In the work bowl of a food processor, place water mixture, grapes, pears, sugar, and corn syrup; process until smooth, about 30 seconds. Strain mixture through a fine-mesh sieve, pressing to extract as much liquid as possible. Stir in rosé reduction. Transfer 1 cup mixture to a jar with a tight-fitting lid. Place remaining mixture in a large jar with a tight-fitting lid. Refrigerate large jar and freeze small jar for at least 4 hours or up to 24 hours.
5. Remove frozen small jar from freezer, and let stand at room temperature for 10 minutes. Scrape frozen base into a large bowl; add refrigerated base, and stir occasionally until frozen base is dissolved. Transfer mixture to an ice cream maker, and churn until color lightens, about 20 minutes.
6. Transfer rosé mixture to prepared bowl or mold. Freeze overnight. (To keep your bowl level in the freezer, place a round cookie cutter underneath to stabilize it.)

To get a perfectly round dome, we used Fat Daddio's Aluminum Hemisphere Pan with a 9-inch width, available on fatdaddios.com.

Note: *With red grapes as its fruit base, our Rosé Sorbet is hard to beat. You can substitute with a high-quality frosé sorbet or raspberry sherbet. We like Jeni's Frosé Sorbet, available on jenis.com and at select grocery stores. (You'll need to order two pints of it.)*

CITRUS GENOISE
Makes 1 (9-inch) cake layer

3   large eggs (150 grams)
½   cup (100 grams) granulated sugar
½   teaspoon orange zest
½   teaspoon (2 grams) vanilla extract
¼   teaspoon kosher salt
½   cup plus 1 tablespoon (69 grams) cake flour
5   tablespoons (40 grams) cornstarch
3   tablespoons (42 grams) unsalted butter, melted
¼   cup (60 grams) dry rosé

1. Preheat oven to 350°F (180°C). Line bottom of a 9-inch round cake pan with parchment paper.
2. In the bowl of a stand mixer fitted with the whisk attachment, whisk together eggs, sugar, zest, vanilla, and salt by hand. Place mixer bowl over a saucepan of simmering water. Cook, whisking

occasionally, until mixture registers 110°F (43°C) on a candy thermometer, about 3 minutes. Carefully return bowl to stand mixer, and beat at high speed until pale yellow and tripled in size, about 3 minutes.

3. In a small bowl, sift together flour and cornstarch. Fold flour mixture into batter.

4. Transfer 1 cup (110 grams) batter to a medium bowl; add melted butter, whisking to combine. Fold butter mixture into remaining batter. Spoon batter into prepared pan.

5. Bake until a wooden pick inserted in center comes out clean, about 15 minutes. Let cool in pan for 10 minutes. Remove from pan, and let cool completely on a wire rack. Brush rosé onto cake layer.

CHOCOLATE GLAZE
Makes 1 cup

- 8 ounces (225 grams) 60% cacao bittersweet chocolate, chopped
- ½ cup (113 grams) unsalted butter
- 3 tablespoons (63 grams) light corn syrup

1. In the top of a double boiler, combine all ingredients. Heat over simmering water, stirring frequently, until melted. Let cool to 100°F (37°C) before glazing bombe.

PLAN IT OUT

Day 1: Make the Rosé Sorbet base in morning. Refrigerate and freeze for 6 hours. Churn Rosé Sorbet. Freeze overnight.

Day 2: Make Citrus Genoise. Assemble bombe. Freeze for 6 hours. Glaze, and serve.

SOMLÓI GALUSKA (SOMLO DUMPLINGS)

Makes 12 servings

Recipe by Szonja Márk

A medley of sponge cake, Pastry Cream, Chocolate Sauce, walnuts, and raisins, this laborious trifle was dreamed up during the 1950s at the storied Budapest, Hungary, restaurant Gundel. To ensure sponge cakes are at their light, fluffy best, speed is essential. Hungarian pastry chef Szonja Márk advises preparing pans and heating the oven in advance because batters lingering on the sidelines won't rise properly during baking, leading to a coarse texture.

¾ cup plus 2½ tablespoons (114 grams) all-purpose flour, divided
⅜ teaspoon kosher salt, divided
½ cup (43 grams) plus 1 tablespoon (5 grams) Dutch process cocoa powder, divided
1⅓ cups (128 grams) ground walnuts, divided
9 large eggs (450 grams), separated
¾ cup plus 3 tablespoons (186 grams) granulated sugar, divided
Rum Raisins (recipe follows)
Pastry Cream (recipe follows)
Chocolate Sauce (recipe follows) and whipped cream, to serve

1. Preheat oven to 350°F (180°C). Line 3 (9-inch) round cake pans with parchment paper.
2. In a small bowl, whisk together ½ cup (63 grams) flour and ⅛ teaspoon salt. In another small bowl, whisk together ½ cup (43 grams) cocoa, 2½ tablespoons (20 grams) flour, and ⅛ teaspoon salt. In a third small bowl, whisk together ⅓ cup (32 grams) ground walnuts, remaining ¼ cup (31 grams) flour, and remaining ⅛ teaspoon salt.
3. In the bowl of a stand mixer fitted with the whisk attachment, beat egg yolks and one-third of sugar (62 grams) at medium speed until pale. Divide egg yolk mixture among 3 medium bowls (70 grams each).
4. Clean bowl of stand mixer and whisk attachment. Using the whisk attachment, beat egg whites at medium speed until soft peaks form. Add remaining sugar (124 grams), and

beat until stiff peaks form. Divide egg white mixture among 3 bowls with yolk mixture (137 grams each). Fold egg yolk and egg white mixtures together in each bowl.
5. Fold flour mixture into one bowl, fold cocoa mixture into another bowl, and fold walnut mixture into third bowl. Pour batters into prepared pans.
6. Bake until a wooden pick inserted in center comes out clean, 12 to 15 minutes. Let cool completely in pans. Remove from pans, and gently peel off parchment.
7. Place plain sponge cake layer on a cake plate, and brush with 5 tablespoons reserved sugar syrup from Rum Raisins. Sprinkle with one-third of Rum Raisins and ⅓ cup (32 grams) ground walnuts. Spread one-third of Pastry Cream over raisins and walnuts. Place cocoa cake layer on top of Pastry Cream, pressing down slightly. Brush with 5 tablespoons reserved syrup. Sprinkle with one-third of Rum Raisins and ⅓ cup (32 grams) ground walnuts. Spread one-third of Pastry Cream over raisins and walnuts. Top with walnut cake layer, and repeat procedure with remaining 5 tablespoons reserved syrup, remaining Rum Raisins, remaining ⅓ cup (32 grams) ground walnuts, and remaining Pastry Cream. Cover and refrigerate overnight.
8. When ready to serve, dust top of cake with remaining 1 tablespoon (5 grams) cocoa. Serve with Chocolate Sauce and whipped cream.

RUM RAISINS
Makes 1½ cups

¾ cup (150 grams) granulated sugar
⅔ cup (151 grams) water
⅔ cup (147 grams) packed raisins
¼ cup (60 grams) dark rum

1. In a small saucepan, bring sugar and ⅔ cup (151 grams) water to a boil. Remove from heat; add raisins and rum. Let cool to room temperature. Strain raisins, and reserve sugar syrup for soaking cake layers.

PASTRY CREAM
Makes 5 cups

4 cups plus 3 tablespoons (1,005 grams) whole milk
1 cup (200 grams) granulated sugar, divided
1 vanilla bean, split lengthwise, seeds scraped and reserved
10 large egg yolks (186 grams)
½ cup plus 2 tablespoons (80 grams) cornstarch
⅛ teaspoon kosher salt

1. In a large saucepan, combine milk, ½ cup (100 grams) sugar, and vanilla bean and reserved seeds. Bring to a boil over medium-low heat.
2. In a large bowl, whisk together egg yolks, cornstarch, salt, and remaining ½ cup (100 grams) sugar. Slowly add hot milk mixture to egg mixture, whisking constantly. Return mixture to pan, and cook until thickened. Immediately transfer to a large bowl. Cover with a piece of plastic wrap, pressing wrap directly onto surface of cream to prevent a skin from forming. Refrigerate until chilled.

CHOCOLATE SAUCE
Makes 1½ cups

1¼ cups (213 grams) 60% cacao dark chocolate chips, chopped
¾ cup plus 2 tablespoons (210 grams) heavy whipping cream

1. Place chopped chocolate in a medium heatproof bowl.
2. In a small saucepan, bring cream to a boil. Pour half of hot cream over chocolate. Let stand for 10 seconds; stir until chocolate is melted. Pour remaining hot cream over melted chocolate, and stir to combine. Let cool slightly.

Note: *If Chocolate Sauce breaks, re-emulsify the cream and chocolate using an immersion blender or food processor to blend until smooth. Make sure it is still warm before blending.*

MATCHA BATTENBERG CAKE

Makes 1 (8-inch) cake

A perfect dessert for anyone who can't decide on their favorite flavor, the Battenberg is constructed with two different cakes and arranged in an iconic check pattern. For our tea take, matcha and almond sponge cakes form the signature checkered pattern, with a layer of apricot jam sandwiched between the cakes and a cover of homemade Marzipan to seal it all together.

1	cup (227 grams) unsalted butter, softened
1	cup (200 grams) granulated sugar
3	large eggs (150 grams)
1	teaspoon (4 grams) almond extract
½	teaspoon (2 grams) vanilla extract
1¾	cups (219 grams) all-purpose flour
2	teaspoons (10 grams) baking powder
½	teaspoon (1.5 grams) kosher salt
1	tablespoon (15 grams) whole milk
1½	teaspoons (3 grams) matcha powder

Confectioners' sugar, for dusting
Marzipan (recipe follows)
¼   cup (80 grams) apricot jam, warmed

1. Preheat oven to 350°F (180°C). Butter and flour an 8-inch square baking pan; line pan with parchment paper. Fold a sheet of foil over 3 to 4 times to create a sturdy 8-inch-long, 1-inch-wide strip. Place in center of prepared pan to form a divider.
2. In the bowl of a stand mixer fitted with the paddle attachment, beat butter and granulated sugar at medium speed until creamy, 3 to 4 minutes, stopping to scrape sides of bowl. Add eggs, one at a time, beating just until combined after each addition. Beat in extracts.

3. In a medium bowl, whisk together flour, baking powder, and salt. With mixer on low speed, gradually add flour mixture to butter mixture, beating just until combined. Pour half of batter into a medium bowl.
4. In a small bowl, stir together milk and matcha powder. Add matcha mixture to remaining batter, and fold to combine. Pour each batter into one side of prepared pan.
5. Bake until a wooden pick inserted in center of each cake comes out clean, 25 to 30 minutes. Let cool in pan for 10 minutes. Remove from pan, and let cool completely on a wire rack. Using a serrated knife, trim off dark outer edges of cake. Cut each cake into 2 (8x1½x1-inch) rectangles.
6. On a work surface lightly dusted with confectioners' sugar, roll Marzipan to ⅛-inch thickness. Brush a 1½-inch side of one piece of matcha cake with warm apricot jam, and place on Marzipan, jam side down. Brush a 1-inch side of matcha cake and a 1½-inch side of one piece of almond cake with jam. Place almond cake next to matcha cake, 1½-inch side down, using jam as a glue. Brush top of matcha cake and a 1-inch side of second piece of almond cake with jam. Place almond cake directly on

top of matcha piece. Brush a 1½-inch side of second piece of matcha cake with jam, and place directly on top of first almond piece. Gently press all cake pieces together. Brush outside of all cake pieces with jam. Carefully wrap Marzipan around cake, gently pressing to smooth out air pockets and seal. Cut off any excess Marzipan. Cut a ½-inch piece off each end of cake. Serve immediately, or refrigerate for up to 2 days.

MARZIPAN
Makes about 4 cups

3½	cups (420 grams) confectioners' sugar
1½	cups (144 grams) almond flour
1	large egg white (30 grams)
2	teaspoons (8 grams) almond extract
1	teaspoon (4 grams) rum extract

1. In the work bowl of a food processor, place confectioners' sugar and flour; pulse until combined. Add egg white and extracts; process until mixture holds together and is the consistency of softened butter. Wrap tightly in plastic wrap, and refrigerate for up to 1 month.

STRAWBERRY LEMON JELLY ROLL

Makes 10 servings

We give plain sponge cake a bright lemon kick and a sweet swirl of luscious berry buttercream. Intense freeze-dried strawberries flavor a rich mascarpone and buttercream filling while fresh ones crown the top of our sunny cake.

¾   cup (94 grams) cake flour, sifted
¾   teaspoon (3.75 grams) baking powder
¼   teaspoon kosher salt
4   large eggs (200 grams), room temperature and separated
⅔   cup (133 grams) granulated sugar, divided
6   tablespoons (18 grams) lemon zest
1   tablespoon (15 grams) fresh lemon juice
1   cup (120 grams) confectioners' sugar
    Strawberry Mascarpone Buttercream (recipe follows)
    Garnish: sliced fresh strawberries

1. Preheat oven to 350°F (180°C). Butter a 15x10-inch jelly roll pan. Line pan with parchment paper; butter pan again.
2. In a small bowl, sift together flour, baking powder, and salt. Set aside.

3. In the bowl of a stand mixer fitted with the whisk attachment, beat egg yolks and ⅓ cup (66.5 grams) granulated sugar at high speed until thick, pale, and ribbonlike. Add lemon zest and juice, beating until combined. Transfer batter to a large bowl; set aside.
4. Clean bowl of stand mixer and whisk attachment. Using the whisk attachment, beat egg whites at medium speed until foamy. Gradually add remaining ⅓ cup (66.5 grams) granulated sugar; increase mixer speed to high, and beat until soft-medium peaks form. Fold egg whites into yolk mixture in 2 additions until no streaks remain. Fold in flour mixture. Quickly spread batter into prepared pan. (Do not overwork batter or it will deflate.)
5. Bake until a wooden pick inserted in center comes out clean, about 8 minutes.
6. Meanwhile, dust confectioners' sugar into a 15x10-inch rectangle on a clean dish towel. Immediately loosen cake from sides of pan, and turn out onto prepared towel. Gently peel off parchment paper. Starting at one short side, roll up cake and towel together, and place seam side down on a wire rack. Let cool completely.

7. Gently unroll cake, and spread with Strawberry Mascarpone Buttercream, leaving a ½-inch border. Reroll cake without towel, and refrigerate for 30 minutes before serving. Garnish with strawberries, if desired.

STRAWBERRY MASCARPONE BUTTERCREAM
Makes 1¾ cups

½   cup (113 grams) unsalted butter, softened
½   cup (112 grams) mascarpone cheese, room temperature
¾   teaspoon (4.5 grams) vanilla bean paste
1   cup (120 grams) confectioners' sugar
3   tablespoons (15 grams) freeze-dried strawberry powder (see Note)
⅛   teaspoon kosher salt

1. In the bowl of a stand mixer fitted with the paddle attachment, beat butter and mascarpone at medium speed until creamy, about 2 minutes. Beat in vanilla bean paste. Gradually add confectioners' sugar, strawberry powder, and salt, beating until smooth.

Note: *To make strawberry powder, place 1 cup (25 grams) freeze-dried strawberries in a plastic bag, and crush with a rolling pin. (Alternatively, process in a food processor.) Sift powder to remove any large pieces of strawberries, then measure.*

DARK CHOCOLATE CAKE WITH WHIPPED CARAMELIZED WHITE CHOCOLATE GANACHE

Makes 1 (9-inch) cake

Recipe by Jesse Szewczyk

With essentially every type of chocolate, this recipe is for all you chocolate fanatics. It's coated in a luxe frosting made with the real star, Caramelized White Chocolate, and the top is showered in shimmering sea salt flakes that crunch like sprinkles. The salt is a nice contrast to the chocolate's sweetness, making this cake dangerously easy to eat.

1   cup (227 grams) unsalted butter, softened
3   cups (660 grams) firmly packed dark brown sugar
4   large eggs (200 grams)
1   cup (227 grams) sour cream
1   tablespoon (13 grams) vanilla extract
2¼   cups (281 grams) all-purpose flour
1   cup (101 grams) black cocoa powder
1   tablespoon (15 grams) baking soda
1   teaspoon (3 grams) kosher salt
1⅓   cups (320 grams) boiling water
Whipped Caramelized White Chocolate Ganache (recipe follows)
Dark Chocolate Drip (recipe follows)
Garnish: flaked sea salt

1. Preheat oven to 350°F (180°C). Butter and flour 3 (9-inch) round cake pans.
2. In the bowl of a stand mixer fitted with the paddle attachment, beat butter and brown sugar at medium speed until fluffy, 3 to 4 minutes, stopping to scrape sides of bowl. Add eggs, and beat until light and fluffy, about 3 minutes. Add sour cream and vanilla, beating just until smooth.
3. In a medium bowl, whisk together flour, black cocoa, baking soda, and kosher salt. With mixer on low speed, gradually add flour mixture to butter mixture, beating just until combined. Slowly add 1⅓ cups (320 grams) boiling water, beating until smooth. Divide batter among prepared pans.
4. Bake until a wooden pick inserted in center comes out clean, about 30 minutes. Let cool in pans for 15 minutes. Remove from pans, and let cool completely on wire racks.
5. Using a serrated knife, trim top of cake layers. Lightly spread Whipped Caramelized White Chocolate Ganache between layers and on top and sides of cake. Pour Dark Chocolate Drip over cake, letting it drip down sides. Let stand until chocolate is set, about 20 minutes. Garnish with sea salt, if desired. Serve immediately, or refrigerate until ready to serve. Let stand at room temperature for 1 hour before serving.

WHIPPED CARAMELIZED WHITE CHOCOLATE GANACHE
Makes about 4 cups

16   ounces (455 grams) Caramelized White Chocolate (recipe on page 371), chopped
1½   cups (360 grams) heavy whipping cream
1   cup (227 grams) unsalted butter, cubed
1   tablespoon (13 grams) vanilla extract
½   teaspoon (1.5 grams) kosher salt

1. Place Caramelized White Chocolate in a large heatproof bowl.
2. In a small saucepan, bring cream and all remaining ingredients to a simmer over medium heat. Pour hot cream mixture over Caramelized White Chocolate; stir until melted. Freeze for 1 hour.
3. Transfer cooled mixture to the bowl of a stand mixer fitted with the paddle attachment. Beat at high speed until light and fluffy, 30 seconds to 1 minute. Use immediately.

Note: *If your chocolate breaks while whipping it, just melt 3 tablespoons ganache in the microwave, and slowly add it back in while whipping. This can happen if it has chilled for too long, but it's easily fixed.*

DARK CHOCOLATE DRIP
Makes about 1½ cups

6   ounces (175 grams) 60% cacao semisweet chocolate, chopped
¾   cup (180 grams) heavy whipping cream
¼   cup (57 grams) unsalted butter

1. Place chocolate in a medium heatproof bowl.
2. In a small saucepan, bring cream and butter to a simmer over medium heat. Pour hot cream mixture over chocolate; stir until melted. Let cool for 20 minutes before using.

PRO TIP
It's best to frost your cake as soon as you make the frosting because the frosting won't go on as smoothly if you wait. (Make sure your layers are cool.) Because it's a whipped ganache, the frosting will deflate a little (but that's OK).

Photo by Mark Weinberg

BIRTHDAY CAKES

We're sharing the classic cakes and unbeatable frostings that should be in every baker's repertoire. Mix and match as you please for the ultimate birthday experience. Find recipes for our mix-and-match cakes and frostings on pages 38 through 43.

YELLOW CAKE

Makes 1 (9-inch) cake

We use extra egg yolks in this cake to give it that signature sunny shade and a deep, buttery flavor. You won't be able to blow out the candles and slice it fast enough.

1	cup (227 grams) unsalted butter, softened
2	cups (400 grams) granulated sugar
3	large eggs (150 grams), room temperature
2	large egg yolks (37 grams), room temperature
1	teaspoon (4 grams) vanilla extract
2⅔	cups (333 grams) all-purpose flour
2½	teaspoons (12.5 grams) baking powder
1	teaspoon (3 grams) kosher salt
1	cup (240 grams) whole buttermilk, room temperature

1. Preheat oven to 350°F (180°C). Butter and flour 2 (9-inch) round cake pans.
2. In the bowl of a stand mixer fitted with the paddle attachment, beat butter and sugar at medium speed until fluffy, 3 to 4 minutes, stopping to scrape sides of bowl. Add eggs and egg yolks, one at a time, beating well after each addition. Beat in vanilla.
3. In a medium bowl, whisk together flour, baking powder, and salt. With mixer on low speed, gradually add flour mixture to butter mixture alternately with buttermilk, beginning and ending with flour mixture, beating just until combined after each addition. Divide batter between prepared pans.
4. Bake until a wooden pick inserted in center comes out clean, 25 to 30 minutes. Let cool in pans for 10 minutes. Remove from pans, and let cool completely on wire racks.

PEANUT BUTTER CAKE

Makes 1 (9-inch) cake

Great for occasions when you don't want to pull out your stand mixer, this cake is the densest of the bunch.

1½	cups (330 grams) firmly packed light brown sugar
½	cup (128 grams) peanut butter*
½	cup (112 grams) vegetable oil
3	large eggs (150 grams), room temperature
1½	teaspoons (6 grams) vanilla extract
2¼	cups (281 grams) all-purpose flour
1	tablespoon (15 grams) baking powder
1	teaspoon (5 grams) baking soda
1	teaspoon (3 grams) kosher salt
1½	cups (360 grams) whole buttermilk, room temperature

1. Preheat oven to 350°F (180°C). Butter and flour 2 (9-inch) round cake pans.
2. In a large bowl, stir together brown sugar, peanut butter, and oil until combined and creamy. Add eggs and vanilla, stirring just until combined.
3. In a medium bowl, sift together flour, baking powder, baking soda, and salt. Gradually add flour mixture to sugar mixture alternately with buttermilk, beginning and ending with flour mixture, stirring just until combined after each addition. Divide batter between prepared pans.
4. Bake until a wooden pick inserted in center comes out clean, 25 to 30 minutes. Let cool in pans for 10 minutes. Remove from pans, and let cool completely on wire racks.

Use regular, smooth, prepackaged peanut butter.

BIRTHDAY CAKE FROSTINGS

PEANUT BUTTER BUTTERCREAM
Makes about 4 cups

This is the lushest buttercream you'll ever make. Use regular, smooth, prepackaged peanut butter. The natural stuff is separated and has more oil, which will alter the texture of the frosting.

¾ cup (170 grams) unsalted butter, softened
⅓ cup (85 grams) creamy peanut butter*
4½ cups (540 grams) confectioners' sugar
½ teaspoon (1.5 grams) kosher salt
6 tablespoons (90 grams) heavy whipping cream, room temperature

1. In the bowl of a stand mixer fitted with the paddle attachment, beat butter and peanut butter at medium speed until smooth. Reduce mixer speed to low. Gradually add confectioners' sugar and salt, beating until combined. Add cream, beating until a spreadable consistency is reached. Use immediately.

We used Jif Creamy Peanut Butter.

BROWN SUGAR CARAMEL SWISS MERINGUE BUTTERCREAM
Makes about 3½ cups

Swiss meringue makes this slightly salty buttercream silkier than regular buttercream, and it's one of the most forgiving frostings to work with. For the ultimate indulgence, couple it with our buttery Yellow Cake (page 38) and drizzle extra Salted Caramel Sauce over your slice.

3 large egg whites (90 grams), room temperature
½ cup (100 grams) granulated sugar
½ cup (110 grams) firmly packed light brown sugar
1½ cups (340 grams) unsalted butter, cubed and softened
Salted Caramel Sauce (recipe follows)

1. In the bowl of a stand mixer fitted with the whisk attachment, whisk together egg whites and sugars by hand. Place mixer bowl over a saucepan of simmering water. Cook, whisking occasionally, until mixture registers 155°F (68°C) to 160°F (71°C) on a candy thermometer.
2. Carefully return bowl to stand mixer, and beat at high speed until medium-stiff peaks form, about 5 minutes. Reduce mixer to low speed. Beat until bowl is cool to the touch, about 8 minutes. Switch to the paddle attachment. With mixer on medium-low speed, add butter, 2 tablespoons at a time, beating until combined. Add Salted Caramel Sauce, and beat until smooth, about 3 minutes. (If buttercream breaks, beat 2 to 3 minutes more, and the emulsion will come back together.) Use immediately, or refrigerate in an airtight container for up to 3 days. If refrigerating, let frosting come to room temperature before using.

SALTED CARAMEL SAUCE
Makes about ½ cup

½ cup (100 grams) granulated sugar
3 tablespoons (42 grams) unsalted butter, cubed and softened
¼ cup (60 grams) heavy whipping cream, room temperature
1 teaspoon (4 grams) vanilla extract
1 teaspoon (3 grams) kosher salt

1. In a medium saucepan, cook sugar over medium heat, stirring occasionally, until deep amber colored. Carefully add butter, a few pieces at a time, stirring until combined. Stirring constantly, slowly drizzle in cream until combined. Remove from heat; stir in vanilla and salt. Let cool completely.

WHIPPED STRAWBERRY FROSTING
Makes about 4 cups

Cream cheese and heavy whipping cream give this frosting its light and airy consistency, which works wonderfully when creating rustic, swoopy designs on your cake. A more effortless frosting design will also keep the strawberry chunks and delicate fluffy texture intact.

⅓ cup (5 grams) freeze-dried strawberries
8 ounces (225 grams) cream cheese, softened
⅔ cup (133 grams) granulated sugar, divided
¼ teaspoon kosher salt
½ cup (85 grams) chopped fresh strawberries
1¼ cups (300 grams) heavy whipping cream, chilled
2 tablespoons (30 grams) fresh lemon juice

1. In the work bowl of a food processor, place freeze-dried strawberries; process until powdered. Set aside.
2. In the bowl of a stand mixer fitted with the paddle attachment, beat cream cheese, ⅓ cup (66.5 grams) sugar, and salt at medium speed until smooth. Add strawberry powder and strawberries, and beat until combined. Transfer to a medium bowl; set aside.
3. Clean bowl of stand mixer. Using the whisk attachment, beat cream and lemon juice at medium speed until foamy. Increase mixer speed to medium-high. Gradually add remaining ⅓ cup (66.5 grams) sugar, beating until stiff peaks form. Fold half of cream mixture into cream cheese mixture. Fold in remaining cream mixture. Use immediately.

Note: *For best results, make sure your heavy whipping cream is cold.*

PRO TIP
Use your cake decorating tools to your advantage. Before using metal tools, run them under hot water, and dry them. The heat from the tool gently melts and evens out frosting to create a smooth finish.

WHITE CAKE WITH VANILLA BUTTERCREAM

Makes 1 (9-inch) cake

This light cake is as versatile as they come. It is the perfect platform for any flavor icing, but we like coating ours in Vanilla Buttercream for a classic combination.

¾   cup (170 grams) unsalted butter, softened
1½ cups (300 grams) granulated sugar
1¼ teaspoons (5 grams) vanilla extract
1   teaspoon (4 grams) almond extract
2¼ cups (281 grams) cake flour
1   tablespoon (15 grams) baking powder
¾   cup (180 grams) whole milk, room temperature
4   large egg whites (120 grams), room temperature
Vanilla Buttercream (recipe follows)

1. Preheat oven to 350°F (180°C). Butter and flour 2 (9-inch) round cake pans.
2. In the bowl of a stand mixer fitted with the paddle attachment, beat butter and sugar at medium speed until fluffy, 3 to 4 minutes, stopping to scrape sides of bowl. Add extracts, beating just until combined.
3. In a medium bowl, sift together flour and baking powder. With mixer on low speed, gradually add flour mixture to butter mixture alternately with milk, beginning and ending with flour mixture, beating just until combined after each addition. Transfer batter to a large bowl; set aside.
4. Clean bowl of stand mixer. Using the whisk attachment, beat egg whites at medium speed until stiff peaks form. Gently fold half of egg whites into batter. Fold in remaining egg whites. Divide batter between prepared pans.
5. Bake until a wooden pick inserted in center comes out clean, 25 to 30 minutes. Let cool in pans for 10 minutes. Remove from pans, and let cool completely on wire racks. Spread Vanilla Buttercream between layers and on top and sides of cake.

VANILLA BUTTERCREAM
Makes about 3¼ cups

This creamy frosting holds its shape beautifully. Buttercream is simple in structure but extravagant in taste—butter melts at body temperature, so it literally melts in your mouth.

¾   cup (170 grams) unsalted butter, softened
5   cups (600 grams) confectioners' sugar, divided
4   tablespoons (60 grams) heavy whipping cream, room temperature and divided
1½ teaspoons (6 grams) vanilla extract
1   vanilla bean, split lengthwise, seeds scraped and reserved

1. In the bowl of a stand mixer fitted with the paddle attachment, beat butter and 2½ cups (300 grams) confectioners' sugar at low speed until combined. Stir in 2 tablespoons (30 grams) cream, vanilla extract, and vanilla bean seeds. Gradually beat in remaining 2½ cups (300 grams) confectioners' sugar and enough remaining cream until a smooth and spreadable consistency is reached. Use immediately.

CHOCOLATE CAKE WITH CHOCOLATE BUTTERCREAM

Makes 1 (9-inch) cake

This cake is so divine, you'd never guess it was a simple stir-together. It's doubly as decadent slathered in our Chocolate Buttercream.

⅔ cup (133 grams) granulated sugar
⅔ cup (147 grams) firmly packed light brown sugar
¼ cup (56 grams) canola oil
1 large egg (50 grams), room temperature
1 large egg yolk (19 grams), room temperature
1½ teaspoons (6 grams) vanilla extract
½ teaspoon (2 grams) almond extract
1⅔ cups (208 grams) all-purpose flour
⅔ cup (50 grams) unsweetened cocoa powder
1¾ teaspoons (8.75 grams) baking powder
¾ teaspoon (2.25 grams) kosher salt
½ teaspoon (2.5 grams) baking soda
1 cup (240 grams) whole milk, room temperature
⅔ cup (160 grams) hot coffee
Chocolate Buttercream (recipe follows)
Garnish: assorted sprinkles and dragées

1. Preheat oven to 350°F (180°C). Butter and flour 2 (9-inch) round cake pans. Line bottom of pans with parchment paper.
2. In a large bowl, stir together sugars and oil. Add egg, egg yolk, and extracts, stirring to combine.
3. In a medium bowl, sift together flour, cocoa, baking powder, salt, and baking soda. Gradually add flour mixture to sugar mixture alternately with milk, beginning and ending with flour mixture, stirring just until combined after each addition. Stir in hot coffee just until combined. Divide batter between prepared pans.
4. Bake until a wooden pick inserted in center comes out clean, 25 to 30 minutes. Let cool in pans for 10 minutes. Remove from pans, and let cool completely on wire racks. Spread Chocolate Buttercream between layers and on top and sides of cake. Garnish with sprinkles and dragées, if desired.

CHOCOLATE BUTTERCREAM
Makes about 4 cups

Glossy, rich, and velvety smooth to the taste, this is our favorite chocolate frosting.

1 cup (227 grams) unsalted butter, softened
1 cup (85 grams) unsweetened cocoa powder
4 cups (480 grams) confectioners' sugar
4 tablespoons (60 grams) heavy whipping cream, room temperature
2 teaspoons (8 grams) vanilla extract
¾ teaspoon (2.25 grams) kosher salt

1. In the bowl of a stand mixer fitted with the paddle attachment, beat butter and cocoa at low speed until well combined. Gradually add confectioners' sugar, 1 cup (120 grams) at a time, alternately with cream, 1 tablespoon (15 grams) at a time, beating until combined. Increase mixer speed to medium-high. Beat until mixture is smooth, about 1 minute. Add vanilla and salt, beating until combined. Use immediately.

BUNDT
CAKES

The iconic Bundt pan yields a cake with deep, sculpted ridges and graphic curves—the perfect versatile vessel for everything from a traditional pound cake to a rum-glazed roasted banana cake.

PEACH POUND CAKE

Makes 1 (10-cup) Bundt cake

A rich, tangy dose of buttermilk and swirls of cream cheese complement the bright sweetness of the peaches in this decadent pound cake.

1½ cups (340 grams) unsalted butter, softened
2⅓ cups (467 grams) granulated sugar, divided
5 large eggs (250 grams)
½ teaspoon (2 grams) almond extract
2¾ cups (344 grams) plus 2 tablespoons (16 grams) all-purpose flour, divided
¼ cup (30 grams) coconut flour
1 teaspoon (3 grams) kosher salt
½ cup (120 grams) plus 2 tablespoons (30 grams) whole buttermilk, room temperature and divided
2 cups (400 grams) diced peeled fresh peaches (about 3 medium peaches)
½ cup (112 grams) cream cheese, softened

Buttermilk Glaze (recipe follows)

1. Preheat oven to 325°F (170°C). Butter and flour a 10-cup Bundt pan.

2. In the bowl of a stand mixer fitted with the paddle attachment, beat butter and 2 cups (400 grams) sugar at medium speed until fluffy, 6 to 8 minutes, stopping to scrape sides of bowl. Add eggs, one at a time, beating well after each addition. Beat in almond extract.

3. In a medium bowl, whisk together 2¾ cups (344 grams) all-purpose flour, coconut flour, and salt. With mixer on low speed, gradually add flour mixture to butter mixture alternately with ½ cup (120 grams) buttermilk, beginning and ending with flour mixture, beating just until combined after each addition. Fold in peaches. Transfer batter to a large bowl; set aside.

4. Clean bowl of stand mixer and paddle attachment. Using the paddle attachment, beat cream cheese, remaining ⅓ cup (67 grams) sugar, and remaining 2 tablespoons (16 grams) all-purpose flour at medium speed until creamy, 3 to 4 minutes, stopping to scrape sides of bowl. Beat in remaining 2 tablespoons (30 grams) buttermilk until well combined.

5. Spoon half of batter into prepared pan. Add cream cheese filling, and top with remaining batter. Using a knife, gently swirl together batter and cream cheese filling.

6. Bake until a wooden pick inserted near center comes out clean, 1 hour and 30 minutes to 1 hour and 35 minutes, covering with foil after 1 hour of baking to prevent excess browning, if necessary. Let cool in pan for 20 minutes. Remove from pan, and let cool completely on a wire rack. Spoon Buttermilk Glaze over cooled cake.

BUTTERMILK GLAZE
Makes about 1½ cups

½ cup (112 grams) cream cheese, softened
1½ tablespoons (21 grams) unsalted butter, softened
½ cup (60 grams) confectioners' sugar
¼ cup plus 2 tablespoons (90 grams) whole buttermilk

1. In the bowl of a stand mixer fitted with the paddle attachment, beat cream cheese and butter at medium speed until creamy, 3 to 4 minutes. Reduce mixer speed to low. Gradually add confectioner's sugar, beating until combined. Add buttermilk, beating until smooth.

CHOCOLATE-FRANGIPANE BUNDT CAKE

Makes 1 (10-cup) Bundt cake

Recipe by Jake Cohen

A hidden pocket of velvety homemade Frangipane and a decadent almond glaze invigorate this Bundt, elevating it from a tasty dessert to a sophisticated masterpiece worthy of serving as the grand finale to a holiday feast.

½   cup (113 grams) unsalted butter
2   cups (480 grams) whole buttermilk
2   large eggs (100 grams), room temperature
1   tablespoon (6 grams) instant espresso powder
1½   teaspoons (6 grams) almond extract, divided
1   teaspoon (4 grams) vanilla extract
2   cups (400 grams) granulated sugar
2   cups (250 grams) all-purpose flour
¾   cup (64 grams) Dutch process cocoa powder, plus more for dusting pan
2   teaspoons (10 grams) baking soda
1⅛   teaspoons (3 grams) kosher salt, divided
1   teaspoon (5 grams) baking powder
Frangipane (recipe follows)
1½   cups (180 grams) confectioners' sugar
3   tablespoons (45 grams) heavy whipping cream
Garnish: toasted sliced almonds

1. Preheat oven to 350°F (180°C). Grease a 10-cup Bundt pan* with butter, and dust generously with cocoa to coat, tapping out excess.
2. In a small saucepan, melt butter over medium heat. Cook, stirring constantly, until butter turns a medium-brown color and has a nutty aroma, 5 to 6 minutes. Remove from heat.
3. In the bowl of a stand mixer fitted with the whisk attachment, beat browned butter, buttermilk, eggs, espresso powder, 1 teaspoon (4 grams) almond extract, and vanilla at medium speed until smooth.
4. In a large bowl, whisk together granulated sugar, flour, cocoa, baking soda, 1 teaspoon (3 grams) salt, and baking powder. Switch to the paddle attachment. With mixer on low speed, gradually add sugar mixture to butter mixture, beating until smooth. Pour half of batter into prepared pan, smoothing top with a spatula. Spoon Frangipane over batter, using the back of a spoon to spread evenly. Top with remaining batter, and smooth with a spatula.
5. Bake until risen and a wooden pick inserted near center comes out clean, 55 to 60 minutes, rotating pan halfway through baking. Let cool in pan for 10 minutes. Remove from pan, and let cool completely on a wire rack.
6. In a medium bowl, whisk together confectioners' sugar, cream, remaining ½ teaspoon (2 grams) almond extract, and remaining ⅛ teaspoon salt until smooth. Drizzle glaze over cooled cake. Garnish with toasted almonds, if desired.

*I used Nordic Ware Anniversary Bundt Pan.

FRANGIPANE
Makes 1⅓ cups

1   cup (96 grams) almond flour
½   cup (100 grams) granulated sugar
½   cup (113 grams) unsalted butter, melted and cooled
1   large egg (50 grams), room temperature
1   tablespoon (8 grams) all-purpose flour
1   teaspoon (4 grams) almond extract
½   teaspoon (1.5 grams) kosher salt

1. In a medium bowl, stir together all ingredients until a smooth paste forms.

Photo by Mark Weinberg

COCONUT ALMOND MARBLE CHIFFON CAKE

Makes 1 (10-inch) cake

A candy bar inspired our modern—and even more indulgent— makeover of the classic chiffon. We piled on coconut, almond, and chocolate for flavors reminiscent of an Almond Joy. Coconut oil, subbed in for the canola oil, adds depth and nuttiness without sacrificing the cake's texture.

1¾ cups (350 grams) granulated sugar, divided
¼ cup (60 grams) hot water
0.5 ounce (15 grams) 56% cacao semisweet chocolate
¼ teaspoon (1.25 grams) baking soda
1¾ cups (219 grams) cake flour
½ cup (48 grams) almond meal
½ cup (42 grams) desiccated coconut
1 tablespoon (15 grams) baking powder
1 teaspoon (3 grams) kosher salt
¾ cup (180 grams) water
½ cup (112 grams) coconut oil
5 large egg yolks (93 grams)
1½ teaspoons (6 grams) almond extract
½ teaspoon (2 grams) vanilla extract
8 large egg whites (240 grams)
⅛ teaspoon cream of tartar
Chocolate Ganache (recipe follows)
Garnish: toasted almonds, toasted unsweetened coconut flakes

1. Preheat oven to 350°F (180°C). Butter and flour the bottom of a 10-inch tube pan.
2. In the top of a double boiler, stir together ¼ cup (50 grams) sugar, ¼ cup (60 grams) hot water, chocolate, and baking soda. Cook over simmering water until chocolate is melted. Remove from heat; let cool.

3. In a large bowl, whisk together flour, almond meal, coconut, baking powder, salt, and remaining 1½ cups (300 grams) sugar. Make a well in center of flour mixture; add ¾ cup (180 grams) water, oil, egg yolks, and extracts, whisking until smooth.
4. In the bowl of a stand mixer fitted with the whisk attachment, beat egg whites at high speed until soft peaks form. Add cream of tartar, and beat until stiff peaks form. Fold one-third of egg whites into flour mixture. Fold in remaining egg whites. Transfer one-third of batter to a medium bowl; add cooled chocolate mixture, stirring until well combined. Alternate pouring yellow and chocolate batters into prepared pan. Using a knife, swirl batters together.
5. Bake until golden brown and a wooden pick inserted near center comes out clean, about 45 minutes. Invert cake in pan over a glass bottle, and let cool completely. Using a knife, loosen cake from sides and center of pan. Gently remove from pan. Pour Chocolate Ganache over cooled cake. Garnish with almonds and coconut, if desired.

CHOCOLATE GANACHE

Makes about 1 cup

6 ounces (175 grams) 56% cacao semisweet chocolate, chopped
3 tablespoons (45 grams) heavy whipping cream
3 tablespoons (42 grams) unsalted butter

1. Place chocolate in a medium heatproof bowl.
2. In a small saucepan, bring cream and butter to a simmer over medium-low heat. Pour hot cream mixture over chocolate. Let stand for 2 minutes; whisk until melted and smooth. Let cool until desired consistency is reached.

WHITE RUSSIAN BUNDT CAKE

Makes 1 (12-cup) Bundt cake

Recipe by Mandy Dixon

During the arctic Alaskan winters, pastry chef Mandy Dixon and her family serve this moist and flavorful coffee cake all winter long. At their family-run resort, they make a homemade version of coffee liqueur for a fun and easy winter activity, but name brand Kahlúa is wonderful here as well.

1   cup (227 grams) unsalted butter, softened
1½   cups (300 grams) granulated sugar
4   large eggs (200 grams)
2   teaspoons (8 grams) vanilla extract
2¾   cups (344 grams) all-purpose flour
1½   teaspoons (7.5 grams) baking powder
1   teaspoon (3 grams) kosher salt
¾   cup (180 grams) heavy whipping cream
¼   cup (60 grams) Kahlúa
Kahlúa Pecan Filling (recipe follows)
Kahlúa Glaze (recipe follows)

1. Preheat oven to 325°F (170°C). Grease a 12-cup fluted Bundt pan.
2. In the bowl of a stand mixer fitted with the paddle attachment, beat butter and sugar at medium speed until fluffy, 3 to 4 minutes, stopping to scrape sides of bowl. Add eggs, one at a time, beating well after each addition. Beat in vanilla.
3. In a medium bowl, whisk together flour, baking powder, and salt. In a small bowl, whisk together cream and Kahlúa. With mixer on low speed, gradually add flour mixture to butter mixture alternately with cream mixture, beginning and ending with flour mixture, beating just until combined after each addition. Pour half of batter into prepared pan. Sprinkle with Kahlúa Pecan Filling. Top with remaining batter.
4. Bake until cake is firm to the touch, about 1 hour. Let cool in pan for 10 minutes. Remove from pan, and let cool completely on a wire rack. Drizzle Kahlúa Glaze over cooled cake.

KAHLÚA PECAN FILLING
Makes about 1 cup

1   cup (113 grams) chopped toasted pecans
½   cup (110 grams) firmly packed light brown sugar
2   tablespoons (30 grams) Kahlúa
1   tablespoon (5 grams) unsweetened cocoa powder
1   teaspoon (2 grams) ground cinnamon

1. In a medium bowl, stir together all ingredients. Use immediately.

KAHLÚA GLAZE
Makes about 1 cup

1   cup (120 grams) confectioners' sugar, sifted
2   tablespoons (30 grams) heavy whipping cream
2   tablespoons (30 grams) Kahlúa

1. In a small bowl, whisk together all ingredients until smooth. Use immediately.

ROASTED BANANA RUM BUNDT CAKE

Makes 1 (10-cup) Bundt cake

Ready for a bolder, more sophisticated take on the simple loaf? Time to bring out the Bundt pan. We roast the bananas and use tangy buttermilk to create an extra-smooth batter and tender crumb that translate beautifully to cake form. Buttery spiced rum paired with the gooey Roasted Bananas equals pure indulgence.

Roasted Bananas (recipe follows)
1   ripe banana (124 grams), mashed
⅔   cup (160 grams) whole buttermilk
1   cup (220 grams) firmly packed dark
     brown sugar
½   cup (112 grams) canola oil
¼   cup (60 grams) dark rum*
2   large eggs (100 grams)
1   teaspoon (4 grams) vanilla extract
2½   cups (312 grams) cake flour
1   teaspoon (5 grams) baking soda
1   teaspoon (5 grams) baking powder
½   teaspoon (1.5 grams) kosher salt
Vanilla Cream Cheese Glaze (recipe follows)

1. Preheat oven to 325°F (170°C). Butter and flour a 10-cup Bundt pan**.
2. In the work bowl of a food processor, place Roasted Bananas, mashed banana, and buttermilk; process until smooth. Transfer to a large bowl; whisk in brown sugar, oil, rum, eggs, and vanilla.
3. In a medium bowl, whisk together flour, baking soda, baking powder, and salt. Fold flour mixture into banana mixture just until combined. Spoon batter into prepared pan. Gently tap pan on counter to release any air bubbles.
4. Bake until a wooden pick inserted near center comes out clean, 40 to 45 minutes. Let cool in pan for 10 minutes. Remove from pan, and let cool completely on a wire rack. Spoon Vanilla Cream Cheese Glaze over cooled cake.

We used The Kraken Black Spiced Rum.

**We used Nordic Ware Premier Brilliance Pan, available on nordicware.com.*

ROASTED BANANAS
Makes 3 bananas

3   medium unpeeled bananas (672 grams)

1. Preheat oven to 400°F (200°C).
2. Place unpeeled bananas on a sheet pan.
3. Roast until completely black, 20 to 25 minutes. Let cool completely; peel bananas.

VANILLA CREAM CHEESE GLAZE
Makes ½ cup

¼   cup (56 grams) cream cheese, softened
½   cup (60 grams) confectioners' sugar
1   tablespoon (15 grams) whole milk
1   tablespoon (15 grams) dark rum*
¼   teaspoon (1.5 grams) vanilla bean paste

1. In the bowl of a stand mixer fitted with the paddle attachment, beat cream cheese at medium speed until smooth. With mixer on low speed, gradually add confectioners' sugar, beating until combined. Add milk, rum, and vanilla bean paste, beating until smooth. Use immediately.

We used The Kraken Black Spiced Rum.

BLACK-AND-WHITE CHOCOLATE MARBLE POUND CAKE WITH VANILLA BEAN AND BLACK COCOA GLAZES

Makes 1 (10-inch) Bundt cake

Recipe by Ben Mims

It never gets old to marble chocolate and plain batters into a pound cake. For a modern update, however, I use black cocoa for the chocolate batter, which gives it a dark richness, and white chocolate in the "plain" batter to offset the bitter cocoa with sweetness. I scoop both batters alternately into the Bundt pan using a spring-loaded scoop to create the marbled design without swirling the batters together, but feel free to pour both batters into the pan and swirl the batter with a table knife if you like.

2   cups (454 grams) unsalted butter, room temperature and divided
3   cups (600 grams) granulated sugar, divided
3   teaspoons (12 grams) vanilla extract, divided
4   large egg whites (120 grams), room temperature
4   ounces (115 grams) white chocolate, melted
2¼   cups (281 grams) cake flour, divided
2   teaspoons (6 grams) kosher salt, divided
2   large eggs (100 grams), room temperature
4   large egg yolks (74 grams), room temperature
¾   cup (64 grams) black cocoa powder*, sifted
½   cup (120 grams) whole buttermilk, room temperature
Vanilla Bean Glaze (recipe follows)
Black Cocoa Glaze (recipe follows)

1. Butter and flour a 10-inch Bundt pan.
2. In the bowl of a stand mixer fitted with the paddle attachment, beat 1 cup (227 grams) butter, 1½ cups (300 grams) sugar, and 1½ teaspoons (6 grams) vanilla at medium speed until fluffy and pale, at least 6 minutes. Add egg whites, one at a time, beating well after each addition, about 15 seconds. Scrape bottom and sides of bowl with a rubber spatula. With mixer on medium-high speed, add melted white chocolate, beating until smooth, about 1 minute. Add 1½ cups (187 grams) flour and 1 teaspoon (3 grams) salt, and stir with a rubber spatula just until combined. Scrape white batter into a bowl, and set aside.
3. Return bowl to stand mixer. Using the paddle attachment, beat remaining 1 cup (227 grams) butter, remaining 1½ cups (300 grams) sugar, and remaining 1½ teaspoons (6 grams) vanilla at medium speed until fluffy and pale, at least 6 minutes. Add eggs, one at a time, beating well after each addition, about 15 seconds. Add egg yolks, two at a time, beating well after each addition, about 15 seconds. Scrape bottom and sides of bowl with a rubber spatula. With mixer on medium-high speed, beat until smooth, about 1 minute. Add black cocoa, remaining ¾ cup (94 grams) flour, and remaining 1 teaspoon (3 grams) salt. With mixer on low speed, add buttermilk, beating just until batter comes together. Scrape bottom and sides of bowl with a rubber spatula, and stir just until combined.

4. Using a large (2- to 3-ounce) spring-loaded scoop, alternately scoop white and black batters into prepared pan. Tap pan lightly on counter to settle batter.
5. Place pan in a cold oven, and bake at 300°F (150°C) until lightly browned on top and a wooden pick inserted near center comes out clean, 1½ to 2 hours. (This bake time depends on how long it takes your oven to preheat. Start checking after 1½ hours, and continue baking in 10-minute intervals until cake is done.) Let cool in pan for 10 minutes. Remove from pan, and let cool completely on a wire rack.
6. Alternately spoon Vanilla Bean Glaze and Black Cocoa Glaze over cooled cake, letting each one drip down grooves of cake. (Alternatively, pour Black Cocoa Glaze over cake, and let stand until hardened, about 10 minutes. Pour Vanilla Bean Glaze over top, and let stand until hardened, about 10 minutes.)

*Black cocoa is available online or in specialty food stores. I used King Arthur Flour Black Cocoa, but any brand will work. Black cocoa is a deeper color than regular cocoa and further alkalized—or "Dutch processed"—to remove virtually all acidity. To make sure it doesn't dry out the cake batter, this recipe has extra buttermilk to provide more moisture and acidity.

VANILLA BEAN GLAZE
Makes about ½ cup

1   cup (120 grams) confectioners' sugar, sifted
2   tablespoons plus 2 teaspoons (40 grams) heavy whipping cream
¼   teaspoon kosher salt
½   plump Bourbon-Madagascar vanilla bean, split lengthwise, seeds scraped and reserved

1. In a small saucepan, combine all ingredients. Cook over low heat, stirring constantly, until smooth and no lumps remain. Pour glaze into a bowl, and let cool until it falls off a spoon in a thick, heavy stream.

BLACK COCOA GLAZE
Makes about ½ cup

¾   cup (90 grams) confectioners' sugar, sifted
¼   cup (21 grams) black cocoa powder, sifted
3   tablespoons (45 grams) heavy whipping cream
¼   teaspoon kosher salt

1. In a small saucepan, combine all ingredients. Cook over low heat, stirring constantly, until smooth and no lumps remain. Pour glaze into a bowl, and let cool until it falls off a spoon in a thick, heavy stream.

PRO TIP
The cold-oven method gives batter extra time to rise, producing an extra-smooth, tender crumb. It is great for cakes like this where there is no leavening besides the air trapped inside the creamed butter and sugar.

ULTIMATE SOUTHERN CREAM CHEESE POUND CAKE

Makes 1 (10-inch) cake

Recipe by Ben Mims

When you say "pound cake" to a Southerner, they usually think of something intensely rich, tall, and capped with a crackling crust of butter and sugar so good that people fight over it. In this cake, the butter, flour, and eggs match in proportion, but the sugar is almost double the weight, which ensures that crackling crust and gives the cake the requisite sweetness that Southern palates are known to love. Cream cheese not only adds extra fat (flavor!) but also moisture, stability, and some tang to balance all that sugar.

1½　cups (340 grams) unsalted butter, room temperature
8　ounces (225 grams) cream cheese, room temperature
3　cups (600 grams) granulated sugar
1　tablespoon (13 grams) vanilla extract
1½　teaspoons (4.5 grams) kosher salt
6　large eggs (300 grams), room temperature
3　cups (375 grams) cake flour

1. Preheat oven to 325°F (170°C). Butter and flour a 10-inch straight-sided tube or angel food cake pan.

2. In the bowl of a stand mixer fitted with the paddle attachment, beat butter, cream cheese, sugar, vanilla, and salt at medium speed until fluffy and pale, at least 8 minutes. Add eggs, one at a time, beating until there are no streaks of yolk left after each addition, about 15 seconds. Scrape bottom and sides of bowl with a rubber spatula. With mixer on medium-high speed, beat until superlight and airy, at least 3 minutes. Add flour, and stir with a rubber spatula just until combined. Spoon batter into prepared pan, and smooth top.

3. Bake until cake has a lightly raised and cracked dome, is golden brown on top, and a wooden pick inserted near center comes out clean, 1 hour and 30 minutes to 1 hour and 40 minutes. Let cool in pan for 10 minutes. Remove from pan, and let cool completely on a wire rack.

PRO TIP

As with all cake recipes, but more so here, having the butter and cream cheese at true room temperature is vital to the two ingredients incorporating smoothly into the batter. Your best bet is take the butter and cream cheese out of the refrigerator the night before you plan to bake. That way, there's no guessing that they're at the perfect temperature and consistency.

PASSION FRUIT AND CHOCOLATE BUNDT CAKE

Makes 1 (12- to 15-cup) Bundt cake

Recipe by Edd Kimber

This cake's texture is between that of a classic pound cake and the incredibly moist texture of a polenta cake. It's the perfect cake for elevenses, what we Brits refer to as a morning coffee or tea break, or when a layer cake seems like too much effort.

8   extra-large eggs (416 grams)
2½ cups (500 grams) castor sugar
2   tablespoons (6 grams) lemon zest
1¼ cups (280 grams) light olive oil
¾   cup (180 grams) yoghurt
¼   cup (50 grams) passion fruit purée
1¾ cups (219 grams) self-raising flour/
    self-rising flour
1   cup (100 grams) ground almonds
⅔   cup (100 grams) fine semolina
½   teaspoon (2.5 grams) baking powder
Passion Fruit Syrup (recipe follows)
Chocolate Glaze (recipe follows)

1. Preheat oven to 350°F (180°C). Butter and flour a 12- to 15-cup Bundt pan.
2. In the bowl of a stand mixer fitted with the whisk attachment, beat eggs, castor sugar, and zest at medium speed until pale and light, about 5 minutes. Add oil, yoghurt, and passion fruit purée, and beat to combine.
3. In a medium bowl, whisk together flour, almonds, semolina, and baking powder. With mixer on low speed, gradually add flour mixture to egg mixture, beating to combine. Pour batter into prepared pan.
4. Bake until a wooden pick inserted near center comes out clean, 50 to 60 minutes, loosely covering with foil during last 10 minutes of baking to prevent excess browning, if necessary. Let cool in pan for 10 minutes before carefully inverting onto a wire rack. Whilst cake is still warm, brush with Passion Fruit Syrup. (This adds both moisture and a stronger passion fruit flavour.) Let cool completely. Pour Chocolate Glaze over cooled cake, allowing it to run down sides of cake. This cake keeps brilliantly, 3 to 4 days in a covered container.

PASSION FRUIT SYRUP

Makes ½ cup

⅓   cup (67 grams) superfine sugar
⅓   cup (67 grams) passion fruit purée

1. In a small saucepan, bring superfine sugar and passion fruit purée to a simmer over medium heat; simmer until reduced, 2 to 3 minutes.

CHOCOLATE GLAZE

Makes 2 cups

5   ounces (150 grams) 65% to 75% cacao bittersweet chocolate, finely chopped
1   cup (240 grams) heavy whipping cream

1. Place chocolate in a large heatproof bowl. Place cream in a saucepan, and bring just to a simmer over medium heat. Pour over chocolate, and allow to sit for a couple minutes before stirring together to form a silky glaze. The glaze will thicken as it cools, so use whilst still a pouring consistency.

Photo by Yuki Sugiura

HUMMINGBIRD BUNDT CAKE

Makes 1 (12-cup) Bundt cake

Think of this Bundt as the frosted layer cake's laid-back cousin. It requires less effort to make but packs all the same spiced, fruity flavor of the original. Bananas and whole milk keep the cake moist and flavorful for days, but the best part is that tangy, spoon-licking Cream Cheese Icing.

½   cup (57 grams) chopped pecans
3⅓ cups (417 grams) all-purpose flour
1⅓ cups (267 grams) granulated sugar
1   teaspoon (5 grams) baking powder
1   teaspoon (3 grams) kosher salt
1   teaspoon (2 grams) ground cinnamon
¾   teaspoon (3.75 grams) baking soda
¼   teaspoon ground nutmeg
1½ cups (341 grams) mashed ripe banana
1   cup (224 grams) canola oil
½   cup (120 grams) whole milk, room temperature
3   large eggs (150 grams), room temperature
1   teaspoon (4 grams) vanilla extract
1   cup (200 grams) finely chopped fresh pineapple
Cream Cheese Icing (recipe follows)
Garnish: chopped toasted pecans

1. Preheat oven to 350°F (180°C). Butter and flour a 12-cup Bundt pan.

2. Sprinkle pecans in bottom of prepared pan.

3. In a large bowl, sift together flour, sugar, baking powder, salt, cinnamon, baking soda, and nutmeg. In a medium bowl, stir together banana, oil, milk, eggs, and vanilla. Make a well in center of flour mixture; add banana mixture, stirring just until moistened. Fold in pineapple. Pour batter over pecans, smoothing top with an offset spatula.

4. Bake until a wooden pick inserted near center comes out clean, 55 to 60 minutes, covering with foil halfway through baking to prevent excess browning. Let cool in pan for 10 minutes. Remove from pan, and let cool completely on a wire rack. Pour Cream Cheese Icing over cooled cake. Top with toasted pecans, if desired.

CREAM CHEESE ICING
Makes about 1½ cups

3   ounces (86 grams) cream cheese, softened
¼   cup (60 grams) whole milk, room temperature
¼   teaspoon (1 gram) vanilla extract
1¾ cups (210 grams) confectioners' sugar

1. In the bowl of a stand mixer fitted with the paddle attachment, beat cream cheese at medium speed until creamy. Add milk and vanilla, beating until combined. Gradually add confectioners' sugar, beating until smooth. Use immediately.

Photo by Stephen DeVries

CRANBERRY-HAZELNUT COFFEE CAKE

Makes 1 (10-inch) cake

Our moist coffee cake blends buttery hazelnuts and bright cranberries while a crunchy Hazelnut Streusel and zesty Orange Glaze finish it off.

½   cup (113 grams) unsalted butter, softened
1¼ cups (275 grams) firmly packed light brown sugar
3   large eggs (150 grams)
3   tablespoons (9 grams) orange zest (about 1 orange)
2   teaspoons (8 grams) vanilla extract
2½ cups (300 grams) plus 1 tablespoon
     (8 grams) all-purpose flour, divided
1   teaspoon (5 grams) baking powder
½   teaspoon (1.5 grams) kosher salt
1   cup (240 grams) crème fraîche
½   cup (64 grams) chopped dry roasted unsalted hazelnuts
1½ cups (143 grams) fresh or frozen cranberries
Hazelnut Streusel (recipe follows)
Orange Glaze (recipe follows)

1. Preheat oven to 350°F (180°C). Butter and flour a 10-inch tube pan.
2. In the bowl of a stand mixer fitted with the paddle attachment, beat butter and brown sugar at medium speed until fluffy, 3 to 4 minutes, stopping to scrape sides of bowl. Reduce mixer speed to low. Add eggs, one at a time, beating well after each addition. Stir in zest and vanilla.
3. In a medium bowl, whisk together 2½ cups (300 grams) flour, baking powder, and salt. Gradually add flour mixture to butter mixture alternately with crème fraîche, beginning and ending with flour mixture, beating just until combined after each addition. Stir in hazelnuts.
4. In a small bowl, toss together cranberries and remaining 1 tablespoon (8 grams) flour. Gently fold cranberries into batter. Spoon batter into prepared pan, smoothing top. Top with Hazelnut Streusel.

5. Bake until a wooden pick inserted near center comes out clean, 45 to 50 minutes, loosely covering with foil during last 15 minutes of baking to prevent excess browning, if necessary. (Cake made with fresh cranberries will bake more quickly—by about 5 minutes—than cake made with frozen cranberries.) Let cool in pan for 30 minutes. Remove from pan, and let cool completely on a wire rack. Drizzle Orange Glaze over cooled cake. Wrap tightly in plastic wrap, and store in an airtight container at room temperature for up to 4 days.

HAZELNUT STREUSEL

Makes 2⅓ cups

⅔   cup (64 grams) hazelnut flour
½   cup (60 grams) all-purpose flour
⅓   cup (67 grams) granulated sugar
3   tablespoons (9 grams) orange zest (about 1 orange)
¾   teaspoon (1.5 grams) ground cinnamon
¼   teaspoon kosher salt
¼   cup (57 grams) cold unsalted butter, cubed
½   cup (64 grams) chopped roasted hazelnuts

1. In a medium bowl, whisk together flours, sugar, zest, cinnamon, and salt. Using your fingers, cut in cold butter until mixture is crumbly and desired consistency is reached. Stir in hazelnuts. Freeze until ready to use.

ORANGE GLAZE

Makes ½ cup

1   cup (120 grams) confectioners' sugar
1   tablespoon plus 2 teaspoons (25 grams) fresh orange juice

1. In a small bowl, whisk together confectioners' sugar and orange juice until smooth. Use immediately.

ONE-LAYER
CAKES

Low in stature but high in sophistication, these one-layer
wonders feature everything from streusel-topped coffee
cakes to caramelized upside-down cakes.

MARMALADE PUDDING

Makes 8 servings

Recipe by Edd Kimber

This is about as traditional as it gets when it comes to old-school British puddings. Traditionally, this would be steamed, but I prefer baked as it is quicker and, frankly, less fiddly to make. The real twist in this pudding is the addition of Earl Grey tea, which for me makes this dessert reminiscent of breakfast—toast with lashings of butter and marmalade served alongside a mug of Earl Grey.

1   teaspoon (2 grams) loose Earl Grey tea, leaves ground to a powder
Scant ¼ cup (60 grams) whole milk
¾   cup plus 2 tablespoons (198 grams) unsalted butter
1   cup (200 grams) castor sugar
6   tablespoons (18 grams) lemon zest
3   large eggs (150 grams)
2   cups (250 grams) self-raising flour/ superfine cake flour*
1   teaspoon (5 grams) baking powder
⅔   cup (213 grams) medium cut marmalade*
Vanilla Custard (recipe follows)

1. Preheat oven to 350°F (180°C). Lightly grease a tall-sided 8-inch round cake pan; line bottom of pan with a slightly damp sheet of parchment paper. (This helps prevent the marmalade from burning.)
2. Place ground tea in a small bowl. In a small saucepan, bring milk to a boil over medium-high heat. Pour hot milk over tea to bloom and bring out its flavor.
3. In the bowl of a stand mixer fitted with the paddle attachment, beat butter, sugar, and zest at medium speed until fluffy, 3 to 4 minutes, stopping to scrape sides of bowl. Add eggs, one at a time, beating well after each addition.
4. In a medium bowl, stir together flour and baking powder. Fold flour mixture into butter mixture. Add warm Earl Grey milk, quickly stirring into batter. Reserve a few tablespoons marmalade. Spread remaining marmalade in prepared pan. Spread batter over marmalade.
5. Bake until pudding springs back when touched in center, 45 to 50 minutes. Let cool in pan for 5 minutes; carefully invert onto a serving plate.
6. In a small saucepan, heat reserved marmalade over medium heat. Spread onto cake. Serve warm with Vanilla Custard.

*I used Bob's Red Mill Super-Fine Unbleached Cake Flour and Wilkin & Sons Tiptree Orange Medium Cut Marmalade.

VANILLA CUSTARD
Makes about 3 cups

2½ cups (600 grams) whole milk
2   teaspoons (12 grams) vanilla bean paste or 1 vanilla pod/bean, split lengthwise, seeds scraped and reserved
6   large egg yolks (112 grams)
3   tablespoons (36 grams) castor sugar
1   tablespoon (8 grams) plain flour/cake flour

1. In a large saucepan, bring milk and vanilla bean paste or vanilla pod and reserved seeds to a simmer over medium heat.
2. In a medium bowl, whisk together egg yolks, sugar, and flour until smooth. Pour hot milk mixture into egg mixture, whisking constantly. Return mixture to saucepan (removing vanilla pod, if using), and cook, stirring constantly, until mixture is thick enough to coat the back of a spoon. Remove from heat, and pour straight into a jug to serve whilst still hot.

Photo by Yuki Sugiura

CHOCOLATE BISCUIT CAKE

Makes 1 (9-inch) cake

We took inspiration from the royal chef for our take on Queen Elizabeth II's all-time favorite cake, but used milk chocolate for a smoother base rather than creaming sugar and butter and stirring in bitter dark chocolate.

5¾ cups (978 grams) milk chocolate chips
2 cups (480 grams) heavy whipping cream
3 tablespoons (42 grams) unsalted butter
1 teaspoon (3 grams) kosher salt
1 (10.5-ounce) package (300 grams) English rich tea biscuits*, broken into 1- to 2-inch pieces
Milk Chocolate Ganache (recipe follows)
Garnish: melted dark chocolate, melted white chocolate

1. Line a 9-inch round cake pan with plastic wrap.
2. Place chocolate chips in a heatproof bowl.
3. In a medium saucepan, heat cream, butter, and salt over medium heat, stirring frequently, just until bubbles form around edges of pan. (Do not boil.) Remove from heat; pour hot cream mixture over chocolate. Let stand for 5 minutes; stir until chocolate is melted and mixture is smooth.
4. Pour enough melted chocolate into prepared pan to cover bottom of pan. Place biscuit pieces in a single layer over chocolate. Repeat layers until pan is full. Refrigerate until chocolate is hardened, about 4 hours.
5. Invert cake onto a wire rack set over a rimmed baking sheet. Pour Milk Chocolate Ganache over cake, letting it drip down sides. Using an offset spatula, smooth Milk Chocolate Ganache over sides of cake. Refrigerate, uncovered, for at least 8 hours or overnight. Drizzle with melted dark chocolate and melted white chocolate, if desired.

We used McVitie's.

MILK CHOCOLATE GANACHE
Makes about 2½ cups

2 cups (340 grams) milk chocolate chips
⅔ cup plus 1 tablespoon (175 grams) heavy whipping cream

1. Place chocolate chips in a heatproof bowl.
2. In a medium saucepan, heat cream over medium heat, stirring frequently, just until bubbles form around edges of pan. (Do not boil.) Remove from heat; pour hot cream over chocolate. Let stand for 5 minutes; stir until chocolate is melted and mixture is smooth. Use immediately.

ROASTED PECAN POUND CAKE WITH SORGHUM STREUSEL

Makes 2 (9x5-inch) cakes

Recipe by Ben Mims

If plain pound cake is your pair of everyday sneakers, then this pound cake is your special-occasion stilettos. Roasted pecans are finely ground with sugar and then whipped with butter into a nutty batter enriched with sour cream. The crumbly cake is topped with a streusel imbued with fragrant sorghum syrup. Sorghum, a cereal grain that grows abundantly and is a popular ingredient in Southern cuisine, complements the pecans with its signature bitter, leathery taste. I love to serve thick slabs of the cake drizzled with an extra shot of sorghum on the corner so you can dip or smear your bites with as much extra syrup as you want.

2   cups (284 grams) whole pecans
1   tablespoon (14 grams) vegetable oil
2   cups (400 grams) granulated sugar,
    divided
1   cup (227 grams) unsalted butter,
    softened
1   tablespoon (13 grams) vanilla extract
1   teaspoon (3 grams) kosher salt
4   large eggs (200 grams),
    room temperature
2   large egg whites (60 grams),
    room temperature
2   cups (250 grams) all-purpose flour
½   cup (120 grams) sour cream,
    room temperature
Sorghum Streusel (recipe follows)
Flaked sea salt, for sprinkling
Sorghum syrup, to serve

1. Preheat oven to 350°F (180°C). Butter 2 (9x5-inch) loaf pans. Line pans with parchment paper, letting excess extend over sides of pans. Butter and flour parchment.
2. Place pecans on a rimmed baking sheet. Drizzle with oil, and toss with your hands until evenly coated. Spread pecans in a single layer on baking sheet.
3. Bake until toasted and fragrant, 8 to 10 minutes. Let cool completely on pan. Reduce oven temperature to 325°F (170°C).

4. In the work bowl of a food processor, place cooled roasted pecans and 1 cup (200 grams) sugar; pulse until pecans are very finely ground and mixed with sugar, about 20 pulses. Transfer pecan sugar to the bowl of a stand mixer fitted with the paddle attachment. Add butter, vanilla, kosher salt, and remaining 1 cup (200 grams) sugar, and beat at medium speed until fluffy and pale, at least 6 minutes. Add eggs, one at a time, beating until there are no streaks of yolk left after each addition, about 15 seconds. Add egg whites, beating well. Scrape bottom and sides of bowl with a rubber spatula. With mixer on medium-high speed, beat until superlight and airy, at least 3 minutes. Add flour and sour cream, and stir with a rubber spatula just until combined.
5. Divide batter between prepared pans, and smooth tops. Break up Sorghum Streusel, and sprinkle over batter in large clumps. (Do not pack it down.) Sprinkle with sea salt.
6. Bake until topping is deep golden brown and a wooden pick inserted in center comes out clean, 1 hour and 30 minutes to 1 hour and 50 minutes, loosely covering with foil after 1 hour of baking to prevent excess browning. Let cool in pans for 10 minutes.

Using excess parchment as handles, remove from pans, and place on a wire rack. Remove parchment, and let cool completely.
7. To serve, cut pound cake into thick slabs, and place on serving plates. Spoon or pour about 1 tablespoon (21 grams) sorghum syrup onto corner of each slice so you can dip bites of cake into syrup for a more intense sorghum flavor.

SORGHUM STREUSEL
Makes about 2½ cups

1   cup (200 grams) granulated sugar
2   tablespoons (42 grams) sorghum syrup
1   cup (125 grams) all-purpose flour
6   tablespoons (84 grams) unsalted
    butter, softened
½   teaspoon (1.5 grams) kosher salt

1. In a medium bowl, combine sugar and sorghum syrup. Rub syrup into sugar with your fingertips until evenly incorporated. (It will look like golden light brown sugar.) Add flour, butter, and salt, and rub together with your fingertips until large clumps form. Freeze until ready to use, up to 1 day.

CRÈME FRAÎCHE STRAWBERRY SWIRL CHEESECAKE

Makes 1 (9-inch) cake

This jam-dotted cheesecake receives its creamy texture from a trio of cream cheese, goat cheese, and crème fraîche.

24 ounces (680 grams) cream cheese, softened
⅔ cup (133 grams) granulated sugar
¼ cup (56 grams) goat cheese, room temperature
2 tablespoons (16 grams) all-purpose flour
2 teaspoons (8 grams) vanilla extract
⅔ cup (160 grams) crème fraîche, room temperature
2 large eggs (100 grams), room temperature
1 large egg yolk (19 grams), room temperature
Strawberry Graham Cracker Crust (recipe follows)
⅓ cup (107 grams) Quick Black Pepper Strawberry Jam (recipe follows)

1. Preheat oven to 325°F (170°C).
2. In the bowl of a stand mixer fitted with the paddle attachment, beat cream cheese, sugar, goat cheese, flour, and vanilla at medium speed until well combined. Beat in crème fraîche. With mixer on low speed, add eggs and egg yolk, one at a time, beating just until combined after each addition. Pour cream cheese mixture into prepared Strawberry Graham Cracker Crust. Drop Quick Black Pepper Strawberry Jam by teaspoonfuls over cream cheese mixture. Using a knife, swirl several times to create a marble effect.
3. Bake until edges are set and center is still slightly jiggly, 35 to 40 minutes. Let cool completely in pan. Run a knife around edges of pan to loosen cake. Remove from pan. Refrigerate until set, at least 4 hours or overnight. Refrigerate for up to 5 days.

STRAWBERRY GRAHAM CRACKER CRUST

Makes 1 (9-inch) crust

⅔ cup (87 grams) graham cracker crumbs
¼ cup (4 grams) freeze-dried strawberries, powdered (see PRO TIP)
2 tablespoons (24 grams) granulated sugar
2 tablespoons (28 grams) unsalted butter, melted

1. Preheat oven to 325°F (170°C).
2. In a medium bowl, stir together all ingredients. Firmly press mixture into bottom of a 9-inch springform pan.
3. Bake for 10 minutes. Let cool completely. Use immediately.

QUICK BLACK PEPPER STRAWBERRY JAM

Makes 2 cups

1 pound (455 grams) fresh strawberries, hulled and chopped
1¼ cups (250 grams) granulated sugar
3 tablespoons (45 grams) fresh lemon juice
½ teaspoon (1 gram) ground black pepper
¼ teaspoon kosher salt

1. In a medium saucepan, bring all ingredients to a boil over medium-high heat. Cook for 5 minutes, stirring frequently. Reduce heat to medium-low; cook, stirring frequently and mashing berries with a potato masher, until mixture thickens, 20 to 45 minutes. (The ripeness of berries can affect the cook time. This jam could take anywhere from 20 minutes for very ripe berries to 45 minutes for less ripe berries.) To test your jam for doneness, scrape the bottom of the saucepan with your spoon—if the jam parts for a few seconds, it is ready. Remove from heat, and let cool for 30 minutes before transferring to a glass jar. Jam will keep refrigerated for up to 2 weeks.

> **PRO TIP**
> To make powdered freeze-dried strawberries, place freeze-dried strawberries in the work bowl of a food processor, and pulse until reduced to a powder.

CHOCOLATE-POPPY SEED CAKE

Makes 1 (8-inch) cake

Recipe by Uri Scheft

This is a great dessert option for the Jewish holy day Pesach when you just can't handle another macaroon. I think chocolate and poppy seed are the perfect combination. The ground poppy seeds give the cake nice structure—not too dense, not dry, but with substance. The chocolate topping on the cake is totally melt-in-your-mouth. The two textures together make this cake for me.

¾   cup plus 1 teaspoon (175 grams) unsalted butter, softened
⅓   cup plus 2 tablespoons (54 grams) confectioners' sugar
1   large egg yolk (19 grams)
1⅓   cups (130 grams) freshly ground poppy seeds*
⅓   cup plus 2 tablespoons (65 grams) whole poppy seeds
⅔   cup (64 grams) almond meal
⅓   cup (32 grams) ground hazelnuts
6   jumbo egg whites (228 grams)
⅔   cup (133 grams) granulated sugar
5   ounces (150 grams) 60% cacao dark chocolate, chopped
½   cup plus 2 tablespoons (150 grams) heavy whipping cream
1   teaspoon (7 grams) corn syrup
Chocolate Truffles (recipe follows)
Garnish: unsweetened cocoa powder

1. Preheat oven to 325°F (170°C). Butter and flour a tall-sided (at least 3 inches) 8-inch round cake pan; line pan with parchment paper.
2. In the bowl of a stand mixer fitted with the paddle attachment, beat butter and confectioners' sugar at medium speed until creamy, 3 to 4 minutes, stopping to scrape sides of bowl. Add egg yolk, and beat until smooth, 2 to 3 minutes. Scrape bottom of bowl, and beat for 1 minute. Gradually add ground and whole poppy seeds, almond meal, and hazelnuts, beating until combined. Scrape bottom of bowl, and beat until combined. Transfer batter to a large bowl; set aside.
3. Clean bowl of stand mixer. Using the whisk attachment, beat egg whites and granulated sugar at low speed until sugar is dissolved. Increase mixer speed to high, and beat until a firm but still elastic meringue is formed. Fold one-third of meringue into poppy seed mixture. Gently fold in remaining meringue. Spread mixture into prepared pan.
4. Bake until golden brown and firm to the touch, 40 to 50 minutes. Let cool in pan for 30 minutes. Remove from pan, and let cool completely on a wire rack.

5. Place chocolate in a medium heatproof bowl. In a small saucepan, heat cream and corn syrup over medium heat, stirring constantly. Pour hot cream mixture over chocolate. Let stand for 1 minute; stir until chocolate is melted and mixture is smooth. Let cool slightly; stir. Pour hot ganache over cake, and spread with a spatula. Refrigerate until firm. Top with Chocolate Truffles. Cover sides of cake with cocoa, if desired.

*It's important to use freshly ground poppy seeds. If you can't find it freshly ground, grind the seeds yourself just before making this cake. Or grind and then freeze immediately, removing from the freezer 1 hour or less before you incorporate into the cake and bake. If you leave ground poppy seeds at room temperature, they will develop an unpleasant bitterness that can overwhelm the cake.

CHOCOLATE TRUFFLES
Makes 10 to 15 truffles

This is a very straightforward recipe for easy-to-make truffles—it's essentially a ganache. Always use the best-quality chocolate you can find. I don't like dark, very bitter chocolate for these truffles because you already get some bitterness from the poppy seed in the cake. Sixty percent is the highest cacao percentage I recommend for this recipe.

3.5   ounces (101 grams) dark chocolate, chopped
¼   cup plus 1 teaspoon (65 grams) heavy whipping cream
1   tablespoon (14 grams) unsalted butter
Unsweetened cocoa powder, for dusting

1. Place chocolate in a medium heatproof bowl. In a small saucepan, heat cream over medium heat, stirring constantly. Pour hot cream over chocolate. Let stand for 1 minute; stir until chocolate is melted and mixture is smooth. Add butter, stirring until mixture is smooth.
2. Pour chocolate mixture into a small flat plastic box or a tin lined with plastic wrap to form a ½-inch layer. Freeze until firm.
3. Remove from box, and cut into ½-inch cubes. Dust with cocoa.

Photo by Ben Yuster

SOURDOUGH CHOCOLATE LOAF CAKE

Makes 1 (9x5-inch) cake

Recipe by Stacey Ballis

This chocolate loaf cake is one of my favorite ways to use sourdough discard. The slight tang enhances the deep chocolate flavor and prevents the cake from being too sweet, which makes it ideal for brunch. Add some whipped cream and berries, and you have an elegant dessert for a dinner party. Add some frosting and sprinkles, and you have a fun cake that the kids will approve of at their next slumber party.

½   **cup (113 grams) unsalted butter, softened**
1   **cup (220 grams) firmly packed light brown sugar**
½   **cup (100 grams) granulated sugar**
1   **large egg (50 grams), room temperature**
1   **cup (275 grams) sourdough starter discard**
½   **cup (120 grams) whole buttermilk, chilled**
1   **teaspoon (4 grams) vanilla extract**
1   **cup (125 grams) all-purpose flour**
¾   **cup (64 grams) Dutch process cocoa powder (see Note)**
½   **teaspoon (2.5 grams) baking powder**
¼   **teaspoon (1.25 grams) baking soda**
¼   **teaspoon kosher salt**
Buttermilk Glaze (recipe follows)

1. Preheat oven to 325°F (170°C). Butter and flour a 9x5-inch loaf pan.
2. In the bowl of a stand mixer fitted with the paddle attachment, beat butter and sugars at medium speed until fluffy, 3 to 4 minutes, stopping to scrape sides of bowl. Add egg, beating well. Add sourdough discard, buttermilk, and vanilla, beating until combined.
3. In a medium bowl, whisk together flour, cocoa, baking powder, baking soda, and salt. (If your cocoa is very lumpy, you can sift it in.) With mixer on low speed, gradually add flour mixture to butter mixture, beating until combined. Give batter a quick fold with a spatula to ensure bottom of bowl doesn't have any unmixed ingredients. Pour batter into prepared pan.
4. Bake until a wooden pick inserted in center comes out clean, 1 hour to 1 hour and 5 minutes. Let cool in pan for 10 to 15 minutes. Remove from pan, and let cool completely on a wire rack. Spoon Buttermilk Glaze over cake before serving. Wrap tightly in plastic wrap, and store at room temperature for up to 5 days.

Note: *It is important to use Dutch process cocoa powder in this recipe. Natural process cocoa powder is much more acidic, and the cake will be both lighter in color and a bit bitter if you substitute. Droste is my favorite Dutch process cocoa powder.*

Buttermilk Glaze
Makes about ¾ cup

2   **cups (240 grams) confectioners' sugar**
5   **tablespoons (75 grams) whole buttermilk**

1. In a small bowl, whisk together confectioners' sugar and buttermilk until smooth. Use immediately.

Photo by Art Meripol

BROWN SUGAR LARDY CAKE

Makes about 12 servings

Recipe by Dan Lepard

My way to eat this traditional British cake requires no effort, just sliced and served warm, or sometimes fried in butter and enjoyed with ice cream, sautéed apples, and a generous glug of whisky poured over it.

1½   cups (360 grams) dark beer or stout
1   cup (240 grams) hot black tea
1   tablespoon (9 grams) active dry yeast
1   large egg (50 grams)
2   cups (256 grams) raisins
¼   cup (55 grams) firmly packed light brown sugar, plus more for sprinkling
2   tablespoons (28 grams) unsalted butter, melted
1½   teaspoons (3 grams) ground ginger
1½   teaspoons (3 grams) ground cinnamon
1½   teaspoons (3 grams) ground mace
6⅔   cups (833 grams) plain/unbleached all-purpose flour
1½   teaspoons (4.5 grams) kosher salt
½   cup (113 grams) rendered leaf lard*, chilled but spreadable
½   cup (113 grams) unsalted butter, softened

1. Place beer and hot tea in a very large mixing bowl; check that mixture is warm and not too hot (leave it to cool if it is). Whisk in yeast until dissolved. Whisk in egg, and stir in raisins, brown sugar, melted butter, ginger, cinnamon, and mace. Add flour and salt, and mix everything evenly to a soft, sticky dough, adding water or more flour if dough seems too dry or soft. Aim for a consistency that holds its shape but stays on the soft side so it's easy to roll out. Cover bowl, and leave for 10 minutes.
2. Lightly flour worktop, and knead dough for just a few minutes to make sure all the fruit and spices are evenly mixed through. Then put dough back in bowl, and leave in a warm, draft-free place (75°F/24°C) until risen between half and double in volume, usually about 90 minutes.
3. Line a 13x9-inch baking tin with nonstick paper, and rub sides with lard to stop dough from sticking. Beat softened butter with remaining lard to combine.
4. Divide dough into 4 pieces. Take a piece of dough, and roll it to about ¼-inch thickness, slightly bigger than the size of the tin, using flour to stop it from sticking. Spread it generously with lard mixture, and sprinkle with brown sugar. Fold it over on

itself, and roll it out again to about ¼-inch thickness. Lay this roughly in prepared tin, scrunched up to make it fit. Brush top with more lard mixture, and sprinkle with more brown sugar. Repeat with remaining pieces of dough. If you have too much dough for the tin, make a small lardy cake in a loaf tin with the excess. Cover dough, and leave in a warm, draft-free place (75°F/24°C) until risen by half in volume.
5. Preheat oven to 400°F (200°C). Brush top of loaf with any leftover lard mixture, and sprinkle with brown sugar. Slash crisscross lines in top with a sharp blade.
6. Bake for 35 to 40 minutes. Reduce oven temperature to 350°F (180°C), and bake 30 minutes more, covering with foil to stop it from burning. Leave until cold in the tin before serving.

*Rendered pork lard is a little tricky to find. You can get it at Cottonwood Farm (cottonwood-farm.com) in Tuscumbia, Alabama.

Photo by Yuki Sugiura

LITTLE LEMON MERINGUE POUND CAKES

Makes 16 (5½x3-inch) cakes

Recipe by Ben Mims

Whipped heavy cream is a frequent addition to pound cakes because it adds the same amount of fat as butter but with additional moisture to produce a particularly smooth, tender cake. Here, the technique is a boon to these small, tangy versions, made with lemon zest in the batter and suffused with a tart Lemon Syrup. The meringue on top is piped with three different-size star tips to mimic the top of a bouquet of flowers, then torched until cooked through and caramelized. If you're a fan of lemon meringue pie but have always wanted it with just a thick crust and meringue, then this cake will be your dream come true.

¾   cup (170 grams) unsalted butter, softened
1⅓   cups (267 grams) plus ¾ cup (150 grams) granulated sugar, divided
3   tablespoons (9 grams) lemon zest
2   teaspoons (8 grams) vanilla extract, divided
1¼   teaspoons (3 grams) kosher salt, divided
1   teaspoon (5 grams) baking powder
3   large eggs (150 grams), room temperature
1¾   cups (219 grams) cake flour
⅓   cup (80 grams) heavy whipping cream, chilled
Lemon Syrup (recipe follows)
3   large egg whites (90 grams), room temperature

1. Preheat oven to 325°F (170°C). Butter and flour 2 (8-cup) mini loaf pan plaques (such as Williams Sonoma Goldtouch) or 16 (5½x3-inch) mini loaf pans.
2. In the bowl of a stand mixer fitted with the paddle attachment, beat butter, 1⅓ cups (267 grams) sugar, zest, 1½ teaspoons (6 grams) vanilla, 1 teaspoon (3 grams) salt, and baking powder at medium speed until fluffy and pale, at least 6 minutes. Add eggs, one at a time, beating until there are no streaks of yolk left after each addition, about 15 seconds. Scrape bottom and sides of bowl with a rubber spatula. With mixer on medium-high speed, beat until superlight and airy, at least 3 minutes. Add flour, and stir with a rubber spatula just until combined.
3. In a small bowl, whisk cream by hand until stiff peaks form. Using a rubber spatula, fold whipped cream into batter until completely smooth. Spoon 3 to 4 tablespoons batter into each prepared loaf cup or pan, and smooth tops.

4. Bake until cakes are slightly raised and golden brown on top and a wooden pick inserted in center comes out clean, 25 to 30 minutes. Let cool in pans for 5 minutes. Invert pans onto wire racks set over rimmed baking sheets or sheets of foil, and unmold from pans. Spoon about 1 tablespoon Lemon Syrup onto bottom of each cake while still warm, letting it soak completely into cake. Let cool completely.
5. In the bowl of a stand mixer fitted with the whisk attachment, whisk together egg whites, remaining ¾ cup (150 grams) sugar, and remaining ¼ teaspoon salt by hand until combined. Place mixer bowl over a saucepan of simmering water. Cook, stirring constantly, until sugar is dissolved and whites are just hot to the touch, 2 to 3 minutes.
6. Immediately remove bowl from saucepan, and add remaining ½ teaspoon (2 grams) vanilla. Carefully return bowl to stand mixer, and beat at medium-high speed until fluffy and cool to the touch and stiff peaks form.
7. Divide meringue among 3 piping bags fitted with 3 different size and shape star tips. (Alternatively, scrape meringue into 1 large piping bag fitted with a medium star tip.) Turn cakes over so they're upright. Pipe 4 to 5 mounds meringue from largest tip onto cakes, spacing evenly apart. Pipe 2 to 3 mounds meringue from medium-size tip onto cakes, filling in some of the gaps in center of each cake. Pipe 5 to 6 mounds meringue from smallest tip onto cakes, filling in any remaining gaps on top of cakes.
8. Using a kitchen torch, carefully brown meringue all over cakes. Serve immediately. Cakes can be made, soaked in Lemon Syrup, and stored in an airtight container for up to 1 day before serving. Make, pipe, and torch meringue just before serving.

LEMON SYRUP

Makes about 1 cup

1   cup (240 grams) fresh lemon juice
½   cup (100 grams) granulated sugar

1. In a small saucepan, bring lemon juice and sugar to a simmer over medium-high heat, stirring occasionally, until sugar is dissolved. Remove from heat, and let cool completely. Lemon Syrup can be made up to 3 days in advance. Let come to room temperature before using.

PEACH UPSIDE-DOWN CAKE

Makes 1 (9-inch) cake

The beauty of an upside-down cake is the golden, caramelized base it creates while the syrupy fruit bottom simmers underneath its topcoat. This cake beats them all—no contest.

1½ cups (188 grams) self-rising flour
1 cup (200 grams) granulated sugar
½ teaspoon (1 gram) ground nutmeg
¼ teaspoon kosher salt
3 large eggs (150 grams)
½ cup (120 grams) whole buttermilk, room temperature
½ teaspoon (2 grams) vanilla extract

¾ cup (170 grams) unsalted butter, softened and divided
1 cup (220 grams) firmly packed light brown sugar
1¼ cups (280 grams) ¼-inch-thick sliced peeled fresh peaches (about 2 medium peaches)

1. Preheat oven to 350°F (180°C). Butter and flour a 9-inch round cake pan.
2. In the bowl of a stand mixer fitted with the paddle attachment, whisk together flour, granulated sugar, nutmeg, and salt by hand. Add eggs, buttermilk, and vanilla, and beat at medium-low speed until smooth. Add

½ cup (113 grams) butter, beating to combine. Set aside.
3. Place remaining ¼ cup (57 grams) butter in prepared pan. Place pan in oven until butter is melted, 2 to 3 minutes. Sprinkle brown sugar over melted butter. Top with peaches, arranging as desired in a single layer. Spoon batter over peaches, smoothing top with an offset spatula.
4. Bake until a wooden pick inserted in center comes out clean, 40 to 50 minutes, covering with foil after 30 minutes of baking to prevent excess browning. Run a knife around edges of pan to loosen cake. Invert cake onto a serving plate, and let cool slightly. Serve warm.

MISSISSIPPI MUD CAKE

Makes about 16 servings

This classic Southern treat features a crumbly chocolate crust layered with heaps of melty marshmallow, crunchy pecans, and a sweet chocolate drizzle.

1½	cups (188 grams) all-purpose flour
1	cup (200 grams) granulated sugar
1	cup (220 grams) firmly packed light brown sugar
½	cup (43 grams) unsweetened cocoa powder
½	teaspoon (2.5 grams) baking soda
½	teaspoon (1.5 grams) kosher salt, divided
1	cup (227 grams) plus 1 tablespoon (14 grams) unsalted butter, melted and divided
4	large eggs (200 grams), lightly beaten
1	teaspoon (4 grams) vanilla extract
1	(10-ounce) package (283 grams) miniature marshmallows
1	cup (113 grams) chopped pecans

Chocolate Glaze (recipe follows)

1. Preheat oven to 350°F (180°C). Butter and flour a rimmed half sheet pan.
2. In a large bowl, whisk together flour, sugars, cocoa, baking soda, and ¼ teaspoon salt. Add 1 cup (227 grams) melted butter, eggs, and vanilla, stirring until combined. Spoon batter into prepared pan, spreading to edges.
3. Bake until a wooden pick inserted in center comes out clean, about 20 minutes. Sprinkle with marshmallows. Bake until marshmallows are softened, about 5 minutes more.
4. In a medium skillet, combine pecans, remaining 1 tablespoon (14 grams) melted butter, and remaining ¼ teaspoon salt. Cook over medium heat, stirring occasionally, until pecans are toasted, about 8 minutes. Sprinkle toasted pecans over marshmallows; drizzle with Chocolate Glaze. Serve warm or at room temperature.

CHOCOLATE GLAZE
Makes about 1 cup

¼	cup (21 grams) unsweetened cocoa powder
¼	cup (60 grams) whole milk
¼	cup (57 grams) unsalted butter
⅛	teaspoon kosher salt
2	cups (240 grams) confectioners' sugar
1	teaspoon (4 grams) vanilla extract

1. In a medium saucepan, bring cocoa, milk, butter, and salt to a simmer over medium heat, whisking constantly. Remove from heat; whisk in confectioners' sugar and vanilla. Use immediately.

PISTACHIO APRICOT CAKE

Makes 1 (9-inch) cake

If a German apricot cake (Aprikosenkuchen) and a Sicilian pistachio cake did the tango, this jammy cake with creamy White Chocolate Ganache and fluffy pistachio frosting would be the result.

½ cup (113 grams) unsalted butter, softened
1 cup (200 grams) granulated sugar
2 large eggs (100 grams)
½ teaspoon (2 grams) vanilla extract
1⅓ cups (167 grams) all-purpose flour
1¼ teaspoons (6.25 grams) baking powder
½ teaspoon (1.5 grams) kosher salt
½ cup (120 grams) whole buttermilk
½ cup (80 grams) chopped fresh apricots
¾ cup (240 grams) Apricot Jam (recipe on page 345), divided
1 tablespoon (15 grams) fresh lemon juice
Pistachio Buttercream (recipe follows)
White Chocolate Ganache (recipe follows)
Candied Apricots (recipe follows)

1. Preheat oven to 350°F (180°C). Butter and flour a tall-sided 9-inch round cake pan.
2. In the bowl of a stand mixer fitted with the paddle attachment, beat butter and sugar at medium speed until fluffy, 3 to 4 minutes, stopping to scrape sides of bowl. Add eggs, one at a time, beating well after each addition. Beat in vanilla.
3. In a medium bowl, whisk together flour, baking powder, and salt. With mixer on low speed, gradually add flour mixture to butter mixture alternately with buttermilk, beginning and ending with flour mixture, beating just until combined after each addition.
4. In a small bowl, stir together apricots, ¼ cup (80 grams) Apricot Jam, and lemon juice. Gently fold apricot mixture into batter. Spoon batter into prepared pan.
5. Bake until a wooden pick inserted in center comes out clean, 35 to 40 minutes. Let cool in pan for 10 minutes. Remove from pan, and let cool completely on a wire rack.
6. Using a serrated knife, cut cake in half horizontally. Spread about ¾ cup Pistachio Buttercream onto one cake layer. Using a pastry bag fitted with a Wilton 1M round tip, pipe about ½ cup Pistachio Buttercream in a circle around edge of frosted cake layer. Spoon remaining ½ cup (160 grams) Apricot Jam onto cake layer, and top with remaining cake layer. Freeze for 15 minutes.
7. Spread remaining Pistachio Buttercream on top and sides of cake. Pour White Chocolate Ganache over top of cake. Refrigerate until chocolate is set, about 15 minutes. Top with Candied Apricots. Serve at room temperature. Cover and refrigerate for up to 5 days.

PISTACHIO BUTTERCREAM
Makes about 4½ cups

1 cup (142 grams) shelled roasted pistachios
1 teaspoon (5 grams) olive oil
3 cups (360 grams) confectioners' sugar
¾ cup (170 grams) unsalted butter, softened
1 tablespoon (15 grams) whole milk

1. In the work bowl of a food processor, place pistachios and oil; pulse until a thick paste forms, about 5 minutes.
2. In the bowl of a stand mixer fitted with the paddle attachment, beat pistachio paste, confectioners' sugar, butter, and milk at medium-low speed until light and fluffy, 2 to 3 minutes. Use immediately, or refrigerate for up to 2 days.

WHITE CHOCOLATE GANACHE
Makes about 1½ cups

8 ounces (225 grams) white chocolate, chopped
½ cup (120 grams) heavy whipping cream

1. Place chocolate in a heatproof bowl.
2. In a small saucepan, bring cream to a boil over medium heat. Pour hot cream over chocolate. Let stand for 1 minute; whisk until smooth. Let cool until slightly thickened, 3 to 5 minutes.

CANDIED APRICOTS
Makes 1 cup

⅓ cup (80 grams) water
¼ cup (50 grams) granulated sugar
2 tablespoons (30 grams) fresh lemon juice
1 tablespoon (21 grams) honey
1 cup (128 grams) sliced dried apricots

1. In a small saucepan, bring ⅓ cup (80 grams) water, sugar, lemon juice, and honey to a boil over medium heat. Whisk in apricots. Reduce heat to medium-low; simmer, stirring occasionally, until apricots are coated in a thick glaze, 7 to 8 minutes.
2. Line a baking sheet with parchment paper. Spread apricots on prepared pan, and let cool until tacky. Cover and refrigerate for up to 1 week.

FLOURLESS BLACK COCOA CAKE

Makes 1 (9-inch) cake

As pure an incarnation of chocolate cake as you can get. Done up with a white chocolate and coconut ganache drizzle, this one-layer cake is simple enough for a weeknight baking project.

1⅓ cups (227 grams) 63% cacao chocolate baking chips*
1 cup (227 grams) unsalted butter, cubed
6 large eggs (300 grams), room temperature
1½ cups (300 grams) granulated sugar
1 teaspoon (4 grams) vanilla extract
¼ teaspoon kosher salt
1 cup (85 grams) black cocoa powder, sifted
White Chocolate Coconut Ganache (recipe follows)

1. Preheat oven to 325°F (170°C). Line bottom of a 9-inch springform pan with parchment paper. Butter and flour sides of pan.
2. In the top of a double boiler, combine chocolate and butter. Cook over simmering water, stirring occasionally, until chocolate is melted and mixture is smooth. Remove from heat, and let cool for 10 minutes.
3. In the bowl of a stand mixer fitted with the paddle attachment, beat eggs, sugar, vanilla, and salt at medium-low speed until pale yellow in color, about 2 minutes. Fold in melted chocolate until combined. Fold in black cocoa. Pour batter into prepared pan.
4. Bake until a wooden pick inserted in center comes out clean, 1 hour and 5 minutes to 1 hour and 10 minutes. Let cool in pan for 1½ hours.
5. Gently remove sides of pan, and invert cake onto a wire rack. Let cool completely. Drizzle White Chocolate Coconut Ganache over cooled cake.

We used Guittard Extra Dark Chocolate Baking Chips.

White Chocolate Coconut Ganache

Makes 1 cup

½ cup (85 grams) white chocolate chips
½ cup (120 grams) coconut milk
½ tablespoon (7 grams) unsalted butter

1. Place white chocolate in a small heatproof bowl.
2. In a microwave-safe bowl, heat coconut milk on high in 15-second intervals, stirring between each, until steaming. Pour hot milk over chocolate. Let stand for 2 to 3 minutes; stir to combine. Add butter, and stir until incorporated. Let cool completely before using, about 3 hours.

PUMPKIN SPICE GOOEY BUTTER CAKE

Makes about 12 servings

Inspired by the gooey butter cake of St. Louis, Missouri, this spiced cake has two textured layers: a chewy brown sugar base and a filling so rich with butter, eggs, and pumpkin purée that the middle sinks down into a creamy, custardy valley.

¾   cup (165 grams) firmly packed dark brown sugar
¼   cup (50 grams) granulated sugar
½   cup (113 grams) plus 6 tablespoons (84 grams) unsalted butter, melted and divided
5   large eggs (250 grams), divided
1½ cups (188 grams) all-purpose flour
2   teaspoons (10 grams) baking powder
½   teaspoon (1.5 grams) kosher salt
8   ounces (225 grams) cream cheese, softened

1   (15-ounce) can (425 grams) pumpkin
3   tablespoons (45 grams) spiced black rum
3¾ cups (450 grams) confectioners' sugar, sifted
1   teaspoon (2 grams) ground cinnamon
¼   teaspoon ground ginger
¼   teaspoon ground nutmeg
⅛   teaspoon ground allspice
⅛   teaspoon ground cloves
Garnish: confectioners' sugar

1. Preheat oven to 350°F (180°C). Grease a 13x9-inch baking pan. Line pan with parchment paper, letting excess extend over sides of pan.

2. In a large bowl, whisk together brown sugar, granulated sugar, 6 tablespoons (84 grams) melted butter, and 2 eggs (100 grams). Add flour, baking powder, and salt, whisking until smooth. Spread into prepared pan; set aside.

3. In the bowl of a stand mixer fitted with the paddle attachment, beat cream cheese at medium-low speed until smooth. Add pumpkin, and beat until combined, 2 to 3 minutes. Add rum, remaining 3 eggs (150 grams), and remaining ½ cup (113 grams) melted butter, beating until smooth. Gradually add confectioners' sugar, cinnamon, ginger, nutmeg, allspice, and cloves, beating until well combined. Pour over cake base, smoothing with an offset spatula.

4. Bake until center is slightly set, about 40 minutes. Let cool completely in pan. Using excess parchment as handles, remove from pan. Dust with confectioners' sugar, if desired.

CONCORD GRAPE UPSIDE-DOWN MINI LOAF CAKES

Makes 3 (5¾x3¾-inch) cakes

Recipe by Laura Kasavan

These petite upside-down loaf cakes highlight Concord grapes in a brown sugar-thyme topping. Serve cakes slightly warm, topped with billows of whipped cream.

⅓ cup (73 grams) firmly packed light brown sugar
½ cup (113 grams) plus 2 tablespoons (28 grams) unsalted butter, softened and divided
1 cup (150 grams) Concord grapes*
½ teaspoon fresh thyme leaves
¾ cup (150 grams) granulated sugar
2 large eggs (100 grams), room temperature
2 cups (250 grams) all-purpose flour
½ teaspoon (1 gram) ground cinnamon
½ teaspoon (2.5 grams) baking powder
¼ teaspoon (1.25 grams) baking soda
¼ teaspoon kosher salt
1/16 teaspoon ground nutmeg
¾ cup (180 grams) low-fat buttermilk, room temperature
Whipped cream, to serve
Garnish: fresh thyme sprigs

1. Preheat oven to 350°F (180°C). Butter and flour 3 mini (5¾x3¾-inch) loaf cake pans.
2. In a medium saucepan, heat brown sugar and 2 tablespoons (28 grams) butter over medium heat, stirring constantly, until mixture is smooth. Remove from heat, and stir in Concord grapes and thyme. Divide mixture among prepared pans; set aside.
3. In the bowl of a stand mixer fitted with the paddle attachment, beat granulated sugar and remaining ½ cup (113 grams) butter at medium speed until fluffy, 3 to 4 minutes, stopping to scrape sides of bowl. Reduce mixer speed to low. Add eggs, one at a time, beating well after each addition.
4. In a medium bowl, whisk together flour, cinnamon, baking powder, baking soda, salt, and nutmeg. Gradually add flour mixture to butter mixture alternately with buttermilk, beginning and ending with flour mixture, beating just until combined after each addition. Spoon about 1 cup batter over topping in each pan, and smooth with an offset spatula.
5. Bake until golden brown and a wooden pick inserted in center comes out clean, 36 to 38 minutes. Let cool in pans for 5 minutes. Invert cakes onto a wire rack, and let cool completely. Using a serrated knife, trim domed bottom off each loaf to create a level bottom. Serve with whipped cream. Garnish with thyme, if desired.

You do not have to seed the grapes. The heat from the oven helps break the seeds down as the loaf cakes bake.

Photo by Laura Kasavan

MAPLE-PECAN APPLE CAKE WITH MAPLE BUTTERCREAM

Makes about 12 servings

To give this cake a richer maple flavor, we use Grade B maple syrup, which has a stronger profile than Grade A.

1   cup (227 grams) unsalted butter, softened
½   cup (110 grams) firmly packed dark brown sugar
2   large eggs (100 grams), room temperature
1   tablespoon (13 grams) vanilla extract
3   cups (375 grams) all-purpose flour
2   teaspoons (10 grams) baking powder
1   teaspoon (3 grams) kosher salt
1   teaspoon (2 grams) ground cinnamon
½   teaspoon (2.5 grams) baking soda
1   cup (336 grams) Grade B maple syrup
¾   cup (180 grams) sour cream
1   Honeycrisp apple (200 grams), peeled and chopped (about 1¼ cups)
¾   cup (85 grams) finely chopped pecans
Maple Buttercream (recipe follows)

1. Preheat oven to 325°F (170°C). Grease a 13x9-inch baking pan. Line pan with parchment paper, letting excess extend over sides of pan.
2. In the bowl of a stand mixer fitted with the paddle attachment, beat butter and brown sugar at medium speed until creamy, 3 to 4 minutes, stopping to scrape sides of bowl. Add eggs, one at a time, beating well after each addition. Beat in vanilla.
3. In a medium bowl, whisk together flour, baking powder, salt, cinnamon, and baking soda. In a small bowl, whisk together maple syrup and sour cream. With mixer on low speed, gradually add flour mixture to butter mixture alternately with maple syrup mixture, beginning and ending with flour mixture, beating just until combined after each addition. Fold in apple and pecans. Pour batter into prepared pan, smoothing top with an offset spatula.
4. Bake until a wooden pick inserted in center comes out clean, 35 to 40 minutes. Let cool completely in pan. Using excess parchment as handles, remove from pan. Spread Maple Buttercream onto cooled cake.

MAPLE BUTTERCREAM
Makes 5 cups

6   large egg whites (180 grams)
½   cup plus 2 tablespoons (124 grams) granulated sugar
1   cup (336 grams) Grade B maple syrup
1¾   cups plus 2 tablespoons (425 grams) unsalted butter, softened
½   teaspoon (1.5 grams) kosher salt
½   teaspoon (2 grams) vanilla extract

1. In the bowl of a stand mixer fitted with the whisk attachment, beat egg whites at medium speed until foamy. Gradually add sugar, beating until medium peaks form.
2. Meanwhile, in a large saucepan, heat maple syrup over medium heat until a candy thermometer registers 240°F (116°C).
3. Slowly pour hot maple syrup into egg white mixture, beating until bowl is cool to the touch. Add butter, 2 tablespoons (28 grams) at a time, beating until combined. (Your buttercream may look slightly runny at this point, but continue whipping until fluffy.) Add salt and vanilla, beating to combine. Use immediately, or refrigerate in an airtight container for up to 3 days. If refrigerating, let frosting come to room temperature before using.

BUTTERSCOTCH CAKE WITH SALTED CARAMEL BUTTERCREAM

Makes about 12 servings

Finished off with a silky Swiss meringue buttercream and a generous pour of salted caramel, this sheet cake is pure butterscotch bliss.

⅔   cup (113 grams) butterscotch chips
¼   cup (60 grams) water
½   cup (113 grams) unsalted butter, softened
1½ cups (330 grams) firmly packed light brown sugar
3   large eggs (150 grams)
1   teaspoon (4 grams) vanilla extract
2¼ cups (281 grams) cake flour
2   teaspoons (10 grams) baking powder
½   teaspoon (1.5 grams) kosher salt
¼   teaspoon (1.25 grams) baking soda
1   cup (240 grams) heavy whipping cream
Salted Caramel Buttercream (recipe follows)
⅔   cup (168 grams) Salted Caramel Sauce (recipe follows)
Garnish: Maldon sea salt

1. Preheat oven to 325°F (170°C). Grease a 13x9-inch baking pan. Line pan with parchment paper, letting excess extend over sides of pan.
2. In a small microwave-safe bowl, combine butterscotch chips and ¼ cup (60 grams) water. Microwave on high in 15-second intervals, stirring between each, until melted and smooth. Let cool to room temperature.
3. In the bowl of a stand mixer fitted with the paddle attachment, beat butter and brown sugar at medium speed until fluffy, 3 to 4 minutes, stopping to scrape sides of bowl. Add eggs, one at a time, beating well after each addition. Beat in butterscotch mixture and vanilla.
4. In a medium bowl, whisk together flour, baking powder, kosher salt, and baking soda. With mixer on low speed, gradually add flour mixture to butter mixture alternately with cream, beginning and ending with flour mixture, beating just until combined after each addition. Pour batter into prepared pan, smoothing top with an offset spatula.
5. Bake until a wooden pick inserted in center comes out clean, about 35 minutes. Let cool completely in pan. Using excess parchment as handles, remove from pan. Spread Salted Caramel Buttercream onto cooled cake. Drizzle with Salted Caramel. Sprinkle with sea salt, if desired.

SALTED CARAMEL BUTTERCREAM
Makes 4 cups

3   large egg whites (90 grams), room temperature
1   cup (200 grams) granulated sugar
1½ cups (340 grams) unsalted butter, cubed and softened
⅔   cup (168 grams) Salted Caramel Sauce (recipe follows)

1. In the bowl of a stand mixer fitted with the whisk attachment, whisk together egg whites and sugar by hand. Place mixer bowl over a saucepan of simmering water. Cook, whisking occasionally, until mixture registers 155°F (68°C) to 160°F (71°C) on a candy thermometer.
2. Carefully return bowl to stand mixer, and beat at high speed until stiff peaks form and bowl is cool to the touch, about 5 minutes. Add butter, 2 tablespoons (28 grams) at a time, beating until combined. Add Salted Caramel Sauce, and beat until smooth, about 3 minutes. (If buttercream breaks, beat 2 to 3 minutes more, and the emulsion will come back together.) Use immediately, or refrigerate in an airtight container for up to 3 days. If refrigerating, let frosting come to room temperature before using.

SALTED CARAMEL SAUCE
Makes about 1⅓ cups

½   cup (120 grams) heavy whipping cream, room temperature
1   teaspoon (3 grams) Maldon sea salt
1   cup (200 grams) granulated sugar
4   tablespoons (60 grams) water, divided
6   tablespoons (84 grams) unsalted butter, cubed and softened
2   teaspoons (8 grams) vanilla extract

1. In a small saucepan, heat cream and salt over very low heat. Simmer until salt is dissolved. Remove from heat, and set aside.
2. In a medium saucepan, heat sugar and 3 tablespoons (45 grams) water over high heat, being careful not to splash sides of pan. (It should be the consistency of wet sand.) Use remaining 1 tablespoon (15 grams) water to brush down sides of pan, and stir to help sugar dissolve. (Do not stir once it starts to boil.) Cook until desired light amber color is reached and a candy thermometer registers 330°F (166°C). Remove from heat; slowly add warm cream mixture, whisking to combine. Add butter, a few pieces at a time, whisking until combined. Stir in vanilla. Let cool completely.

TOMATO CARAMEL CORNMEAL
UPSIDE-DOWN CAKE

Makes 1 (9-inch) cake

Recipe by Steven Satterfield

The recipe is a mash-up of tomato pie and upside-down cake. The caramel surrounding the roasted plum tomatoes brings their sweeter side to life.

6   ripe plum tomatoes (603 grams), sliced ½ inch thick and seeded
1   teaspoon (3 grams) kosher salt
1   cup (220 grams) firmly packed light brown sugar
1¼   cups (284 grams) unsalted butter, softened and divided
2   teaspoons (10 grams) fresh lemon juice
½   cup (100 grams) granulated sugar
4   large eggs (200 grams), room temperature
1   cup (240 grams) whole buttermilk
2   cups (300 grams) fine yellow cornmeal
3   tablespoons (9 grams) lemon zest

1½   teaspoons (7.5 grams) baking powder
1   teaspoon (3 grams) fine sea salt
1   teaspoon fresh thyme leaves

1. Preheat oven to 350°F (180°C).
2. Sprinkle tomato slices with salt, and place in a roasting pan.
3. Roast for 40 minutes. Remove from oven, and let cool. Discard skins from cooled tomatoes. Set roasted tomato slices aside, and reserve any liquids that may have collected from roasting pan.
4. In a large saucepan, combine reserved tomato drippings, brown sugar, ¼ cup (57 grams) butter, and lemon juice. Heat over medium-high heat until sugar is dissolved and large bubbles form, about 4 minutes.
5. Spray a 9-inch cast-iron skillet with cooking spray. Pour caramel into prepared pan. Arrange roasted tomato slices across bottom of pan neatly and tightly to cover entire surface.

6. In the bowl of a stand mixer fitted with the paddle attachment, beat granulated sugar and remaining 1 cup (227 grams) butter at medium speed until creamy, 3 to 4 minutes, stopping to scrape sides of bowl. Add eggs, one at a time, beating well after each addition. Beat in buttermilk.
7. In a medium bowl, whisk together cornmeal, zest, baking powder, sea salt, and thyme. Add cornmeal mixture to butter mixture, stirring by hand until well combined. Spoon batter over tomato layer in pan.
8. Bake until cake is set and sides have sprung from edges of skillet, about 1 hour. Loosen edges of cake with a small knife or spatula while still warm. Let cool for 15 minutes before carefully inverting onto a platter. Let cool completely before serving.

Photo by Angie Mosier

BROWNED BUTTER APPLE POKE CAKE WITH CREAM CHEESE ICING

Makes about 12 servings

The secret to this apple-intense poke cake? Boiled Cider, a tangy reduction of fresh apple cider. Take a bite of this tender cake, and you'll find the best kind of surprise: pockets of tart cider syrup hiding under a thick coat of cream cheese frosting.

¾ cup plus 2 tablespoons (198 grams) unsalted butter
2 cups (400 grams) granulated sugar
3 large eggs (150 grams)
1½ teaspoons (9 grams) vanilla bean paste
3 cups (375 grams) cake flour
2 teaspoons (10 grams) baking powder
1 teaspoon (3 grams) kosher salt
½ teaspoon (2.5 grams) baking soda
1 cup (240 grams) whole buttermilk
Boiled Cider (recipe follows)
Cream Cheese Icing (recipe follows)

1. In a medium saucepan, melt butter over medium heat. Cook until butter turns a medium-brown color and has a nutty aroma, about 10 minutes. Remove from heat, and place in a small bowl. Let cool in an ice bath, stirring every 5 minutes, until butter solidifies, about 20 minutes.

2. Preheat oven to 325°F (170°C). Grease a 13x9-inch baking pan. Line pan with parchment paper, letting excess extend over sides of pan.

3. In the bowl of a stand mixer fitted with the paddle attachment, beat browned butter and sugar at medium speed until fluffy, 3 to 4 minutes, stopping to scrape sides of bowl. Add eggs, one at a time, beating well after each addition. Beat in vanilla bean paste.

4. In a medium bowl, whisk together flour, baking powder, salt, and baking soda. With mixer on low speed, gradually add flour mixture to butter mixture alternately with buttermilk, beginning and ending with flour mixture, beating just until combined after each addition. Pour batter into prepared pan, smoothing top with an offset spatula.

5. Bake until a wooden pick inserted in center comes out clean, 35 to 40 minutes. Let cool completely in pan. Using a wooden skewer, poke holes all over cake. Pour cooled Boiled Cider over cake. Spread Cream Cheese Icing onto cake.

BOILED CIDER
Makes about 1 cup

4 quarts (3,840 grams) apple cider

1. In a large saucepan, bring cider just to a boil over medium-high heat. Reduce heat to low, and simmer, stirring occasionally, until the consistency of maple syrup is reached, about 2 hours. Let cool completely before using.

CREAM CHEESE ICING
Makes 6 cups

16 ounces (455 grams) cream cheese, softened
1 cup (227 grams) unsalted butter, softened
2 teaspoons (12 grams) vanilla bean paste
3¾ cups (450 grams) confectioners' sugar

1. In the bowl of a stand mixer fitted with the paddle attachment, beat cream cheese at medium speed until smooth. Add butter, and beat until creamy, about 4 minutes. Beat in vanilla bean paste. Gradually add confectioners' sugar, beating until smooth, about 2 minutes. Use immediately.

PEAR CAKE WITH WHIPPED CHOCOLATE GANACHE

Makes about 12 servings

A hint of cardamom lends a little warmth to this rich buttermilk batter swirled with a fragrant pear spread. Unlike jam, fruit spreads don't have any added sugar, so they infuse a more natural, delicate sweetness to baked goods. If you like your cake extra sweet, though, jam works just as well.

¾   cup (170 grams) unsalted butter, softened
1   cup (200 grams) granulated sugar
½   cup (110 grams) firmly packed light brown sugar
4   large eggs (200 grams)
1   teaspoon (4 grams) vanilla extract
2¾   cups (344 grams) cake flour
1   teaspoon (5 grams) baking powder
1   teaspoon (5 grams) baking soda
1   teaspoon (3 grams) kosher salt
¼   teaspoon ground cardamom
1¾   cups (560 grams) pear spread or jam*
¾   cup (180 grams) whole buttermilk
Whipped Chocolate Ganache (recipe follows)
Garnish: shaved chocolate (see Note)

1. Preheat oven to 325°F (170°C). Grease a 13x9-inch baking pan. Line pan with parchment paper, letting excess extend over sides of pan.
2. In the bowl of a stand mixer fitted with the paddle attachment, beat butter and sugars at medium speed until fluffy, 3 to 4 minutes, stopping to scrape sides of bowl. Add eggs, one at a time, beating well after each addition. Beat in vanilla.
3. In a medium bowl, whisk together flour, baking powder, baking soda, salt, and cardamom. In a small bowl, whisk together pear spread and buttermilk. With mixer on low speed, gradually add flour mixture to butter mixture alternately with pear spread mixture, beginning and ending with flour mixture, beating just until combined after each addition. Pour batter into prepared pan, smoothing top with an offset spatula.

4. Bake until a wooden pick inserted in center comes out clean, 40 to 45 minutes. Let cool completely in pan. Using excess parchment as handles, remove from pan. Spread Whipped Chocolate Ganache onto cooled cake. Garnish with shaved chocolate, if desired.

We used St. Dalfour Gourmet Pear 100% Fruit Spread, available at specialty food stores or online.

Note: *To create shaved chocolate, microwave a block of chocolate in 5-second intervals to soften it slightly. Using a vegetable peeler, thinly shave off pieces of chocolate. We used Callebaut 60.3% Cacao Dark Chocolate.*

WHIPPED CHOCOLATE GANACHE
Makes 2½ cups

10.5   ounces (315 grams) 60% cacao chocolate, chopped
1¼   cups (300 grams) heavy whipping cream
2   tablespoons (28 grams) unsalted butter, softened
1   teaspoon (4 grams) vanilla extract

1. Place chopped chocolate in a large heatproof bowl.
2. In a small saucepan, bring cream to a boil over medium-low heat. Pour half of hot cream over chocolate; let stand for 30 seconds. Starting in center of bowl, slowly stir with a rubber spatula until combined. Add remaining hot cream, and slowly stir to combine. Add butter and vanilla, stirring until fully incorporated. Let ganache come to room temperature. Cover and refrigerate for at least 2 hours.
3. Place ganache in the bowl of a stand mixer fitted with the whisk attachment. With mixer on low speed, beat ganache until light in color and thickened. (If ganache texture starts to look granular, you've overwhipped.) Use immediately.

BOURBON-WALNUT BROWN SUGAR CAKE WITH MASCARPONE BUTTERCREAM

Makes about 12 servings

There's nothing like a little bourbon to warm the soul when the weather turns cool and crisp, which is why we let the aromatic Kentucky-made spirit star in this grown-up version of your favorite brown sugar cake. Mascarpone thickens and brings a slight tang to the frosting.

1   cup (227 grams) unsalted butter, softened
1½ cups (330 grams) firmly packed dark brown sugar
4   large eggs (200 grams)
1   teaspoon (6 grams) vanilla bean paste
3   cups (375 grams) cake flour
2   teaspoons (10 grams) baking powder
1   teaspoon (2 grams) ground cinnamon
½   teaspoon (2.5 grams) baking soda
½   teaspoon (1.5 grams) kosher salt
1   cup (240 grams) whole milk
½   cup (120 grams) bourbon
¾   cup (85 grams) chopped walnuts
Mascarpone Buttercream (recipe follows)
Garnish: chopped walnuts

1. Preheat oven to 325°F (170°C). Grease a 13x9-inch baking pan. Line pan with parchment paper, letting excess extend over sides of pan.
2. In the bowl of a stand mixer fitted with the paddle attachment, beat butter and brown sugar at medium speed until fluffy, 3 to 4 minutes, stopping to scrape sides of bowl. Add eggs, one at a time, beating well after each addition. Beat in vanilla bean paste.
3. In a medium bowl, whisk together flour, baking powder, cinnamon, baking soda, and salt. In a small bowl, whisk together milk and bourbon. With mixer on low speed, gradually add flour mixture to butter mixture alternately with milk mixture, beginning and ending with flour mixture, beating just until combined after each addition. Fold in walnuts. Pour batter into prepared pan, smoothing top with an offset spatula.
4. Bake until a wooden pick inserted in center comes out clean, 35 to 40 minutes. Let cool completely in pan. Using excess parchment as handles, remove from pan. Spread Mascarpone Buttercream onto cooled cake. Garnish with walnuts, if desired.

MASCARPONE BUTTERCREAM
Makes 3 cups

1   cup (227 grams) unsalted butter, softened
2   cups (240 grams) confectioners' sugar
2   teaspoons (10 grams) heavy whipping cream
2   teaspoons (12 grams) vanilla bean paste
⅛   teaspoon kosher salt
8   ounces (225 grams) mascarpone cheese

1. In the bowl of a stand mixer fitted with the paddle attachment, beat butter at medium speed until creamy. Increase mixer speed to medium-high. Gradually add confectioners' sugar, beating until fluffy, 3 to 4 minutes. Add cream, vanilla bean paste, and salt; beat until combined. Fold in mascarpone, and stir until combined. (Be careful not to overmix mascarpone. It will begin to separate and start to weep.) Use immediately.

SPICE CAKE WITH GINGER PORT-POACHED FIGS

Makes 1 (9-inch) cake

Recipe by Marian Cooper Cairns

This moist cake is the perfect backdrop for any fall fruit, but there's something transcendent about covering it with aromatic port-poached figs. A final dollop of crème fraîche brings a cool, tangy finish to this warmly spiced slice of heaven.

1   cup (200 grams) granulated sugar
¾   cup (180 grams) whole buttermilk
¾   cup (168 grams) vegetable oil
½   cup (170 grams) molasses
1   large egg (50 grams), lightly beaten
2   teaspoons (8 grams) vanilla extract
3   cups (375 grams) cake flour
1½   teaspoons (3 grams) ground cinnamon
1   teaspoon (5 grams) baking soda
1   teaspoon (5 grams) baking powder
1   teaspoon (3 grams) kosher salt
¼   teaspoon ground nutmeg
Scant ¼ teaspoon ground cloves
Crème fraîche and Ginger Port-Poached
       Figs (recipe follows), to serve

1. Preheat oven to 350°F (180°C). Lightly grease and flour a 9-inch square baking pan.
2. In the bowl of a stand mixer fitted with the paddle attachment, beat sugar, buttermilk, oil, molasses, egg, and vanilla at medium speed until well combined.
3. In a medium bowl, whisk together flour, cinnamon, baking soda, baking powder, salt, nutmeg, and cloves. With mixer on low speed, gradually add flour mixture to sugar mixture, beating just until combined. Pour batter into prepared pan.
4. Bake until a wooden pick inserted in center comes out clean, 50 to 1 hour. Let cool in pan for 15 minutes. Remove from pan, and let cool on a wire rack for 1 hour. Serve with crème fraîche and Ginger Port-Poached Figs.

GINGER PORT-POACHED FIGS
Makes 8 servings

1¼   cups (300 grams) ruby port wine
¼   cup (60 grams) fresh orange juice
3   tablespoons (63 grams) honey
4   slices fresh ginger
1   star anise pod
¼   teaspoon black peppercorns
8   large firm ripe fresh figs (307 grams)

1. In a small saucepan, bring port, orange juice, honey, ginger, star anise, and peppercorns to a boil over medium heat. Reduce heat to low, and simmer until slightly thickened, 10 to 15 minutes. Add figs; cook, stirring occasionally, until figs are just beginning to soften, 3 to 5 minutes. Remove from heat, and let cool completely. Discard star anise and peppercorns.

Photo by Matt Armendariz

STICKY TOFFEE PUDDING

Makes 8 servings

Recipe by Edd Kimber

I think it is pretty much impossible to dislike Sticky Toffee Pudding. It is surely the one thing we can all agree on. (If you're not a fan, I am sorry, but we can't be friends.) Whilst I would like to say this love is about the pudding itself, I would be lying. For me, this is about lashings of Butterscotch Sauce served with plenty of cream (clotted cream if you're being extravagant) or ice cream.

1½ cups (263 grams) pitted Medjool dates, roughly chopped
¾ cup (180 grams) water
7 tablespoons (105 grams) rum
⅓ cup (76 grams) unsalted butter, softened
¾ cup (165 grams) firmly packed light brown sugar
2 tablespoons (42 grams) golden syrup or honey
½ teaspoon (2 grams) vanilla extract
2 large eggs (100 grams), room temperature

1¾ cups (219 grams) self-raising flour/ self-rising flour
2 teaspoons (4 grams) ground ginger
2 teaspoons (4 grams) ground cinnamon
1 (1-inch) piece ginger root, grated
1½ teaspoons (7.5 grams) bicarbonate of soda/baking soda
Clotted cream and Butterscotch Sauce (recipe follows), to serve

1. Preheat oven to 350°F (180°C). Grease a 9-inch square cake pan; line pan with parchment paper, and place on a baking sheet.
2. In a medium saucepan, heat dates, ¾ cup (180 grams) water, and rum over medium-high heat. Reduce heat, and simmer until most of water has been absorbed. Using an immersion blender, process until smooth; set aside.
3. In the bowl of a stand mixer fitted with the paddle attachment, beat butter, brown sugar, golden syrup, and vanilla at medium speed until smooth and combined, about 5 minutes. Add eggs, one at a time, beating well after each addition. Fold in flour, ground ginger, and cinnamon.

4. Stir grated ginger and bicarbonate of soda into date mixture, and pour into batter; quickly fold to combine. Spoon batter into prepared pan.
5. Bake until pudding springs back when touched in center and a wooden pick inserted in center comes out clean, 45 to 55 minutes. Let cool in pan for 5 minutes. Remove from pan; serve warm clotted cream and with Butterscotch Sauce.

BUTTERSCOTCH SAUCE
Makes 1¼ cups

¼ cup (57 grams) unsalted butter
½ cup (110 grams) firmly packed light brown sugar
⅛ teaspoon flaked sea salt
Scant ½ cup (120 grams) heavy whipping cream

1. In a small tall-sided saucepan, heat butter over medium heat. Whisk in brown sugar and sea salt. Add cream, and bring to a boil; cook for 3 minutes.

Photo by Yuki Sugiura

FIGGY OAT COFFEE CAKE

Makes 12 servings

Recipe by Marian Cooper Cairns

We updated the classic streusel coffee cake with fresh ripe figs and almonds. No need to distinguish between breakfast and dessert—it's an eat-it-anytime-you-crave-it cake.

1½	cups (188 grams) all-purpose flour
¾	cup (60 grams) old-fashioned oats
2	teaspoons (10 grams) baking powder
½	teaspoon (1.5 grams) kosher salt
½	cup (113 grams) unsalted butter, softened
¾	cup (150 grams) granulated sugar
2	large eggs (100 grams)
1	teaspoon (4 grams) vanilla extract
½	teaspoon (2 grams) almond extract
¾	cup (180 grams) plain yogurt
2	cups (220 grams) chopped fresh figs

Oatmeal Almond Streusel (recipe follows)

1. Preheat oven to 350°F (180°C). Lightly grease and flour a 9-inch square baking pan.
2. In the work bowl of a food processor, place flour, oats, baking powder, and salt; pulse until oats are ground, 6 to 7 times.
3. In the bowl of a stand mixer fitted with the paddle attachment, beat butter and sugar at medium speed until fluffy, 3 to 4 minutes, stopping to scrape sides of bowl. Add eggs, one at a time, beating well after each addition. Beat in extracts.
4. With mixer on low speed, gradually add oats mixture to butter mixture alternately with yogurt, beginning and ending with oats mixture, beating just until combined after each addition. Gently fold in figs. Spread batter in prepared pan. Sprinkle with Oatmeal Almond Streusel.
5. Bake until golden brown and a wooden pick inserted in center comes out clean, 55 to 60 minutes. Let cool in pan for 20 minutes. Serve warm or at room temperature.

OATMEAL ALMOND STREUSEL

Makes about 1½ cups

½	cup (63 grams) all-purpose flour
⅓	cup (27 grams) old-fashioned oats
¼	cup (55 grams) firmly packed light brown sugar
¼	teaspoon kosher salt
5	tablespoons (70 grams) cold unsalted butter, cubed
½	cup (57 grams) chopped fresh figs
⅓	cup (38 grams) sliced almonds

1. In a small bowl, whisk together flour, oats, brown sugar, and salt. Using a pastry blender, cut in cold butter until mixture is crumbly. Stir in figs and almonds.

Photo by Matt Armendariz

FIG AND VANILLA BEAN UPSIDE-DOWN CORNMEAL CAKE

Makes 1 (9-inch) cake

Recipe by Marian Cooper Cairns

A toothsome, crunchy cornmeal cake and velvety caramelized fig layer combine to create a dessert that triumphs in both texture and taste.

¾ cup (170 grams) unsalted butter, softened and divided
½ cup (110 grams) firmly packed light brown sugar
12 fresh figs (467 grams), sliced ¼ inch thick
¾ cup (150 grams) granulated sugar
3 large eggs (150 grams)
1 cup (150 grams) fine yellow cornmeal
⅔ cup (83 grams) all-purpose flour
1½ teaspoons (7.5 grams) baking powder
¾ teaspoon (2.25 grams) kosher salt
¾ cup (180 grams) whole buttermilk
2 teaspoons (12 grams) vanilla bean paste

1. Preheat oven to 350°F (180°C). Line bottom of a 9-inch round cake pan with parchment paper; grease pan and parchment.
2. In a small saucepan, melt ¼ cup (57 grams) butter over low heat; stir in brown sugar. Pour into prepared pan. Arrange figs slightly overlapping on top of brown sugar mixture. Set aside.
3. In the bowl of a stand mixer fitted with the paddle attachment, beat granulated sugar and remaining ½ cup (113 grams) butter at medium speed until fluffy, 3 to 4 minutes, stopping to scrape sides of bowl. Add eggs, one at a time, beating well after each addition.
4. In a medium bowl, whisk together cornmeal, flour, baking powder, and salt. In a small bowl, whisk together buttermilk and vanilla bean paste. With mixer on low speed, gradually add cornmeal mixture to butter mixture alternately with buttermilk mixture, beginning and ending with flour mixture, beating just until combined after each addition. Pour batter over figs.
5. Bake until a wooden pick inserted in center comes out clean, 55 to 60 minutes. Let cool in pan for 15 minutes. Run a knife around edges of cake. Turn out onto a serving plate. Serve warm.

Photo by Matt Armendariz

ONE-LAYER GINGERBREAD CAKE

Makes 1 (9-inch) cake

A generous portion of minced fresh ginger is folded directly into the batter of this stunner. Swoopy Meringue Frosting gives it the whimsical appearance of a snowcapped mountain.

1 cup (200 grams) granulated sugar
½ cup (170 grams) unsulphured molasses
½ cup (170 grams) light corn syrup
1 cup (240 grams) freshly squeezed orange juice with pulp
1 cup (227 grams) unsalted butter, melted
2 large eggs (100 grams)
½ cup (70 grams) minced fresh ginger
2½ cups (313 grams) all-purpose flour
1 teaspoon (5 grams) baking soda
1 teaspoon (2 grams) ground cinnamon
½ teaspoon (1.5 grams) kosher salt
½ teaspoon (1 gram) ground cloves
1 cup (113 grams) chopped pecans
¼ cup (35 grams) diced candied orange zest*

Meringue Frosting (recipe follows)
Gingerbread Ski Chalet (see Note)
Garnish: confectioners' sugar

1. Preheat oven to 350°F (180°C). Line bottom of a tall-sided 9-inch springform pan with parchment paper. Wrap bottom and sides of pan with a double layer of foil

2. In the bowl of a stand mixer fitted with the paddle attachment, beat granulated sugar, molasses, corn syrup, orange juice, melted butter, eggs, and ginger at medium speed until combined.

3. In a medium bowl, whisk together flour, baking soda, cinnamon, salt, and cloves. With mixer on low speed, gradually add flour mixture to sugar mixture, beating until combined. Fold in pecans and candied orange zest. Pour batter into prepared pan.

4. Bake until a wooden pick inserted in center comes out with a few moist crumbs, 55 to 60 minutes. Let cool completely in pan.

5. Remove cake from pan, and place on a serving plate or cake stand. Spread Meringue Frosting on top of cake, piling it high and creating mounds of "snow." Place Gingerbread Ski Chalet on one side. Dust cake with confectioners' sugar, if desired. Store at room temperature for up to 2 days.

*We used the peels of Trader Joe's Sweetened Dried Orange Slices, available at Trader Joe's or on amazon.com.

Note: *For our Gingerbread Ski Chalet recipe, visit bakefromscratch.com/gingerbread-ski-chalet.com.*

MERINGUE FROSTING
Makes about 8 cups

2 cups (400 grams) granulated sugar
½ cup (120 grams) water
6 large egg whites (180 grams)
¼ teaspoon cream of tartar

1. In a medium saucepan, bring sugar and ½ cup (120 grams) water to a boil over high heat. Reduce heat to medium-high; cook until mixture registers 248°F (120°C) on a candy thermometer.

2. Meanwhile, in the bowl of a stand mixer fitted with the whisk attachment, beat egg whites and cream of tartar at high speed until stiff peaks form. With mixer running, pour hot sugar syrup into egg whites in a slow, steady stream. Beat until bowl cools to the touch and frosting reaches a spreadable consistency, about 10 minutes. Use immediately.

PLUM SKILLET CAKE

Makes 1 (9- or 10-inch) cake

Recipe by Kelsey Siemens

Our plum trees are among the tallest in my family's orchard at Willow View Farms in British Columbia. The trees are pure magic to walk through when they're heavy with ripe fruit. Purple-skinned with yellow flesh, Italian plums are always a showstopper. I like to keep things simple when baking with them as their natural sweet flavor should be front and center. For this Plum Skillet Cake, I added a bit of cardamom, a spice that works very well with the plums.

½ cup (113 grams) unsalted butter, softened
1 cup (200 grams) plus 2 tablespoons (24 grams) granulated sugar, divided
2 large eggs (100 grams)
2 teaspoons (8 grams) vanilla extract
1⅓ cups (167 grams) all-purpose flour
1¼ teaspoons (6.25 grams) baking powder
½ teaspoon (1 gram) ground cardamom
¼ teaspoon fine sea salt
½ cup (120 grams) sour cream
5 to 7 Italian plums* (about 300 grams), halved and pitted
¼ teaspoon ground cinnamon
Garnish: confectioners' sugar

1. Preheat oven to 350°F (180°C). Butter a 9- or 10-inch cast-iron skillet.
2. In the bowl of a stand mixer fitted with the paddle attachment, beat butter and 1 cup (200 grams) granulated sugar at medium speed until fluffy, 3 to 4 minutes, stopping to scrape sides of bowl. Add eggs, one at a time, beating well after each addition. Beat in vanilla.
3. In a medium bowl, whisk together flour, baking powder, cardamom, and sea salt. With mixer on low speed, gradually add half of flour mixture to butter mixture, beating just until combined. Beat in sour cream.

Gradually add remaining flour mixture, beating just until combined. Spread batter in prepared skillet.
4. Gently press plum halves, cut side down, into batter. In a small bowl, combine cinnamon and remaining 2 tablespoons (24 grams) granulated sugar. Sprinkle cinnamon sugar over cake.
5. Bake until a wooden pick inserted in center comes out clean, 50 to 1 hour. Let cool slightly. Dust with confectioners' sugar, if desired. Serve warm.

The size of your plums (and skillet) will determine how many you can fit on your cake.

Note: *Black plum halves or frozen plum halves also work for this recipe. Do not thaw frozen plum halves beforehand.*

Photo by Kelsey Siemens

RIGÓ JANCSI

Makes 12 servings

Recipe by Szonja Márk

A classic Hungarian dessert, Rigó Jancsi is an intense amalgamation of chocolate: a cube of sponge cake and whipped ganache capped in a thin, fudge-like strip.

9   large eggs (450 grams), separated
¾   cup plus 2½ tablespoons (180 grams) granulated sugar, divided
1   cup plus 1 tablespoon (90 grams) Dutch process cocoa powder
¾   cup (94 grams) all-purpose flour
¼   teaspoon kosher salt
Chocolate Whipped Cream (recipe follows)
Chocolate Coating (recipe follows)

1. Preheat oven to 350°F (180°C). Line a half sheet pan with parchment paper.
2. In the bowl of a stand mixer fitted with the whisk attachment, beat egg whites at medium speed until soft peaks form. Add two-thirds of sugar (120 grams), and beat until stiff peaks form. Transfer to a large bowl; set aside.
3. Clean bowl of stand mixer and whisk attachment. Using the whisk attachment, beat egg yolks and remaining sugar (60 grams) at medium speed until pale and fluffy. Fold egg whites into egg yolks.
4. In a medium bowl, sift together cocoa, flour, and salt. Carefully fold cocoa mixture into egg mixture. Spread batter on prepared pan.
5. Bake for 10 minutes. Let cool completely on pan. Turn out cake, and gently peel off parchment. Cut cake in half to create 2 (11x8-inch) rectangles.
6. Line a 13x9-inch baking pan with plastic wrap, letting excess extend over sides of pan. Place one half of sponge cake in prepared pan. Spread with Chocolate Whipped Cream. Top with remaining half of sponge cake. Fold plastic wrap over top of cake to cover. Freeze until set, at least 2 hours.
7. Pour Chocolate Coating over frozen cake, smoothing top with as few strokes as

possible. Freeze until set, about 5 minutes. Trim edges to create a clean 10x7½-inch rectangle. Using a hot, dry knife, slice cake into 12 squares.

CHOCOLATE WHIPPED CREAM
Makes 2¾ cups

8   ounces (225 grams) 60% cacao chocolate, chopped
2   cups (480 grams) heavy whipping cream

1. Place chopped chocolate in a medium heatproof bowl.
2. In a large saucepan, bring cream to a boil. Pour half of hot cream over chocolate. Let stand for 10 seconds; stir until chocolate is melted. Pour remaining hot cream over melted chocolate, and stir to combine. Let cool to room temperature, then refrigerate for at least 4 hours.
3. In the bowl of a stand mixer fitted with the paddle attachment, beat chilled chocolate mixture at medium-high speed until stiff peaks form, about 30 seconds. Use immediately.

CHOCOLATE COATING
Makes 1½ cups

1¼   cups (213 grams) 60% cacao dark chocolate chips, chopped
¾   cup plus 2 tablespoons (210 grams) heavy whipping cream

1. Place chopped chocolate in a medium heatproof bowl.
2. In a small saucepan, bring cream to a boil. Pour half of hot cream over chocolate. Let stand for 10 seconds; stir until chocolate is melted. Pour remaining hot cream over melted chocolate, and stir to combine. Use immediately.

PRO TIP

If Chocolate Whipped Cream becomes granular, you've overwhipped it. To fix, place the mixing bowl over a warm water bath for 10 seconds. Remove from heat, whisk gently, and repeat until it is smooth. Return to mixer, and whip again.

MÁKOS GUBA
(POPPY SEED "GOOBAH" CAKE)

Makes 1 (9-inch) cake

Recipe by Szonja Márk

Mákos Guba is a savory-sweet Hungarian bread pudding dominated by auspicious poppy seeds, which symbolize luck and wealth in the new year. This rendition takes the shape of a circular cake gussied up with Meringue. Use either stale or fresh sweet bread, like challah or the challah-like kalács for a silkier feel.

15   cups (613 grams) (1-inch) cubed challah
4   cups plus 3 tablespoons (1,005 grams) whole milk
2   tablespoons (42 grams) honey
1   tablespoon (14 grams) unsalted butter
1   vanilla bean, split lengthwise, seeds scraped and reserved
1   large egg (50 grams)
1   large egg yolk (19 grams)
1   cup (120 grams) confectioners' sugar, divided
1   teaspoon (4 grams) almond extract
1   cup (142 grams) poppy seeds, ground
Meringue (recipe follows)
Sour Cherry Topping (recipe follows)

1. Preheat oven to 325°F (170°C). Spray a 9-inch springform pan with cooking spray. Line bottom of pan with parchment paper.
2. Place cubed challah in a large bowl.
3. In a medium saucepan, combine milk, honey, butter, and vanilla bean and reserved seeds. Bring to a boil over medium-low heat.
4. In a large bowl, whisk together egg, egg yolk, ½ cup (60 grams) confectioners' sugar, and almond extract. Add a small amount of hot milk mixture to egg mixture, and whisk to combine. Gradually add remaining hot milk mixture to egg mixture, whisking constantly. Pour mixture over cubed bread, and let soak for 10 minutes.
5. In a small bowl, stir together ground poppy seeds and remaining ½ cup (60 grams) confectioners' sugar. Sprinkle over soaked bread, and toss well to combine. Pour bread mixture into prepared pan.
6. Bake until an instant-read thermometer inserted in center registers 165°F (74°C) to 170°F (77°C), 45 to 50 minutes. Let cool completely in pan. Remove from pan.
7. Spoon Meringue into a piping bag fitted with a smooth or star tip. Pipe Meringue

stars around edges of cake, leaving center empty. Using a kitchen torch, carefully brown Meringue. Pour Sour Cherry Topping onto center of cake. Serve immediately.

MERINGUE
Makes 2¼ cups

½   cup plus 2 tablespoons (124 grams) granulated sugar, divided
2   tablespoons (28 grams) water
2   large egg whites (60 grams), room temperature

1. In a small saucepan, combine two-thirds of sugar (83 grams) and 2 tablespoons (28 grams) water. Heat over high heat until mixture registers 250°F (121°C) on a candy thermometer.
2. Meanwhile, in the bowl of a stand mixer fitted with the whisk attachment, beat egg whites at medium speed until soft peaks form. Add remaining sugar (41 grams), and beat until stiff peaks form.
3. With mixer running, slowly pour in hot sugar syrup. Increase mixer speed to high, and beat until bowl is cool to the touch. Use immediately.

SOUR CHERRY TOPPING
Makes 2 cups

3¼   cups (632 grams) frozen pitted sour cherries
½   cup (100 grams) granulated sugar
3   tablespoons (24 grams) cornstarch

1. In a medium saucepan, combine frozen cherries and sugar. Bring to a boil over medium-high heat; reduce heat to medium-low.
2. Place cornstarch in a small bowl. Add 3 tablespoons cooking liquid from pan, and whisk until smooth. Add cornstarch mixture to cherries, and cook, whisking constantly, until thickened. Remove from heat, and let cool to room temperature. Refrigerate until ready to use.

POMEGRANATE MOLASSES GINGERBREAD CAKE

Makes 1 (8-inch) cake

Melding the warm spices of gingerbread with the tart power of Pomegranate Molasses, our one-layer cake is a sophisticated spin on a holiday favorite. A final luxurious coat of vanilla frosting rounds out this simple stunner.

½   cup (113 grams) unsalted butter, softened
½   cup (100 grams) granulated sugar
2   large eggs (100 grams)
½   cup (170 grams) Pomegranate Molasses (recipe on page 131)
2   teaspoons (2 grams) lemon zest
2   teaspoons (10 grams) grated fresh ginger
1½   cups (188 grams) all-purpose flour
1   teaspoon (2 grams) ground ginger
¾   teaspoon (3.75 grams) baking soda
¾   teaspoon (2.25 grams) kosher salt
½   teaspoon (1 gram) ground cloves
¼   teaspoon ground black pepper
½   cup (120 grams) whole milk
⅓   cup (50 grams) diced crystallized ginger
Vanilla Cream Cheese Frosting (recipe follows)
Garnish: pomegranate arils

1. Preheat oven to 350°F (180°C). Spray an 8-inch springform pan with cooking spray; line bottom of pan with parchment paper.
2. In the bowl of a stand mixer fitted with the paddle attachment, beat butter and sugar at medium speed until creamy, 3 to 4 minutes, stopping to scrape sides of bowl. Add eggs, one at a time, beating well after each addition. Add Pomegranate Molasses, zest, and grated ginger, and beat until combined.

3. In a medium bowl, whisk together flour, ground ginger, baking soda, salt, cloves, and pepper. With mixer on low speed, gradually add flour mixture to butter mixture alternately with milk, beginning and ending with flour mixture, beating just until combined after each addition. Fold in crystallized ginger. Pour batter into prepared pan, smoothing top.
4. Bake until a wooden pick inserted in center comes out clean, 30 to 35 minutes. Let cool in pan for 10 minutes. Remove sides of pan, and turn cake over. Remove bottom of pan, and gently peel off parchment. Return cake to bottom of pan, right side up. Let cool completely. Spread Vanilla Cream Cheese Frosting onto cooled cake. Sprinkle with pomegranate arils, if desired.

VANILLA CREAM CHEESE FROSTING
Makes about 2 cups

½   cup (112 grams) cream cheese, softened
¼   cup (57 grams) unsalted butter, softened
½   teaspoon (2 grams) vanilla extract
1   vanilla bean, split lengthwise, seeds scraped and reserved
¼   teaspoon kosher salt
2½   cups (300 grams) confectioners' sugar

1. In the bowl of a stand mixer fitted with the paddle attachment, beat cream cheese, butter, vanilla extract, vanilla bean seeds, and salt at medium speed until smooth. With mixer on low speed, add confectioners' sugar, ½ cup (60 grams) at a time, beating until well combined. Use immediately, or cover and refrigerate for up to 3 days.

BREAD

QUICK
BREADS

Weeknight baking is a cinch with these scones, muffins, and loaf breads. Highlighting flavors like spicy gingerbread and juicy stone fruit, these recipes span the seasons.

ORANGE BLOSSOM HONEYCOMB SCONES

Makes 8 scones

Inspired by the busy bees of spring, we paired chopped honeycomb and orange blossom water to create a delicate floral and honey scone. Crowned with golden honeycomb chunks and a generous drizzle of white chocolate, these baked goods offer a surprising flavor combination you didn't know you needed until now.

3   cups (375 grams) all-purpose flour
½   cup (100 grams) granulated sugar
1   tablespoon (15 grams) baking powder
¾   teaspoon (2.25 grams) kosher salt
1   vanilla bean, split lengthwise, seeds scraped and reserved
¾   cup (170 grams) cold unsalted butter, grated
½   cup (84 grams) chopped honeycomb*
¾   cup (180 grams) whole milk
2   large eggs (100 grams), divided
1   teaspoon (4 grams) vanilla extract
¾   teaspoon (3 grams) orange blossom water
1   tablespoon (15 grams) heavy whipping cream
8   ounces (225 grams) white chocolate, chopped
Garnish: chopped honeycomb

1. Preheat oven to 400°F (200°C). Line a baking sheet with parchment paper.
2. In a large bowl, whisk together flour, sugar, baking powder, salt, and vanilla bean seeds. Add cold butter, tossing to coat. Cover and freeze for 15 minutes. Stir in honeycomb.
3. In a small bowl, whisk together milk, 1 egg (50 grams), vanilla extract, and orange blossom water. Add milk mixture to flour mixture, stirring and folding just until moistened. Turn out dough onto a heavily floured surface. Using well-floured hands, knead dough 5 to 10 times, about 1 minute.

Roll dough to ¾- to 1-inch thickness. Using a 2¾-inch round cutter, cut dough, rerolling scraps only once. Place on prepared pan.
4. In a small bowl, whisk together cream and remaining 1 egg (50 grams). Brush egg wash onto scones.
5. Bake until golden brown, 12 to 15 minutes.
6. In the top of a double boiler, melt chocolate over simmering water. (Alternatively, in a large microwave-safe bowl, microwave chocolate on medium in 30-second intervals, stirring between each, until melted and smooth.) Drizzle over scones. Garnish with honeycomb, if desired.

*Use raw honeycomb not packed in honey. You can find this information on the package. If packed in honey, the comb will disintegrate while being chopped and bubble out of the scone when baked. Honeycomb is available in specialty food stores and on amazon.com.

HUMMINGBIRD LOAF

Makes 1 (9x5-inch) loaf

This may be the most vivacious loaf bread you've ever tasted. Little bits of dried apricot deliver intermittent bursts of sweet-tart flavor, and an ample pour of spiced rum turns up the va-va-voom. The pecan- and oat-packed streusel topping and the rich cream cheese mixed in with the batter ensure the perfect dose of tender crumble and crunch in every bite.

1   cup (240 grams) spiced rum
½   cup (64 grams) diced dried pineapple pieces
½   cup (64 grams) diced dried apricots
4   ounces (115 grams) cream cheese, softened
⅓   cup (76 grams) unsalted butter, softened
1   cup (200 grams) granulated sugar
1   large egg (50 grams), room temperature
½   teaspoon (2 grams) vanilla extract
1½   cups (188 grams) all-purpose flour
1   teaspoon (2 grams) ground cinnamon
½   teaspoon (1.5 grams) kosher salt
½   teaspoon (2.5 grams) baking powder

¼   teaspoon (1.25 grams) baking soda
¼   teaspoon ground nutmeg
¾   cup (171 grams) mashed banana
½   cup (57 grams) chopped pecans
Pecan-Oat Streusel (recipe follows)
Vanilla Glaze (recipe follows)

1. In a small saucepan, bring rum, pineapple, and apricots to a boil over medium heat. Reduce heat to low, and simmer until fruit is plump and liquid has evaporated, about 20 minutes. Remove from heat, and let cool completely.
2. Preheat oven to 350°F (180°C). Butter and flour a 9x5-inch loaf pan. Line pan with parchment paper, letting excess extend over sides of pan.
3. In the bowl of a stand mixer fitted with the paddle attachment, beat cream cheese and butter at medium speed until creamy. Add sugar, and beat until fluffy, 3 to 4 minutes, stopping to scrape sides of bowl. Add egg, beating well. Beat in vanilla.
4. In a medium bowl, whisk together flour, cinnamon, salt, baking powder, baking soda, and nutmeg. With mixer on low speed, gradually add flour mixture to cream cheese

mixture, beating until combined. Fold in rehydrated fruit, mashed banana, and pecans. Spoon batter into prepared pan. Top with Pecan-Oat Streusel.
5. Bake until golden brown and a wooden pick inserted in center comes out clean, 1 hour to 1 hour and 10 minutes, covering with foil halfway through baking to prevent excess browning. Let cool in pan for 10 minutes. Using excess parchment as handles, remove from pan, and let cool completely on a wire rack. Drizzle Vanilla Glaze over cooled loaf. Store in an airtight container at room temperature for up to 4 days.

PECAN-OAT STREUSEL
Makes about ½ cup

¼   cup (28 grams) chopped pecans
¼   cup (20 grams) old-fashioned oats
¼   cup (55 grams) firmly packed light brown sugar
¼   cup (31 grams) all-purpose flour
¼   teaspoon kosher salt
¼   teaspoon ground nutmeg
3   tablespoons (42 grams) unsalted butter, cubed

1. In a small bowl, whisk together pecans, oats, brown sugar, flour, salt, and nutmeg. Using a pastry blender, cut in butter until pea-size crumbs remain. Squeeze mixture into small and large clumps. Refrigerate in an airtight container for up to 3 days.

VANILLA GLAZE
Makes about ½ cup

2   cups (240 grams) confectioners' sugar
3   tablespoons (45 grams) whole milk, room temperature
1   teaspoon (4 grams) vanilla extract
¼   teaspoon kosher salt

1. In a small bowl, whisk together all ingredients until smooth. Use immediately.

Photo by Stephen DeVries

TRADITIONAL ENGLISH SCONES

Makes 8 scones

Recipe by Edd Kimber

I don't think there are many things better than a scone topped with clotted cream and jam. Scones are known the world over for a good reason! My recipe is fairly traditional but incorporates a slightly unusual kneading and resting technique I was taught at Le Manoir, a two-star Michelin restaurant I spent a little time in after competing on The Great British Bake Off. If you don't have time for the resting, don't worry—bake them as soon as they have been formed. They will still taste excellent; they just won't look quite the same.

2¾ cups (344 grams) plain/cake flour
1 tablespoon (15 grams) baking powder
½ teaspoon (1.5 grams) kosher salt
¼ cup (57 grams) unsalted butter, cubed
½ cup (100 grams) castor sugar
½ cup (64 grams) raisins or sultanas, soaked in hot water for 10 minutes and drained
⅓ cup plus 1 tablespoon (95 grams) whole milk
3 large eggs (150 grams), divided
Clotted cream and jam, to serve

1. In a medium bowl, whisk together flour, baking powder, and salt. Using a pastry blender or your fingertips, rub in butter until mixture is crumbly. Stir in sugar.
2. In a small bowl, combine drained raisins, milk, and 2 eggs (100 grams). Make a well in center of flour mixture. Add raisin mixture, and using a knife, stir together just until a soft, wet dough forms.
3. Turn out dough onto a heavily floured surface, and sprinkle with flour. Gently knead dough by folding in half and then turning through 45 degrees. Repeat until dough is smooth and springs back slightly when pressed. (Be careful not to overwork the dough. This is a light, very brief action. You are not kneading bread; it is more of a folding motion to create a smooth dough and incorporate a little air.)
4. Line a baking sheet with parchment paper. Lightly sprinkle dough with flour, and roll to about 1-inch thickness. Using a 3-inch round cutter, cut dough, rerolling scraps as necessary. (When cutting scones, push the cutter into the dough using a straight up-and-down motion.) Place on prepared pan. Let rest for 1 hour. (Resting gives the scones a more refined, less rustic look. The baking powder gets to work, and the dough will puff out slightly, giving a slightly wider base, which, when baked, looks more like something you'd get at a hotel afternoon tea.)
5. Preheat oven to 390°F (200°C).
6. In a small bowl, whisk remaining 1 egg (50 grams). Brush egg wash over top of scones. (Avoid getting any egg on the sides, as this will prevent the scones from rising properly.)
7. Bake until golden brown on top, about 12 minutes. Let cool slightly before serving with clotted cream and jam.

Photo by Yuki Sugiura

STRAWBERRY BASIL SCONES

Makes 12 scones

Welcome the year's first haul of strawberries with these tender basil-scented scones. Sprinkle with sanding sugar for a breakfast that sparkles.

4   cups (500 grams) all-purpose flour
½   cup (100 grams) granulated sugar
1   tablespoon (15 grams) baking powder
¾   teaspoon (2.25 grams) kosher salt
¾   cup (170 grams) cold unsalted butter, grated
1   cup (147 grams) diced fresh strawberries
2   tablespoons (4 grams) chopped fresh basil

¾   cup (180 grams) whole milk
2   large eggs (100 grams), divided
1   tablespoon (15 grams) heavy whipping cream
Garnish: sanding sugar

1. Preheat oven to 400°F (200°C). Line a baking sheet with parchment paper.
2. In a large bowl, whisk together flour, granulated sugar, baking powder, and salt. Add cold butter, tossing to coat. Cover and freeze for 15 minutes. Stir in strawberries and basil.
3. In a small bowl, whisk together milk and 1 egg (50 grams). Add milk mixture to flour mixture, stirring and folding just until moistened. Turn out dough onto a heavily floured surface. Using well-floured hands, knead dough 5 to 10 times, about 1 minute. Roll dough to ¾- to 1-inch thickness. Using a 2¾-inch round cutter, cut dough, rerolling scraps only once. Place on prepared pan.
4. In a small bowl, whisk together cream and remaining 1 egg (50 grams). Brush egg wash onto scones. Sprinkle with sanding sugar, if desired.
5. Bake until golden brown, 12 to 15 minutes. Let cool slightly; serve warm.

GRUYÈRE PROSCIUTTO SCONES

Makes 8 scones

A sophisticated reboot of the classic ham and cheese coupling, this savory scone pairs nutty Gruyère with the salty punch of prosciutto. Fresh dill introduces a taste of springtime bounty.

3   cups (375 grams) all-purpose flour
¼   cup (50 grams) granulated sugar
1   tablespoon (15 grams) baking powder
¾   teaspoon (2.25 grams) kosher salt
½   teaspoon (1 gram) ground black pepper
½   cup (113 grams) cold unsalted butter, grated
½   cup (50 grams) freshly grated Gruyère cheese
¼   pound (115 grams) prosciutto, chopped
2   tablespoons (4 grams) chopped fresh dill
1   cup (240 grams) whole milk
2   large eggs (100 grams), divided
1   tablespoon (15 grams) heavy whipping cream
Garnish: sea salt, ground black pepper
Softened butter, to serve

1. Preheat oven to 400°F (200°C). Line a baking sheet with parchment paper.
2. In a large bowl, whisk together flour, sugar, baking powder, salt, and pepper. Add cold butter and Gruyère, tossing to coat. Cover and freeze for 15 minutes. Stir in prosciutto and dill.
3. In a small bowl, whisk together milk and 1 egg (50 grams). Add milk mixture to flour mixture, stirring and folding just until moistened. Turn out dough onto a heavily floured surface. Using well-floured hands, knead dough 5 to 10 times, about 1 minute. Shape dough into an 8-inch circle. Using a bench scraper or sharp knife, cut into 8 wedges. Place about 1½ inches apart on prepared pan.
4. In a small bowl, whisk together cream and remaining 1 egg (50 grams). Brush egg wash onto scones. Sprinkle with sea salt and pepper, if desired.
5. Bake until golden brown, 12 to 17 minutes. Let cool slightly; serve warm with butter.

LEMON STREUSEL SCONES

Makes 8 scones

Doubling down on bright citrus flavors with a Lemon Glaze and zesty dough, these sunny scones are topped off with a warm cardamom streusel to cut through the tang.

3   cups (375 grams) all-purpose flour
½   cup (100 grams) granulated sugar
1   tablespoon (15 grams) baking powder
1   tablespoon (3 grams) lemon zest
¾   teaspoon (2.25 grams) kosher salt
¾   cup (170 grams) cold unsalted butter, grated
½   cup (57 grams) sliced almonds
1   cup (240 grams) whole milk
1   large egg (50 grams)
Cardamom Streusel Topping (recipe follows)
Lemon Glaze (recipe follows)

1. Preheat oven to 400°F (200°C). Line a baking sheet with parchment paper.
2. In a large bowl, whisk together flour, sugar, baking powder, zest, and salt. Add cold butter, tossing to coat. Cover and freeze for 15 minutes. Stir in almonds.
3. In a small bowl, whisk together milk and egg. Add milk mixture to flour mixture, stirring and folding just until moistened. Turn out dough onto a heavily floured surface. Using well-floured hands, knead dough 5 to 10 times, about 1 minute. Shape dough into an 8-inch circle. Top with Cardamom Streusel Topping. Using a bench scraper or sharp knife, cut into 8 wedges. Place about 1½ inches apart on prepared pan. Freeze for 10 minutes.
4. Bake until golden brown, 12 to 18 minutes. Let cool completely. Drizzle Lemon Glaze over cooled scones.

CARDAMOM STREUSEL TOPPING
Makes about ½ cup

¼   cup (55 grams) firmly packed light brown sugar
¼   cup (31 grams) all-purpose flour
½   teaspoon (1 gram) ground cardamom
2   tablespoons (28 grams) unsalted butter, cubed and softened

1. In a small bowl, whisk together brown sugar, flour, and cardamom. Add butter, pinching with fingers to incorporate. Squeeze mixture into large clumps. Use immediately, or refrigerate in an airtight container for up to 3 days.

LEMON GLAZE
Makes about 1 cup

1   cup (120 grams) confectioners' sugar
1   tablespoon (3 grams) lemon zest
2   tablespoons (30 grams) fresh lemon juice

1. In a small bowl, whisk together all ingredients until smooth. Use immediately.

CHERRY WALNUT SOURDOUGH SCONES

Makes 8 scones

Recipe by Stacey Ballis

These scones are a wonderful and flexible recipe made from sourdough discard that is simple enough for everyday breakfast and elegant enough for your next brunch or high tea. Barely sweet, they are a great foil for cream and jam or honey butter. You can add any dried fruit, nut, and/or chocolate chip or chunk combination you like. We love them with dried cherries and walnuts. If you like a bit of spice, try adding a pinch of cinnamon and some chopped candied ginger.

1½ cups (188 grams) all-purpose flour
3   tablespoons (36 grams) granulated sugar
1   tablespoon (15 grams) baking powder
½   teaspoon (1.5 grams) kosher salt
5   tablespoons (70 grams) cold unsalted butter, cubed
½   cup (64 grams) chopped dried cherries
½   cup (57 grams) chopped walnuts
1   cup (275 grams) sourdough starter discard
½   cup (120 grams) heavy whipping cream, plus more for brushing
1   tablespoon (12 grams) Demerara or turbinado sugar

1. Preheat oven to 425°F (220°C). Line a baking sheet with parchment paper.
2. In the work bowl of a food processor, place flour, granulated sugar, baking powder, and salt; pulse until combined, about 3 times. Add cold butter, and pulse until mixture is crumbly with some larger pieces of butter remaining, 10 to 12 quick pulses. Turn out dough into a large bowl, and stir in cherries and walnuts.
3. In a medium bowl, stir together sourdough discard and cream until combined. Add discard mixture to flour mixture, stirring with a fork just until dough comes together. Turn out dough onto a lightly floured surface, and knead a few times until a slightly sticky dough forms.
4. Gently pat dough into an 8-inch circle, about 1 inch thick. Cut into 8 wedges. (You can also shape dough into a square, and cut into 9 square scones, if you like.) Place scones on prepared pan. Brush top of scones with cream, and sprinkle with Demerara sugar.
5. Bake until tops and edges are lightly golden brown, 12 to 15 minutes. Let cool on pan for 10 minutes. Serve warm or at room temperature.

PRO TIP
You can make these scones using mix-ins of your choice. Use ½ cup (57 grams) chopped nuts, ½ cup (64 grams) dried fruit, or ½ cup (85 grams) chocolate chips.

Photo by Art Meripol

CARROT CAKE SCONES

Makes 8 scones

The queen of spring cakes, now in a tender scone. Though we trade the traditional cream cheese frosting for a honeyed Crème Fraîche Icing, we keep the base faithful to the original with a veggie-rich, well-spiced batter and plenty of chopped walnuts to add crunch.

3   cups (375 grams) all-purpose flour
½   cup (100 grams) granulated sugar
1   tablespoon (15 grams) baking powder
1   teaspoon (2 grams) ground cinnamon
¾   teaspoon (2.25 grams) kosher salt
½   teaspoon (1 gram) ground ginger
¼   teaspoon ground cloves
¾   cup (170 grams) cold unsalted butter, grated
1   cup (99 grams) grated carrot
⅓   cup (43 grams) golden raisins
⅓   cup (38 grams) chopped walnuts
¾   cup (180 grams) whole milk
2   large eggs (100 grams), divided
1   tablespoon (15 grams) heavy whipping cream
Crème Fraîche Icing (recipe follows)
Garnish: chopped walnuts

1. Preheat oven to 400°F (200°C.) Line a baking sheet with parchment paper.
2. In a large bowl, whisk together flour, sugar, baking powder, cinnamon, salt, ginger, and cloves. Add cold butter, tossing to coat. Cover and freeze for 15 minutes. Stir in carrot, raisins, and walnuts.
3. In a small bowl, whisk together milk and 1 egg (50 grams). Add milk mixture to flour mixture, stirring and folding just until moistened. Turn out dough onto a heavily floured surface. Using well-floured hands, knead dough 5 to 10 times, about 1 minute. Shape dough into an 8-inch circle. Using a bench scraper or sharp knife, cut into 8 wedges. Place about 1½ inches apart on prepared pan.
4. In a small bowl, whisk together cream and remaining 1 egg (50 grams). Brush egg wash onto scones.
5. Bake until golden brown, 12 to 19 minutes. Let cool completely. Spoon Crème Fraîche Icing over cooled scones. Garnish with walnuts, if desired.

CRÈME FRAÎCHE ICING
Makes about 2 cups

2½   cups (300 grams) confectioners' sugar
½   cup (120 grams) crème fraîche, softened
1   tablespoon (21 grams) honey

1. In a medium bowl, stir together all ingredients until smooth and spreadable. Use immediately.

NUTELLA BANANA BREAD

Makes 1 (8½x4½-inch) loaf

Yes, Nutella makes everything better—but the true star of this nutty quick bread is the streusel.

1⅓ cups (208 grams) all-purpose flour
½ teaspoon (1.5 grams) kosher salt
½ teaspoon (2.5 grams) baking soda
¼ teaspoon (1.25 grams) baking powder
1⅛ cups (255 grams) mashed banana (about 3 medium bananas)
¾ cup (150 grams) granulated sugar
2 large eggs (100 grams)
⅓ cup plus 2 teaspoons (85 grams) canola oil
¼ cup (60 grams) whole milk
1 teaspoon (4 grams) vanilla extract
½ cup (128 grams) Nutella
Chocolate Hazelnut Streusel (recipe follows)

1. Preheat oven to 325°F (170°C). Butter and flour an 8½x4½-inch loaf pan.
2. In a medium bowl, whisk together flour, salt, baking soda, and baking powder. In a large bowl, whisk together mashed banana, sugar, eggs, oil, milk, and vanilla. Fold in flour mixture just until combined.
3. In a small microwave-safe bowl, heat Nutella on high in 15-second intervals, stirring between each (about 30 seconds total). Spoon half of batter into prepared pan; spoon half of warm Nutella over batter. Top with remaining batter and remaining Nutella; swirl together using a knife. Top with Chocolate Hazelnut Streusel.
4. Bake until a wooden pick inserted in center comes out clean, about 1 hour and 25 minutes. Let cool in pan for 10 minutes. Remove from pan, and let cool completely on a wire rack.

CHOCOLATE HAZELNUT STREUSEL

Makes about 2 cups

½ cup (63 grams) all-purpose flour
3 tablespoons (42 grams) firmly packed light brown sugar
1½ tablespoons (7.5 grams) Dutch process cocoa powder
1 teaspoon (2 grams) ground cinnamon
½ teaspoon (1.5 grams) kosher salt
¼ cup (57 grams) cold unsalted butter, cubed
⅓ cup (38 grams) chopped hazelnuts
⅓ cup (57 grams) chopped 60% cacao bittersweet chocolate chips

1. In the bowl of a stand mixer fitted with the paddle attachment, combine flour, brown sugar, cocoa, cinnamon, and salt. With mixer on low speed, add cold butter, beating until mixture is crumbly. Stir in hazelnuts and chocolate chips. Refrigerate until ready to use.

BLACK COCOA BANANA BREAD

Makes 1 (8½x4½-inch) loaf

Unlike regular cocoa, black cocoa is void of any acidity, so it's able to deliver a deep cocoa punch without overpowering the banana flavor. This indulgent loaf is brimming with chocolate chips and smooth chunks of mashed banana.

⅓   cup plus 2 teaspoons (86 grams) unsalted butter, softened
¾   cup plus 3 tablespoons (207 grams) firmly packed dark brown sugar
2   large eggs (100 grams)
1⅓ cups (167 grams) all-purpose flour
¼   cup plus 2 tablespoons (31 grams) black cocoa powder*
1   teaspoon (3 grams) kosher salt
¾   teaspoon (3.75 grams) baking powder
¼   teaspoon (1.25 grams) baking soda
1½ cups (341 grams) mashed banana (about 3 medium bananas)
⅓   cup plus 1 tablespoon (95 grams) sour cream
1½ teaspoons (6 grams) vanilla extract
½   cup (85 grams) 60% cacao bittersweet chocolate chips
3   tablespoons (36 grams) turbinado sugar

1. Preheat oven to 325°F (170°C). Butter and flour an 8½x4½-inch loaf pan.
2. In the bowl of a stand mixer fitted with the paddle attachment, beat butter and brown sugar at medium speed until fluffy, 3 to 4 minutes, stopping to scrape sides of bowl. Add eggs, one at a time, beating well after each addition.
3. In a medium bowl, whisk together flour, black cocoa, salt, baking powder, and baking soda. In a small bowl, whisk together mashed banana, sour cream, and vanilla. With mixer on low speed, add banana mixture to butter mixture, beating until combined. Gradually add flour mixture, beating just until combined. Fold in chocolate chips. Spoon batter into prepared pan, smoothing top with an offset spatula. Sprinkle with turbinado sugar.
4. Bake until a wooden pick inserted in center comes out clean, about 1 hour and 10 minutes. Let cool in pan for 10 minutes. Remove from pan, and let cool completely on a wire rack.

Black cocoa is available online or in specialty food stores. We used King Arthur Flour Black Cocoa, but any brand will work.

MINI TROPICAL BANANA BREAD

Makes 4 (5½x3-inch) loaves

A bite of these mini loaves takes you on an island flavor vacation. Sweet pineapple, chewy coconut, and a tangy burst of Citrus Glaze combine for a sunny take on the original.

½	cup (113 grams) unsalted butter, softened
⅔	cup (147 grams) firmly packed light brown sugar
3	tablespoons (60 grams) guava jam
2	large eggs (100 grams)
2¼	cups (281 grams) all-purpose flour
1	teaspoon (5 grams) baking soda
1	teaspoon (5 grams) baking powder
½	teaspoon (1.5 grams) kosher salt
1½	cups (341 grams) mashed banana (about 3 medium bananas)
⅓	cup (80 grams) coconut milk
¼	teaspoon (1 gram) coconut extract
½	cup (100 grams) finely diced fresh pineapple
½	cup (60 grams) sweetened flaked coconut

Citrus Glaze (recipe follows)

1. Preheat oven to 325°F (170°C). Butter and flour 4 (5½x3-inch) loaf pans.

2. In the bowl of a stand mixer fitted with the paddle attachment, beat butter and brown sugar at medium speed until fluffy, 3 to 4 minutes, stopping to scrape sides of bowl. Beat in jam until well combined. Add eggs, one at a time, beating well after each addition.

3. In a medium bowl, whisk together flour, baking soda, baking powder, and salt. In a small bowl, whisk together mashed banana, coconut milk, and coconut extract; whisk in pineapple and coconut. With mixer on low speed, add banana mixture to butter mixture, beating until combined. Gradually add flour mixture, beating just until combined. Divide batter among prepared pans, smoothing tops with an offset spatula.

4. Bake until a wooden pick inserted in center comes out clean, about 40 minutes. Let cool in pans for 10 minutes. Remove from pans, and let cool completely on wire racks. Spoon Citrus Glaze over cooled loaves.

CITRUS GLAZE
Makes ½ cup

1	cup (120 grams) confectioners' sugar
1	lemon (99 grams), zested and juiced
1	lime (90 grams), zested and juiced

1. In a medium bowl, combine confectioners' sugar and zests. In a small bowl, combine lemon juice and lime juice. Add 2 to 3 tablespoons (30 to 45 grams) citrus juice to confectioners' sugar mixture, stirring until desired consistency is reached. Use immediately.

BLUEBERRY-ALMOND BANANA BREAD

Makes 1 (8½x4½-inch) loaf

We spiked the traditional banana bread formula with a double dose of crème fraîche (in the batter and the glaze) to tenderize the crumb and offer a touch of tang to round out the flavor.

⅓ cup plus 2 teaspoons (86 grams) unsalted butter, softened
½ cup (100 grams) granulated sugar
2 large eggs (100 grams)
1⅔ cups (208 grams) all-purpose flour
¾ teaspoon (3.75 grams) baking soda
¾ teaspoon (3.75 grams) baking powder
½ teaspoon (1.5 grams) kosher salt
1⅛ cups (255 grams) mashed banana (about 3 medium bananas)
¼ cup (60 grams) crème fraîche
¼ cup (85 grams) honey
1 teaspoon (4 grams) vanilla extract
½ teaspoon (2 grams) almond extract

1 cup (170 grams) fresh blueberries
¾ cup (85 grams) slivered almonds
Crème Fraîche Glaze (recipe follows)
Garnish: toasted sliced almonds

1. Preheat oven to 325°F (170°C). Butter and flour an 8½x4½-inch loaf pan.
2. In the bowl of a stand mixer fitted with the paddle attachment, beat butter and sugar at medium speed until fluffy, 3 to 4 minutes, stopping to scrape sides of bowl. Add eggs, one at a time, beating well after each addition.
3. In a medium bowl, whisk together flour, baking soda, baking powder, and salt. In a small bowl, whisk together mashed banana, crème fraîche, honey, and extracts. With mixer on low speed, add banana mixture to butter mixture, beating until combined. Gradually add flour mixture, beating just until combined. Fold in blueberries and almonds.

Spoon batter into prepared pan, smoothing top with an offset spatula.
4. Bake for 30 minutes. Cover with foil, and bake until a wooden pick inserted in center comes out clean, about 40 minutes more. Let cool in pan for 10 minutes. Remove from pan, and let cool completely on a wire rack. Spoon Crème Fraîche Glaze over cooled loaf. Garnish with almonds, if desired.

CRÈME FRAÎCHE GLAZE
Makes ½ cup

½ cup (60 grams) confectioners' sugar
¼ cup (60 grams) crème fraîche
½ tablespoon (7.5 grams) whole milk

1. In a small bowl, whisk together all ingredients until smooth. Use immediately.

CARAMELIZED BANANA BREAD

Makes 1 (8½x4½-inch) loaf

Think of this as a breakfast bread version of bananas Foster. Crowned with golden Caramelized Banana halves and offering a hint of cinnamon flavor, this loaf is all about taking the banana to the nth power of sweetness.

1⅔ cups (208 grams) all-purpose flour
½ teaspoon (1.5 grams) kosher salt
½ teaspoon (2.5 grams) baking soda
¼ teaspoon (1.25 grams) baking powder
1⅛ cups (255 grams) mashed banana (about 3 medium bananas)
¾ cup (165 grams) firmly packed light brown sugar
⅓ cup plus 2 teaspoons (86 grams) unsalted butter, melted
¼ cup (60 grams) sour cream
2 large eggs (100 grams)
1 teaspoon (4 grams) vanilla extract
½ teaspoon (1 gram) ground cinnamon
Caramelized Banana (recipe follows)

1. Preheat oven to 325°F (170°C). Butter and flour an 8½x4½-inch loaf pan.
2. In a medium bowl, whisk together flour, salt, baking soda, and baking powder. In a large bowl, whisk together mashed banana, brown sugar, melted butter, sour cream, eggs, vanilla, and cinnamon. Fold flour mixture into banana mixture just until combined. Spoon batter into prepared pan. Place Caramelized Banana halves, cut side up, on top of batter.
3. Bake until a wooden pick inserted in center comes out clean, about 50 minutes. Let cool in pan for 10 minutes. Remove from pan, and let cool completely on a wire rack.

CARAMELIZED BANANA
Makes 2 halves

1 tablespoon (14 grams) unsalted butter
2 tablespoons (28 grams) firmly packed light brown sugar
1 medium banana (124 grams), halved lengthwise

1. In a small skillet, melt butter over medium-low heat.
2. Gently press brown sugar onto each cut side of banana. Place bananas, cut side down, in skillet; cook until bananas are golden brown and caramelized, 4 to 5 minutes. Gently turn, and cook 2 minutes more. Remove from heat; set aside until ready to use.

DROP BISCUITS

Makes 11 biscuits

This recipe is a breezy wonder, with craggy peaked tops that offer a bit of crunch with the signature soft interior. The final brush with butter? Consider that its brush with greatness.

½ cup (113 grams) cold unsalted butter
1¾ cups (219 grams) all-purpose flour
1½ cups (187 grams) cake flour
2 tablespoons (24 grams) granulated sugar
1 tablespoon (15 grams) baking powder
1 teaspoon (3 grams) kosher salt
1¾ cups (420 grams) whole buttermilk, chilled
2 tablespoons (28 grams) salted butter, melted

1. Preheat oven to 400°F (200°C). Line a baking sheet with parchment paper.
2. Using a bench scraper, cut cold butter into cubes, and freeze until ready to use.
3. In a large bowl, stir together flours, sugar, baking powder, and salt. Place three-fourths of flour mixture in the work bowl of a food processor; add cold butter, and pulse until mixture is crumbly with some pea-size pieces of butter remaining.
4. Return mixture to large bowl, and stir to combine with remaining flour mixture. (Alternatively, cut cold butter into flour mixture using a pastry blender.) Add cold buttermilk, stirring just until combined. (Dough will be sticky and wet.)

5. Using a ¼-cup measuring cup, scoop dough, and drop 2 inches apart onto prepared pan. Brush top of biscuits with melted butter.
6. Bake for 8 minutes. Reduce oven temperature to 375°F (190°C), and bake until golden brown, 8 to 10 minutes more. Brush with melted butter; serve hot.

SWEET CORN, CHEDDAR & JALAPEÑO SCONES

Makes 12 to 14 scones

Recipe by Steven Satterfield

I love a biscuit or a scone in just about any form. So, imagine my delight when I discovered how perfectly fresh corn both sweetens and moisturizes the scone dough, spiked with jalapeño, tangy Cheddar, and spices.

2½ cups (313 grams) all-purpose flour
1 tablespoon (12 grams) granulated sugar
1 tablespoon (15 grams) baking powder
2 teaspoons (6 grams) fine sea salt
1 teaspoon (2 grams) ground cumin
1 teaspoon (2 grams) chili powder
½ cup (113 grams) very cold unsalted butter, cubed
2½ cups (250 grams) shredded extra-sharp white Cheddar cheese
1 bunch (81 grams) scallions, thinly sliced
1 jalapeño (34 grams), minced, including seeds
2 large eggs (100 grams)
2½ cups (380 grams) fresh corn kernels, coarsely chopped in food processor
½ cup (120 grams) plus 2 tablespoons (30 grams) half-and-half, divided
Flaked sea salt, for sprinkling

1. Preheat oven to 450°F (230°C). Line a baking sheet with parchment paper.
2. In a large bowl, whisk together flour, sugar, baking powder, fine sea salt, cumin, and chili powder. Work cold butter into flour mixture, flattening fat between your thumb and forefinger and breaking it up into pea-size pieces until mixture is crumbly. (It is fine to have a few larger chunks of butter here and there.) Add Cheddar, scallions, and jalapeño to flour mixture, stirring to combine.

3. In a small bowl, whisk together eggs, corn, and ½ cup (120 grams) half-and-half. Add egg mixture to flour mixture, stirring just until combined and dough holds together.
4. Turn out dough onto a lightly floured surface. Dust top of dough lightly with flour, and roll to 1-inch thickness. (The dough will be sticky, so you will need to keep your hands and the rolling pin floured as well.) Using a 2½-inch square cutter, cut dough. Using a sharp knife, slice each piece of dough diagonally. Place on prepared pan. Refrigerate for 15 minutes, or freeze for 5 minutes.
5. Brush dough with remaining 2 tablespoons (30 grams) half-and-half, and sprinkle with flaked sea salt.
6. Bake until golden brown, about 15 minutes. Serve hot or at room temperature.

Photo by Angie Mosier

PEACH AND BLUEBERRY CORNMEAL MUFFINS

Makes 14 jumbo muffins

In the South, bigger is always better, and these jumbo blueberry-peach muffins are no exception. Doubling down on crunchy texture with cornmeal and the almond-flecked streusel, these fruity quick breads are the best way to enjoy peaches for breakfast.

1   cup (227 grams) unsalted butter, softened
2½ cups (550 grams) firmly packed light brown sugar
4   large eggs (200 grams), room temperature
2   teaspoons (8 grams) vanilla extract
3   cups (375 grams) all-purpose flour
1   cup (150 grams) cornmeal
1½ teaspoons (7.5 grams) baking powder
½   teaspoon (2.5 grams) baking soda
1   teaspoon (3 grams) kosher salt
1   cup (240 grams) whole buttermilk, room temperature
1   cup (240 grams) peach purée*
3   cups (675 grams) diced fresh peaches (about 4 medium peaches)
1   cup (170 grams) fresh blueberries
Almond Streusel (recipe follows)

1. Preheat oven to 425°F (225°C). Line 14 jumbo muffin cups with parchment or paper liners, or spray wells with cooking spray.
2. In the bowl of stand mixer fitted with the paddle attachment, beat butter and brown sugar at medium speed until fluffy, 3 to 4 minutes, stopping to scrape sides of bowl. Add eggs, one at a time, beating well after each addition. Beat in vanilla.
3. In a medium bowl, whisk together flour, cornmeal, baking powder, baking soda, and salt. With mixer on low speed, gradually add flour mixture to butter mixture alternately with buttermilk and peach purée, beginning and ending with flour mixture, beating just until combined after each addition. Fold in peaches and blueberries. Spoon batter into prepared muffin cups, filling three-fourths full. Top each muffin with ½ cup Almond Streusel.
4. Bake for 5 minutes. Reduce oven temperature to 350°F (180°C), and bake until golden brown and a wooden pick

inserted in center comes out clean, 30 to 35 minutes more, loosely covering with foil after 15 minutes of baking to prevent excess browning.

To make peach purée, slice and peel 2 medium peaches (334 grams). Place in the work bowl of a food processor, and purée until smooth. Makes about 1 cup (240 grams) purée.

ALMOND STREUSEL
Makes about 7 cups

3   cups (375 grams) all-purpose flour
1½ cups (170 grams) sliced almonds
1½ cups (330 grams)) firmly packed light brown sugar
1   teaspoon (3 grams) kosher salt
1   cup (227 grams) unsalted butter, melted

1. In a small bowl, whisk together flour, almonds, brown sugar, and salt. Add melted butter, stirring until mixture is crumbly. Refrigerate in an airtight container for up to 2 weeks.

PASSOVER BUNS

Makes 15 buns

Recipe by Uri Scheft

Normally I don't try to find a replacement bread for Passover. It's one week of the year when you just don't eat bread. It's not that hard. I make bread for a living, and I can go a week without it. Let's eat matzah. Over the years, people certainly asked for Pesach (Passover) buns, and I always refused. Then I made these. And now I think I've changed my mind. They are flourless buns built on matzo meal and potato starch, but they are light and airy and perfect for a Pesach table. The trick is to closely follow the methodology of the recipe. It's not very forgiving, unfortunately. And the depth of color of your buns will depend on the brand of matzo meal you use.

1½ cups (360 grams) room temperature water
½ cup (112 grams) vegetable oil
5 teaspoons (20 grams) granulated sugar
1 tablespoon (9 grams) kosher salt
1 cup plus 3 tablespoons (150 grams) matzo meal
⅓ cup (50 grams) potato starch
¾ teaspoon (3.75 grams) baking powder
3 large eggs (150 grams)

1. Preheat oven to 350°F (180°C). Line baking sheets with parchment paper.
2. In a small stockpot, bring 1½ cups (360 grams) water, oil, sugar, and salt to a boil over medium-high heat.
3. In the bowl of a stand mixer fitted with the paddle attachment, beat matzo meal, potato starch, and baking powder at medium speed until combined. With mixer on low speed, add boiled liquid, beating until combined. Let cool for 10 minutes. Add eggs, one at a time, beating until mixture is smooth.
4. Using wet hands, shape dough into 20 buns (about ¼ cup [50 grams] each). Place ¾ inch apart on prepared pans.
5. Bake until lightly browned, 35 to 40 minutes.

Photo by Ben Yuster

HOMEMADE MATZO

Makes 12 matzos

Recipe by Uri Scheft

This thin and crisp cracker-like recipe is based on a matzah recipe I learned from Mitchell Davis of the James Beard Foundation. We were cooking a dinner at the James Beard House, and Mitchell made the best matzah ball soup I've ever had—even better than my mom's. He shared the base matzah recipe with me, and I've worked it into this homemade version. I love it because you can be very playful with the flavors. We used caraway seeds, but if you don't like caraway, you can use dried cumin seeds, dried herbs, or whatever you like. It's a flavorful take on what's often a pedestrian part of Pesach meals.

4¾ cups (594 grams) all-purpose flour
1 tablespoon (9 grams) kosher salt
1½ teaspoons (3 grams) ground black pepper
4 large eggs (200 grams), beaten
¼ cup (85 grams) date honey
¼ cup (60 grams) room temperature water
½ onion (30 grams), grated and drained
2½ tablespoons (5 grams) chopped fresh thyme
4 teaspoons (20 grams) olive oil
2 teaspoons (6 grams) caraway seeds

1. In a large bowl, stir together flour, salt, and pepper until combined. Make a well in center of flour mixture; add eggs, date honey, ¼ cup (60 grams) water, onion, thyme, and oil, and stir with a fork until a stiff dough forms. Knead by hand until mixture is smooth, about 1 minute. Cover with plastic wrap, and let rest for 30 minutes.
2. Preheat oven to 400°F (200°C).
3. Divide dough into 12 equal pieces (70 grams each), and shape each piece into a ball. On a lightly floured surface, roll each ball into a thin 8-inch circle. Use a pastry brush to gently brush any excess flour off dough. Sprinkle caraway onto each piece of dough. Using a fork, prick holes in dough.
4. Bake 2 at a time on a baking sheet for 10 to 12 minutes. Let cool before serving.

Photo by Ben Yuster

ROLL-OUT BISCUITS

Makes 12 biscuits

We took the formula for a roll-out buttermilk biscuit one step further and threw in a flaky twist. A quick brush with buttermilk and a tri-fold of the dough creates light layers in this golden biscuit, making it perfect to split open and butter.

1½   cups (340 grams) cold unsalted butter
2½   cups (313 grams) all-purpose flour
2½   cups (312 grams) cake flour
¼   cup (50 grams) granulated sugar
3½   tablespoons (52.5 grams) baking powder
4   teaspoons (12 grams) kosher salt
2   cups (480 grams) plus 2 tablespoons
     (30 grams) whole buttermilk, chilled
     and divided
2   tablespoons (28 grams) salted butter,
     melted

1. Line a baking sheet with parchment paper.
2. Using a bench scraper, cut cold butter into cubes, and freeze for 10 minutes.
3. In a large bowl, stir together flours, sugar, baking powder, and salt. Place three-fourths of flour mixture in the work bowl of a food processor; add cold butter, and pulse until mixture is crumbly with some pea-size pieces of butter remaining, 5 to 7 times.
4. Return mixture to large bowl, and stir to combine with remaining flour mixture. Add 2 cups (480 grams) cold buttermilk, stirring with a fork just until combined. (Do not overmix. You want to keep the ingredients cold.)
5. Using a bowl scraper, turn out dough onto a heavily floured surface, and pat into a 15x6-inch rectangle. Brush dough with remaining 2 tablespoons (30 grams) cold buttermilk. Fold dough into thirds. Reflour

work surface, and roll dough to 1-inch thickness. Using a 2½-inch round cutter dipped in flour, cut dough without twisting cutter. (Since this dough is laminated, it cannot be rerolled like normal roll-out biscuits. The rerolls will not match the final product from the first roll.) Place biscuits about ½ inch apart on prepared pan. Refrigerate for at least 30 minutes.
6. Preheat oven to 375°F (190°C).
7. Brush top of biscuits with melted butter.
8. Bake until golden brown, 16 to 18 minutes. Brush with melted butter; serve hot.

BUTTERMILK BISCUITS

Makes 10 biscuits

Our recipe for pillowy Buttermilk Biscuits creates a fine-crumbed and crisp-crusted biscuit that would be a treasured addition to any dinner table.

3½ cups (438 grams) all-purpose flour
1½ cups (187 grams) cake flour
¼   cup (50 grams) granulated sugar
3½ tablespoons (52.5 grams) baking powder
4   teaspoons (12 grams) kosher salt
1½ cups (340 grams) cold unsalted butter, cubed
2   cups (480 grams) whole buttermilk, chilled
2   tablespoons (28 grams) salted butter, melted
Jam, to serve

1. Line 2 baking sheets with parchment paper.
2. In a large bowl, whisk together flours, sugar, baking powder, and salt. Using a pastry blender, cut in cold butter until mixture is crumbly. Gradually add cold buttermilk, stirring just until combined.
3. Turn out dough onto a heavily floured surface, and roll to 1-inch thickness. Using a 3½-inch round cutter dipped in flour, cut dough without twisting cutter, rerolling scraps only once. Place 2 inches apart on prepared pans. Refrigerate for 30 minutes.
4. Preheat oven to 375°F (190°C).
5. Brush top of biscuits with melted butter.
6. Bake until golden brown, 18 to 20 minutes. Brush with melted butter; serve hot with jam.

DOUBLE GINGERBREAD SCONES

Makes 8 scones

Our scones earn their double gingerbread title from the twofold dose of ground and candied ginger in the dough. We also added old-fashioned oats to this treat to make your winter morning breakfast a little heartier.

2   cups (250 grams) all-purpose flour
¾   cup (60 grams) old-fashioned oats
¼   cup (55 grams) firmly packed light brown sugar
1   tablespoon (15 grams) baking powder
1½   teaspoons (3 grams) ground ginger
½   teaspoon (1 gram) ground cinnamon
¼   teaspoon ground nutmeg
¼   teaspoon ground cloves
½   cup (113 grams) cold unsalted butter, cubed
½   cup (80 grams) diced candied ginger
¼   cup (60 grams) plus 2 tablespoons
     (30 grams) heavy whipping cream, divided
¼   cup (85 grams) unsulphured molasses
1   large egg (50 grams)
Turbinado sugar, for sprinkling
Scone Glaze (recipe follows)

1. Preheat oven to 425°F (220°C). Line a baking sheet with parchment.
2. In a large bowl, whisk together flour, oats, brown sugar, baking powder, ground ginger, cinnamon, nutmeg, and cloves. Using a pastry blender, cut in cold butter until mixture is crumbly. Add candied ginger, tossing to combine.
3. In a small bowl, combine ¼ cup (60 grams) cream, molasses, and egg. Add cream mixture to flour mixture, stirring until combined.
4. Turn out dough onto a lightly floured surface, and gently knead up to 10 times. Pat dough into a 7-inch circle, about 1 inch thick. Cut dough into 8 wedges, and place on prepared pan. Brush top of scones with remaining 2 tablespoons (30 grams) cream, and sprinkle with turbinado sugar.
5. Bake until dough no longer looks wet around the edges, 13 to 14 minutes. Let cool completely. Drizzle Scone Glaze over cooled scones.

SCONE GLAZE
Makes ⅓ cup

1   cup (120 grams) confectioners' sugar
1½   tablespoons (22 grams) whole milk

1. In a small bowl, stir together confectioners' sugar and milk. Use immediately.

STRAWBERRY RICOTTA MUFFINS

Makes 16 muffins or 7 to 8 jumbo muffins

Recipe by Shiran Dickman

Ricotta cheese and sour cream give these delicate muffins an ultra-moist texture and richer taste. The touch of tang balances out the sweetness from the fresh bits of strawberry.

2¼ cups (281 grams) all-purpose flour, sifted
¾ cup (150 grams) granulated sugar
2 teaspoons (10 grams) baking powder
½ teaspoon (3 grams) fine sea salt
1 cup (225 grams) ricotta cheese
2 large eggs (100 grams)
⅔ cup (160 grams) whole milk
¼ cup (56 grams) canola or vegetable oil
2 teaspoons (8 grams) vanilla extract

1¼ cups (184 grams) diced fresh strawberries
Garnish: confectioners' sugar

1. Preheat oven to 350°F (180°C). Spray 16 muffin cups or 8 jumbo muffin cups with cooking spray, or line cups with paper liners.
2. In a large bowl, combine flour, granulated sugar, baking powder, and sea salt. Set aside.
3. In a medium bowl, whisk ricotta cheese until smooth. Add eggs and milk, and whisk until smooth. Add oil and vanilla, and stir until well combined. Add ricotta mixture to flour mixture, and fold with a wooden spoon or a rubber spatula just until combined. Gently fold in strawberries. Divide batter among prepared muffin cups, filling about three-fourths full.

4. Bake until a wooden pick inserted in center comes out clean, 15 to 20 minutes for regular muffins or 22 to 27 minutes for jumbo muffins. Let cool in pans for 10 minutes. Remove from pans, and let cool completely on wire racks. Garnish with confectioners' sugar, if desired. Muffins are best the same day they are made, but they can be stored in an airtight container at room temperature or in refrigerator for up to 3 days.

Note: *This recipe was developed with a standard muffin pan with a capacity of 80 to 100 milliliters and a jumbo muffin pan with a capacity of 160 to 180 milliliters.*

Photo by Shiran Dickman

PEANUT BUTTER AND JELLY MUFFINS

Makes 12 muffins or 5 to 6 jumbo muffins

Recipe by Shiran Dickman

Inspired by your favorite childhood treat, these muffins are incredibly fluffy (thanks to the peanut butter), but the oozy jam surprise at the muffin's center is the real game changer. We used strawberry, but you can use any flavor jam you like.

1½ cups (188 grams) all-purpose flour, sifted
2   teaspoons (10 grams) baking powder
½   teaspoon (3 grams) fine sea salt
¾   cup (150 grams) granulated sugar
⅔   cup (170 grams) creamy peanut butter
½   cup (120 grams) whole milk
2   large eggs (100 grams)

¼   cup (56 grams) canola or vegetable oil
1   teaspoon (4 grams) vanilla extract
½   cup (160 grams) strawberry jam

1. Preheat oven to 375°F (190°C). Spray 12 muffin cups or 6 jumbo muffin cups with cooking spray, or line cups with paper liners.
2. In the bowl of a stand mixer fitted with the whisk attachment, stir together flour, baking powder, and sea salt by hand. Add sugar, peanut butter, milk, eggs, oil, and vanilla, and beat at medium-low speed just until combined.
3. Fill prepared muffin cups halfway full with batter. Using the back of a teaspoon, make a small well in center of each cup; spoon 1 to 2 teaspoons jam into each well. Divide remaining batter among muffin cups, filling about three-fourths full.

4. Bake until a wooden pick inserted in center comes out clean, 15 to 20 minutes for regular muffins or 22 to 27 minutes for jumbo muffins. Let cool in pans for 5 minutes. Remove from pans, and let cool completely on wire racks. Muffins are best the same day they are made, but they can be stored in an airtight container at room temperature or in refrigerator for up to 3 days.

Note: *This recipe was developed with a standard muffin pan with a capacity of 80 to 100 milliliters and a jumbo muffin pan with a capacity of 160 to 180 milliliters.*

Photo by Shiran Dickman

RASPBERRY LEMON POPPY SEED MUFFINS

Makes 12 muffins or 5 to 6 jumbo muffins

Recipe by Shiran Dickman

Fresh raspberries bring a surge of summertime to the classic lemon-poppy seed combo. When folding the berries into the batter, be gentle so as not to crush them. Otherwise, you won't get those concentrated bursts of red in the final muffin. With yogurt used in place of milk, these offer a super-tender texture layered with just the right amount of crunch from the poppy seeds.

¾   cup (150 grams) granulated sugar
2   teaspoons (2 grams) lemon zest
2   cups (250 grams) all-purpose flour, sifted
2   tablespoons (18 grams) poppy seeds
1½ teaspoons (7.5 grams) baking powder
2   teaspoons (10 grams) baking soda
¼   teaspoon fine sea salt

2   large eggs (100 grams)
¾   cup (180 grams) plain yogurt
¼   cup plus 2 tablespoons (85 grams) unsalted butter, melted and slightly cooled
¼   cup (60 grams) fresh lemon juice
1   cup (170 grams) fresh or unthawed frozen raspberries

1. Preheat oven to 375°F (190°C). Spray 12 muffin cups or 6 jumbo muffin cups with cooking spray, or line cups with paper liners.
2. In a large bowl, whisk together sugar and zest. (This helps bring out the lemon flavor.) Add flour, poppy seeds, baking powder, baking soda, and sea salt, and stir until combined.
3. In a medium bowl, whisk together eggs, yogurt, melted butter, and lemon juice until combined and smooth. Pour egg mixture into flour mixture, and stir with a wooden spoon or a rubber spatula just until combined. Gently fold in raspberries, being careful not to mash. Divide batter among prepared muffin cups, filling about three-fourths full.
4. Bake until a wooden pick inserted in center comes out clean, 15 to 20 minutes for regular muffins or 22 to 27 minutes for jumbo muffins. Let cool in pans for 5 minutes. Remove from pans, and let cool completely on wire racks. Muffins are best the same day they are made, but they can be stored in an airtight container at room temperature or in refrigerator for up to 3 days.

Note: *This recipe was developed with a standard muffin pan with a capacity of 80 to 100 milliliters and a jumbo muffin pan with a capacity of 160 to 180 milliliters.*

Photo by Shiran Dickman

LEMON AND WHITE CHOCOLATE MUFFINS

Makes 12 muffins or 5 to 6 jumbo muffins

Recipe by Shiran Dickman

These indulgent quick breads are a guaranteed win for your next potluck brunch. The key? A double dose of white chocolate—both in the batter and drizzled on top post-bake—enhanced by the subtle citrus punch from a touch of lemon zest. If you like your muffins sweet, these are for you.

2 cups (250 grams) all-purpose flour, sifted
⅔ cup (133 grams) granulated sugar
2½ teaspoons (12.5 grams) baking powder
¼ teaspoon fine sea salt
1 large egg (50 grams)
¾ cup (180 grams) whole milk
⅓ cup (75 grams) canola or vegetable oil
2 teaspoons (2 grams) lemon zest

2 tablespoons (30 grams) fresh lemon juice
1 teaspoon (4 grams) vanilla extract
⅔ cup (113 grams) coarsely chopped white chocolate
½ cup (100 grams) melted white chocolate

1. Preheat oven to 375°F (190°C). Spray 12 muffin cups or 6 jumbo muffin cups with cooking spray, or line cups with paper liners.
2. In a large bowl, whisk together flour, sugar, baking powder, and sea salt.
3. In a medium bowl, whisk together egg, milk, oil, lemon zest and juice, and vanilla. Pour egg mixture into flour mixture, and fold with a rubber spatula or wooden spoon just until combined. Stir in chopped white chocolate. Divide batter among prepared muffin cups, filling about three-fourths full.

4. Bake until a wooden pick inserted in center comes out clean, 15 to 20 minutes for regular muffins or 22 to 27 minutes for jumbo muffins. Let cool in pans for 10 minutes. Remove from pans, and let cool completely on wire racks. Drizzle melted white chocolate over cooled muffins. Muffins are best the same day they are made, but they can be stored in an airtight container at room temperature or in refrigerator for up to 3 days.

Note: *This recipe was developed with a standard muffin pan with a capacity of 80 to 100 milliliters and a jumbo muffin pan with a capacity of 160 to 180 milliliters.*

Photo by Shiran Dickman

PEACHES AND CREAM MUFFINS

Makes 12 muffins or 5 to 6 jumbo muffins

Recipe by Shiran Dickman

This epic flavor profile translates beautifully into muffin form. The batter is strong enough to hold an ample amount of fresh, diced peaches. Heavy cream keeps the crumb light and tender, and you still get a burst of juicy peach in every bite.

½ cup (113 grams) unsalted butter, softened
¾ cup (150 grams) granulated sugar
2 large eggs (100 grams)
¾ cup (180 grams) heavy whipping cream
1½ teaspoons (6 grams) vanilla extract
1¾ cups (219 grams) all-purpose flour, sifted
2 teaspoons (10 grams) baking powder
¼ teaspoon fine sea salt
¼ teaspoon ground cinnamon (optional)
1 cup (225 grams) (½-inch) diced peaches, fresh and peeled, or canned and drained well

1. Preheat oven to 375°F (190°C). Spray 12 muffin cups or 6 jumbo muffin cups with cooking spray, or line cups with paper liners.
2. In the bowl of a stand mixer fitted with the paddle attachment, beat butter and sugar at medium speed until fluffy, 2 to 3 minutes, stopping to scrape sides of bowl. Add eggs, one at a time, beating well after each addition. Add cream and vanilla, beating until combined.
3. In a medium bowl, whisk together flour, baking powder, salt, and cinnamon (if using). With mixer on low speed, gradually add flour mixture to butter mixture, beating just until combined. Stir in peaches. Divide batter among prepared muffin cups, filling about three-fourths full.
4. Bake until a wooden pick inserted in center comes out clean, 15 to 20 minutes for regular muffins or 22 to 27 minutes for jumbo muffins. Let cool in pans for 10 minutes. Remove from pans, and let cool completely on wire racks. Muffins are best the same day they are made, but they can be stored in an airtight container at room temperature or in refrigerator for up to 3 days.

Note: *This recipe was developed with a standard muffin pan with a capacity of 80 to 100 milliliters and a jumbo muffin pan with a capacity of 160 to 180 milliliters.*

Photo by Shiran Dickman

MEYER LEMON POMEGRANATE MUFFINS

Makes 24 muffins

When life gives you Meyer lemons, something more epic than lemonade is called for. These muffins zip with lemon, poppy seeds, and a double dose of pomegranate with arils in the dough and a generous drizzle of homemade Pomegranate Molasses on top.

3   cups (375 grams) all-purpose flour
2   cups (400 grams) granulated sugar
¾   teaspoon (3.75 grams) baking soda
½   teaspoon (1.5 grams) kosher salt
1½   cups (249 grams) pomegranate arils
1   cup (240 grams) sour cream, room temperature
1   cup (227 grams) unsalted butter, melted
4   large eggs (200 grams)
1   tablespoon (9 grams) poppy seeds
1   tablespoon (3 grams) Meyer lemon zest
1   tablespoon (15 grams) fresh Meyer lemon juice
Poppy Seed Streusel (recipe follows)
Pomegranate Molasses (recipe follows)

1. Preheat oven to 350°F (180°C). Butter and flour 2 (12-cup) muffin pans.
2. In a large bowl, sift together flour, sugar, baking soda, and salt. Stir in pomegranate arils.
3. In another large bowl, whisk together sour cream, melted butter, eggs, poppy seeds, and lemon zest and juice. Fold flour mixture into sour cream mixture until well combined. Divide batter among prepared muffin cups. Sprinkle each muffin with about 1 tablespoon Poppy Seed Streusel.
4. Bake until golden brown, 20 to 25 minutes. Let cool in pans for 5 minutes. Remove from pans, and let cool completely on wire racks. Drizzle Pomegranate Molasses over cooled muffins.

POPPY SEED STREUSEL

Makes about 1½ cups

⅔   cup (133 grams) granulated sugar
⅔   cup (83 grams) all-purpose flour
1   teaspoon (3 grams) poppy seeds
¼   teaspoon kosher salt
¼   cup (57 grams) unsalted butter, cubed and softened

1. In a small bowl, whisk together sugar, flour, poppy seeds, and salt. Using a pastry blender, cut in butter until mixture is crumbly. Use immediately.

POMEGRANATE MOLASSES

Makes ¾ cup

3   cups (720 grams) pomegranate juice
½   cup (100 grams) granulated sugar
1½   tablespoons (22.5 grams) fresh lemon juice
¼   teaspoon kosher salt
¼   teaspoon ground black pepper

1. In a medium saucepan, bring all ingredients to a boil over medium-high heat. Reduce heat to medium-low, and simmer until thickened, syrupy, and reduced by about two-thirds, 25 to 30 minutes. Let cool completely, then refrigerate overnight. Refrigerate in an airtight container until ready to use.

STRAWBERRY SHORTCAKES

Makes 8 shortcakes

We pump up the strawberry flavor in these shortcakes by stirring fresh and freeze-dried berries into the sweet biscuit dough and the tangy whipped Greek yogurt.

1½ cups (188 grams) self-rising flour
⅓ cup (50 grams) yellow cornmeal
2 tablespoons (24 grams) granulated sugar
¾ teaspoon (2.25 grams) kosher salt
¼ teaspoon ground black pepper
6 tablespoons (84 grams) cold unsalted butter, cubed
½ cup (73 grams) diced fresh strawberries
¾ cup (180 grams) whole buttermilk, plus more for brushing
Strawberry Whipped Greek Yogurt (recipe follows)
Strawberry Coulis (recipe follows)

1. Preheat oven to 375°F (190°C). Line a baking sheet with parchment paper.
2. In a medium bowl, whisk together flour, cornmeal, sugar, salt, and pepper. Using a pastry blender, cut in cold butter until mixture is crumbly. Stir in strawberries. Stir in buttermilk just until flour is moistened.
3. On a lightly floured surface, roll dough to 1-inch thickness. Using a 2-inch round cutter, cut dough, rerolling scraps only once. (When cutting biscuits, push the cutter into dough using a straight up-and-down motion. Do not twist cutter.) Place on prepared pan. Brush top of shortcakes with buttermilk.
4. Bake until golden, 12 to 15 minutes. Let cool completely. Cut shortcakes in half horizontally. Spoon 3 to 4 tablespoons Strawberry Whipped Greek Yogurt onto bottom half of shortcakes. Top with about 2 tablespoons Strawberry Coulis. Cover with top half of shortcakes. Serve immediately.

STRAWBERRY WHIPPED GREEK YOGURT
Makes about 4 cups

1 cup (240 grams) whole-milk plain Greek yogurt
¾ cup (180 grams) heavy whipping cream
¼ cup (4 grams) freeze-dried strawberries, powdered (see PRO TIP)
3 tablespoons (63 grams) honey
¼ teaspoon kosher salt
¼ teaspoon (1 gram) rose water

1. In the bowl of a stand mixer fitted with the whisk attachment, beat all ingredients at low speed until well combined and slightly thickened. Increase mixer speed to high, and beat until thick and stiff, about 5 minutes. Use immediately, or refrigerate for up to 2 days.

> **PRO TIP**
> To make powdered freeze-dried strawberries, place freeze-dried strawberries in the bowl of a food processor; pulse until reduced to a powder.

STRAWBERRY COULIS
Makes about 1 cup

2 cups (270 grams) halved fresh strawberries
¼ cup (55 grams) firmly packed light brown sugar
2 tablespoons (30 grams) fresh lemon juice
2 tablespoons (30 grams) water
1 teaspoon (3 grams) cornstarch
½ cup (76 grams) quartered fresh strawberries

1. In a small saucepan, bring halved strawberries, brown sugar, and lemon juice to a simmer over medium heat. Reduce heat to low; cover and cook for 15 minutes, stirring and mashing any larger strawberry pieces.
2. In a small bowl, stir together 2 tablespoons (30 grams) water and cornstarch. Add cornstarch mixture to hot strawberry mixture, and bring to a simmer; cook until thickened. Remove from heat, and stir in quartered strawberries. Let cool completely. Refrigerate in an airtight container for up to 1 week.

CARDAMOM RHUBARB SHORTCAKES

Makes 12 shortcakes

Recipe by Claire Ptak

I made these shortcakes with rhubarb flavoured with cardamom pods and orange peel for a winter feel. Shortcakes work best with acidic fruit jam like raspberry, plum, and rhubarb.

5   cups (625 grams) all-purpose flour
2   tablespoons (30 grams) baking powder
½   cup (100 grams) castor sugar
½   teaspoon (1.5 grams) kosher salt
1   cup (227 grams) cold unsalted butter
2½   cups (600 grams) double/heavy
     whipping cream
1   medium egg (47 grams), lightly beaten
Roasted Rhubarb (recipe follows) or
     good-quality jam and freshly whipped
     cream, to serve

1. Line a baking tray with parchment paper.
2. In a large bowl, sift together flour and baking powder; stir in sugar and salt.
3. Cut cold butter into small pieces, and rub through dry ingredients with a pastry cutter, the back of a fork, or your fingers, or use an electric mixer or food processor. Any which way you like to get a coarse crumbly result. Pour cream over top, and stir with a wooden spoon until just combined.
4. Turn mixture out onto a lightly floured surface, and press together into a block. Let dough rest for 5 minutes.
5. When ready, roll dough to 1-inch (2½-centimeter) thickness, and use a 2¼-inch (6-centimeter) round pastry cutter to stamp out even rounds, but try not to handle the dough too much. Transfer shortcakes to prepared pan. Cover with cling film (plastic wrap), and refrigerate or freeze for 10 to 20 minutes. This will help the shortcakes keep their shape while baking.
6. Preheat oven to 400°F (200°C).
7. Brush shortcakes with egg.
8. Bake for 18 to 25 minutes, depending on their size. Remove scones from oven, and transfer to a wire rack to allow them to cool completely. To serve, split scones in half, spread with Roasted Rhubarb, and fill with cream.

ROASTED RHUBARB

Makes about 12 servings

7½   cups (750 grams) chopped rhubarb
6   tablespoons (72 grams) castor sugar
12   cardamom pods (crushed in a mortar
     and pestle)
3   tablespoons (9 grams) orange zest
3   tablespoons (45 grams) orange juice

1. Preheat oven to 350°F (180°C). Line a baking tray with parchment paper.
2. Place rhubarb in a single layer on prepared pan. Sprinkle with sugar and all remaining ingredients. Cover with foil.
3. Roast for 10 to 20 minutes. Uncover and roast until rhubarb retains its shape but is almost jammy, about 10 minutes more.

Photo by Yuki Sugiura

YEAST
BREADS

Whether you're an expert baker or new to kneading, our recipes will help you harness the natural leavening power of yeast to bake the bread of your dreams, from fruit-filled babkas to rustic Dutch oven boules.

CINNAMON SWIRL BUNS

Makes 12 buns

Recipe by John Whaite

Improving upon the universally beloved cinnamon buns, this recipe has tang and crunch with a lemon glaze and generous sprinkling of pearl sugar.

Dough:
2	cups (254 grams) strong white/bread flour, plus extra for dusting
2	cups (250 grams) plain/all-purpose flour
2½	teaspoons (10 grams) castor sugar
1	teaspoon (3 grams) kosher salt
¼	teaspoon ground cardamom
2	teaspoons (6 grams) fast-action/instant yeast
⅔	cup (160 grams) warm water (105°F/41°C to 110°F/43°C)
½	cup (120 grams) whole milk
1	large egg (50 grams)
3	tablespoons (42 grams) unsalted butter, softened

Flavourless oil, for greasing

Cinnamon Filling:
9	tablespoons (126 grams) unsalted butter
½	cup (110 grams) firmly packed dark brown muscovado sugar
¼	cup (31 grams) plain/all-purpose flour
2	tablespoons (12 grams) ground cinnamon
3	tablespoons (9 grams) lemon zest (about 1 lemon)
1	teaspoon (2 grams) ground cardamom

Lemon Glaze:
¾	cup (90 grams) icing sugar/confectioners' sugar
3	tablespoons (45 grams) fresh lemon juice

Garnish: pearl sugar

1. For dough: In the bowl of a stand mixer fitted with the dough hook attachment, add flours. Whisk in castor sugar, salt, and cardamom. Add yeast, and whisk into flour mixture. With mixer on low speed, add water, milk, and egg. Increase speed to medium, and add softened butter. Beat until a smooth, elastic dough forms, about 5 minutes. Place dough in an oiled bowl, cover with cling film (plastic wrap), and allow to rise until doubled in size, usually an hour but it could be longer if your kitchen is cool.

2. For cinnamon filling: In a medium bowl, combine all ingredients. (Use your hands as that helps to soften the butter and combine the ingredients more quickly.)

3. On a floured workspace, roll dough into a rectangle of about 15 to 17 inches (38 to 43 centimeters). Spread cinnamon filling all over dough. Roll up in a tight spiral. (As you roll, pull toward you to create this tight spiral.) Push each end toward centre to compress roll. Trim off messy ends, then cut roll into 12 equal slices. (I use dental floss for this, which I slide under the dough to where I want to cut, then bring across the two ends, up and over the dough, pulling it tight to cut through—just like a cheese wire.) Place buns, spiral side up, in a 13x9-inch (33x22-centimeter) baking pan, leaving a little space between each one. Allow to rise until buns are swollen and wobble slightly when touched, about 30 minutes.

4. Preheat oven to 425°F (220°C).

5. Bake until risen and golden, 12 to 15 minutes.

6. For lemon glaze: In a small bowl, add confectioners' sugar. Whisk in lemon juice until combined. As soon as buns come out of the oven, glaze with lemon glaze, and sprinkle with pearl sugar, if desired.

Photo by Yuki Sugiura

SOURDOUGH BISCUITS

Makes 12 biscuits

Recipe by Stacey Ballis

When I met my Kentucky-born husband, I had never made a biscuit in my life. Lucky for me, my mother-in-law was willing to teach me her technique. One morning, with no buttermilk in the house, I adapted the recipe to use my sourdough discard, and we've never gone back. My husband loves these light, flaky biscuits with butter and sorghum syrup, but I like them with just a bit of jam. I mix up a large jar of the dry ingredients, and then I just have to remember that for every 1 cup of dry mix, add ¾ cup discard, ¼ cup cream, and ½ cup butter, which makes this recipe great for quick breakfasts for any size group.

2 cups (250 grams) all-purpose flour
4 teaspoons (20 grams) baking powder
2 teaspoons (6 grams) kosher salt
1 cup (227 grams) cold unsalted butter, cubed
1½ cups (413 grams) sourdough starter discard, room temperature
½ cup (120 grams) heavy whipping cream
2 tablespoons (28 grams) salted butter, melted

1. Position oven rack in upper third of oven, and preheat oven to 425°F (220°C). Line a baking sheet with parchment paper.
2. In a large bowl, stir together flour, baking powder, and salt. Using a pastry blender, cut in cold butter until mixture is crumbly with some larger pieces of butter remaining. In a small bowl, stir together sourdough discard and cream. Add discard mixture to flour mixture, and stir with a fork until a cohesive dough forms.
3. Turn out dough onto a lightly floured surface, and knead gently just until dough comes together. Pat dough into a 10x7½-inch rectangle, 1 inch thick. (The thickness is more important than the size of the rectangle; you want the dough no less than 1 inch thick so that the biscuits puff up beautifully.) Using a sharp knife, cut dough into 12 squares. (If you prefer round biscuits, cut dough using a 2½-inch round cutter, rerolling scraps only once. I find that biscuits formed from scraps never get the loft of the regular biscuits, and squares are just easier.) Place biscuits 2 inches apart on prepared pan. Lightly brush top of biscuits with melted butter.
4. Bake until golden brown, 13 to 15 minutes, turning pan halfway through baking. Let cool on pan for 3 minutes; serve warm.

Photo by Art Meripol

SOURDOUGH BANANA CHOCOLATE CHIP MUFFINS

Makes 12 muffins

Recipe by Stacey Ballis

These muffins are really fast to pull together since they use oil instead of butter, which eliminates the need to plan ahead for softened butter. If you keep overripe bananas in the freezer (see Note), then you can mix the batter in no longer than it will take your oven to preheat, and you'll have fresh muffins in about half an hour.

1¼ cups (156 grams) all-purpose flour
½ cup (110 grams) firmly packed light brown sugar
⅓ cup (67 grams) granulated sugar
2 teaspoons (10 grams) baking powder
1 teaspoon (5 grams) baking soda
½ teaspoon (1.5 grams) kosher salt
1 cup (275 grams) sourdough starter discard, room temperature

5 tablespoons (70 grams) canola oil
1 cup (227 grams) well-mashed ripe banana
½ cup (120 grams) cold sour cream
1 large egg (50 grams), lightly beaten
1 teaspoon (4 grams) vanilla extract
1 cup (170 grams) 60% cacao dark chocolate chips

1. Preheat oven to 375°F (190°C). Line a 12-cup muffin pan with parchment or paper liners.
2. In a large bowl, stir together flour, sugars, baking powder, baking soda, and salt. In a medium bowl, stir together sourdough discard and oil until well combined. In a small bowl, stir together mashed banana, sour cream, egg, and vanilla. Add banana mixture to discard mixture, whisking until smooth. Add banana mixture to flour mixture, and fold to combine. Stir in chocolate chips. Spoon batter into prepared muffin cups,

filling two-thirds to three-fourths full.
3. Bake until lightly browned and a wooden pick inserted in center comes out clean, 20 to 25 minutes. Let cool in pan for 10 to 15 minutes. Remove from pan, and let cool completely on a wire rack. Store in an airtight container at room temperature for up to 4 days, or freeze for up to 1 month.

Note: *The best bananas for baking are ones that you have let go overripe on your counter, fully brown speckled, and then frozen in their peels in a heavy-duty resealable plastic bag. Once thawed, the frozen bananas will mash easily and have lost all of their starchy aspects, bringing moisture and deep banana flavor to any cake, muffin, or sweet bread.*

Photo by Art Meripol

TRADITIONAL ENGLISH MUFFINS

Makes 8 English muffins

Though often seen as the perfect base for eggs Benedict, this stalwart classic works as a wholesome breakfast all on its own. Try one toasted with butter and honey or with a slather of tart marmalade. With our straightforward and tasty recipe at your disposal, your days of buying English muffins will be numbered.

2½	cups (318 grams) bread flour
¾	cup (180 grams) warm whole milk (120°F/49°C to 125°F/52°C)
1	large egg (50 grams)
1	tablespoon (14 grams) unsalted butter, cubed and softened
1	tablespoon (12 grams) granulated sugar
2	teaspoons (6 grams) instant yeast
1	teaspoon (3 grams) kosher salt
1	teaspoon (5 grams) baking powder
¾	cup (112.5 grams) semolina flour
¼	cup (38 grams) cornmeal

1. In the bowl of a stand mixer fitted with the paddle attachment, beat bread flour, warm milk, egg, butter, sugar, yeast, salt, and baking powder at low speed until combined. Switch to the dough hook attachment. With mixer on medium-low speed, beat until smooth and elastic, about 5 minutes.

2. Spray a large bowl with cooking spray. Place dough in bowl, turning to grease top. Cover and let rise in refrigerator overnight. (Alternatively, cover and let rise in a warm, draft-free place [75°F/24°C] until doubled in size, about 1 hour.)

3. In a small bowl, whisk together semolina flour and cornmeal. Sprinkle semolina mixture over a well-seasoned cast-iron griddle. Line a rimmed baking sheet with parchment paper. Sprinkle semolina mixture over prepared baking sheet. Butter 8 (3¾x1-inch) English muffin rings. For a small, single-burner griddle, place 4 rings on griddle; set aside remaining 4 rings. For a large, double-burner griddle, place all 8 rings on griddle.

4. Let dough come to room temperature. On a lightly floured surface, divide dough into 8 equal portions. Shape each portion into a ball, and roll each ball into a 3½-inch disk. Place 1 disk in each prepared muffin ring. Sprinkle tops lightly with semolina mixture. Cover loosely with plastic wrap, and let rise in a warm, draft-free place (75°F/24°C) for 20 minutes.

5. Preheat oven to 350°F (180°C).

6. Place griddle on stove, and heat over medium-low heat, allowing muffins to come to temperature with pan. Cook, moving pan around occasionally for even heat, until muffins are golden brown on bottom, 5 to 7 minutes. Turn muffins, and remove rings; cook until golden brown on both sides and an instant-read thermometer inserted in center registers 190°F (88°C), about 5 minutes more. If muffins register below 190°F (88°C) but are golden brown, place on prepared baking sheet, and cover with foil.

7. Bake for 5 to 10 minutes. Let cool completely on a wire rack. If using a single-burner griddle, remove pan from heat, and allow to return to room temperature. Wipe pan clean, and sprinkle with remaining semolina mixture. Place remaining 4 muffins on griddle. Place griddle on stove, and heat over medium-low heat, allowing muffins to come to temperature with pan. Repeat procedure as directed. Store in an airtight container for up to 5 days.

FOUGASSE

Makes 2 fougasse

Recipe by John Whaite

A classic Provençal recipe, fougasse is marked by the slashed pattern running along its sides, resembling a wheat stalk. This rosemary-scented flatbread is destined to become the delightful savoury centerpiece of dinner.

1 tablespoon (14 grams) salted butter
1 small red onion (200 grams), thinly sliced
1 teaspoon (4 grams) castor sugar
1 teaspoon (5 grams) balsamic vinegar
2 cups (254 grams) strong white/bread flour, plus more for dusting
¾ cup (180 grams) warm water (105°F/41°C to 110°F/43°C)
3 tablespoons (6 grams) finely chopped fresh rosemary (or herb of your choice)
3½ teaspoons (10.5 grams) fast-action/instant yeast
1⅓ teaspoons (5 grams) kosher salt
Polenta/cornmeal, for rolling

1. In a frying pan, melt butter over medium heat. Add red onion, and cook, stirring occasionally, until very soft, a good 15 minutes at least. Add castor sugar and vinegar, and cook until caramelised, about 5 minutes more. Allow to cool completely.
2. In the bowl of a stand mixer fitted with the dough hook attachment, beat cooled onion, flour, water, rosemary, yeast, and salt at medium speed until smooth and elastic. This will be a fairly wet dough, but don't add any extra flour, or you'll make it tough. Just keep kneading it, and as gluten forms in the dough, it will become less sticky. Cover with cling film (plastic wrap), and allow to rise until doubled in size.
3. Dust a baking sheet liberally with flour/semolina and polenta/cornmeal, and dust your counter top, too. Gently tip risen dough out onto counter, using a dough scraper to help remove it from the bowl. When mound of dough is on the counter, cut in half using a sharp knife or dough scraper. Take one portion of dough, and shape it with your hands into a rough triangle shape. Using the thin edge of the dough scraper, cut a line down the middle from the tip of the triangle to the flat edge. You are cutting right through the depth of the dough, but not to each end, because you do not want to cut the dough in half. (There needs to be ¾ inch [2 centimeters] of dough uncut at either end of the line.) This line will be like a centre vein on a leaf. Then, on either side of that line, at a 45-degree angle, cut 3 little "veins" in the same way. Stretch the dough so the holes open up. Repeat with the other piece of dough. Place on the well-floured and polenta/cornmeal-dusted baking sheet. Use 2 sheets if there isn't enough room on one. Allow to proof for 30 minutes.
4. Preheat oven to 450°F (230°C). Place 2 baking sheets in oven to heat up. (Slide breads off their baking sheets directly onto hot sheets in oven.)
5. Bake until golden and crispy, 12 to 15 minutes.

Photo by Yuki Sugiura

LADY GREY CHELSEA BUNS

Makes 12 buns

We added golden raisins and Lady Grey Tea Jelly to the standard currant bun, a sticky, sweet treat often enjoyed at teatime. Proof the dough in the fridge overnight for an impressive and quick breakfast.

4   cups (508 grams) bread flour
2   tablespoons (24 grams) granulated sugar
2¼   teaspoons (7 grams) instant yeast
1   teaspoon (3 grams) kosher salt
1¼   cups (300 grams) warm whole milk (120°F/49°C to 125°F/52°C)
¼   cup (57 grams) unsalted butter, melted
1   large egg (50 grams)
Tea Jelly Filling (recipe follows)
¼   cup (80 grams) Lady Grey Tea Jelly (recipe follows), melted

1. In the bowl of a stand mixer fitted with the dough hook attachment, combine flour, sugar, yeast, and salt.
2. In a large measuring cup, stir together warm milk and melted butter. With mixer on low speed, slowly add milk mixture and egg to flour mixture, beating until a soft dough forms, stopping to scrape sides of bowl, if necessary. Increase mixer speed to medium, and beat until smooth and elastic, about 7 minutes.
3. Spray a large bowl with cooking spray. Place dough in bowl, turning to grease top. Cover with plastic wrap, and let rise in a warm, draft-free place (75°F/24°C) until doubled in size, about 1 hour.
4. Line a rimmed baking sheet with parchment paper.
5. On a lightly floured surface, roll dough into a 14x10-inch rectangle. Spread Tea Jelly Filling onto dough, leaving a ½-inch border on one long side. Starting with opposite long side, roll up dough, jelly roll style; pinch seam to seal. Trim ends, and slice into 12 rolls. Place on prepared pan. Let rise in a warm, draft-free place (75°F/24°C) until puffed, about 30 minutes.
6. Preheat oven to 375°F (190°C).
7. Bake until golden brown and puffed, 20 to 25 minutes. Brush with melted Lady Grey Tea Jelly. Let cool slightly on a wire rack. Serve warm. Store in an airtight container at room temperature for up to 5 days.

TEA JELLY FILLING
Makes about 1 cup

1   cup (240 grams) water
2   bags (4 grams) Lady Grey tea
½   cup (64 grams) golden raisins
½   cup (64 grams) currants
¼   cup (57 grams) unsalted butter, softened
¼   cup (80 grams) Lady Grey Tea Jelly (recipe follows), room temperature
¼   cup (55 grams) firmly packed light brown sugar

1. In a small saucepan, bring 1 cup (240 grams) water and tea bags to a boil over high heat; discard tea bags. Add raisins and currants. Reduce heat to low; simmer until fruit is plump, 15 to 20 minutes. Remove from heat, and let cool for 10 minutes.
2. In a small bowl, stir together rehydrated fruit, butter, Lady Grey Tea Jelly, and brown sugar. Use immediately.

LADY GREY TEA JELLY
Makes about 3 cups

1¾   cups (420 grams) water
12   bags (24 grams) Lady Grey tea
3   cups (600 grams) granulated sugar
2   tablespoons (6 grams) lemon zest
¼   cup (60 grams) fresh lemon juice
1   tablespoon (2 grams) grated fresh ginger
1   (3-ounce) package (86 grams) liquid pectin

1. In a medium saucepan, bring 1¾ cups (420 grams) water and tea bags to a boil over high heat; remove from heat. Cover and let steep for 30 minutes; remove tea bags, gently pressing to release any excess tea.
2. Add sugar, lemon zest and juice, and ginger; bring to a boil over medium heat. Cook for 2 minutes; remove from heat, and stir in pectin. Return to a boil; cook, stirring constantly, until thickened, 1 to 2 minutes. Let cool completely. Cover and refrigerate until set, about 4 hours.

STRAWBERRY POPPY SEED BUNS

Makes 12 buns

Triple your berry intake in the morning with these richly frosted buns. Slathered with Strawberry Cream Cheese Frosting and packed with poppy seeds and Strawberry Cream Cheese, these are the splurge that you—and your strawberries—deserve.

4   cups (508 grams) bread flour
2   tablespoons (24 grams) granulated sugar
2¼   teaspoons (7 grams) instant yeast
2   teaspoons (6 grams) poppy seeds
1   teaspoon (3 grams) kosher salt
1¼   cups (300 grams) warm whole milk (120°F/49°C to 125°F/52°C)
¼   cup (57 grams) unsalted butter, melted
1   large egg (50 grams)
½   recipe Strawberry Cream Cheese (recipe follows)
⅓   cup (76 grams) unsalted butter, softened
Strawberry Cardamom Sugar (recipe follows)
Strawberry Cream Cheese Frosting (recipe follows)

1. In the bowl of a stand mixer fitted with the dough hook attachment, combine flour, sugar, yeast, poppy seeds, and salt.
2. In a large measuring cup, stir together warm milk and melted butter. With mixer on low speed, gradually add milk mixture and egg to flour mixture, beating until a soft dough forms, stopping to scrape sides of bowl, if necessary. Increase mixer speed to medium, and beat until smooth and elastic, about 7 minutes.
3. Spray a large bowl with cooking spray. Place dough in bowl, turning to grease top. Cover and let rise in a warm, draft-free place (75°F/24°C) until doubled in size, about 1 hour.
4. On a lightly floured surface, roll dough into a 14x10-inch rectangle. Spread Strawberry Cream Cheese onto dough. Fold dough into thirds, like a letter. Cover with plastic wrap, and let rest for 10 minutes.
5. Butter and flour a 13x9-inch baking pan.
6. On a lightly floured surface, roll dough into a 14x10-inch rectangle. Spread butter onto dough, leaving a ½-inch border on one long side. Sprinkle with Strawberry Cardamom Sugar. Starting with one long side, roll dough into a log, pinching seam to seal. Trim ends. Slice into 12 rolls. Place in prepared pan. Let rise in a warm, draft-free place (75°F/24°C) until puffed, about 45 minutes.
7. Preheat oven to 375°F (190°C).
8. Bake until golden brown and puffed, 25 to 30 minutes. Let cool on a wire rack. Drizzle with Strawberry Cream Cheese Frosting. Serve warm.

STRAWBERRY CREAM CHEESE
Makes about 1 cup

8   ounces (225 grams) cream cheese, softened
½   cup (8 grams) freeze-dried strawberries, powdered (see PRO TIP)
½   cup (73 grams) diced fresh strawberries

1. In the bowl of a stand mixer fitted with the paddle attachment, beat all ingredients at medium-low speed until well combined. Refrigerate in an airtight container for up to 4 days.

STRAWBERRY CARDAMOM SUGAR
Makes about 1 cup

¾   cup (150 grams) granulated sugar
⅓   cup (5 grams) freeze-dried strawberries
1   teaspoon (2 grams) ground cardamom
1   teaspoon (1 gram) lemon zest

1. In the work bowl of a food processor, place all ingredients; process until well combined. Store in an airtight container at room temperature for up to 1 week.

STRAWBERRY CREAM CHEESE FROSTING
Makes about 1 cup

4   ounces (115 grams) cream cheese, softened
1½   tablespoons (21 grams) unsalted butter, softened
1½   cups (180 grams) confectioners' sugar
¼   cup (4 grams) freeze-dried strawberries, powdered (see PRO TIP)
2 to 3 tablespoons (30 to 45 grams) whole milk

1. In the bowl of a stand mixer fitted with the paddle attachment, beat cream cheese and butter at medium speed until creamy. With mixer on low speed, gradually add confectioners' sugar and freeze-dried strawberries, beating until combined. Add milk, 1 tablespoon (15 grams) at a time, beating until desired consistency is reached. Use immediately.

> **PRO TIP**
> To make powdered freeze-dried strawberries, place freeze-dried strawberries in the bowl of a food processor; pulse until reduced to a powder.

CAST IRON SWEET POTATO CARDAMOM BREAD

Makes 1 (10-inch) loaf

Recipe by Mandy Dixon

In my recipe, I use bread flour, which helps the dough to rise, and milk, which softens the dough and makes it tender. The sweet potato provides a natural sweetness, but the bread itself isn't too sweet or cloying. This is particularly good if there is some tartness or acid added, so consider adding in chopped fruit or citrus to the mix.

2¼ cups (268 grams) bread flour, divided
¼ cup (60 grams) warm milk (120°F/49°C to 130°F/54°C)
1 tablespoons plus ½ teaspoon (10 grams) active dry yeast
⅓ cup (92 grams) sweet potato purée (see PRO TIP)
⅓ cup (75 grams) unsalted butter, softened
2 large eggs (100 grams)
⅛ cup (25 grams) granulated sugar
1 tablespoon (3 grams) orange zest
1 teaspoon (3 grams) kosher salt
Cardamom Filling (recipe follows)
½ cup (56 grams) toasted pecans, chopped
Lemon-Vanilla Glaze (recipe follows)

1. In the bowl of a stand mixer fitted with the paddle attachment, stir together ⅓ cup (42 grams) flour, warm milk, and yeast. Let stand until mixture is foamy, about 5 minutes.
2. Add sweet potato purée, butter, eggs, sugar, zest, salt, and remaining flour, and beat at low speed until combined. Turn out dough onto a heavily floured surface, and knead until smooth and elastic, 4 to 5 minutes.
3. Spray a large bowl with cooking spray. Place dough in bowl, turning to grease top. Cover and let rise in a warm, draft-free place (75°F/24°C) until doubled in size, about 1 hour.
4. Grease a 10-inch cast-iron skillet.
5. Turn out dough onto a heavily floured surface, and roll into an 18x10-inch rectangle. Spread Cardamom Filling onto dough. Sprinkle pecans on top of filling, leaving a 1-inch border. Starting at one long

side, roll up dough, jelly roll style, pinching seam to seal. Place seam side down. Using a serrated knife, cut roll in half lengthwise. Carefully twist dough pieces around each other, cut sides up, and form into a circle. Place in prepared pan. Wrap pan tightly in plastic wrap, and refrigerate overnight.
6. Uncover and bring dough to room temperature. Cover and let rise in a warm, draft-free place (75°F/24°C) for about 30 minutes.
7. Preheat oven to 350°F (180°C).
8. Bake for 25 minutes. Reduce oven temperature to 325°F (170°C), and bake 15 minutes more, covering with foil to prevent excess browning, if necessary. Drizzle Lemon-Vanilla Glaze over bread. Let glaze soak in a bit, and serve warm.

CARDAMOM FILLING
Makes about ¾ cup

½ cup (110 grams) firmly packed light brown sugar
⅓ cup (75 grams) unsalted butter, softened
1½ teaspoons (3 grams) ground cinnamon
½ teaspoon (1 gram) ground cardamom

1. In a medium bowl, stir together all ingredients. Use immediately.

LEMON-VANILLA GLAZE
Makes about ½ cup

1 cup (120 grams) confectioners' sugar
1 tablespoon (15 grams) whole milk
1 teaspoon (5 grams) fresh lemon juice
½ teaspoon (2 grams) vanilla extract

1. In a small bowl, stir together all ingredients. Use immediately.

> **PRO TIP**
> Preheat oven to 425°F (220°C). Rub 1 medium sweet potato with canola or grapeseed oil. Prick potato with a fork, and season with sea salt. Wrap potato in foil. Bake until potato is completely soft, about 45 minutes. Let cool. Peel, and purée in the container of a blender. We always bake potatoes rather than boil for more intense flavor.

CHOCOLATE ALMOND PULL-APART BREAD

Makes 2 (8x4-inch) loaves

Chocolate, almond, and rich, fluffy bread dough combine for the ultimate pull-apart recipe. Whether enjoying it as breakfast, dessert, or an outrageous snack, this compulsively eatable chocolate-rich bread will reign as a new favorite in your baking wheelhouse.

4¼ cups (531 grams) all-purpose flour
¼ cup (50 grams) granulated sugar
2¼ teaspoons (7 grams) instant yeast
1 teaspoon (3 grams) kosher salt
¾ cup (180 grams) warm whole milk (120°F/49°C to 125°F/52°C)
2 large eggs (100 grams), room temperature
1 large egg yolk (19 grams), room temperature
1 teaspoon (4 grams) vanilla extract
1 teaspoon (4 grams) almond extract
½ cup (113 grams) unsalted butter, cubed and softened
½ cup (57 grams) sliced almonds

½ cup (85 grams) finely chopped 45% cacao milk chocolate*
Milk Chocolate-Almond Filling (recipe follows)
1.5 ounces (45 grams) 45% cacao milk chocolate, melted
1.5 ounces (45 grams) white chocolate, melted

1. In the bowl of a stand mixer fitted with the paddle attachment, combine flour, sugar, yeast, and salt.
2. In a small bowl, whisk together warm milk, eggs, egg yolk, and extracts. With mixer on low speed, gradually add milk mixture to flour mixture, beating just until combined. Switch to the dough hook attachment. With mixer on medium-low speed, add butter, 2 tablespoons (28 grams) at a time, beating until combined after each addition. Increase mixer speed to medium, and beat until smooth and elastic, 3 to 5 minutes. Add almonds and chopped chocolate, beating until combined.
3. Spray a large bowl with cooking spray.

Place dough in bowl, turning to grease top. Cover with plastic wrap, and let rise in a warm, draft-free place (75°F/24°C) until doubled in size, about 1 hour.
4. Knead dough 5 times, and shape into a ball; return to greased bowl. Cover and refrigerate overnight.
5. Preheat oven to 350°F (180°C). Butter and flour 2 (8x4-inch) loaf pans. Line pans with parchment paper.
6. On a lightly floured surface, roll dough into a 20x18-inch rectangle. Spread Milk Chocolate-Almond Filling onto dough. Using a sharp knife, cut dough widthwise into 5 (4-inch) strips. Stack strips one on top of the other, and cut into 4x2½-inch rectangles. Stand prepared pans vertically on one short side, and starting at bottom, carefully layer dough rectangles, cut side up, one on top of the other in pans. Turn loaf pans upright onto bottoms.
7. Bake until golden and an instant-read thermometer inserted in center registers 190°F (88°C), 30 to 45 minutes, covering with foil to prevent excess browning, if necessary. Let cool in pans for 15 minutes. Remove from pans, and drizzle with melted milk and white chocolates. Serve warm.

We used Guittard 45% Cacao Soleil D'Automne Milk Chocolate.

MILK CHOCOLATE-ALMOND FILLING
Makes about 1 cup

½ cup (85 grams) chopped 45% cacao milk chocolate
¼ cup (60 grams) heavy whipping cream
3 tablespoons (42 grams) unsalted butter
2 tablespoons (24 grams) granulated sugar
¼ teaspoon kosher salt
½ cup (57 grams) chopped almonds

1. In a small microwave-safe bowl, combine chocolate, cream, butter, sugar, and salt. Microwave on high in 30-second intervals, stirring between each, until melted and smooth. Stir in almonds. Cover and refrigerate until thickened, at least 30 minutes or up to 4 days.

STRAWBERRY COCONUT BABKA

Makes 2 (9x5-inch) loaves

Coconut flakes lend a delicate nuttiness to the sweet filling in this yeasted bread. We slather strawberry jam over the warm loaves post-bake.

¾ cup (180 grams) warm whole milk (105°F/41°C to 110°F/43°C)
1 tablespoon (9 grams) active dry yeast
5½ cups (688 grams) all-purpose flour
¾ cup (150 grams) granulated sugar
5 large eggs (250 grams), divided
1 teaspoon (4 grams) vanilla extract
1 cup (227 grams) unsalted butter, softened
1 tablespoon (9 grams) kosher salt
1 tablespoon (15 grams) water
Strawberry Coconut Filling (recipe follows)
¼ cup (80 grams) melted strawberry preserves (optional)
Confectioners' Sugar Glaze (recipe follows) (optional)

1. Place warm milk in a small bowl. Gradually add yeast, whisking until completely dissolved. Let stand for 5 minutes.
2. In the bowl of a stand mixer fitted with the dough hook attachment, stir together flour and sugar until combined. With mixer on low speed, add yeast mixture, 4 eggs (200 grams), and vanilla, beating until mixture comes together, 2 to 3 minutes. (Mixture will be dry and crumbly.) Add butter, 1 tablespoon (14 grams) at a time, letting each piece incorporate before adding the next. Add salt, beating just until combined, about 3 minutes. Increase mixer speed to medium, and beat until a smooth and elastic dough forms and pulls away from sides of bowl.
3. Spray a large bowl with cooking spray. Place dough in bowl, turning to grease top. Cover with a double layer of plastic wrap, and let rise in refrigerator overnight until almost doubled in size.
4. Line 2 (9x5-inch) loaf pans with parchment paper; spray with cooking spray.
5. In a small bowl, lightly whisk together 1 tablespoon (15 grams) water and remaining 1 egg (50 grams).
6. Remove dough from refrigerator, and divide in half. On a floured surface, roll each half of dough into a 16x12-inch rectangle. Spread half of Strawberry Coconut Filling onto each rectangle, leaving a 1-inch border on all sides. Brush edges of dough with egg wash. Starting at one short side, roll up dough, jelly roll style; pinch edges to seal. Using a serrated knife, cut each roll in half lengthwise, leaving 1 inch at top intact. Carefully turn each half cut side up, and twist dough pieces around each other, pinching ends to seal. Transfer to prepared pans. Cover and let rise in a warm, draft-free place (75°F/24°C) until almost doubled in size, about 1 hour.
7. Preheat oven to 350°F (180°C).
8. Bake for 25 minutes. Cover with foil, and bake until an instant-read thermometer inserted in center registers 190° (88°F) to 200°F (92°C), 40 to 45 minutes more. Brush melted preserves onto warm loaves while still in pans, if desired. Let cool for 20 minutes. Remove from pans, and let cool completely on a wire rack. Drizzle with Confectioners' Sugar Glaze, if desired. Store in an airtight container at room temperature for up to 2 days.

STRAWBERRY COCONUT FILLING
Makes about 2 cups

3 tablespoons (24 grams) cornstarch
3 tablespoons (45 grams) fresh lemon juice
1½ cups (480 grams) strawberry preserves
1½ cups (98 grams) unsweetened flaked coconut

1. In a small saucepan, stir together cornstarch and lemon juice until smooth. Stir in preserves; bring to a boil over medium heat, stirring frequently. Reduce heat; simmer, stirring constantly, until thickened, 6 to 8 minutes. Transfer to a bowl; stir in coconut. Let cool completely.

CONFECTIONERS' SUGAR GLAZE
Makes about 1 cup

2 cups (240 grams) confectioners' sugar
3 tablespoons (45 grams) whole milk
⅛ teaspoon kosher salt

1. In a small bowl, stir together all ingredients until smooth. Use immediately.

Photo by Stephen DeVries

CHERRY TOMATO FOCACCIA

Makes about 12 servings

This fluffy Italian flatbread is the perfect family-size recipe for your next get-together, impressing both the eyes and the taste buds.

Poolish:
1   cup plus 2 tablespoons (255 grams) water (70°F/21°C)
⅛   teaspoon instant yeast
2   cups (250 grams) all-purpose flour

Dough:
1¼   cups (284 grams) water (85°F/29°C)
4½   teaspoons (14 grams) instant yeast
4   cups (500 grams) all-purpose flour
¼   cup (56 grams) olive oil
2   tablespoons (24 grams) granulated sugar
5   teaspoons (15 grams) kosher salt

Topping:
3   tablespoons (42 grams) warm water (80°F/27°C)
2   tablespoons (28 grams) olive oil
½   medium red onion (55 grams), thinly sliced
1   dry pint (270 grams) cherry tomatoes (see Note)
2   tablespoons (4 grams) fresh rosemary leaves
1   tablespoon (9 grams) coarse kosher salt
1   (8-ounce) ball (226 grams) fresh mozzarella, thinly sliced

1. For poolish: In a large bowl, stir together 1 cup plus 2 tablespoons (255 grams) water and yeast. Add flour, and stir thoroughly by hand until smooth and there are no dry bits

of flour remaining. Cover bowl with plastic wrap, and let stand at room temperature for 14 to 16 hours.
2. For dough: In the bowl of a stand mixer fitted with the paddle attachment, combine poolish, 1¼ cups (284 grams) water, and yeast. Add flour, oil, sugar, and salt. Beat at low speed until dough starts to pull away from sides of bowl, 5 to 7 minutes.
3. Turn out dough onto a floured surface, and knead until smooth. Test dough using the windowpane method. (See PRO TIP on page 152.) If dough is not ready, knead a couple more times, and test again.
4. Grease a large bowl with olive oil. Place dough in bowl, and rub a little oil on top of dough. Cover surface of dough with plastic wrap, and let rise in a warm, draft-free place (75°F/24°C) for 1 hour.
5. Spray a rimmed 18x13-inch sheet pan with cooking spray; brush with olive oil.
6. Turn out dough onto prepared pan, and gently stretch to completely fill bottom of pan. If dough is tight and will not stretch completely, let dough rest for 5 to

10 minutes, and then try again. Cover with plastic wrap, and let rise for 30 minutes.
7. Uncover dough, and dimple using your fingertips. You want your fingertips to touch the bottom of the sheet pan but without tearing through the dough. Cover and let rise until dough is level with sides of pan, about 30 minutes.
8. Preheat oven to 425°F (220°C).
9. For topping: Sprinkle dough with 3 tablespoons (42 grams) warm water; drizzle with oil. Add onion, tomatoes, rosemary, and coarse salt.
10. Bake for 15 minutes. Add sliced mozzarella, and bake until cheese is melted and focaccia is golden, 5 to 10 minutes more. Immediately transfer focaccia to a wire rack. Enjoy hot out of the oven, or let cool slightly, and serve warm. Focaccia is best the day it's made, but leftovers can be reheated in the oven the next day.

Note: *The weight of the tomatoes may vary based on the size of each tomato used. You can also use grape tomatoes.*

SWEET AND SPICY ROASTED GARLIC- AND BRIE-STUFFED FLATBREADS

Makes 9 flatbreads

Recipe by Erin Jeanne McDowell

With spicy jelly and melted cheese, these are perfect as a meal alongside a big salad or just as a comforting snack.

2	medium heads garlic (200 grams)
⅓	cup (75 grams) plus 2 teaspoons (10 grams) extra-virgin olive oil, divided
5	cups (625 grams) all-purpose flour
1½	cups (360 grams) warm water (95°F/35°C)
3	tablespoons (63 grams) honey
1	tablespoon plus 1 teaspoon (12 grams) instant yeast
2	teaspoons (6 grams) fine sea salt
1	large egg (50 grams)
1	tablespoon (15 grams) water
18	ounces (520 grams) Brie cheese, thickly sliced
1	cup plus 2 tablespoons (360 grams) hot pepper jelly

Garnish: smoked salt or coarse sea salt

1. Preheat oven to 325°F (170°C).

2. Cut ⅓ inch off top end of garlic, keeping cloves intact. Place each head of garlic, cut side up, on a sheet of foil. Drizzle with 2 teaspoons (10 grams) oil, and wrap garlic in foil. Place on a baking sheet.

3. Bake until soft, about 1 hour. Let cool completely. Squeeze pulp into a small bowl.

4. In the bowl of a stand mixer fitted with the dough hook attachment, beat flour, 1½ cups (360 grams) warm water, honey, yeast, sea salt, and remaining ⅓ cup (75 grams) oil at low speed for 2 minutes. Increase mixer speed to medium, and beat for 2 minutes.

5. Spray a large bowl with cooking spray. Place dough in bowl, turning to grease top. Cover with plastic wrap, and let rise in a warm, draft-free place (75°F/24°C) until nearly doubled in size, about 1 hour.

6. On a lightly floured surface, divide dough into 9 (128-gram) pieces. Loosely cover with plastic wrap, and let rest for 20 minutes.

7. Preheat oven to 500°F (260°C). Line 2 baking sheets with parchment paper.

8. Working with one piece of dough at a time, press dough with fingers into a 6x5-inch rectangle, about ⅓ inch thick. In a small bowl, whisk together egg and 1 tablespoon (15 grams) water. Brush egg wash onto left half of rectangle. Place 1 tablespoon (8 grams) roasted garlic in center of left side of each rectangle, and spread in an even layer. Top with 2 ounces Brie and 2 tablespoons (40 grams) pepper jelly. Fold dough over filling, and press edges firmly to seal. Place on prepared pans. Brush dough with egg wash, and sprinkle with smoked or coarse salt, if desired.

9. Bake until deep golden brown, 8 to 10 minutes. Let cool for 5 to 10 minutes before serving.

Photo by Mark Weinberg

DEMI BAGUETTES

Makes 4 loaves

A compact recipe for the French classic offers home bakers a chance to bring the art of boulangerie to their small-scale but no-less-artisan home operation.

Poolish:
1 cup plus 1 tablespoon (241 grams) tepid water (70°F/21°C)
¹⁄₁₆ teaspoon instant yeast
1¾ cups plus 2½ tablespoons (242 grams) bread flour

Dough:
1 cup plus 2½ tablespoons (262 grams) water (for temperature, see Note)
1 teaspoon (3 grams) instant yeast
3¾ cups (476 grams) bread flour
1½ tablespoons (14 grams) kosher salt

1. For poolish: In a large bowl, stir together 1 cup plus 1 tablespoon (241 grams) tepid water and yeast. Add flour, and stir thoroughly by hand until smooth and there are no dry bits of flour remaining. Cover bowl with plastic wrap, and let stand at room temperature for 14 to 16 hours.
2. For dough: In the bowl of a stand mixer fitted with the dough hook attachment, combine poolish, 1 cup plus 2½ tablespoons (262 grams) water, and yeast. Add flour and salt. Beat at medium-low speed for 3 minutes; beat at medium speed for 3 minutes. Test dough using the windowpane method. (See PRO TIP.) If dough is not ready, beat 1 minute more, and test again. Final dough should be smooth.
3. Spray a large glass bowl with cooking spray. Place dough in bowl, turning to grease top. Cover with a kitchen towel, and let rise in a warm, draft-free place (75°F/24°C) for 1½ hours, folding after 45 minutes.
4. Turn out dough onto a floured surface, and divide into 4 equal parts (each weighing 300 grams). Shape each baguette into a blunt log by gently flattening dough into a rectangle. (There is no set size or thickness that the rectangle should be. The proof will determine these dimensions.) Take top edge of short side of dough, and tuck top third toward center, sealing it with your thumbs. Fold dough again by taking top edge and folding it down and sealing it with your thumbs. Roll dough until seam side is down. Cover with a kitchen towel, and let rest for 15 minutes.
5. Shape baguettes by gently flattening dough into a rectangle. Take top edge of long side of dough, and fold top third toward center, pressing to seal. Turn dough 180 degrees, and repeat folding top third to meet other fold in center. Take top edge of long side of dough, and tuck it to center, and going left to right, seal it by pressing firmly with the heal of your hand. Turn dough 180 degrees, and tuck top third over the rest of the dough, sealing it by pressing firmly with the heal of your hand. Roll seal to bottom, and using both hands, gently roll from center out toward ends, lengthening the dough as you go, and tapering ends. Baguettes should be about 14 inches long. Place baguettes on baguette pans. Cover and let rise for 45 to 60 minutes.
6. Soak a kitchen towel with water, and place on a rimmed sheet tray. Place in oven, and pour enough water in pan to cover bottom. Preheat oven to 500°F (260°C).
7. Using a lame, score bread. Place bread in oven, and immediately reduce oven temperature to 480°F (249°C).
8. Bake for 10 minutes. Remove sheet pan with towel (it should be dry now), and continue baking until baguettes are a rich golden brown, 5 to 10 minutes more. Let cool on a wire rack before cutting or storing.

Note: *This recipe was developed in a 71°F environment, so the water temperature used in this recipe was 58°F/14°C. There is an equation to figure out the correct temperature of the water based on the temperature of your environment. Use Fahrenheit temperatures. Take the desired dough temperature (75°F), and multiply by 4 to get 300°F. Then subtract the preferment temperature (the temperature of your poolish), room temperature, flour temperature, and friction factor. (Friction factor is the amount that mixing increases the dough's temperature. Each mixer will have a slightly different friction factor, but a good place to start is 25°F.)*

Example equation:
75°F (desired dough temperature) x 4 = 300°F
300°F - 79°F (preferment temperature) - 71°F (room temperature) - 67°F (flour temperature) - 25°F (friction factor) = 58°F (water temperature for final dough)

PRO TIP
Test the dough for proper gluten development using the windowpane test. Pinch off a small piece of dough. (Make sure you don't tear the dough.) Slowly pull the dough out from the center. If the dough is ready, you will be able to stretch it until it's thin and translucent like a windowpane. If the dough tears, it's not quite ready.

CHEESY BABKA WITH
SUN-DRIED TOMATOES

Makes 1 (9x5-inch) loaf

This savory babka has the flavor palate of a grown-up pizza, with rich ripples of cheese and chopped sun-dried tomatoes balanced out by the mild herbaceous notes of basil.

3	cups (375 grams) all-purpose flour
¼	cup (50 grams) granulated sugar
2¾	teaspoons (8.25 grams) instant yeast
2	teaspoons (6 grams) kosher salt
3	large eggs (150 grams)
2	large egg yolks (37 grams)
⅔	cup (160 grams) warm whole milk (120°F/49°C to 130°F/54°C)
¾	cup (170 grams) unsalted butter, softened
1	large egg white (30 grams)
1	tablespoon (15 grams) water
1½	cups (150 grams) shredded Italian cheese blend
¾	cup (82.5 grams) oil-packed julienned sun-dried tomatoes, drained
⅓	cup (11 grams) chopped fresh basil
1	clove garlic (5 grams), minced

1. In the bowl of a stand mixer fitted with the paddle attachment, combine flour, sugar, yeast, and salt. Stir in eggs and egg yolks. With mixer on low speed, gradually add warm milk, beating until dough comes together. Increase mixer speed to medium-high, and beat for 6 to 8 minutes. Test dough using the windowpane test. (See PRO TIP.) If dough is not ready, beat 1 minute more, and test again.
2. Switch to the dough hook attachment. With mixer on medium-high speed, add butter in three additions, letting each incorporate before adding the next. Beat until a smooth and elastic dough forms and pulls away from sides of bowl.
3. Spray a large bowl with cooking spray. Place dough in bowl, turning to grease top. Cover surface of dough with plastic wrap, and let rise in a warm, draft-free place (75°F/24°C) until doubled in size, 1½ to 2 hours.
4. Refrigerate dough for 30 minutes. (Alternatively, dough can be made 1 day in advance, and the entire rise may take place in the refrigerator overnight. Remove dough from refrigerator, and let come to room temperature before proceeding.)

5. Spray a 9x5-inch loaf pan with cooking spray.
6. In a small bowl, whisk together egg white and 1 tablespoon (15 grams) water.
7. On a heavily floured surface, roll dough into 16x12-inch rectangle. Brush edges of dough with egg wash. Sprinkle dough with cheese, tomatoes, basil, and garlic. Starting with one short side, roll up dough, jelly roll style, and pinch seam to seal. Using a bench scraper, cut roll in half lengthwise. Carefully twist dough pieces tightly around each other, pinching ends to seal. Place in prepared pan, cut sides up. Tuck ends and sides tightly into pan. Cover and let rise in a warm, draft-free place (75°F/24°C) until doubled in size, 30 minutes to 1 hour.
8. Preheat oven to 350°F (180°C).
9. Bake for 20 minutes. Cover with foil, and bake until an instant-read thermometer inserted in center registers 190°F (88°C), 40 to 45 minutes more. Let cool in pan for 10 minutes. Remove from pan, and let cool completely on a wire rack.

PRO TIP
Test the dough for proper gluten development using the windowpane test. Pinch off (make sure you don't tear the dough) a small piece of dough. Slowly pull the dough out from the center. If the dough is ready, you will be able to stretch it until it's thin and translucent like a windowpane. If the dough tears, it's not quite ready.

STRAWBERRY BRIOCHE WITH PEARL SUGAR

Makes 1 (9x5-inch) loaf

Sticky-sweet strawberry filling is smeared, rolled, and twisted into a buttery brioche dough, and a final sprinkling of pearl sugar offers an element of elegant crunch.

3   cups (375 grams) all-purpose flour
¼   cup (50 grams) granulated sugar
2   teaspoons (6 grams) instant yeast
2   teaspoons (6 grams) kosher salt
4   large eggs (200 grams)
½   cup (120 grams) warm whole milk (120°F/49°C to 130°F/54°C)
¾   cup (170 grams) unsalted butter, softened
1   tablespoon (3 grams) lemon zest
1   large egg white (30 grams)
1   tablespoon (15 grams) water
Strawberry Jam Filling (recipe follows)
Pearl sugar, for sprinkling

1. In the bowl of a stand mixer fitted with the paddle attachment, combine flour, granulated sugar, yeast, and salt. Stir in eggs. With mixer on low speed, gradually add warm milk, beating until dough comes together. Increase mixer speed to medium-high, and beat for 6 to 8 minutes. Test dough using the windowpane test. (See PRO TIP on page 154.) If dough is not ready, beat 1 minute more, and test again.

2. Switch to the dough hook attachment. With mixer on medium-high speed, add butter in three additions, letting each incorporate before adding the next. Beat until a smooth and elastic dough forms and pulls away from sides of bowl. Add zest, and beat until combined.

3. Spray a large bowl with cooking spray. Place dough in bowl, turning to grease top. Cover surface of dough with plastic wrap, and let rise in a warm, draft-free place (75°F/24°C) until doubled in size, 1½ to 2 hours.

4. Refrigerate dough for 30 minutes. (Alternatively, dough can be made 1 day in advance, and the entire rise may take place in the refrigerator overnight. Remove dough from refrigerator, and let come to room temperature before proceeding.)

5. Spray a 9x5-inch loaf pan with cooking spray; line pan with parchment paper, letting excess extend over sides of pan.

6. In a small bowl, whisk together egg white and 1 tablespoon (15 grams) water.

7. On a heavily floured surface, roll dough into 16x12-inch rectangle. Brush edges of dough with egg wash. Spread Strawberry Jam Filling onto dough, leaving a 1-inch border on all sides. Starting with one short side, roll up dough, jelly roll style, and pinch seam to seal. Using a bench scraper, cut roll in half lengthwise. Carefully twist dough pieces tightly around each other, pinching ends to seal. Place in prepared pan, cut sides up. Cover and let rise in a warm, draft-free place (75°F/24°C) until doubled in size, 30 minutes to 1 hour.

8. Preheat oven to 350°F (180°C).

9. Brush top of loaf with egg wash, and sprinkle with pearl sugar.

10. Bake for 20 minutes. Cover with foil, and bake until an instant-read thermometer inserted in center registers 190°F (88°C), 40 to 45 minutes more. Let cool in pan for 10 minutes. Using excess parchment as handles, remove from pan, and let cool completely on a wire rack.

STRAWBERRY JAM FILLING
Makes 1 cup

1   cup (320 grams) strawberry preserves
2   tablespoons (16 grams) cornstarch
2   tablespoons (30 grams) fresh lemon juice

1. In a small saucepan, heat all ingredients over medium heat until slightly thickened, about 5 minutes. Remove from heat; let cool completely. Once cooled, refrigerate for 30 minutes before using.

PRALINE PECAN BABKA

Makes 1 (9x5-inch) loaf

Developed in the early 19th century in New Orleans, pralines are creamy, cookie-size candies made of brown sugar, butter, and nuts. We commemorate the confection's sweet nuttiness and melt-in-your mouth magic with a pillowy pecan-laden babka.

½   cup (120 grams) warm whole milk (105°F/41°C to 110°F/43°C)
1¼ teaspoons (3.75 grams) active dry yeast
2½ cups (313 grams) all-purpose flour
3½ tablespoons (42 grams) granulated sugar
2¼ teaspoons (6.75 grams) kosher salt, divided
2   large eggs (100 grams)
1   large egg yolk (19 grams)
1   teaspoon (4 grams) vanilla extract
¾   cup plus 2 tablespoons (198 grams) unsalted butter, softened and divided
1   large egg white (30 grams)
1   tablespoon (15 grams) water
1½ cups (330 grams) firmly packed dark brown sugar
¾   cup (85 grams) finely chopped pecans
Caramel Pecan Glaze (recipe follows)

1. In a small bowl, stir together warm milk and yeast. Let stand until mixture is foamy, about 5 minutes.
2. In the bowl of a stand mixer fitted with the paddle attachment, combine flour, granulated sugar, and 1¾ teaspoons (5.25 grams) salt. Stir in eggs, egg yolk, and vanilla. With mixer on low speed, gradually add yeast mixture, beating until dough comes together. Increase mixer speed to medium-high, and beat for 5 to 7 minutes. Test dough using the windowpane test. (See PRO TIP.) If dough is not ready, beat 1 minute more, and test again.
3. Switch to the dough hook attachment. With mixer on medium-high speed, add ½ cup plus 2 tablespoons (141 grams) butter in three additions, letting each incorporate before adding the next. Beat until a smooth and elastic dough forms and pulls away from sides of bowl.
4. Spray a large bowl with cooking spray. Place dough in bowl, turning to grease top. Cover surface of dough with plastic wrap, and let rise in a warm, draft-free place (75°F/24°C) until doubled in size, 1½ to 2 hours.
5. Refrigerate dough for at least 30 minutes. (Alternatively, dough can be made 1 day in advance, and the entire rise may take place in the refrigerator overnight.)
6. Spray a 9x5-inch loaf pan with cooking spray. Line pan with parchment paper, letting excess extend over sides of pan.
7. In a small bowl, whisk together egg white and 1 tablespoon (15 grams) water.

8. On a heavily floured surface, roll dough into 16x12-inch rectangle. Brush edges of dough with egg wash. Spread remaining ¼ cup (57 grams) butter onto dough. In a small bowl, combine brown sugar, pecans, and remaining ½ teaspoon (1.5 grams) salt. Sprinkle sugar mixture over butter, and gently press into dough. Starting with one short side, roll up dough, jelly roll style, and pinch seam to seal. (If dough is getting too warm and difficult to work with, refrigerate for 15 to 20 minutes before proceeding.) Using a bench scraper, trim ends, and cut roll in half lengthwise. Carefully twist dough pieces tightly around each other, cut sides up, pinching and tucking ends to seal. Place in prepared pan, cut sides up. Cover and let rest in a warm, draft-free place (75°F/24°C) for 30 minutes.
9. Preheat oven to 350°F (180°C).
10. Bake for 30 minutes. Cover with foil, and bake until an instant-read thermometer inserted in center registers 190°F (88°C), 30 to 35 minutes more. Let cool in pan for 10 minutes. Using excess parchment paper as handles, remove from pan, and let cool completely on a wire rack. Drizzle Caramel Pecan Glaze over cooled loaf.

PRO TIP

Test dough for proper gluten development. Pinch off (make sure you don't tear dough) a small piece of dough. Slowly pull dough out from center. If dough is ready, you will be able to stretch it until it's thin and translucent like a windowpane. If dough tears, it's not ready.

CARAMEL PECAN GLAZE
Makes 1¼ cups

¼   cup (57 grams) unsalted butter
½   cup (110 grams) firmly packed dark brown sugar
½   cup (120 grams) heavy whipping cream
½   teaspoon (2 grams) vanilla extract
⅛   teaspoon kosher salt
¼   cup (28 grams) chopped toasted pecans

1. In a medium saucepan, melt butter over medium heat. Add brown sugar; cook for 1 minute, stirring constantly. Add cream, vanilla, and salt, and bring to a boil; boil for 2 minutes, stirring constantly. Remove from heat; stir in pecans. Let cool slightly before using.

PAIN AU LEVAIN

Makes 2 loaves

Made with the dependable workhorse of the kitchen, the Dutch oven, this sourdough boule is a humble but mighty loaf that will bring rustic charm to your spread.

Leaven:
- ¾ cup plus 2 tablespoons (200 grams) water (60°F/15°C)
- 1 tablespoon plus 1 teaspoon (24 grams) sourdough culture
- 1½ cups plus 1 tablespoon (199 grams) bread flour

Dough:
- 3½ cups plus 1 teaspoon (800 grams) warm water (80°F/27°C), divided
- 5¾ cups plus 2½ tablespoons (750 grams) bread flour
- 1¾ cups plus 3 tablespoons (252 grams) whole wheat flour
- 2 tablespoons plus 1 teaspoon (21 grams) kosher salt

Buckwheat flour, for dusting

1. For leaven: In a large bowl, stir together ¾ cup plus 2 tablespoons (200 grams) water and sourdough culture. Add flour, and stir thoroughly by hand until smooth and there are no dry bits of flour remaining. Cover bowl with plastic wrap, and let stand at room temperature overnight.

2. For dough: In a large bowl, stir together 3¼ cups (738 grams) warm water and 1¼ cups plus 1 teaspoon (350 grams) leaven. (Reserve remaining 50 grams leaven; it is now your starter.) Add flours, and stir by hand until there are no dry bits of flour remaining. Let rest for 30 minutes.

3. Add salt and remaining ¼ cup plus 1 teaspoon (62 grams) warm water, and squeeze dough to combine. (The dough will seem to separate, but it will re-form as you knead dough by folding it on top of itself.)

4. Place dough in a thick glass bowl. Cover with a kitchen towel, and let rise in a warm, draft-free place (75°F/24°C) until dough feels smooth and soft, 3 to 4 hours, turning every 30 minutes. (To complete a turn, grab underside of dough, stretch it up, and then fold it to center of dough. Do this 3 to 4 times around the bowl.)

5. Turn out dough onto a lightly floured surface, and divide in half. Preshape dough by folding each loaf in half, and then work dough into a tight, smooth ball. Let dough rest, covered with a kitchen towel, for 20 to 30 minutes.

6. For final shape, turn over one loaf, grab bottom edge, and gently stretch and fold bottom third over center third. Stretch right side out, and fold right third over center; repeat with left side. Finish by folding top third over previous folds. Roll loaf away from you, and using both hands, cup dough, and pull it toward you to seal. Repeat with remaining loaf. Place in separate bowls or baskets lined with kitchen towels heavily dusted with buckwheat flour. Let rise for 3 hours.

7. Preheat oven to 500°F (260°C). Place a Dutch oven in oven to preheat.

8. Carefully remove Dutch oven, and turn out one loaf into hot pan. Be very careful not to touch sides. Score loaf. Place lid on Dutch oven, and put it back in oven. Immediately reduce oven temperature to 450°F (230°C).

9. Bake for 20 minutes. Remove lid, and bake until bread is deep golden brown, 15 to 20 minutes more. Immediately place loaf on a wire rack to let cool.

10. Increase oven temperature to 500°F (260°C), preheat Dutch oven again, and repeat procedure with remaining loaf.

ANGEL BISCUITS

Makes 11 biscuits

A cross between a buttermilk biscuit and a Parker House roll, these Angel Biscuits will impress any and all at the dinner table. With its pillowy softness and golden buttery top, take one bite and you'll never question its name again.

¼ cup (57 grams) all-vegetable shortening
¼ cup (57 grams) cold unsalted butter
2 tablespoons (30 grams) warm water (105°F/41°C to 110°F/43°C)
1 teaspoon (3 grams) active dry yeast
2 tablespoons (24 grams) granulated sugar
1½ cups (188 grams) all-purpose flour
1¼ cups (156 grams) cake flour
2 teaspoons (6 grams) kosher salt
½ teaspoon (2.5 grams) baking powder
¼ teaspoon (1.25 grams) baking soda
1 cup (240 grams) whole buttermilk
2 tablespoons (28 grams) salted butter, melted

1. Line a baking sheet with parchment paper.
2. Using a bench scraper, cut shortening and cold butter into cubes, and freeze until ready to use.
3. In a small bowl, stir together 2 tablespoons (30 grams) warm water and yeast until yeast is dissolved. Stir in sugar, and let stand until mixture is foamy, about 5 minutes.
4. In a medium bowl, whisk together flours, salt, baking powder, and baking soda. Place three-fourths of flour mixture in the work bowl of a food processor; add cold shortening and cold butter, and pulse until mixture is crumbly with some pea-size pieces of butter remaining. Return mixture to large bowl, and stir to combine with remaining flour mixture. (Alternatively, cut cold shortening and cold butter into flour mixture using a pastry blender.) Add yeast mixture and buttermilk, stirring just until dry ingredients are moistened. Cover and refrigerate for 1 hour.
5. Turn out dough onto a lightly floured surface, and knead 4 or 5 times. Pat dough to ¾-inch thickness. Using a 2½-inch round cutter, cut dough, re-patting scraps only once. Place on prepared pan. Cover and let rise in a warm, draft-free place (75°F/24°C) until puffed, about 1 hour.
6. Preheat oven to 375°F (190°C).
7. Brush biscuits with melted butter.
8. Bake until golden brown, 12 to 15 minutes. Let cool on pan for 5 minutes; serve warm.

MILK BREAD

Makes 2 (9x5-inch) loaves or 24 rolls

Sweet, downy Milk Bread gets its unparalleled texture from Tangzhong, a milk and flour mixture that is heated on the stove until thickened into a creamy paste. The second crucial part of the Milk Bread recipe? A rolled and spiraled shaping method, which gives the loaf its towering height and the iconic swirling imprint on the side crust.

1⅓ cups (320 grams) warm whole milk (100°F/38°C to 110°F/43°C)
⅔ cup (133 grams) granulated sugar
4½ teaspoons (14 grams) active dry yeast
5½ cups (699 grams) bread flour*
Tangzhong (recipe follows)
3 large eggs (150 grams), divided
2 teaspoons (6 grams) kosher salt
6 tablespoons (84 grams) unsalted butter, room temperature
1 tablespoon (15 grams) whole milk

1. In a small bowl, whisk together warm milk, sugar, and yeast. Let stand until mixture is foamy, about 10 minutes.
2. In the bowl of a stand mixer fitted with the dough hook attachment, stir together yeast mixture, flour, Tangzhong, 2 eggs (100 grams), and salt with a wooden spoon until combined. With mixer on low speed, beat for 5 minutes. Add butter, and beat at medium-low speed for 6 minutes. Scrape sides of bowl, and turn dough over. Beat 2 minutes more. Check dough's gluten development by using the windowpane test. (See PRO TIP.) Cover and let rise in a warm, draft-free place (75°F/24°C) until doubled in size, about 1 hour.
3. Spray 2 (9x5-inch) loaf pans (for loaves) or 2 (13x9-inch) baking pans (for rolls) with cooking spray.
4. For loaves: Divide dough into 6 equal portions (252 grams each). Shape each portion into a ball. Roll each ball into a 12x5-inch oval. Fold right third (lengthwise) over middle third. Fold left side over middle. Using a rolling pin, flatten dough, and reroll into a 12x5-inch oval. Starting with one short side, roll dough away from you into a cylinder. Place seam side down in prepared pan. Repeat with remaining dough, placing 3 portions in each prepared pan. Cover and let rise in a warm, draft-free place (75°F/24°C) until doubled in size, about 1 hour.
5. For rolls: Divide dough into 24 equal portions. Roll each portion into a ball. Using a rolling pin, roll each portion into a

7x3-inch oval. Fold right third (lengthwise) over middle third. Fold left side over middle. Using a rolling pin, flatten dough, and roll into a 7x2½-inch oval. Starting with one short side, roll dough away from you into a cylinder. Place seam side down in prepared pan. Repeat with remaining dough, placing 12 rolls in each prepared pan. Cover and let rise in a warm, draft-free place (75°F/24°C) until doubled in size, about 1 hour.
6. Preheat oven to 350°F (180°C).
7. In a small bowl, whisk together milk and remaining 1 egg (50 grams). Brush top of dough with egg wash.
8. For loaves: Bake until an instant-read thermometer inserted in center registers 190°F (88°C), about 30 minutes, covering with foil during last 10 minutes of baking. Immediately remove from pans, and let cool completely on a wire rack before slicing.
9. For rolls: Bake until golden brown, about 20 minutes. Let cool in pans for 15 to 20 minutes. Remove from pans, and let cool on a wire rack. Serve warm or at room temperature.

*We used King Arthur Bread Flour.

TANGZHONG
Makes about ¾ cup

The magic of Milk Bread can be chalked up to the Tangzhong, a paste made from milk and flour that's slowly heated to exactly 149°F (65°C). It resembles a white, loose roux and has two purposes: extend the bread's shelf life for up to 4 days and lock in moisture without making the bread heavy.

¾ cup (180 grams) whole milk
¼ cup (32 grams) bread flour*

1. In a small saucepan, whisk together milk and flour. Cook over medium-low heat, whisking constantly, until mixture thickens and registers 149°F (65°C) on an instant-read thermometer and whisk leaves lines on bottom of saucepan. Transfer to a small bowl, and let cool to room temperature before using.

*We used King Arthur Bread Flour.

PRO TIP
Test the dough for proper gluten development using the windowpane test. Pinch off (make sure you don't tear the dough) a small piece of dough. Slowly pull the dough out from the center. If the dough is ready, you will be able to stretch it until it's thin and translucent like a windowpane. If the dough tears, it's not quite ready.

APRICOT NOYAUX SKOLEBRØD

Makes 15 buns

The traditional Norwegian cardamom bun, skolebrød, gets a stone fruit twist in this recipe that uses the whole apricot, from pit to flesh. Noyaux, the nutlike kernel found in the heart of the fruit, gives the pastry cream an almond flavor.

1⅔ cups (400 grams) plus 2 tablespoons (30 grams) whole milk, divided
¼ cup (57 grams) unsalted butter
⅔ cup (133 grams) granulated sugar
2½ teaspoons (7.5 grams) instant yeast
4½ cups (563 grams) all-purpose flour
1½ teaspoons (3 grams) ground cardamom
½ teaspoon (1.5 grams) kosher salt
⅓ cup (107 grams) Apricot Jam (recipe on page 345)
Noyaux Pastry Cream (recipe follows)
1 large egg (50 grams)
1 teaspoon (5 grams) water
1 cup (120 grams) confectioners' sugar
⅔ cup (40 grams) toasted sweetened desiccated coconut

1. In a medium saucepan, heat 1⅔ cups (400 grams) milk and butter over medium heat, stirring frequently, until butter is melted and a candy thermometer registers 125°F (52°C).

2. In a small bowl, whisk together granulated sugar and yeast. Add yeast mixture to warm milk mixture, whisking to combine. Let stand until mixture is foamy, about 10 minutes.

3. In the bowl of a stand mixer fitted with the dough hook attachment, combine flour, cardamom, and salt. With mixer on low speed, gradually add milk mixture, beating until combined. Increase mixer speed to medium, and beat until smooth and elastic, 8 to 10 minutes.

4. Spray a large bowl with cooking spray. Place dough in bowl, turning to grease top. Cover dough directly with plastic wrap, and let rise in a warm, draft-free place (75°F/24°C) until doubled in size, about 1 hour.

5. Turn out dough onto a lightly floured surface. Divide dough into 15 (72-gram) pieces, and shape into balls. Cover with plastic wrap, and let rise until doubled in size, about 30 minutes.

6. Preheat oven to 375°F (190°C). Line 2 baking sheets with parchment paper.

7. Make an indentation in center of each ball with two fingers of each hand, pressing from center outward, leaving a 1-inch border. Press bottom of indentation flat, leaving a nickel-size circle in center. (This ensures the jam will remain in roll while baking.) Spoon 1 teaspoon (7 grams) Apricot Jam into center of each bun. Place Noyaux Pastry Cream in a pastry bag fitted with a Wilton #12 round tip. Pipe enough Noyaux Pastry Cream to cover jam in a spiral motion working from outside inward. Place on prepared pans.

8. In a small bowl, whisk together egg and 1 teaspoon (5 grams) water. Brush egg wash onto outside of each bun.

9. Bake until golden and risen, about 20 minutes, rotating pans and covering with foil halfway through baking to prevent excess browning. Let cool on wire racks for 20 minutes.

10. In a small bowl, whisk together confectioners' sugar and remaining 2 tablespoons (30 grams) milk. Spoon glaze over buns, and sprinkle with coconut. Store in an airtight container at room temperature for up to 3 days.

NOYAUX PASTRY CREAM
Makes about 1 cup

1⅓ cups (320 grams) whole milk
1 tablespoon (8 grams) ground noyaux*
3 large egg yolks (56 grams)
⅓ cup (67 grams) granulated sugar
2 tablespoons (16 grams) cornstarch
½ teaspoon (2 grams) almond extract
½ teaspoon (2 grams) vanilla extract

1. In a medium saucepan, bring milk and noyaux to a boil over medium heat. Remove from heat; cover and let steep for 20 minutes. Strain cream mixture, gently pressing on solids. Return mixture to pan, and bring to a boil over medium heat.

2. In a medium bowl, whisk together egg yolks, sugar, cornstarch, and extracts. Slowly add warm milk mixture to egg mixture, whisking constantly. Return mixture to pan, and cook, whisking constantly, until thickened. Pour into a small bowl. Cover directly with plastic wrap, and refrigerate for at least 1 hour or up to 2 days.

*Noyaux is the nutlike kernel found within the pits of stone fruit. The easiest way to acquire noyaux is to toast pits on a lined baking sheet at 350°F (180°C) for 7 minutes. Let cool slightly. Place pits in rows on a kitchen towel, and cover with another kitchen towel. Crack each pit by firmly tapping with the bottom of a dowel rolling pin.

BLUEBERRY MASCARPONE BABKA WITH LEMON CURD GLAZE

Makes 1 (9x5-inch) loaf

Freeze-dried blueberries are a wonderful alternative to fresh berries, whose high water content makes them difficult to incorporate into this already wet dough.

½ cup (120 grams) warm whole milk (105°F/41°C to 110°F/43°C)
1¼ teaspoons (4 grams) active dry yeast
2½ cups (313 grams) all-purpose flour
3½ tablespoons (42 grams) granulated sugar
2 teaspoons (2 grams) lemon zest
1½ teaspoons (4.5 grams) kosher salt
2 large eggs (100 grams)
1 large egg yolk (19 grams)
1 teaspoon (4 grams) vanilla extract
½ cup plus 2 tablespoons (141 grams) unsalted butter, cubed and softened
1 large egg white (30 grams)
1 tablespoon (15 grams) water
Mascarpone Filling (recipe follows)
1 cup (46 grams) freeze-dried blueberries
Lemon Curd Glaze (recipe follows)

1. In a small bowl, gradually whisk together warm milk and yeast. Let stand until mixture is foamy, about 5 minutes.
2. In the bowl of a stand mixer fitted with the paddle attachment, combine flour, sugar, zest, and salt. Stir in eggs, egg yolk, and vanilla. With mixer on low speed, gradually add yeast mixture, beating until dough comes together. Increase mixer speed to medium-high, and beat for 5 to 7 minutes. Test dough using the windowpane test. (See PRO TIP.) If dough is not ready, beat 1 minute more, and test again.
3. Switch to the dough hook attachment. With mixer on medium-high speed, add butter in three additions, letting each incorporate before adding the next. Beat until a smooth and elastic dough forms and pulls away from sides of bowl, 4 to 6 minutes.
4. Spray a large bowl with cooking spray. Place dough in bowl, turning to grease top. Cover surface of dough with plastic wrap, and refrigerate overnight.

5. Spray a 9x5-inch loaf pan with cooking spray.
6. In a small bowl, whisk together egg white and 1 tablespoon (15 grams) water. On a heavily floured surface, roll dough into a 16x12-inch rectangle. Brush edges of dough with egg wash. Spread Mascarpone Filling onto dough, leaving a ½-inch border.
7. In the container of a blender, blend freeze-dried blueberries to a fine powder. Sprinkle ¼ cup (32 grams) blueberry powder over Mascarpone Filling.
8. Starting with one long side, roll up dough, jelly roll style; pinch seam to seal. (If dough is getting too warm and difficult to work with, refrigerate for 15 to 20 minutes before proceeding.) Using a bench scraper, trim 1 inch off ends, and place ends in center of prepared pan. Cut roll in half lengthwise. Carefully twist dough pieces tightly around each other, pinching and tucking ends to seal. Place loaf, cut sides up, over trimmed ends in prepared pan. (Gently compress ends of loaf to fit in pan.) Brush dough with egg wash. Cover and let rest in a warm, draft-free place (75°F/24°C) for 30 minutes.
9. Preheat oven to 350°F (180°C).
10. Bake for 15 minutes. Cover with foil, and bake until an instant-read thermometer inserted in center registers 205°F (96°C), 55 minutes to 1 hour and 5 minutes more, rotating pan every 15 minutes. Let cool in pan for 15 minutes. Remove from pan, and let cool completely on a wire rack. Drizzle Lemon Curd Glaze over cooled loaf.

MASCARPONE FILLING

Makes ½ cup

4 ounces (115 grams) mascarpone cheese
2 tablespoons (15 grams) lightly beaten egg whites
1 tablespoon (7 grams) confectioners' sugar

1. In a small bowl, stir together all ingredients until combined.

LEMON CURD GLAZE

Makes ¼ cup

¼ cup (85 grams) Lemon Curd (recipe follows)
2 tablespoons (14 grams) confectioners' sugar
1½ teaspoons (7.5 grams) heavy whipping cream

1. In a small bowl, stir together all ingredients until combined. Use immediately.

LEMON CURD

Makes 1 cup

½ cup (120 grams) fresh lemon juice
¼ cup (57 grams) unsalted butter
2 large egg yolks (37 grams)
¼ cup plus 1 tablespoon (62 grams) granulated sugar
1 tablespoon (8 grams) cornstarch

1. In a small saucepan, heat lemon juice and butter over medium heat until butter is melted.
2. In a medium bowl, whisk together egg yolks, sugar, and cornstarch until pale yellow. Add a small amount of hot lemon mixture to egg mixture, whisking constantly. Add egg mixture to remaining hot lemon mixture in pan, whisking to combine. Cook, stirring constantly, until thickened and beginning to boil, about 3 minutes. Transfer curd to a glass bowl. Cover and refrigerate until ready to use.

PRO TIP
Test the dough for proper gluten development using the windowpane test. Pinch off (make sure you don't tear the dough) a small piece of dough. Slowly pull the dough out from the center. If the dough is ready, you will be able to stretch it until it's thin and translucent like a windowpane. If the dough tears, it's not quite ready.

BAGEL WREATH

Makes 1 (8-bagel) wreath

Recipe by Erin Jeanne McDowell

This wreath will wow at any brunch, weaving dough together to achieve an epic pull-apart round perfect for serving a crowd. Bagels are traditionally boiled to get their signature chewy exterior. In this recipe, the wreath is brushed with water and baked at a slightly reduced temperature. The combination yields a delightfully chewy eight-bagel wreath. You can use different toppings on each bagel so there's a little something for everyone.

4½ cups (572 grams) bread flour
1 tablespoon (12 grams) granulated sugar
1 tablespoon (9 grams) instant yeast
1 tablespoon (9 grams) fine sea salt
1½ cups plus 2 tablespoons (390 grams) warm water (95°F/35°C)
Boiling water, for finishing
Toppings: sesame seeds, poppy seeds, fine sea salt, grated Asiago cheese

1. In the bowl of a stand mixer fitted with the dough hook attachment, beat flour, sugar, yeast, and salt at low speed until combined, 15 to 30 seconds. Add 1½ cups plus 2 tablespoons (390 grams) warm water, and beat for 4 minutes. Increase mixer speed to medium, and beat for 3 minutes.

2. Spray a large bowl with cooking spray. Place dough in bowl, turning to grease top. Cover with plastic wrap, and let rise in a warm, draft-free place (75°F/24°C) until nearly doubled in size, 30 minutes to 1 hour.

3. On a lightly floured surface, divide dough into 8 (113-gram) pieces. Loosely cover dough with plastic wrap, and let rest for 20 minutes.

4. Working with one piece of dough at a time, press dough into a slightly oblong shape by pushing it flat with your fingers. Starting at top of dough (the edge farthest away from you), fold one-third of dough over onto itself. Press firmly with your fingertips or with the heel of your hand to seal. Continue folding dough over and pressing to seal until a log is formed.

5. Starting with very light pressure in center of log, roll dough between your hands and work surface until log is about 12 inches long. Repeat with remaining dough.

6. Preheat oven to 400°F (200°C). Place a sheet of parchment paper on a work surface, and lightly brush parchment with oil. Have a bowl of cool water ready.

7. Place one piece of dough onto prepared parchment, and shape into a circle. Lightly brush one end with cool water, and adhere other end by pressing firmly to seal. Take next piece of dough, and weave it through the first round. Once it's been threaded through, use water on one end, and press firmly to seal. Continue this process until you've used and woven all pieces of dough to create the Bagel Wreath. Gently transfer Bagel Wreath on parchment to a baking sheet. Brush surface of wreath 2 to 3 times with boiling water. Sprinkle with toppings as desired.

8. Bake until lightly golden brown, 12 to 15 minutes. Let cool completely before serving.

Photos by Mark Weinberg

CONCORD GRAPE FOCACCIA

Makes 1 (14x12-inch) loaf

Recipe by Laura Kasavan

This Concord grape-studded focaccia bakes up golden and chewy, the perfect starter for any fall dinner party. With a sprinkle of fresh rosemary and sea salt to complement the Concord grapes, this bread is an unexpected sweet-meets-savory way to celebrate the harvest.

4   cups (500 grams) all-purpose flour
2   teaspoons (6 grams) instant yeast
3   teaspoons (9 grams) kosher salt, divided
1½   cups (360 grams) warm water (120°F/49°C)
5   tablespoons (70 grams) extra-virgin olive oil, divided
2   tablespoons (24 grams) granulated sugar
2   cups (300 grams) Concord grapes*
2   tablespoons (4 grams) chopped fresh rosemary

1. In a large bowl, whisk together flour, yeast, and 2 teaspoons (6 grams) salt with a dough whisk until combined. Add 1½ cups (360 grams) warm water and 2 tablespoons (28 grams) oil, stirring just until combined. Cover and let stand in a warm, draft-free place (75°F/24°C) until puffed, 1½ to 2 hours.

2. Preheat oven to 400°F (200°C).
3. Turn out dough onto a lightly floured surface, and shape into a ball. Line a rimmed baking sheet with parchment paper. Brush parchment with 1 tablespoon (14 grams) oil. Transfer dough to prepared pan, and gently press or roll dough into a 14x12-inch rectangle. Cover and let rest for 10 minutes.
4. Coat dough generously with remaining 2 tablespoons (28 grams) oil. Sprinkle with sugar, and top with Concord grapes, pressing gently into dough. Sprinkle with rosemary and remaining 1 teaspoon (3 grams) salt.
5. Bake until golden brown, 30 to 35 minutes. Let cool for 30 minutes before slicing.

*The heat from the oven helps break down the Concord grape seeds as the focaccia bakes. If you prefer seedless grapes, you can use Thomcord grapes, a hybrid of the Thompson Seedless grape and Concord grape, instead.

Photo by Laura Kasavan

CLASSIC DUTCH OVEN BREAD

Makes 1 loaf

This humble recipe is endlessly customizable (see our Cheddar Sage [page 171] and Cherry Walnut [page 172] variations) but also a rustic triumph in its base form. Let it have a long, cold rest in the refrigerator for the best flavor—then let a very hot Dutch oven and 35-minute bake take you the rest of the way.

3   cups (381 grams) bread flour
1   cup (130 grams) whole wheat flour
1   tablespoon (9 grams) kosher salt
2¼ teaspoons (7 grams) instant yeast
1¾ cups plus 2 tablespoons (425 grams) warm water (105°F/41°C to 110°F/43°C)
Corn flour, for dusting

1. In a large bowl, place bread flour, whole wheat flour, salt, and yeast. Add 1¾ cups plus 2 tablespoons (425 grams) warm water, and stir with hands until fully incorporated and a sticky dough forms. (Alternatively, place bread flour, whole wheat flour, salt, and yeast in the bowl of a stand mixer fitted with the paddle attachment. Add 1¾ cups plus 2 tablespoons [425 grams] warm water, and beat at medium speed until a sticky dough forms, about 30 seconds.) Cover and let rise in a warm, draft-free place (75°F/24°C) for 2 hours.
2. Refrigerate for at least 2 hours (preferably overnight) or up to 5 days*.
3. Turn out dough onto a lightly floured surface, and gently press dough just to level and even it out. Starting on left side of dough and working clockwise, fold edges of dough toward center, pressing lightly. Turn dough ball over, and using both hands, cup dough, and pull it toward you. Turn dough 90 degrees, and repeat until you have a smooth, tight, sealed round. (See *Shape Your Boule*.)
4. Heavily dust a sheet of parchment paper with corn flour; place dough on parchment, seam side up. Cover and let rise in a warm, draft-free place (75°F/24°C) for 1 hour.
5. When dough has 30 minutes left to rise, place a 6- to 7-quart Dutch oven and lid in a cold oven. Preheat oven to 500°F (260°C).
6. Carefully remove hot Dutch oven from oven; remove lid, and quickly turn bread into Dutch oven so seam is now on bottom.

Score top of bread (being careful not to touch hot sides of Dutch oven). Cover with lid, and place back in oven.
7. Immediately reduce oven temperature to 450°F (230°C). Bake for 25 minutes. Remove lid, and bake until an instant-read thermometer inserted in center registers 190°F (88°C), about 10 minutes more. Immediately remove loaf from Dutch oven, and let cool completely on a wire rack.

*The longer the dough stands, the more the flavor will develop.

SHAPE YOUR BOULE
Use gentle tucks, folds, and rolls to help you shape the domed Dutch oven loaf.

1. Place your dough on a lightly floured surface. Fold one outer edge into the center, pressing lightly to hold it in place.

2. Moving clockwise, continue to tuck the edges into the center. Press dough folds in gently as you tuck, being careful not to overwork the dough. As this is a no-knead recipe, any excess handling will just make your bread tougher.

3. Turn the dough ball seam side down. Cup the dough, and gently drag it toward you. Repeat this process several times. You want to feel the ball sticking slightly, tugging the sides and stretching the dough into a taut ball.

CHEDDAR SAGE DUTCH OVEN BREAD

Makes 1 loaf

Half a pound of white Cheddar and sage pump up the savory, herbaceous volume in our Classic Dutch Oven Bread formula.

(8-ounce) block (226 grams) extra-sharp aged white Cheddar cheese*

teaspoon (2 grams) rubbed sage

Classic Dutch Oven Bread (recipe on page 170)

1. Divide block of Cheddar into 2 (113-gram) pieces. Cut one half into ½-inch cubes, and finely grate other half. In a small bowl, stir together grated cheese and sage.

2. In step 3 of Classic Dutch Oven Bread recipe, after you turn out dough onto a lightly floured surface, dust dough lightly with flour, and roll to 1-inch thickness. Sprinkle roughly two-thirds of cubed cheese and two-thirds of grated cheese-sage mixture onto dough. Starting on left side and working clockwise, fold edges of dough toward center, pressing lightly. Reroll dough to 1-inch thickness, sprinkle with remaining cubed cheese and remaining grated cheese-sage mixture, and repeat folding dough to center. Turn dough ball over, and using both hands, cup dough, and pull it toward you. Turn dough 90 degrees, and repeat until you have a tight, sealed round. It is OK if some of the cheese cubes are poking out through the dough. (See *Shape Your Boule* on page 170.)

3. Proceed as directed. Add 5 minutes to bake time after you remove the lid.

*We used Cabot's Seriously Sharp Premium Naturally Aged Cheddar Cheese.

CHERRY WALNUT DUTCH OVEN BREAD

Makes 1 loaf

Chewy dried cherries add texture and tart flavor.

1   cup (113 grams) chopped walnuts
¾   cup (120 grams) dried cherries
Classic Dutch Oven Bread (recipe on page 170)

1. In a small bowl, stir together walnuts and cherries.

2. In step 3 of Classic Dutch Oven Bread recipe, after you turn out dough onto a lightly floured surface, dust dough lightly with flour, and roll to 1-inch thickness. Sprinkle roughly two-thirds of walnut mixture onto dough. Starting on left side and working clockwise, fold edges of dough toward center, pressing lightly. Reroll dough to 1-inch thickness; sprinkle with remaining walnut mixture, and repeat folding dough to center. Turn dough ball over, and using both hands, cup dough, and pull it toward you. Turn dough 90 degrees, and repeat until you have a tight, sealed round. It is OK if some of the walnuts and cherries are poking out through the dough. (See *Shape Your Boule* on page 170.)

3. Proceed as directed. Add 5 minutes to bake time after you remove the lid.

MULTIGRAIN DUTCH OVEN BREAD

Makes 1 loaf

hearty trinity of rye, whole wheat, and bread
ours forms a flavorful dough while oats and
eeds become aromatic mix-ins and a crunchy
opping.

cups (254 grams) bread flour
¼ cups (128 grams) dark rye flour, plus
more for dusting
cup (130 grams) whole wheat flour
cup (53 grams) old-fashioned oats
cup (36 grams) raw shelled sunflower
seeds
tablespoons (28 grams) firmly packed
light brown sugar
tablespoon (9 grams) kosher salt
tablespoon (9 grams) black sesame seeds
tablespoon (9 grams) flax seeds
¼ teaspoons (7 grams) instant yeast
teaspoon (2 grams) fennel seeds
¾ cups plus 2½ tablespoons (432 grams)
warm water (105°F/41°C to
110°F/43°C)
Multi-Seed Topping (recipe follows)

. In a large bowl, place flours, oats, sunflower
eeds, brown sugar, salt, sesame seeds, flax
eeds, yeast, and fennel seeds. Add 1¾ cups

plus 2½ tablespoons (432 grams) warm water,
and stir by hand until fully incorporated and
a sticky dough forms. (Alternatively, place
flours, oats, sunflower seeds, brown sugar, salt,
sesame seeds, flax seeds, yeast, and fennel
seeds in the bowl of a stand mixer fitted with
the paddle attachment. Add 1¾ cups plus
2½ tablespoons [432 grams] warm water, and
beat at medium speed until a sticky dough
forms, about 30 seconds.) Cover and let rise in
a warm, draft-free place (75°F/24°C) for
2 hours.

2. Refrigerate for at least 2 hours (preferably
overnight).

3. Turn out dough onto a lightly floured
surface, and gently press dough just to level
and even it out. Starting on left side and
working clockwise, fold edges of dough toward
center, pressing lightly. Turn dough ball over,
and using both hands, cup dough, and pull
it toward you. Turn dough 90 degrees, and
repeat until you have a smooth, tight, sealed
round. (See *Shape Your Boule* on page 170.)

4. Dust a sheet of parchment paper with rye
flour; place dough on parchment, seam side
up. Cover and let rise in a warm, draft-free
place (75°F/24°C) for 1 hour.

5. When dough has 30 minutes left to rise,
place a 6- to 7-quart Dutch oven and lid in a

cold oven. Preheat oven to 500°F (260°C).

6. Carefully remove hot Dutch oven from
oven; remove lid, and quickly turn bread
into Dutch oven so seam is now on bottom.
Brush top of loaf with water, and sprinkle
with Multi-Seed Topping. Score top of bread
(being careful not to touch hot sides of
Dutch oven). Cover with lid, and place back
in oven.

7. Immediately reduce oven temperature
to 450°F (230°C). Bake for 25 minutes.
Remove lid, and bake until an instant-read
thermometer inserted in center registers
190°F (88°C), about 15 minutes more.
Immediately remove loaf from Dutch oven,
and let cool completely on a wire rack.

Multi-Seed Topping
Makes about ¼ cup

1   tablespoon (5 grams) old-fashioned oats
2   teaspoons (6 grams) raw shelled
sunflower seeds
1½ teaspoons (4.5 grams) black sesame seeds
1½ teaspoons (4.5 grams) flax seeds
1   teaspoon (3 grams) fennel seeds

1. In a small bowl, stir together all
ingredients.

SWEET POTATO DUTCH OVEN BREAD

Makes 1 loaf

This Dutch oven bread is tender, with a brilliant orange hue and a touch of sweetness.

4   cups (508 grams) bread flour
1½   cups (380 grams) lightly mashed baked
      sweet potato (see Note)
1   tablespoon (9 grams) kosher salt
2¼   teaspoons (7 grams) instant yeast
1¼   cups (284 grams) warm water
      (105°F/41°C to 110°F/43°C)
Corn flour, for dusting

1. In a large bowl, place bread flour, sweet potato, salt, and yeast. Add 1¼ cups (284 grams) warm water, and stir by hand until fully incorporated and a sticky dough forms. (Alternatively, place bread flour, sweet potato, salt, and yeast in the bowl of a stand mixer fitted with the paddle attachment. Add 1¼ cups [284 grams] warm water, and beat at medium speed until a sticky dough forms, about 30 seconds.) Cover and let rise in a warm, draft-free place (75°F/24°C) for 2 hours.

2. Refrigerate for at least 2 hours (preferably overnight).

3. Turn out dough onto a lightly floured surface, and gently press dough just to level and even it out. Starting on left side and working clockwise, fold edges of dough toward center, pressing lightly. Turn dough ball over, and using both hands, cup dough, and pull it toward you. Turn dough 90 degrees, and repeat until you have a smooth, tight, sealed round. (See *Shape Your Boule* on page 170.)

4. Heavily dust a sheet of parchment paper with corn flour; place dough on parchment, seam side up. Cover and let rise in a warm, draft-free place (75°F/24°C) for 1 hour.

5. When dough has 30 minutes left to rise, place a 6- to 7-quart Dutch oven and lid in a cold oven. Preheat oven to 500°F (260°C).

6. Carefully remove hot Dutch oven from oven, remove lid, and quickly turn bread into Dutch oven so seam is now on bottom. Score top of bread (being careful not to touch hot sides of Dutch oven). Cover with lid, and place back in oven.

7. Immediately reduce oven temperature to 450°F (230°C). Bake for 25 minutes. Remove lid, and bake until an instant-read thermometer inserted in center registers 190°F (88°C), 10 to 15 minutes more. Immediately remove loaf from Dutch oven, and let cool completely on a wire rack.

Note: *For mashed sweet potatoes: Wash sweet potatoes, prick with a fork, and bake in a 425°F (220°C) oven for 30 to 40 minutes.*

APPLE-CRANBERRY PULL-APART BREAD

Makes 1 (9x5-inch) loaf

Recipe by Kelsey Siemens

How can anyone resist the smell of fresh, homemade bread? Pulling apart the pieces while they're still warm is ideal, and the tart apple pieces and dried cranberries combine to create wonderful pops of flavor.

½   cup (120 grams) whole milk
2¼   teaspoons (7 grams) active dry yeast
¼   cup (57 grams) unsalted butter, softened
¾   cup (150 grams) granulated sugar, divided
2   large eggs (100 grams)
2   teaspoons (8 grams) vanilla extract
1   teaspoon (3 grams) kosher salt
2¾   cups plus 3 tablespoons (368 grams) all-purpose flour
2   teaspoons (4 grams) ground cinnamon
2   medium tart apples (280 grams), diced
¼   cup (32 grams) dried cranberries
2½   tablespoons (35 grams) unsalted butter, melted
Maple Glaze (recipe follows)

1. In a small saucepan, heat milk over medium heat, stirring constantly, until steaming but not boiling, being careful not to heat past 110°F (43°C). (Alternatively, microwave milk in 15-second intervals until steaming but not boiling.) Remove from heat, and stir in yeast. Let stand until mixture is foamy, about 5 minutes.

2. In the bowl of a stand mixer fitted with the paddle attachment, beat butter, ¼ cup (50 grams) sugar, eggs, vanilla, and salt at low speed until combined. Beat in yeast mixture. Gradually add flour, beating until dough comes together and pulls away from sides of bowl, about 5 minutes. Turn out dough onto a lightly floured surface, and knead into a smooth ball.

3. Spray a large bowl with cooking spray. Place dough in bowl, turning to grease top. Cover with plastic wrap, and let rise in a warm, draft-free place (75°F/24°C) until doubled in size, about 1 hour.

4. Spray a 9x5-inch loaf pan with cooking spray.

5. In a small bowl, stir together cinnamon and remaining ½ cup (100 grams) sugar. In a medium bowl, stir together apples and cranberries.

6. On a lightly floured surface, roll dough into a 16x12-inch rectangle. Brush melted butter onto dough. Sprinkle with cinnamon sugar mixture.

7. Cut dough lengthwise into 4 equal strips. Carefully stack strips one on top of the other,

adding apple-cranberry mixture between each layer; cut into 5 equal squares. Layer squares in prepared pan. Cover with a clean kitchen towel, and let rise in a warm, draft-free place (75°F/24°C) for 30 minutes.

8. Preheat oven to 350°F (180°C).

9. Bake for 20 minutes. Cover with foil, and bake until an instant-read thermometer inserted in center registers 205°F (96°C), 40 to 45 minutes more. Let cool in pan for 5 to 10 minutes. Remove from pan, and drizzle with Maple Glaze. Serve warm.

MAPLE GLAZE
Makes about 1½ cups

8   ounces (225 grams) cream cheese, softened
½   cup (170 grams) Grade A maple syrup
½   cup (60 grams) confectioners' sugar
⅛   teaspoon kosher salt

1. In the bowl of a stand mixer fitted with the paddle attachment, beat cream cheese at medium speed until smooth. Gradually add maple syrup, beating until combined. Beat in confectioners' sugar and salt. Use immediately.

GINGERBREAD MORNING BUNS

Makes 12 buns

We are obsessed with The Vanilla Bean Blog creator Sarah Kieffer's brilliant idea to bake her cinnamon buns in copper soufflé molds. The copper's superior conductive quality helps caramelize the sugary filling and produces perfect scrolls of pastry.

4⅔ cups (583 grams) all-purpose flour
4½ teaspoons (14 grams) active dry yeast
4 teaspoons (8 grams) ground ginger
2 teaspoons (4 grams) ground cinnamon
1 teaspoon (3 grams) kosher salt
½ teaspoon (1 gram) ground mace or
   2 teaspoons (4 grams) ground nutmeg
½ teaspoon (1 gram) ground allspice
1½ cups (360 grams) whole milk
6 tablespoons (126 grams) unsulphured molasses
¼ cup (57 grams) unsalted butter, melted, plus more for brushing
½ cup (100 grams) granulated sugar
Gingerbread Filling (recipe follows)
Simple Glaze (recipe follows)

1. In the bowl of a stand mixer fitted with the paddle attachment, combine flour, yeast, ginger, cinnamon, salt, mace (or nutmeg), and allspice.

2. In a small microwave-safe bowl, stir together milk, molasses, and melted butter. Microwave on high until an instant-read thermometer registers 120°F (49°C) to 130°F (54°C). With mixer on low speed, add warm milk mixture to flour mixture, beating until combined. Increase mixer speed to medium, and beat for 2 minutes.

3. On a lightly floured surface with lightly floured hands, knead dough until smooth and elastic, about 6 minutes.

4. Spray a large bowl with cooking spray. Place dough in bowl, turning to grease top. Cover and let rise in a warm, draft-free place (75°F/24°C) until doubled in size, 45 minutes to 1 hour.

5. Brush 12 ramekins, jumbo muffin cups, or soufflé molds* with melted butter, and sprinkle with sugar. Place dishes on a small sheet pan. (The filling tends to overflow a little.)

6. Divide dough in half. On a lightly floured surface, roll half of dough into a 16x12-inch rectangle. Spread half of Gingerbread Filling onto dough. Starting with one long side, roll dough into a log. Using a serrated knife, cut log into 6 (2½-inch-thick) slices. Repeat with remaining dough and remaining Gingerbread Filling. Place rolls in prepared pans. Cover and let rise in a warm, draft-free place (75°F/24°C) until doubled in size, 20 to 30 minutes.

7. Preheat oven to 350°F (180°C).

8. Bake until golden brown, 20 to 30 minutes. Let cool slightly, about 5 minutes. Remove from molds or pans using a small offset spatula. Drizzle with Simple Glaze.

We used Mauviel M'Passion Mini Copper Soufflé Molds.

GINGERBREAD FILLING
Makes 1½ cups

1 cup (227 grams) unsalted butter, softened
1 cup (220 grams) firmly packed light brown sugar
2½ teaspoons (5 grams) ground ginger
2½ teaspoons (5 grams) ground cinnamon
½ teaspoon (1.5 grams) kosher salt
½ teaspoon (1 gram) ground mace

1. In a medium bowl, stir together all ingredients.

SIMPLE GLAZE
Makes 1½ cups

2 cups (240 grams) confectioners' sugar
½ cup (120 grams) whole milk

1. In a small bowl, stir together confectioners' sugar and milk.

CONCHAS

Makes 15 rolls

To give our version of this Mexican sweet roll an even more tender, heightened pillowy texture than the traditional recipe, we enrich the dough with more butter and milk. The classic crunchy, sugary streusel topping is delicious as is, but you'll adore our two indulgent flavor variations of Mexican chocolate and Chinese five-spice.

4¼ cups (531 grams) all-purpose flour, divided
⅓ cup (67 grams) granulated sugar
2¼ teaspoons (7 grams) active dry yeast
1 teaspoon (3 grams) kosher salt
⅔ cup (150 grams) evaporated milk
⅓ cup (80 grams) water
6 tablespoons (84 grams) unsalted butter, cubed and softened
2 large eggs (100 grams)
Egg Streusel Topping Three Ways (recipe follows)

1. In the bowl of a stand mixer fitted with the paddle attachment, beat 2 cups (250 grams) flour, sugar, yeast, and salt at low speed until combined.

2. In a small saucepan, heat evaporated milk, ⅓ cup (80 grams) water, and butter over medium heat until a candy thermometer registers 120°F (49°C) to 130°F (54°C). With mixer on low speed, add hot milk mixture to flour mixture. Increase mixer speed to medium, and beat for 2 minutes. Add eggs and 1 cup (125 grams) flour; beat at high speed for 2 minutes. Gradually add remaining 1¼ cups (156 grams) flour, beating until a soft dough forms.

3. Switch to the dough hook attachment; beat at medium speed until dough is smooth but still sticky, about 5 minutes. Turn out dough onto a lightly floured surface, and knead until very soft, smooth, and no longer sticky, about 1 minute. If dough seems too sticky, add ¼ cup (31 grams) more flour. (Dough should be on the soft side, so don't add too much flour, or buns won't be as soft.)

4. Spray a large bowl with cooking spray. Place dough in bowl, turning to grease top. Cover with plastic wrap, and let rise in a warm, draft-free place (75°F/24°C) until doubled in size, 1 to 1½ hours.

5. Line 3 baking sheets with parchment paper.

6. Punch down dough, and turn out onto a lightly floured surface. Divide dough into 15 equal portions (65 grams each), and shape each portion into a smooth ball. Flatten each ball into a 3-inch round, and place on prepared pans. Top with Egg Streusel

Topping Three Ways. Using a small paring knife, carefully cut a scallop shell or crisscross design into streusel, leaving a ¼-inch border. Let rise in a warm, draft-free place (75°F/24°C) until almost doubled in size, 45 minutes to 1 hour.

7. Preheat oven to 375°F (190°C).

8. Bake until topping is just beginning to brown, 15 to 20 minutes. Serve warm or at room temperature. Store in an airtight container at room temperature for up to 2 days.

EGG STREUSEL TOPPING THREE WAYS

Makes 3 cups

1½ cups (188 grams) plus 1 tablespoon (8 grams) all-purpose flour, divided
½ cup (100 grams) granulated sugar
⅛ teaspoon kosher salt
7 tablespoons (98 grams) cold unsalted butter, cubed
1 large egg (50 grams)
1 large egg yolk (19 grams)
2 tablespoons (8 grams) finely grated Mexican chocolate
1 teaspoon (2 grams) unsweetened cocoa powder
1 tablespoon (14 grams) firmly packed dark brown sugar
1 teaspoon (2 grams) ground cinnamon
½ teaspoon (1 gram) Chinese five-spice powder

1. In a medium bowl, stir together 1½ cups (188 grams) flour, granulated sugar, and salt. Using a pastry blender, cut in cold butter until mixture is crumbly. In a small bowl, whisk together egg and egg yolk; stir egg mixture into flour mixture until clumps form.

2. Divide mixture into 3 equal portions of 1 cup each. Using hands, form each portion into a paste, making sure all ingredients are well combined and emulsified with no butter chunks left over. Place one portion in a small bowl, and stir in finely grated chocolate and cocoa until combined. Place second portion in another bowl. Stir in brown sugar, cinnamon, five-spice powder, and remaining 1 tablespoon (8 grams) flour. Leave third portion as is.

3. Beginning with plain streusel mixture, divide and shape each portion into 5 balls. (You will have a total of 15 balls.) On a lightly floured surface, press each ball into a 4-inch patty. Place on a large plate, separating layers with plastic wrap or parchment paper to keep from sticking together. Cover with plastic wrap, and refrigerate until ready to use.

PUMPKIN-DATE BABKA

Makes 1 (12- to 13-inch) round loaf

This tightly woven babka is visually impressive, and braiding the dough to create the design is easier than you think. The tender pumpkin bread is layered with spiraling waves of Date-Hazelnut Filling gently spiced with a dash of cardamom. We like slicing into the round like you would a pie and drizzling wedges with the tangy Crème Fraîche Honey Glaze before serving.

¼   cup (60 grams) warm whole milk (105°F/41°C to 110°F/43°C)
4   tablespoons (48 grams) granulated sugar, divided
1   tablespoon (9 grams) active dry yeast
3¾ cups (469 grams) all-purpose flour, divided
1½ teaspoons (4.5 grams) kosher salt
¾   cup (183 grams) canned pumpkin
3   large eggs (150 grams), divided
1   teaspoon (4 grams) vanilla extract
½   cup (113 grams) unsalted butter, softened
Date-Hazelnut Filling (recipe follows)
1   tablespoon (15 grams) water
2   tablespoons (24 grams) sanding sugar
¼   teaspoon ground cinnamon
Crème Fraîche Honey Glaze (recipe follows)

1. In the bowl of a stand mixer fitted with the paddle attachment, whisk together warm milk, 2 tablespoons (24 grams) granulated sugar, and yeast by hand until yeast is dissolved. Let stand for 10 minutes.
2. With mixer on low speed, add ¾ cup (94 grams) flour, beating until smooth, about 30 seconds. Cover and let rise in a warm, draft-free place (75°F/24°C) until doubled in size, about 45 minutes.
3. Add salt, remaining 3 cups (375 grams) flour, and remaining 2 tablespoons (24 grams) granulated sugar. Add pumpkin, 2 eggs (100 grams), and vanilla, and using the dough hook attachment, beat at low speed until combined, 2 to 3 minutes. Scrape sides of bowl, and increase mixer speed to medium-low; beat until dough pulls away from sides of bowl, 7 to 9 minutes. Add butter, 1 tablespoon

(14 grams) at a time, letting each piece incorporate before adding the next. Shape dough into a ball.
4. Spray a large bowl with cooking spray. Place dough in bowl, turning to grease top. Cover with plastic wrap, and let rise in a warm, draft-free place (75°F/24°C) until doubled in size, 1 to 1½ hours.
5. Punch down dough, and divide in half (about 490 grams each). On a lightly floured large surface, roll each half of dough into an 18x9-inch rectangle. Spread half of Date-Hazelnut Filling onto each rectangle, leaving a 1-inch border on all sides. Starting with one long side, roll up dough, jelly roll style; pinch edges to seal. Place rolls, seam side down, on work surface. Using a bench scraper, cut each roll in half lengthwise; turn halves cut side up.
6. To prepare loaf for braiding, lay two strands side by side horizontally across your work surface. Place remaining strands perpendicular to them over center. To weave the center, carefully fold back the top half of the left vertical strand and the left side of the top horizontal strand. Return the vertical strand to its previous position, then lay the horizontal strand over it. Repeat by folding back the bottom half of the right vertical strand and the right half of the bottom horizontal strand. Return the vertical strand to its previous position, then lay the horizontal strand over it. The four strands should now be closely woven at center.
7. To braid loose ends, lift each "under" strand over the strand to its right until you've gone clockwise one full circle. Repeat procedure in a counterclockwise direction, lifting each "under" strand over the strand to its left until you've gone one full circle. Repeat braiding in alternating directions until you've reached ends. Tuck ends under.
8. Transfer to a parchment paper-lined baking sheet. Cover loosely with plastic wrap, and let rise in a warm, draft-free place (75°F/24°C) until almost doubled in size, about 30 minutes.
9. Preheat oven to 350°F (180°C).
10. In a small bowl, whisk together 1 tablespoon (15 grams) water and remaining 1 egg

(50 grams). In another small bowl, stir together sanding sugar and cinnamon. Brush egg wash onto dough, and sprinkle with cinnamon sugar mixture.
11. Bake until an instant-read thermometer inserted in center registers 205°F (96°C), 55 to 60 minutes, covering with foil after 25 minutes of baking. Let cool completely on a wire rack. Drizzle Crème Fraîche Honey Glaze over cooled loaf.

DATE-HAZELNUT FILLING
Makes about 1¼ cups

1½ cups (262.5 grams) whole pitted dates
⅓   cup (80 grams) water
2   tablespoons (24 grams) granulated sugar
1   teaspoon (2 grams) ground cinnamon
½   teaspoon (2 grams) vanilla extract
¼   teaspoon kosher salt
⅛   teaspoon ground cardamom
1   cup (113 grams) finely chopped hazelnuts

1. In a small microwave-safe bowl, combine dates and ⅓ cup (80 grams) water. Loosely cover and microwave on high for 2 minutes.
2. Place dates, any remaining water, sugar, cinnamon, vanilla, salt, and cardamom in the work bowl of a food processor; process until smooth. Transfer to a bowl, and let cool completely. Stir in hazelnuts.

CRÈME FRAÎCHE HONEY GLAZE
Makes about ¾ cup

½   cup (120 grams) crème fraîche
½   cup (60 grams) confectioners' sugar
2   tablespoons (42 grams) honey
¼   teaspoon (1 gram) vanilla extract
⅛   teaspoon kosher salt

1. In a small bowl, whisk together all ingredients until smooth. Use immediately.

TRADITIONAL STOLLEN

Makes 2 loaves

Our stollen recalls the sophisticated flavor of times past: slightly sweet yeasted bread dough loaded with dried fruit rehydrated in brandy. To finish, we shape our dough in the traditional ceremonial form and cover it in a luxurious, snowy blanket of butter and confectioners' sugar.

1   cup (128 grams) dried cherries
¾   cup (96 grams) chopped dried apricots
¾   cup (96 grams) dried currants
1   cup (240 grams) apricot brandy
1   cup (240 grams) warm whole milk
    (105°F/41°C to 110°F/43°C), divided
2¼ teaspoons (7 grams) active dry yeast
4¼ cups (531 grams) all-purpose flour,
    divided
⅔   cup (150 grams) plus ¼ cup (57 grams)
    unsalted butter, melted and divided
1   large egg (50 grams)
¼   cup (50 grams) granulated sugar
1   tablespoon (3 grams) lemon zest
1   teaspoon (3 grams) kosher salt
Candied Zest (recipe follows)
¾   cup (85 grams) slivered almonds,
    chopped
Confectioners' sugar, for dusting

1. In a medium bowl, toss together cherries, apricots, and currants. Pour brandy over fruit. Cover and let stand overnight or up to 3 days. (The longer it stands, the stronger the flavor.)

2. In the bowl of a stand mixer fitted with the paddle attachment, combine ½ cup (120 grams) warm milk and yeast. Let stand until mixture is foamy, about 10 minutes. Add 1 cup (125 grams) flour, and beat at low speed until a smooth dough forms, about 1 minute. Cover and let rise in a warm, draft-free place (75°F/24°C) until doubled in size, about 30 minutes.

3. Using the dough hook attachment, add ⅔ cup (150 grams) melted butter, egg, granulated sugar, lemon zest, salt, remaining 3¼ cups (406 grams) flour, and remaining ½ cup (120 grams) warm milk, beating at very low speed until combined, about 2 minutes, stopping to scrape sides of bowl as needed. Increase mixer speed to low, and beat until a smooth dough forms, about 18 minutes.

4. Spray a large bowl with cooking spray. Place dough in bowl, turning to grease top. Cover and let rise in a warm, draft-free place (75°F/24°C) until doubled in size, about 1 hour.

5. Punch down dough in center; turn out dough onto a lightly floured surface. Strain fruit, discarding any liquid. Knead fruit mixture, Candied Zest, and almonds into dough until evenly dispersed. (Be patient while kneading. If any fruit pieces or nuts fall out, just place them back in dough, and keep kneading.) Cover and let stand for 10 minutes.

6. Line 2 baking sheets with parchment paper.

7. Divide dough in half (about 815 grams each). On a lightly floured surface, roll half of dough into a 13x9-inch oval. Fold dough almost in half lengthwise, leaving a 1-inch border uncovered. Place on a prepared pan, and cover with plastic wrap. Repeat with remaining dough. Lightly brush loaves with some of remaining ¼ cup (57 grams) melted butter. Cover and let rise in a warm, draft-free place (75°F/24°C) until puffed, about 45 minutes.

8. Preheat oven to 350°F (180°C).

9. Bake until golden brown, a wooden pick inserted in center comes out clean, and an instant-read thermometer inserted in center registers 190°F (88°C), 30 to 35 minutes. While still hot, brush loaves with some of remaining melted butter. Liberally dust with confectioners' sugar. Let stand for 5 minutes. Brush with remaining melted butter, and dust with confectioners' sugar again. Let cool completely. Dust with confectioners' sugar once more before serving. Wrap tightly in plastic wrap, and store at room temperature for up to 2 weeks.

CANDIED ZEST
Makes about 1½ cups

2   large navel oranges (650 grams)
2   large lemons (238 grams)
2   cups (480 grams) water
1   cup (200 grams) granulated sugar
1   vanilla bean, split lengthwise, seeds
    scraped and reserved
¼   cup (48 grams) vanilla sugar*

1. Using a serrated knife, remove zest from oranges and lemons in 1-inch-long strips. Remove most of pith from zest.

2. In a medium saucepan, bring zest and cold water to cover to a boil. Drain, and repeat procedure. Pat zest dry, and cut into 1x¼-inch strips.

3. In same saucepan, bring 2 cups (480 grams) water, granulated sugar, and vanilla bean and reserved seeds to a boil over medium heat. Cook, stirring constantly, until sugar is dissolved. Add zest; simmer, stirring occasionally, until translucent and tender, about 25 minutes. Let cool in syrup. Strain zest, reserving syrup for another use, if desired. Let zest dry on a wire rack set over a baking sheet for 1 hour.

4. Toss zest in vanilla sugar; dice zest. Store in an airtight container for up to 1 week.

*We used Heilala Vanilla Pure Vanilla Bean Sugar.

SHAPE YOUR STOLLEN

1. Roll dough into a 13x9-inch oval. Gently press any dried fruit or other mix-ins that have fallen out back into the dough.

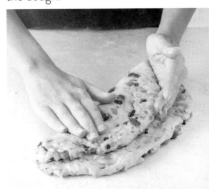

2. Fold dough in half lengthwise, leaving just a 1-inch border uncovered. (Think of the appearance of a tightly swaddled baby—that's what it should look like.)

STOLLEN WREATHS

Makes 2 small wreaths

Combining the visual beauty of holiday wreath bread with the fruit- and brandy-laced flavor of stollen, these sweet rings have nutty grated marzipan and a medley of dried cranberries, figs, and raisins kneaded directly into the dough.

½	cup (64 grams) dried cranberries
½	cup (64 grams) golden raisins
½	cup (64 grams) chopped dried black mission figs
½	cup (120 grams) brandy
¼	cup (60 grams) dark rum
1	cup (240 grams) warm whole milk (105°F/41°C to 110°F/43°C), divided
2¼	teaspoons (7 grams) active dry yeast
4¼	cups (531 grams) all-purpose flour, divided
1	cup (227 grams) unsalted butter, melted and divided
1	large egg (50 grams)
½	cup (100 grams) granulated sugar, divided
3	tablespoons (9 grams) orange zest
1	tablespoon (3 grams) lemon zest
1	teaspoon (3 grams) kosher salt
2	teaspoons (4 grams) ground cinnamon
½	teaspoon (1 gram) ground ginger
½	teaspoon (1 gram) ground nutmeg

Vanilla Bean Marzipan (recipe on page 186)
Confectioners' sugar, for dusting

1. In a medium bowl, toss together cranberries, raisins, and figs. Pour brandy and rum over fruit. Cover and let stand overnight or up to 3 days. (The longer it stands, the stronger the flavor.)

2. In the bowl of a stand mixer fitted with the paddle attachment, combine ½ cup (120 grams) warm milk and yeast. Let stand until mixture is foamy, about 10 minutes. Add 1 cup (125 grams) flour, and beat at low speed until a smooth dough forms, about 1 minute. Cover and let rise in a warm, draft-free place (75°F/24°C) until doubled in size, about 30 minutes.

3. Using the dough hook attachment, add ⅔ cup (150 grams) melted butter, egg, ¼ cup (50 grams) granulated sugar, zests, salt, remaining 3¼ cups (406 grams) flour, and remaining ½ cup (120 grams) warm milk, beating at very low speed until combined, about 2 minutes, stopping to scrape sides of bowl as needed. Increase mixer speed to low, and beat until a smooth dough forms, about 18 minutes.

4. Spray a large bowl with cooking spray. Place dough in bowl, turning to grease top. Cover and let rise in a warm, draft-free place (75°F/24°C) until doubled in size, about 1 hour.

5. Punch down dough in center; turn out dough onto a lightly floured surface. Divide dough in half. Cover and let stand for 10 minutes.

6. In a small bowl, stir together cinnamon, ginger, nutmeg, and remaining ¼ cup (50 grams) granulated sugar. Grate Vanilla Bean Marzipan, and divide in half (150 grams each). Strain fruit, discarding any liquid. Divide fruit mixture in half (119 grams each).

7. Preheat oven 350°F (180°C).

8. On a lightly floured surface, roll half of dough into a 22x9-inch rectangle. Liberally brush with some of remaining ⅓ cup (77 grams) melted butter. Sprinkle with half of sugar mixture, half of Vanilla Bean Marzipan, and half of fruit mixture, leaving a 1-inch border. Starting with one long side, roll up dough, jelly roll style; pinch edges to seal. Place roll, seam side down, on work surface. Using a bench scraper, cut roll in half lengthwise; turn halves cut side up. Carefully twist dough pieces tightly around each other. Place a sheet of parchment paper on work surface. Carefully move twist onto parchment; form twist into a circle, tucking ends under. (If any pieces of fruit or Vanilla Bean Marzipan fall out, place them back on wreath.) Place wreath on a baking sheet. Brush with some of remaining melted butter. Cover while repeating with remaining dough, sugar mixture, Vanilla Bean Marzipan, and fruit mixture.

9. Bake until golden brown, a wooden pick inserted in center comes out clean, and an instant-read thermometer inserted near center registers 190°F (88°C), 30 to 35 minutes. While still hot, brush wreaths with remaining melted butter. Let cool completely on pans. Lightly dust with confectioners' sugar just before serving.

SHAPE YOUR STOLLEN

1. Starting with one long side, roll up dough, jelly roll style. Pinch edges to seal.

2. Using a bench scraper, cut roll in half lengthwise. Turn halves cut side up.

3. Carefully twist dough pieces tightly around each other.

4. Form twist into a wreath, tucking ends under. Gently press any fruit or marzipan that has come free back into wreath.

MINI STOLLEN LOAVES

Makes 12 mini loaves

These mini loaves each contain a generous serving of chopped chocolate and kirsch-soaked dates and cherries while a decadent vanilla marzipan core lies tucked in the middle.

¾   cup (96 grams) dried cherries
¾   cup (96 grams) chopped dried dates
½   cup (120 grams) cherry brandy (kirschwasser)
1   cup (240 grams) warm whole milk (105°F/41°C to 110°F/43°C), divided
2¼ teaspoons (7 grams) active dry yeast
4¼ cups (531 grams) all-purpose flour, divided
⅔   cup (150 grams) plus ¼ cup (57 grams) unsalted butter, melted and divided
1   large egg (50 grams)
¼   cup (50 grams) granulated sugar
3   tablespoons (9 grams) orange zest
1   teaspoon (3 grams) kosher salt
1   vanilla bean, split lengthwise, seeds scraped and reserved
¼   teaspoon ground cardamom
¾   cup (128 grams) chopped bittersweet chocolate
½   cup (57 grams) finely chopped roasted chestnuts*
Vanilla Bean Marzipan (recipe follows)
Confectioners' sugar, for dusting

1. In a medium bowl, toss together cherries and dates. Pour brandy over fruit. Cover and let stand overnight or up to 3 days. (The longer it stands, the stronger the flavor.)
2. In the bowl of a stand mixer fitted with the paddle attachment, combine ½ cup (120 grams) warm milk and yeast. Let stand until mixture is foamy, about 10 minutes. Add 1 cup (125 grams) flour, and beat at low speed until a smooth dough forms, about 1 minute. Cover and let rise in a warm, draft-free place (75°F/24°C) until doubled in size, about 30 minutes.
3. Using the dough hook attachment, add ⅔ cup (150 grams) melted butter, egg, granulated sugar, zest, salt, vanilla bean seeds, cardamom, remaining 3¼ cups (406 grams) flour, and remaining ½ cup (120 grams) warm milk, beating at very low

speed until combined, about 2 minutes, stopping to scrape sides of bowl as needed. Increase mixer speed to low, and beat until a smooth dough forms, about 18 minutes.
4. Spray a large bowl with cooking spray. Place dough in bowl, turning to grease top. Cover and let rise in a warm, draft-free place (75°F/24°C) until doubled in size, about 1 hour.
5. Punch down dough in center; turn out dough onto a lightly floured surface. Strain fruit, discarding any liquid. Knead fruit mixture, chocolate, and chestnuts into dough until evenly dispersed. (Be patient while kneading. If any fruit pieces or nuts fall out, just place them back in dough, and keep kneading.) Cover and let stand for 10 minutes.
6. Divide Vanilla Bean Marzipan into 12 pieces (about 20 grams each). Roll each piece into a 3½-inch log. Set aside.
7. Line 2 baking sheets with parchment paper.
8. Divide dough into 12 pieces (about 117 grams each). On a lightly floured surface, roll each piece of dough into a 5x3½-inch rectangle. Place 1 piece of Vanilla Bean Marzipan in center of each rectangle. Fold top half of dough over Vanilla Bean Marzipan, then fold bottom half over top. Gently roll loaves to seal seam. Pinch ends under, and place loaves on prepared pans, seam side down. (Final loaves should be 4½ inches long.) Lightly brush loaves with some of remaining ¼ cup (57 grams) melted butter. Cover and let rise in a warm, draft-free place (75°F/24°C) until puffed, about 45 minutes.
9. Preheat oven to 350°F (180°C).
10. Bake until golden brown, a wooden pick inserted in center comes out clean, and an instant-read thermometer inserted in center registers 190°F (88°C), 25 to 30 minutes. While still hot, brush loaves with some of remaining melted butter. Liberally dust with confectioners' sugar. Let stand for 5 minutes. Brush with remaining melted butter, and dust with confectioners' sugar again. Let cool completely. Dust with confectioners' sugar once more before serving. Wrap tightly in plastic wrap, and store at room temperature for up to 2 weeks.

We used Gefen Organic Whole Roasted & Peeled Chestnuts.

VANILLA BEAN MARZIPAN

Makes about 1 cup

1⅓ cups (128 grams) almond flour
⅔   cup (80 grams) confectioners' sugar
¼   cup (50 grams) granulated sugar
1   large egg white (30 grams)
1   teaspoon (6 grams) vanilla bean paste
½   teaspoon (2.5 grams) fresh orange juice

1. In the work bowl of a food processor, place flour and sugars; pulse until combined. Add egg white, vanilla bean paste, and orange juice; process until mixture holds together. Wrap tightly in plastic wrap, and refrigerate for up to 1 month.

SHAPE YOUR STOLLEN

1. After dividing dough into 12 pieces, roll out each one into a 5x3½-inch rectangle. Using your finger, press a neat, 3½-inch-long dent into center of dough. Nestle log of marzipan into divot.

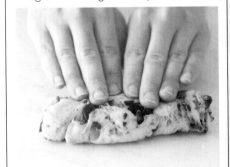

2. Tuck both sides of dough over marzipan log, covering it. Using your cupped hand, gently roll mini stollen logs to seal seams.

OVERNIGHT LEVAIN PIZZA DOUGH

Makes 3 regular or 5 thin-crust dough balls

Recipe by Ken Forkish

I was never convinced that a pizza crust made with natural leavening from a wild yeast (a.k.a. sourdough) culture would make a better pizza than one made from a long-fermented dough based on commercial yeast. Then I ate pizza made by the master, Franco Pepe, at Pepe in Grani in Italy. Franco's pizza crusts have a delicate, incredibly light texture and flavors of ripe lactic fermentation. Making pizza dough from a wild yeast culture takes a bit more time and planning, but once you get familiar with the routine, there's nothing difficult about it.

Note: *If you don't already have your levain built, you'll need to start building the levain 6 days before you start making your pizza dough—that is, 7 to 8 days before you bake the pizza.*

Levain Starter:
100 grams (⅓ cup plus 4 teaspoons) water (100°F/38°C)

50 grams (2 tablespoons plus 1 teaspoon) Wild Yeast (Levain) Culture (recipe on page 189)

100 grams (¾ cup plus 2 teaspoons) high-protein bread flour (may also substitute all-purpose or 00 flour)

Final Dough:
225 grams (scant 1 cup) water (90°F/32°C to 95°F/35°C) (70%)

14 grams (2½ teaspoons) fine sea salt (2.8%)

250 grams (1 cup) Levain Starter (25%)

375 grams (scant 3 cups) white flour, preferably 00 (100%)

1. Measure and Combine Levain Starter Ingredients. The evening of the day before you plan to make pizza, use your digital scale to measure 100 grams water (100°F/38°C) into a quart-size plastic container with a lid. (If you live in a warm climate and have warm inside temperatures overnight, mix the levain with cooler water—for example,

at 75°F [24°C] instead of 100°F [38°C].) Measure 50 grams from container of Wild Yeast (Levain) Culture in your refrigerator right into water, and mix by hand. (Don't worry about completely dissolving starter.) Measure 100 grams bread flour into levain mixture, and mix by hand until it all comes together in a semiliquid batter. Put lid on it, and let stand overnight at room temperature. (The warmer the location, the more lactic fermentation flavors will go into your crust, up to a point.) Overdo it with the starter's fermentation, and you will then get an excess of alcohol in the culture, producing more acetic acid flavors.

2. Measure and Combine Dough Ingredients. Ten to 12 hours after you mix Levain Starter, it should be bubbly, goopy, and lively. Now make the dough. Measure 225 grams water (90°F/32°C to 95°F/35°C) into a 6-quart dough tub. Sprinkle salt into water, and swirl around to dissolve. Add in all of Levain Starter, and blend it briefly by hand with water and salt, using a pincer motion to cut it into chunks. (Don't worry about dissolving it completely—it won't.) Add 375 grams flour to water-salt-starter mixture.

3. Mix Dough. Mix by hand, first by stirring your hand around inside dough tub to integrate flour, water, salt, and yeast into a single mass of dough. Then use pincer method to cut dough in sections with your hand, alternating with folding dough to develop it back into a unified mass. Continue for just 30 seconds to 1 minute. The target dough temperature at the end of the mix is 80°F (27°C); use your probe thermometer to check it.

4. Knead and Rise. Let dough rest for 20 minutes, then knead it on a work surface with a very light dusting of flour for 30 seconds to 1 minute. The skin of the dough should be very smooth. Place dough ball, seam side down, in lightly oiled dough tub. Cover with a tight-fitting lid. Hold dough for 3 hours at room temperature (assuming 70°F/21°C to 74°F/23°C) for first rise. This timeline is flexible, so if you

need to shape after 2 hours, don't stress; just make up your dough balls a little early and add the difference in time to the next stage.

5. Shape. Moderately flour a work surface about 2 feet wide. With floured hands, gently ease dough out of tub. With your hands still floured, pick up dough, and ease it back down on work surface in a somewhat even shape. Dust entire top of dough with flour, then cut it into 3 or 5 equal-size pieces, depending on style of pizza. Use your scale to get evenly sized dough balls. Take a piece of dough, and stretch one-third of it sideways until it resists, then fold it back over main piece of dough. Repeat, working your way around dough and forming it into a medium-tight round, working gently and being careful not to tear dough. Stop when dough ball is in a roughly circular shape. Then flip it over, and put seam on work surface in an area cleared of flour. Cup your hands around back of dough ball as you face it, and with pinky fingers of both hands, make contact with dough ball where it meets surface of your countertop. Pull entire dough ball 4 or 5 inches toward you on clean, unfloured surface, leading with your pinkies and applying enough downward pressure as you pull so dough ball grips your work surface. Give dough a turn, and repeat this tightening step 1 or 2 more times until dough ball is rounded.

6. Second Fermentation. Place dough balls on lightly floured dinner plates or a baking sheet, leaving space between balls to allow for expansion. Lightly flour tops to prevent sticking, cover with plastic wrap, and let stand at room temperature (assuming 70°F/21°C) for about 5 hours. Dough balls should hold for 4 hours for making pizza. Or refrigerate dough balls 4 hours after shaping them, then use them to make pizza the next day.

7. Make Pizza. This dough is fantastic for any pizza.

Note: *Baker's percentage is listed in parentheses after each ingredient.*

OVERNIGHT LEVAIN PIZZA DOUGH

A wild yeast culture is created when yeast in the air and in the flour combine to form a living culture that makes bread dough, pizza dough, and even pancakes rise. You can create your own by mixing flour and water daily for 7 days.

Levain Volume Conversions
Measure your levain ingredients by weight rather than volume; volume conversions are approximate.

100 grams whole wheat flour = ¾ cup plus ½ tablespoon
100 grams water = ½ cup plus 4 teaspoons
50 grams levain = 2 tablespoons plus 1 teaspoon

Making the Levain
Start with one empty container with a lid that fits. A medium size bowl will work. Weigh the container, and write down its empty weight on a piece of tape that you then attach to the outside of the container.

Any time of day: By hand, mix 100 grams water (100°F/38°C) with 100 grams room temperature whole wheat flour in your container. Let stand at room temperature without its lid for a couple hours, then put lid on it.

Day 1 Evening: Next, 24 to 36 hours after first feeding of your new culture, add 100 grams water (100°F/38°C) and 100 grams room temperature whole wheat flour. Mix by hand until integrated, and let stand on counter. Leave lid off for a couple hours to capture some of the natural yeast floating around in the air, then cover it.

Day 2 Evening: Remove about half of mixture from container (with a wet hand is easiest), and throw it away. Add to remainder 100 grams water (100°F/38°C) and 100 grams room temperature whole wheat flour, and mix it all together by hand. Let stand at room temperature, covered.

Day 3 Evening: Remove about three-fourths of bubbly mixture, and throw that away, then add 100 grams water (between 85°F [29°C] and 90°F [32°C]), and 100 grams room temperature whole wheat flour to your new culture. Mix by hand until integrated. Let stand at room temperature, covered.

Day 4 Evening: Using the weight of the empty container for reference, remove and discard all but 50 grams culture. Add 150 grams water (85°F/29°C) plus 75 grams room temperature whole wheat flour and 75 grams room temperature all-purpose white flour. Mix by hand until integrated. Let stand at room temperature, covered.

Day 5 Evening: Remove and discard all but 50 grams culture, and add 100 grams water (85°F/29°C) and 100 grams room temperature all-purpose white flour. Mix by hand until integrated. Let stand overnight, covered.

Day 6 Morning: The culture should feel gassy and goopy and like there's life in there, and it will have a nice lactic, slightly alcoholic fragrance. Pop it in the fridge. Tonight, you can mix a starter, and tomorrow morning, you can make a pizza dough for pizza the evening of day 8.

Photo by Alan Weiner

OVERNIGHT LEVAIN PIZZA DOUGH TIMELINE

Build Wild Yeast (Levain) Culture: 6 days

Make Levain Starter: 10 to 12 hours (overnight)

Mix Final Dough: 10 minutes; knead 20 minutes later

Bulk Fermentation: 3 hours

Divide, Shape, and Cover Dough: 10 minutes

Second Fermentation: 5 to 6 hours at room temperature, with a hold time of 3 to 4 hours

SATURDAY PIZZA DOUGH

Makes 3 regular or 5 thin-crust dough balls

Recipe by Ken Forkish

This same-day dough is the answer when you wake up in the morning and decide you want pizza for dinner. This dough was inspired by the Associazione Verace Pizza Napoletana (AVPN) pizza dough rules. After mixing, the dough rests for 2 hours. Then dough balls (panetti) are made and set aside, covered, and held at room temperature in their second stage of fermentation for 6 hours. The dough balls are ready to make pizza anytime following the second fermentation and hold for 4 hours at room temperature. The dough will be a little gassy, very easily stretched, and a little delicate near the end of its 4-hour hold time.

350 grams (1½ cups) water (90°F/32°C to 95°F/35°C) (70%)

15 grams (2¾ teaspoons) fine sea salt (3%)

0.3 grams (⅓ of ¼ teaspoon) instant dried yeast (0.6%)

500 grams (scant 4 cups) white flour, preferably 00 (100%)

1. Measure and Combine Ingredients. Use your digital scale to measure 350 grams water (90°F/32°C to 95°F/35°C) into a 6-quart dough tub. Sprinkle salt into water, and swirl around to dissolve. Add yeast to water; let rest for 1 minute to hydrate, then swish it around until dissolved. Add 500 grams flour (preferably 00) to water-salt-yeast mixture.

2. Mix Dough. Mix by hand, first by stirring your hand around inside dough tub to integrate flour, water, salt, and yeast into a single mass of dough. Then, using a pincer motion, squeeze big chunks of dough, tightening your grip to cut through dough, alternating with folding dough to develop it back into a unified mass. Continue for just 30 seconds to 1 minute. The target dough temperature at the end of the mix is 80°F (27°C); use your probe thermometer to check it.

3. Knead and Rise. Let dough rest for 20 minutes, then knead it on a work surface with a very light dusting of flour for 30 seconds to 1 minute. The skin of the dough should be very smooth. Place dough ball, seam side down, in lightly oiled dough

tub. Cover with a tight-fitting lid. Hold dough for 2 hours at room temperature (assuming 70°F/21°C to 74°F/23°C) for first rise. This timeline is flexible, so if you need to do this after 1 or 1½ hours, don't stress; just make up your dough balls a little early and add the difference in time to the next stage.

4. Shape. Moderately flour a work surface about 2 feet wide. With floured hands, gently ease dough out of tub. With your hands still floured, pick up dough, and ease it back down onto work surface in a somewhat even shape. Dust entire top of dough with flour, then cut it into 3 or 5 equal-size pieces, depending on style of pizza. Use your scale to get evenly sized dough balls. Shape each piece of dough into a medium-tight round, working gently and being careful not to tear dough.

5. Second Fermentation. Place dough balls on lightly floured dinner plates or a baking sheet, leaving space between them to allow for expansion. Lightly flour tops, cover airtight with plastic wrap, and let rest at room temperature for 6 hours for second fermentation. Alternatively, you

can rest dough balls for 4 hours at room temperature, and then refrigerate to hold for up to the next evening.

6. Make Pizza. Without refrigeration, the dough balls can be used anytime in the 4 hours following the second fermentation. If you refrigerate the dough balls, let them come to room temperature for 1 hour while you preheat the oven and prepare your toppings.

Note: *Baker's percentage is listed in parentheses after each ingredient.*

SATURDAY PIZZA DOUGH TIMELINE

Bulk Fermentation: 2 hours

Divide, Shape, and Cover Dough: 10 minutes

Second Fermentation: 6 hours

Hold Time for Use at Room Temperature: 4 hours, or refrigerate to extend the use until the next evening

---

Photo by Alan Weiner

CHERRY BOMB

Makes 1 (12-inch) pizza

Recipe by Ken Forkish

An abundance of fresh cherry tomatoes and quality salami make this pizza. The sweet tomatoes perfectly balance the salami's salty, spicy bite.

- dough ball (260 to 300 grams)*
- 12 ripe cherry tomatoes (101 grams)
- 2 tablespoons (30 grams) extra-virgin olive oil, plus more for drizzling
- ¾ teaspoon (5 grams) red wine vinegar or another tasty vinegar
- ¼ cup (39 grams) sliced sweet onion, cut in half and sliced vertically
- (2-ounce) salami stick (60 grams), such as soppressata, thinly sliced into 12 to 15 pieces
- 4 ounces (115 grams) fresh mozzarella, cut into ½-inch-thick pieces
- 0.25 ounce (7 grams) Pecorino Romano cheese, grated

1. If you use a dough recipe that calls for refrigeration, remove dough ball from refrigerator 1 to 1½ hours before baking pizza. Put your pizza steel or stone on an upper rack in your oven no more than 8 inches below broiler. Preheat oven to 550°F (290°C) for 45 minutes. (If your oven won't go that high, preheat oven to 500°F [260°C].)
2. Slice cherry tomatoes in half, and put them in a mixing bowl. Add oil and vinegar. Toss by hand, and set aside. Cook onion very lightly—not to translucent—over moderate heat with just enough oil to keep onions from sticking to pan. Set aside in a small bowl. (If you like, soak onion slices in cold water for 10 minutes before sweating to remove oniony bite.)
3. Set up your pizza assembly station. Give yourself about 2 feet of width on countertop. Moderately flour work surface. Position your wooden peel next to floured area, and lightly drizzle it with oil. (If you don't have a peel, you can use a well-floured cookie sheet instead.) Have prepped cherry tomatoes, onions, sliced salami, and cheeses at hand. Switch oven to

broil 10 minutes before loading pizza.
4. Shape pizza dough. (See *How to Shape Your Pizza* on page 192.)
5. Drizzle a small amount of oil over top of pizza, and top it with cherry tomatoes, onion, salami, and mozzarella, in that order. Then sprinkle Pecorino over top before baking.
6. Turn off broiler, then gently slide pizza onto pizza steel or stone. Close oven door, and change setting to bake at 550°F (290°C). Bake until rim is golden, about 5 minutes. (If baking at 500°F [260°C], bake about 9 minutes.) Change oven setting from bake to broil, and broil until cheese is melted and crust is golden with spots of brown and a few small spots of char, about 2 minutes. (Check after 1 minute to be safe.) Use tongs or a fork to slide pizza from pizza steel or stone onto a large plate. Serve sliced.

Use Overnight Levain Pizza Dough (page 188) or Saturday Pizza Dough (page 190).

Photo by Alan Weiner

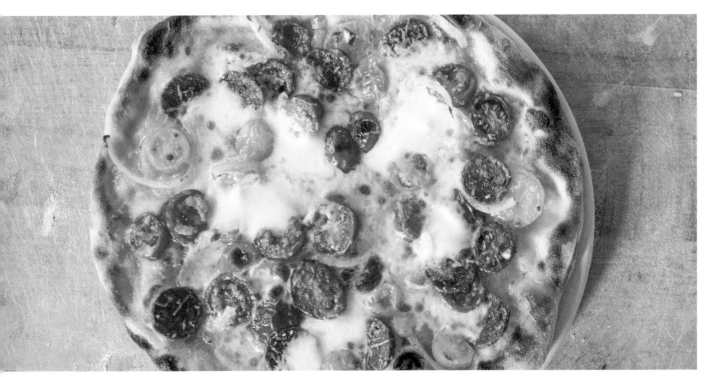

PIZZA MARGHERITA

Makes 1 (12-inch) pizza

Recipe by Ken Forkish

The best possible ingredients—a simple tomato sauce, fresh fior di latte mozzarella, and basil—and a great dough make this Italian classic a perennial star. Rub a little olive oil on the basil leaves before you put the pizza in the oven. The oil helps the leaves slightly fry in the oven and helps preserve the vibrant green color.

1 dough ball (260 to 300 grams)*
¼ to ⅓ cup (54 to 92 grams) Basic Tomato Sauce (recipe follows)
1 tablespoon (14 grams) extra-virgin olive oil, plus more for drizzling
Scant ¼ cup (10 to 15 grams) grated Pecorino Romano or Parmigiano-Reggiano cheese
3.5 to 4 ounces (80 to 100 grams) fresh whole-milk mozzarella cheese (fior di latte) or brine-packed mozzarella di bufala, sliced into short strips about ½ inch thick
3 to 5 fresh whole basil leaves
Sliced cherry tomatoes (optional)

1. If you use a dough recipe that calls for refrigeration, remove dough ball from refrigerator 1 to 1½ hours before baking pizza.

Put your pizza steel or stone on an upper rack in your oven no more than 8 inches below broiler. Preheat oven to 550°F (290°C) for 45 minutes. (If your oven won't go that high, preheat oven to 500°F [260°C].)
2. Set up your pizza assembly station. Give yourself about 2 feet of width on countertop. Moderately flour work surface. Position your wooden peel next to floured area, and lightly drizzle it with oil. (If you don't have a peel, you can use a well-floured cookie sheet instead.) Have sauce, oil, cheeses, and basil at hand, with a ladle or large spoon for sauce. Switch oven to broil 10 minutes before loading pizza.
3. Shape pizza dough. (See *How to Shape Your Pizza.*)
4. Spread Basic Tomato Sauce over dough to within ½ inch of edge, smoothing it with the back of the spoon or ladle. Turn off broiler, then gently slide pizza onto pizza stone or steel. Close oven door, and change setting to bake at 550°F (290°C). Bake until rim is just starting to turn golden, about 4 minutes. (If baking at 500°F [260°C], bake about 8 minutes.) Use a pair of tongs to remove pizza onto a plate. Drizzle oil on top of pizza, then sprinkle Pecorino evenly over sauce. Layer mozzarella and basil leaves evenly over pizza. Using your hands, place pizza back onto pizza steel or stone, and bake 1 to 2 minutes more.

5. Change oven setting from bake to broil, and broil until cheese is softly melted and crust is golden with spots of brown and a few small spots of char, about 2 minutes. (Check after 1 minute to be safe.) Add sliced cherry tomatoes as soon as pizza comes out of the oven for a margherita "extra," if desired. Use tongs or a fork to slide pizza from pizza steel or stone onto a large plate. Drizzle a small amount of oil over pizza, and serve whole or sliced in half.

*Use Overnight Levain Pizza Dough (page 188) or Saturday Pizza Dough (page 190).

BASIC TOMATO SAUCE
Makes about 4 cups or enough sauce for 7 (12-inch) pizzas

1 (28-ounce) can (800 grams) whole peeled tomatoes
1½ teaspoons (8 grams) fine sea salt

1. Place tomatoes and salt in the container of a blender; pulse on lowest speed setting very, very briefly, just until tomatoes are blended.
2. Pour sauce into a sealable container. I use a quart-size deli container with a lid. Label the container with the date, and refrigerate or freeze what you don't use. It should keep for 1 week in refrigerator.

Photos by Alan Weiner

HOW TO SHAPE YOUR PIZZA

1. To shape pizza, put dough ball on floured work surface, and flip to coat both sides moderately with flour. Leaving about a ½ inch of outer rim undeflated, punch down middle with your fingertips, pushing air toward rim of disk, then flip dough over, and repeat.

2. Using floured hands, grab rim at about 10 o'clock and 2 o'clock positions, and lift so crust hangs down vertically; preserve outer rim by placing thumbs about a ½ inch from edge. Let gravity pull rest of dough down to stretch it. Run rim between your hands, working around circumference of dough several times.

3. Make two fists, and position them just inside rim, with crust hanging vertically. Gently stretch and turn dough repeatedly, letting bottom of dough pull down, expanding surface. Keep a close eye on thickness of dough. You want the dough thin, but you don't want it so thin that it tears.

4. Transfer disk of pizza dough to peel, and run your hands around perimeter to relax it and work out the kinks.

CORN PIE

Makes 1 (12-inch) pizza

Recipe by Ken Forkish

In the summer, there's nothing like fresh corn. In this pie, I like to blend different cheeses to give the pizza greater complexity of flavor without detracting from the unadulterated corn, sweet and bursting with flavor.

1   dough ball (260 to 300 grams)*
1   tablespoon (14 grams) extra-virgin olive oil
3.5 ounces (100 grams) fresh mozzarella, cut into cubes
1   fresh jalapeño pepper (28 grams), chopped
½   cup (73 grams) (or to taste) fresh corn kernels cut from cob
2   ounces (55 grams) ricotta salata or Cotija cheese, crumbled
Black pepper, to taste
Salsa Verde (recipe follows)

1. If you use a dough recipe that calls for refrigeration, remove dough ball from refrigerator about 1 hour before baking pizza. Put your pizza steel or stone on an upper rack in your oven about 8 inches below broiler. Preheat oven to 550°F (290°C) for 45 minutes.(If your oven won't go that high, preheat oven to 500°F [260°C].)
2. Switch oven to broil 10 minutes before loading pizza.
3. Shape pizza dough. (See *How to Shape Your Pizza* on page 192.)
4. Drizzle dough with oil, then sprinkle mozzarella evenly over top of dough. Add jalapeño and corn. Sprinkle ricotta salata or Cotija cheese over top, then generously grate fresh black pepper over all.
5. Turn off broiler, then gently slide pizza onto pizza stone or steel. Close oven door, and change setting to bake at 550°F (290°C). Bake for 5 minutes. (If baking at 500°F [260°C], bake about 9 minutes.) Change oven setting from bake to broil, and broil for 1 to 2 minutes. Remove from oven; add dollops of Salsa Verde to taste. Serve sliced.

SALSA VERDE
Makes about ½ cup

1   cup (14 grams) fresh flat-leaf parsley
½   cup (7 grams) fresh mint or basil
⅓   cup (75 grams) olive oil, with some in reserve
1   anchovy fillet (2 grams)
4 to 5 cloves fresh garlic (11 to 15 grams)
1   tablespoon (18 grams) Champagne vinegar
½   teaspoon (2.5 grams) fine sea salt

1. Combine all ingredients in a small food processor (or chop herbs and garlic finely), and blend until combined. Do not mix into a purée; a little rough texture is fine. Add more oil if needed to get a thick consistency, not at all dry, a little thinner than a paste. Reserve into a covered container. This will go on the pizza in dollops right after it comes out of the oven.

*Use Overnight Levain Pizza Dough (page 188) or Saturday Pizza Dough (page 190).

Photo by Alan Weiner

CRESCENT ROLLS

Makes 24 rolls

Is there any roll that sets the scene for a convivial holiday dinner better than a bread basket piled high with buttery Crescent Rolls? If you're anything like us, you and the crescent go way back. Dressed up with sea salt, this roll's timeless shape and versatility make it a family favorite as well as a busy baker's go-to recipe. (The dough can be made ahead for a worry-free addition to the dinner table.)

4¼	cups (510 grams) bread flour
4½	teaspoons (14 grams) instant yeast
1	tablespoon (9 grams) kosher salt
1	cup (240 grams) whole milk
½	cup (113 grams) unsalted butter
2	tablespoons (24 grams) granulated sugar
2	tablespoons (42 grams) honey
1	large egg (50 grams), room temperature
1	large egg yolk (19 grams), room temperature
¼	cup (57 grams) unsalted butter, melted

Garnish: flaked sea salt

1. In the bowl of a stand mixer fitted with the dough hook attachment, combine flour, yeast, and kosher salt.

2. In a small saucepan, heat milk, butter, sugar, and honey over medium-low heat until an instant-read thermometer registers 120°F (49°C) to 130°F (54°C). Add warm milk mixture to flour mixture, and beat at low speed just until combined, about 2 minutes. Add egg and egg yolk, and beat until a smooth and elastic dough forms, about 6 minutes.

3. Spray a large bowl with cooking spray. Place dough in bowl, turning to grease top. Cover and let rise in a warm, draft-free place (75°F/24°C) until doubled in size, 35 to 45 minutes. Line 2 baking sheets with parchment paper.

4. Punch down dough. On a lightly floured surface, divide dough in half (about 490 grams each). Working with 1 half at a time (keep remaining dough covered to prevent it from drying out), roll dough into a 14-inch circle.

Using a pastry wheel, cut dough into 12 equal triangles. Starting from widest end of triangle, roll up dough, pinching pointed end to seal. Place rolls, pointed side down, on prepared pans. Repeat with remaining dough. Cover and let rise in a warm, draft-free place (75°F/24°C) until doubled in size, 35 to 45 minutes.

5. Preheat oven to 375°F (190°C).

6. Brush rolls with melted butter.

7. Bake until golden brown, 10 to 11 minutes. Brush with melted butter again, and sprinkle with sea salt, if desired. Serve warm or at room temperature. Store in an airtight container at room temperature for up to 4 days.

CLOVER BEER ROLLS

Makes 24 rolls

We infused this dough with a light amber ale because it offers subtle notes of toasty malt and sweet citrus that balance out the savory Parmesan and Roasted Garlic. A hoppy beer (like an IPA) would make the bread too bitter. Place three dough balls into a muffin cup to yield a charming clover shape.

1¾ cups plus 2 tablespoons (450 grams) warm amber ale* (105°F/41°C to 110°F/43°C), divided
4½ teaspoons (14 grams) active dry yeast
1½ tablespoons (31.5 grams) honey
5⅔ cups (680 grams) bread flour
10 ounces (280 grams) coarsely grated Parmesan cheese, divided
Roasted Garlic (recipe follows)
2 tablespoons (24 grams) granulated sugar
2 tablespoons (4 grams) chopped fresh parsley
1 tablespoon (9 grams) kosher salt
¼ cup (57 grams) unsalted butter, melted
Garnish: flaked sea salt, chopped fresh parsley

1. In a small bowl, stir together 1 cup (240 grams) warm beer, yeast, and honey. Let stand until mixture is foamy, about 5 minutes.
2. In the bowl of a stand mixer fitted with the dough hook attachment, combine flour, 8 ounces (225 grams) Parmesan, Roasted Garlic, sugar, parsley, and salt. Add yeast mixture and remaining ¾ cup plus 2 tablespoons (210 grams) warm beer, and beat at low speed until a smooth and elastic dough forms, 8 to 9 minutes.
3. Spray a large bowl with cooking spray. Place dough in bowl, turning to grease top. Cover and let rise in a warm, draft-free place (75°F/24°C) until doubled in size, 30 to 40 minutes.
4. Spray 2 (12-cup) muffin pans with cooking spray.
5. Punch down dough, and turn out onto a lightly floured surface. Divide dough into 24 (60-gram) portions. Working with 1 portion at a time (keep remaining dough covered to prevent it from drying out),

divide each portion into 3 (20-gram) pieces. Roll each piece into a ball. Place 3 dough balls in each prepared muffin cup. Cover and let rise in a warm, draft-free place (75°F/24°C) until doubled in size, about 40 minutes. (Alternatively, cover tightly and refrigerate overnight. When ready to bake, let stand at room temperature for 30 minutes.)
6. Preheat oven to 400°F (200°C).
7. Brush rolls with melted butter, and sprinkle with remaining 2 ounces (55 grams) Parmesan.
8. Bake until golden brown and an instant-read thermometer inserted in center registers 190°F (88°C), 8 to 10 minutes, rotating pans halfway through baking. Brush with melted butter again, and sprinkle with sea salt and parsley, if desired. Serve warm or at room temperature. Store in an airtight container at room temperature for up to 4 days.

*We used Bell's Amber Ale, but any amber or brown ale will do. You can also use a pale ale, but it does have more hops than amber ale, so it will affect your rolls' flavor slightly.

ROASTED GARLIC

Makes 1 head

1 large (2½-inch) head garlic (about 73 grams)
1 teaspoon (5 grams) olive oil
¼ teaspoon kosher salt

1. Preheat oven to 350°F (180°C).
2. Cut ¼ inch off top end of garlic, keeping cloves intact. Place garlic, cut side up, on foil. Drizzle with oil, and sprinkle with salt; wrap garlic in foil.
3. Bake until soft, 1 hour to 1 hour and 10 minutes. Let cool completely. Squeeze pulp into a small bowl, and mash with a fork.

PULL-APART ROLLS ·

Makes 24 rolls

Peppery, freshly grated Comté cheese and Caramelized Shallots team up for a flavor blowout in these hearty rolls. This method is a cinch. Throw these Pull-Apart Rolls on a platter, and watch everyone tear off their own piece of pillowy perfection.

1	cup (240 grams) warm whole milk (105°F/41°C to 110°F/43°C)
1	cup (240 grams) warm water (105°F/41°C to 110°F/43°C)
1	tablespoon (9 grams) active dry yeast
2	large eggs (100 grams), room temperature
¼	cup (50 grams) granulated sugar
½	cup (113 grams) unsalted butter, melted and divided
1	tablespoon (9 grams) kosher salt
6¼	cups (750 grams) bread flour
7	ounces (200 grams) coarsely grated Comté cheese

Caramelized Shallots (recipe follows)
Garnish: flaked sea salt

1. In the bowl of a stand mixer fitted with the paddle attachment, whisk together warm milk, 1 cup (240 grams) warm water, and yeast by hand. Let stand until mixture is foamy, about 10 minutes. Whisk in eggs, sugar, ¼ cup (57 grams) melted butter, and salt. Add flour, cheese, and Caramelized Shallots. With mixer on low speed, beat until well combined, about 1 minute. Cover and let rise in a warm, draft-free place (75°F/24°C) until doubled in size, about 1 hour.
2. Spray 2 (9-inch) square baking pans with cooking spray. Line pans with parchment paper, letting excess extend over sides of pans; spray pans again.
3. With lightly floured hands, turn out dough onto a lightly floured surface, and knead 3 to 4 times. (If there is too much flour on the work surface, you won't be able to shape the rolls properly.) Divide dough into 24 (71-gram) pieces. Gently shape each piece into a ball, and place 12 balls in each prepared pan in 3 rows of 4, leaving no space between each ball. Cover and let rise in a warm, draft-free place (75°F/24°C) until puffed, 30 to 45 minutes. (Alternatively, cover tightly and refrigerate overnight. When ready to bake, let stand at room temperature for 30 minutes.)
4. Preheat oven to 375°F (190°C).

5. Brush rolls with remaining ¼ cup (57 grams) melted butter.
6. Bake until an instant-read thermometer inserted in centers registers 190°F (88°C), about 27 minutes, covering with foil and rotating pans halfway through baking to prevent excess browning. Brush with melted butter again, and sprinkle with sea salt, if desired. Serve warm or at room temperature. Store in an airtight container at room temperature for up to 4 days.

CARAMELIZED SHALLOTS
Makes ½ cup

5	large shallots (215 grams)
1	teaspoon (5 grams) olive oil
1	tablespoon (14 grams) unsalted butter
½	teaspoon (2 grams) granulated sugar
¼	teaspoon kosher salt
⅛	teaspoon ground black pepper

1. Peel shallots, and cut lengthwise into quarters. Slice into ⅛-inch pieces.
2. In a medium skillet, heat oil over medium heat. Add shallots and butter, and sprinkle with sugar, salt, and pepper. Cook until shallots begin to brown evenly; reduce heat to low, and cook, stirring frequently, until shallots are very soft, 10 to 15 minutes. Let cool to room temperature.

SOUR CREAM KNOTS

Makes 33 knots

Your traditional sour cream roll deserves some va-va-voom this holiday season. We added heaps of melty extra-sharp Cheddar and shaped the dough into eye-catching knots. (Don't let the new look fool you. Our shaping technique is easy!) With tangy sour cream and fresh cracked pepper, these no-knead rolls embody everything comfort food should be.

½   cup (120 grams) warm water (105°F/41°C to 110°F/43°C)
2   tablespoons (18 grams) active dry yeast
2   cups (480 grams) sour cream
½   cup (113 grams) unsalted butter
½   cup (100 grams) granulated sugar
1   tablespoon (9 grams) kosher salt
2   large eggs (100 grams), room temperature
6¼ cups (750 grams) bread flour
10 ounces (280 grams) coarsely grated extra-sharp Cheddar cheese*
1   tablespoon (6 grams) ground black pepper
¼   cup (57 grams) unsalted butter, melted
Garnish: flaked sea salt

1. In the bowl of a stand mixer fitted with the paddle attachment, combine ½ cup (120 grams) warm water and yeast. Let stand until mixture is foamy, about 5 minutes.
2. In a medium saucepan, heat sour cream, butter, sugar, and salt over medium-low heat, stirring constantly, until butter is melted, 3 to 4 minutes. Let mixture cool to 110°F (43°C), about 10 minutes. Add eggs, whisking to combine. Add sour cream mixture to yeast mixture, whisking until combined.
3. Add flour, Cheddar, and pepper to yeast mixture, and beat at low speed until well combined, about 1 minute. Cover and let rise in a warm, draft-free place (75°F/24°C) until doubled in size, about 1 hour.
4. Line 4 baking sheets with parchment paper.
5. Divide dough into 33 (57-gram) pieces. With lightly floured hands, working with 1 piece at a time (keep remaining dough covered to prevent it from drying out), roll each piece into a 12-inch-long rope. Tie a loose knot in center of rope, leaving about 2 inches of dough at each end. Wrap one end up and over loop and the other end down and under. Pinch two ends together at center. Place on prepared

pans. Cover and let rise in a warm, draft-free place (75°F/24°C) until doubled in size, 30 to 40 minutes. (Alternatively, cover tightly and refrigerate overnight. When ready to bake, let stand at room temperature for 30 minutes.)
6. Preheat oven to 375°F (190°C).
7. Brush rolls with melted butter.
8. Bake until golden brown and an instant-read thermometer inserted in center registers 190°F (88°C), 10 to 11 minutes, rotating pans halfway through baking. Brush with melted butter again, and sprinkle with sea salt, if desired. Serve warm or at room temperature. Store in an airtight container at room temperature for up to 4 days.

We used Tillamook Extra Sharp Cheddar Cheese.

PUMPKIN PRETZELS

Makes 12 pretzels

Recipe by Kelsey Siemens

At my family's farm in British Columbia, I am constantly collecting pumpkins as soon as they're ripe in our fields. I usually bring home one or two specialty varieties a week until my little home is full to the brim. Pink, blue, white, green, beige, red, orange—we grow over 50 different kinds! Soft pretzels have been a longtime favorite in my family, and adding in a hint of pumpkin makes them a delightful fall treat.

¼ cup (60 grams) warm water (95°F/35°C to 105°F/41°C)
2¼ teaspoons (7 grams) active dry yeast
1 teaspoon (4 grams) granulated sugar
4½ cups (563 grams) all-purpose flour
1 cup (240 grams) water
½ cup (122 grams) pumpkin purée
1 teaspoon (3 grams) kosher salt
½ teaspoon (1 gram) ground allspice
¼ cup (57 grams) unsalted butter, melted
Cinnamon Sugar Pretzel Topping (recipe follows)

1. In a small bowl, combine ¼ cup (60 grams) warm water, yeast, and sugar. Let stand until mixture is foamy, about 5 minutes.
2. In the bowl of a stand mixer fitted with the dough hook attachment, beat flour, 1 cup (240 grams) water, pumpkin, salt, and allspice at low speed until combined. With mixer on medium speed, add yeast mixture, beating until a smooth dough forms and pulls away from sides of bowl, 4 to 5 minutes. If dough seems too sticky, add more flour, ¼ cup (31 grams) at a time. Alternatively, turn out dough onto a lightly floured surface, and knead by hand 40 to 50 times. (Dough should be on the tacky side, so don't add too much flour, or it can make the dough tougher.)
3. Spray a large bowl with cooking spray. Place dough in bowl, turning to grease top. Cover with plastic wrap, and let rise in a warm, draft-free place (75°F/24°C) until doubled in size, about 1 hour.
4. Line 2 baking sheets with parchment paper.
5. Divide dough into 12 equal pieces. Roll one piece of dough into an 18-inch-long rope by rolling from center of rope toward ends to gently lengthen. Bring ends of dough up to form a "U" shape, then bring ends down diagonally across bottom of pretzel. Where dough meets, wet with a small amount of water to help seal. Repeat with remaining dough. Place on prepared pans. Let rise in a warm, draft-free place (75°F/24°C) for 45 minutes.
6. Preheat oven to 400°F (200°C).
7. Bake for 12 to 15 minutes. Let cool for 3 minutes. Brush with melted butter while still warm, and sprinkle with Cinnamon Sugar Pretzel Topping.

CINNAMON SUGAR PRETZEL TOPPING
Makes about ½ cup

½ cup (100 grams) granulated sugar
2 teaspoons (4 grams) ground cinnamon

1. In a small bowl, stir together sugar and cinnamon until combined.

Photo by Kelsey Siemens

EGGNOG BABKA KNOTS

Makes 12 knots

Our favorite holiday quaff imbues these babka knots with warm notes of nutmeg and velvety vanilla custard. For an extra dose of holiday decadence, we made a rich Brandy Crème Anglaise as the perfect dunking sauce for our elegant babka twists.

¼   cup (60 grams) warm water (105°F/41°C to 110°F/43°C)
2¼   teaspoons (7 grams) active dry yeast
4¼   cups (531 grams) all-purpose flour
¼   cup (50 grams) granulated sugar
1½   teaspoons (4.5 grams) kosher salt
¾   cup (191 grams) warm eggnog (105°F/41°C to 110°F/43°C)
½   cup (113 grams) unsalted butter, melted
2   large eggs (100 grams), room temperature and divided
1   tablespoon (18 grams) vanilla bean paste*
1   teaspoon (4 grams) vanilla extract*
1   cup plus 2 tablespoons (248 grams) firmly packed light brown sugar
¼   teaspoon freshly ground nutmeg
¼   cup (57 grams) unsalted butter, softened
1   tablespoon (15 grams) cold water
Brandy Crème Anglaise (recipe follows)

1. In a small bowl, stir together ¼ cup (60 grams) warm water and yeast. Let stand until mixture is foamy, about 10 minutes.
2. In the bowl of a stand mixer fitted with the dough hook attachment, combine flour, granulated sugar, and salt. Add yeast mixture, warm eggnog, melted butter, 1 egg (50 grams), vanilla bean paste, and vanilla extract. With mixer on low speed, beat until dough comes together, 2 to 3 minutes. Continue beating until dough is smooth and elastic, about 8 minutes.
3. Spray a large bowl with cooking spray. Shape dough into a smooth round, and place in bowl, turning to grease top. Cover surface of dough with plastic wrap, and let rise in a warm, draft-free place (75°F/24°C) until doubled in size, 1 to 1½ hours.
4. Line 2 baking sheets with parchment paper.
5. On a lightly floured surface, divide dough into 12 (83-gram) pieces. Roll each piece into a 9x4½-inch rectangle.
6. In a small bowl, combine brown sugar and nutmeg. Spread 1 teaspoon (5 grams) butter onto each rectangle. Spoon 1½ tablespoons brown sugar mixture onto each rectangle.
7. Starting with one long side, roll up dough, jelly roll style, and place seam side down on surface. Using a bench scraper, cut each roll in half lengthwise. Shaping one at a time, cross

2 pieces in center, cut sides up, then twist pieces around each other tightly, pinching each end to seal. Form dough into a spiral with cut sides up, tucking and pinching end underneath roll to seal. Place at least 3 inches apart on prepared pans. Cover and let rise in a warm, draft-free place (75°F/24°C) for 45 minutes.
8. Preheat oven to 350°F (180°C).
9. In a small bowl, whisk together 1 tablespoon (15 grams) cold water and remaining 1 egg (50 grams). Brush eggwash onto knots.
10. Bake until an instant-read thermometer inserted in center registers 190°F (88°C), 16 to 18 minutes. (If you want your knots light in color like the ones pictured, cover with foil halfway through baking.) Let cool on pans for 10 minutes. Serve warm, or let cool completely on a wire rack. Serve with Brandy Crème Anglaise.

*We used Heilala Vanilla Extract and Vanilla Bean Paste.

BRANDY CRÈME ANGLAISE
Makes 2¾ cups

1   cup (240 grams) heavy whipping cream
1   cup (240 grams) whole milk
½   cup (100 grams) granulated sugar, divided
1   tablespoon (18 grams) vanilla bean paste
⅛   teaspoon flaked sea salt
5   large egg yolks (93 grams)
2   tablespoons (30 grams) brandy

1. In a medium saucepan, heat cream, milk, ¼ cup (50 grams) sugar, vanilla bean paste, and salt over medium-low heat, stirring frequently, just until steaming. (Do not boil.)
2. In a medium bowl, whisk together egg yolks and remaining ¼ cup (50 grams) sugar. Slowly pour about half of warm cream mixture into egg mixture, whisking constantly. Add egg mixture to remaining warm cream mixture, whisking to combine. Cook, whisking constantly, until mixture starts to thicken and coats the back of a spoon and an instant-read thermometer registers 180°F (82°C). Immediately pour anglaise into a fine-mesh sieve over a medium bowl. Place in an ice bath to cool quickly, or cover with a piece of plastic wrap, pressing wrap directly onto surface, and refrigerate until completely cool. Once cool, stir in brandy. Cover and refrigerate for up to 4 days.

ST. LUCIA BUNS

Makes 19 buns

These Swedish saffron buns are made with sour cream and vodka. The traditional version requires the saffron to infuse in vodka overnight so it can develop an intense color, but our method is much faster.

⅓ cup (67 grams) plus 1 tablespoon (12 grams) granulated sugar, divided
½ teaspoon saffron, lightly crushed
1 tablespoon (15 grams) vodka
⅔ cup (160 grams) plus 1 tablespoon (15 grams) whole milk, divided
1 tablespoon (9 grams) active dry yeast
⅓ cup (80 grams) sour cream, room temperature
2 large eggs (100 grams), room temperature and divided
4 cups (500 grams) all-purpose flour
1 tablespoon (9 grams) kosher salt
½ cup (113 grams) unsalted butter, softened
Garnish: Swedish pearl sugar*

1. Using a mortar and pestle, grind together 1 tablespoon (12 grams) granulated sugar and saffron. Place in a small bowl, and add vodka. Let stand for at least 20 minutes.
2. In a small saucepan, heat ⅔ cup (160 grams) milk and remaining ⅓ cup (67 grams) granulated sugar over low heat, stirring occasionally, until mixture registers 110°F (43°C) on an instant-read thermometer. Remove from heat. Whisk in yeast; let stand until mixture is foamy, about 10 minutes. Whisk in sour cream and 1 egg (50 grams); whisk in saffron mixture.

3. In a large bowl, combine flour and salt. In the bowl of a stand mixer fitted with the dough hook attachment, place yeast mixture. With mixer on low speed, gradually add half of flour mixture, beating until incorporated, 2 to 3 minutes. Add butter, 1 tablespoon (14 grams) at a time, letting each piece incorporate before adding the next, about 5 minutes, stopping to scrape sides of bowl as needed. Gradually add remaining flour mixture, beating until incorporated. Continue beating until dough is smooth and elastic, about 16 minutes.
4. Spray a large bowl with cooking spray. Shape dough into a smooth round, and place in bowl, turning to grease top. Cover and let rise in a warm, draft-free place (75°F/24°C) until doubled in size, about 1½ hours.
5. Line 2 baking sheets with parchment paper. Punch down dough, and turn out onto a lightly floured surface. Divide dough into 19 (50-gram) pieces. (Keep dough covered while shaping so it does not dry out.) Roll each portion into a 12- to 13-inch rope, letting ends taper. Roll each end into a tight spiral in opposite directions, meeting in the middle to create an "S" shape. Place at least 3 inches apart on prepared pans. Cover and let rise in a warm, draft-free place (75°F/24°C) for 45 minutes.
6. Preheat oven to 400°F (200°C).
7. In a small bowl, whisk together remaining 1 egg (50 grams) and remaining 1 tablespoon (15 grams) milk. Brush top and sides of each bun with egg wash. Top with pearl sugar, if desired.
8. Bake until golden brown, 7 to 10 minutes, rotating pans halfway through baking. Let cool on a wire rack. Store in an airtight container at room temperature for up to 4 days.

We used Lars Own Swedish Pearl Sugar.

PIES AND TARTS

PIES

A rich combo of flaky crust and sweet flavor-packed filling, pies are an all-American tradition. From an apple stunner to a triple chocolate icebox dream, find our classic and contemporary favorites here.

BANOFFEE PIE

Makes 1 (9-inch) pie

We incorporated two British standards into our take on this rich banana-topped treat. Normally served as an accompaniment to a strong cuppa, malted rich tea biscuits form our crumb crust while bergamot, the bitter citrus flavor behind Earl Grey tea, offers a complementary tang to the sticky toffee filling for a well-balanced and truly British bite.

1½	cups (195 grams) finely ground English rich tea biscuits*
4½	tablespoons (63 grams) firmly packed light brown sugar
¼	teaspoon kosher salt
7	tablespoons (98 grams) unsalted butter, melted

Bergamot Filling (recipe follows)

½	cup (100 grams) granulated sugar
¼	cup (60 grams) water
2	bananas (248 grams), cut into ½-inch slices

Sweetened Whipped Cream (recipe follows)
Garnish: chocolate curls

1. Preheat oven to 350°F (180°C). Lightly grease a 9-inch pie plate.

2. In a medium bowl, stir together ground biscuits, brown sugar, and salt. Add melted butter, stirring with a fork until moistened. Using the bottom of a measuring cup, press mixture into bottom and up sides of prepared plate.

3. Bake until lightly browned, 10 to 12 minutes. Let cool completely on a wire rack.

4. Pour warm Bergamot Filling into prepared crust. Let cool completely. Refrigerate for at least 8 hours.

5. In a small skillet, heat granulated sugar and ¼ cup (60 grams) water over medium-high heat. Cook, swirling pan occasionally (do not stir) and brushing sides of pan, until mixture begins to turn amber colored. Remove from heat. Add banana slices, a few at a time, and coat both sides with caramel, about 30 seconds. Remove bananas using a slotted spoon, and let cool on a parchment paper-lined baking sheet for 10 minutes.

6. Arrange caramelized banana slices over Bergamot Filling, and top with Sweetened Whipped Cream. Garnish with chocolate curls, if desired.

*We used McVitie's.

BERGAMOT FILLING
Makes about 2 cups

½	cup plus 2 tablespoons (150 grams) heavy whipping cream
½	cup plus 1 teaspoon (125 grams) sweetened condensed milk
1	cup (200 grams) granulated sugar
¾	cup (255 grams) golden syrup
¼	cup (60 grams) water
¼	cup (57 grams) unsalted butter, softened
3	tablespoons (39 grams) bergamot extract
1	teaspoon (3 grams) kosher salt

1. In a medium saucepan, heat cream and condensed milk over low heat, stirring frequently, just until bubbles form around edges of pan. (Do not boil.) Remove from heat, and keep warm.

2. In a large saucepan, heat sugar, golden syrup, and ¼ cup (60 grams) water over low heat, stirring occasionally, until sugar is dissolved. Increase heat to medium. Cook, without stirring, until mixture is amber colored and registers 240°F (116°C) on a candy thermometer. Remove from heat, and carefully stir in cream mixture. (Caramel will bubble up vigorously.) Return to heat, and cook, stirring constantly, until mixture registers 240°F (116°C) on a candy thermometer. Remove from heat. Stir in butter, bergamot extract, and salt. Use immediately.

SWEETENED WHIPPED CREAM
Makes about 2 cups

1	cup (240 grams) heavy whipping cream
2	tablespoons (14 grams) confectioners' sugar

1. In the bowl of a stand mixer fitted with the whisk attachment, beat cream and confectioners' sugar at high speed until stiff peaks form, 2 to 3 minutes. Use immediately.

RUSSIAN SALMON HAND PIES

Makes 6 hand pies

Recipe by Mandy Dixon

Alaskan pastry chef Mandy Dixon shapes her version of the Russian coulibiac (or pirok) into hand pies for dogsled drivers, known as mushers, to "grab and go" along the Iditarod Trail. This recipe can also be made in a jumbo muffin pan.

- tablespoon (14 grams) unsalted butter
- cup (95 grams) minced yellow onion
- clove garlic (5 grams), minced
- cup (100 grams) shredded green cabbage
- cup (62 grams) mushrooms, cleaned and torn
- teaspoon chopped fresh thyme
- teaspoon (1.5 grams) caraway seeds
- Kosher salt and ground black pepper, to taste
- pound (227 grams) Alaskan salmon, skinned and boned
- Puff Pastry (recipe follows)
- cup (75 grams) cooked short-grain brown rice
- medium egg (102 grams), hard-cooked and chopped
- cup (50 grams) shredded Manchego cheese

⅓ cup (45 grams) fine bread crumbs
¼ cup (60 grams) heavy whipping cream
1 medium egg (47 grams), beaten

1. Preheat oven to 375°F (190°C). Butter 6 (4-inch-round, 2-inch-high) ring molds.
2. In a large sauté pan, melt butter over low heat. Add onion and garlic; sauté until softened, about 7 minutes. Add cabbage, mushrooms, thyme, and caraway. Increase heat to medium; add more butter, if necessary. (Sometimes I sprinkle in a bit of water or chicken stock to create steam and help soften the cabbage.) Cook until cabbage and mushrooms are tender, about 6 minutes. Season with salt and pepper.
3. Poach, bake, grill, or pan-sear the salmon. Each of these techniques offers a little variation in flavor and texture. If you prepare the salmon any way other than poaching, I usually like to rub it with a good-quality olive oil and season with salt and pepper. This prevents the fish from sticking to the pan surface and protects the flesh from drying out before cooking. The salmon can be a little undercooked because it will cook additionally in the pie. Let salmon cool, and flake it into medium chunks.
4. On a lightly floured surface, roll out one sheet of Puff Pastry. Cover remaining sheet with a cloth or plastic wrap so it doesn't

dry out. Using a 5-inch round cutter, cut dough into 6 rounds, and place in prepared molds. Place a layer of rice onto pastry. Add chopped egg. Layer with salmon, cheese, bread crumbs, and cabbage mixture. (You can mix them all together if you want, but the layers look nice when you bite into the pie. The sequence of these events doesn't matter as much as your own personal taste. Some people feel very strongly about where the hard-cooked eggs are placed!) Season with salt and pepper. Pour cream over pies.
5. On a lightly floured surface, roll out remaining sheet of Puff Pastry. Using a 5-inch round cutter, cut dough into 6 rounds. Brush rims of filled pies with a little water, and place rounds on top of each pie. Crimp edges together to seal. (Some people do this with a fork or between two fingers to make a decorative edge. Use any leftover dough to cut out shapes, if desired.) Cut vents in top of dough to release steam. Brush dough with beaten egg.
6. Bake on top rack of oven until pastry is golden brown, 35 to 40 minutes. Serve warm.

PUFF PASTRY
Makes 2 sheets (or enough for 6 hand pies)

4 cups (508 grams) bread flour
2 teaspoons (6 grams) kosher salt
2 cups (454 grams) cold unsalted butter, cubed
½ cup (120 grams) cold water

1. In a large bowl, sift together flour and salt. Add cold butter, and rub flour and butter between your fingers. Make a well in center of flour mixture; pour in some cold water, mixing until you have a firm, rough dough, adding additional water if needed. Cover and refrigerate for about 20 minutes.
2. Turn out dough onto a lightly floured surface; knead gently. Roll dough into an 18x12-inch rectangle. Fold dough into thirds, like a letter. Turn dough 90 degrees. Roll dough into an 18x12-inch rectangle again. Fold dough into thirds, like a letter, again. Divide dough in half, and wrap in plastic wrap. Refrigerate for at least 20 minutes.

APPLE PIE

Makes 1 (9-inch) pie

The combination of spiced apple filling and buttery double crust is as close to simple perfection as a dessert can get. Remember, cold ingredients and limited handling of the dough create the flakiest crust.

Piecrust Dough (recipe follows)
⅓   cup (67 grams) granulated sugar
⅓   cup (73 grams) firmly packed light brown sugar
3   tablespoons (24 grams) cornstarch
1   teaspoon (2 grams) apple pie spice
¼   teaspoon kosher salt
4   cups (670 grams) sliced Gala or Fuji apples (about 2½ pounds)
1   tablespoon (15 grams) fresh lemon juice
1   large egg (50 grams)
1   tablespoon (15 grams) water

1. Preheat oven to 375°F (190°C).
2. Let Piecrust Dough stand at room temperature until slightly softened, about 15 minutes. On a lightly floured surface, roll half of dough into a 12-inch circle. Transfer to a 9-inch pie plate, pressing into bottom and up sides. Trim excess dough to ½ inch beyond edge of plate.
3. In a large bowl, whisk together sugars, cornstarch, apple pie spice, and salt. Add apples and lemon juice, tossing to coat. Spoon apple mixture into prepared crust.
4. On a lightly floured surface, roll remaining dough into a 12-inch circle. Using a sharp knife or a fluted pastry wheel, cut 6 (1-inch-wide) strips. Arrange strips in a lattice design on top of filling. Trim strips to ½ inch beyond edge of plate. Fold edges under, and crimp as desired.
5. In a small bowl, whisk together egg and 1 tablespoon (15 grams) water. Brush egg wash onto dough.
6. Bake until crust is golden brown and apples are tender, 50 to 60 minutes, loosely covering with foil after 30 minutes of baking to prevent excess browning.

Piecrust Dough
Makes 1 (9-inch) double crust

4   cups (500 grams) all-purpose flour
½   cup (100 grams) granulated sugar
½   teaspoon (1.5 grams) kosher salt
¾   cup (170 grams) cold unsalted butter, cubed
¾   cup (180 grams) ice water

1. In the work bowl of a food processor, place flour, sugar, and salt; pulse until combined. Add cold butter, and pulse until mixture is crumbly. With processor running, add ¾ cup (180 grams) ice water in a slow, steady stream until a dough forms.
2. Turn out dough onto a lightly floured surface, and divide in half. Shape each half into a disk, and wrap tightly in plastic wrap. Refrigerate for at least 30 minutes or overnight.

DOUBLE BERRY HAND PIES

Makes about 8 hand pies

Juicy hand pies bursting with a double berry filling are held together with a buttery strawberry-scented pie dough.

Strawberry Pie Dough (recipe follows)
1   cup (152 grams) quartered fresh strawberries
¾   cup (128 grams) fresh blueberries
2   tablespoons (28 grams) firmly packed light brown sugar
2   tablespoons (16 grams) all-purpose flour
1   teaspoon (1 gram) lemon zest
1   tablespoon (15 grams) fresh lemon juice
1   teaspoon chopped fresh thyme
¼   teaspoon kosher salt
1   large egg (50 grams)
1   tablespoon (15 grams) water
2   tablespoons (24 grams) turbinado sugar
Strawberry Balsamic Reduction (recipe follows)

1. Line 2 baking sheets with parchment paper.
2. Roll half of Strawberry Pie Dough to ⅛-inch thickness. Using a 4½-inch round cutter, cut dough, rerolling scraps only once. Repeat with remaining Strawberry Pie Dough. Place rounds between sheets of parchment paper, and refrigerate for 5 to 7 minutes.
3. In a medium bowl, stir together strawberries, blueberries, brown sugar, flour, lemon zest and juice, thyme, and salt. In a small bowl, whisk together egg and 1 tablespoon (15 grams) water. Brush edges of dough with egg wash. Place 1½ tablespoons berry mixture in center of half of rounds. Top with remaining rounds, and press edges with a fork to seal. Place on prepared pans, and freeze for 15 minutes.
4. Preheat oven to 375°F (190°C).
5. Brush frozen hand pies with egg wash, and sprinkle with turbinado sugar. Cut small vents in top of dough to release steam.
6. Bake until golden brown, about 20 minutes. Drizzle with Strawberry Balsamic Reduction. Serve warm.

STRAWBERRY PIE DOUGH
Makes dough for 8 hand pies

2½   cups (313 grams) all-purpose flour
½   cup (8 grams) freeze-dried strawberries
1   tablespoon (2 grams) fresh thyme leaves
1   teaspoon (3 grams) kosher salt
1   teaspoon (4 grams) granulated sugar
1   cup (227 grams) cold unsalted butter, cubed
4 to 8 tablespoons (60 to 120 grams) ice water

1. In the work bowl of a food processor, place flour, freeze-dried strawberries, thyme, salt, and sugar; process until well combined. Add cold butter, and pulse until mixture is crumbly. With processor running, add ice water, 1 tablespoon (15 grams) at a time, just until dough comes together.
2. Turn out dough onto a lightly floured surface, and divide in half. Shape each half into a disk, and wrap in plastic wrap. Refrigerate for at least 2 hours.

STRAWBERRY BALSAMIC REDUCTION
Makes about 1 cup

⅓   cup (80 grams) white balsamic vinegar
1⅓   cups (202 grams) quartered fresh strawberries
2   tablespoons (28 grams) firmly packed light brown sugar
¼   teaspoon kosher salt
¼   teaspoon lemon zest

1. In a small saucepan, bring vinegar to a boil over medium heat. Reduce heat to low; simmer until slightly thickened, 2 to 4 minutes. Stir in strawberries, brown sugar, salt, and zest. Increase heat to medium, and bring to a boil. Reduce heat to low; simmer until strawberries have released their juices and softened, about 5 minutes.
2. Using the back of a wooden spoon, crush strawberries against sides of pan. Continue simmering until sauce has thickened slightly. Remove from heat, and transfer to the container of a blender; purée until smooth. Let cool completely. Refrigerate in an airtight container for up to 6 days.

CARAMELIZED WHITE CHOCOLATE CHESS PIE

Makes 1 (9-inch) pie

Recipe by Jesse Szewczyk

Chess pie is delicious, but it's not always the prettiest—so dust the top of this baby in confectioners' sugar, and call it a day. Chess pie will form a crunchy top while it bakes. This is a sign of a good chess pie and to be expected, but it can also make the surface crack and sink. If you want your pie to have a flatter top, bake it in a water bath, and let cool in the warm oven before removing it.

Pie Dough (recipe follows)
½   cup (113 grams) unsalted butter, cubed
4   ounces (115 grams) Caramelized White Chocolate (recipe on page 371), coarsely chopped
1   cup (200 grams) granulated sugar
4   large eggs (200 grams)
2   tablespoons (18 grams) yellow cornmeal
1   teaspoon (4 grams) vanilla extract
¼   teaspoon kosher salt
1   tablespoon (7 grams) confectioners' sugar

1. Preheat oven to 350°F (180°C).
2. On a lightly floured surface, roll Pie Dough into a 12-inch circle. Transfer to a 9-inch pie pan, pressing into bottom and up sides. Trim excess dough to ½ inch beyond edge of pan. Fold edges under, and crimp as desired. Prick bottom of dough all over with a fork. Freeze for 15 minutes.
3. Top dough with a piece of parchment paper, letting ends extend over edges of pan. Add pie weights.
4. Bake for 15 minutes. Let cool completely on a wire rack. Reduce oven temperature to 325°F (170°C).

5. In the top of a double boiler, combine butter and Caramelized White Chocolate. Cook over simmering water, stirring frequently, until melted, about 5 minutes. Remove from heat; add granulated sugar, eggs, cornmeal, vanilla, and salt, whisking until smooth. Pour filling into prepared crust.
6. Bake until center is set and no longer jiggly, about 40 minutes. Let cool for 2 hours. To make a stripe pattern, lay 1-inch strips of parchment paper over pie. Dust with confectioners' sugar, and carefully remove parchment. Serve immediately, or refrigerate until ready to serve. Let stand at room temperature for 1 hour before serving.

PIE DOUGH
Makes 1 (9-inch) crust

1½   cups (188 grams) all-purpose flour
1   teaspoon (4 grams) granulated sugar
½   teaspoon (1.5 grams) kosher salt
½   cup (113 grams) unsalted butter, cubed
4 to 5 tablespoons (60 to 75 grams) cold water

1. In the work bowl of a food processor, place flour, sugar, and salt; pulse until combined. Add butter, and pulse until mixture is crumbly. With processor running, add cold water, 1 tablespoon (15 grams) at a time, just until a dry dough forms.
2. Turn out dough, and shape into a disk. Wrap in plastic wrap, and refrigerate for 1 hour.

Photo by Mark Weinberg

BERRIES AND CREAM PIE

Makes 1 (9-inch) pie

Recipe by Kate Wood

With a tangy buttermilk filling, pecan-laced crust, and sweet berry topping, this pie represents everything I've come to know and love about quintessentially Southern desserts. Berries fit perfectly with this pie, but peaches, plums, and dark cherries would be a great addition.

5   large egg yolks (93 grams)
¼   cup plus 6 tablespoons (122 grams) granulated sugar, divided
2½   tablespoons (20 grams) cornstarch
½   teaspoon (1.5 grams) kosher salt
2¾   cups (660 grams) heavy whipping cream, divided
⅔   cup (160 grams) whole buttermilk
1   teaspoon (6 grams) vanilla bean paste
¾   teaspoon lemon zest
     Graham Cracker-Pecan Crust (recipe follows)
1   cup (170 grams) mixed fresh berries, hulled, washed, and dried

1. In a medium bowl, whisk together egg yolks, ¼ cup plus 3 tablespoons (86 grams) sugar, cornstarch, and salt.

2. In a medium saucepan, bring 1¾ cups (420 grams) cream, buttermilk, and vanilla bean paste to a simmer over medium-low heat, whisking occasionally. Slowly drizzle a small amount of hot cream mixture into egg mixture, whisking constantly. Slowly add remaining hot cream mixture to egg mixture, whisking constantly. Pour mixture back into saucepan, and cook, stirring constantly, until slightly thickened (about the consistency of mayonnaise), about 4 minutes. Remove from heat; stir in zest. Let cool for 10 minutes, stirring frequently.

3. Pour filling into prepared Graham Cracker-Pecan Crust, smoothing top with an offset spatula. Cover with a piece of plastic wrap, pressing wrap directly onto surface of filling to prevent a skin from forming. Refrigerate overnight.

4. In the bowl of a stand mixer fitted with the paddle attachment, beat remaining 1 cup (240 grams) cream and remaining 3 tablespoons (36 grams) sugar at medium-high speed until stiff peaks form. Spread whipped cream onto pie. Top with berries. Refrigerate until ready to serve.

GRAHAM CRACKER-PECAN CRUST
Makes 1 (9-inch) crust

1   cup (130 grams) finely crushed graham crackers
¾   cup (85 grams) finely chopped pecans
¼   cup (50 grams) granulated sugar
½   teaspoon (1.5 grams) kosher salt
7   tablespoons (98 grams) unsalted butter, melted

1. Preheat oven to 350°F (180°C).
2. In a medium bowl, stir together graham crackers, pecans, sugar, and salt. Add melted butter, and stir until mixture comes together in a wet sand consistency. Pat mixture into bottom and halfway up sides of a 9-inch springform pan*.
3. Bake until set, 8 to 10 minutes. Let cool completely in pan. Remove ring to release crust.

*This crust can also be made in a 9-inch pie plate. Pat mixture all the way up sides of plate.

FRIED APPLE HAND PIES

Makes about 20 hand pies

It is a truth universally acknowledged in the Deep South: Everything is better fried. Apple pie is no exception. These half-moon pastries take all that is good about the original and add a hefty dose of crispy, crunchy (and cinnamon sugar-coated) crust by deep-frying them.

1⅓ cups (267 grams) granulated sugar, divided

⅓ cup (73 grams) firmly packed light brown sugar

3 tablespoons (24 grams) cornstarch

1 teaspoon (3 grams) apple pie spice

¼ teaspoon kosher salt

4 cups (525 grams) diced peeled Gala or Fuji apples (about 2½ pounds)

1 tablespoon (15 grams) fresh lemon juice

Piecrust Dough (recipe on page 210)

1 large egg (50 grams)
1 tablespoon (15 grams) water
1 gallon (3,790 grams) peanut oil
1 tablespoon (6 grams) ground cinnamon

1. In a large skillet, whisk together ⅓ cup (67 grams) granulated sugar, brown sugar, cornstarch, apple pie spice, and salt. Add apples and lemon juice, tossing to coat. Cook over medium heat until apples are tender and filling is thickened, about 20 minutes. Let cool for 10 minutes.

2. Let Piecrust Dough stand at room temperature until slightly softened, about 15 minutes. On a lightly floured surface, roll half of dough to ⅛-inch thickness. Using a 4½-inch round cutter, cut dough, rerolling scraps only once. Repeat with remaining dough.

3. In a small bowl, whisk together egg and 1 tablespoon (15 grams) water. Brush edges of dough with egg wash. Place 2 teaspoons filling in center of each round. Fold dough over filling. Crimp from center to edges, gently pressing in any filling as you go. Pick up and pinch edges to seal. Freeze for 20 minutes.

4. In a large stockpot, heat oil over medium-high heat until a deep-fry thermometer registers 360°F (182°C). Place paper towels on a wire rack.

5. In a small bowl, whisk together cinnamon and remaining 1 cup (200 grams) granulated sugar.

6. Working in batches, fry hand pies until golden brown, 5 to 7 minutes. Carefully remove from hot oil, and immediately toss in cinnamon sugar mixture. Let drain on prepared rack. Serve warm.

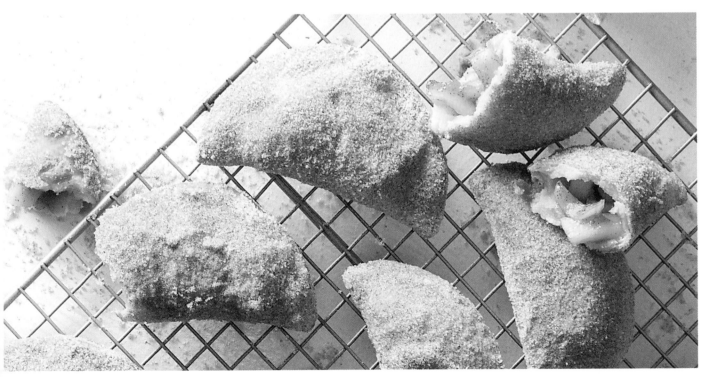

BALSAMIC FIG & RASPBERRY HAND PIES

Makes 12 hand pies

Recipe by Marian Cooper Cairns

Come for the crisp, buttery crust, stay for the jammy filling. This hand pie, which combines tart raspberries, juicy figs, and acidic balsamic vinegar, packs a lot into one neat pastry package.

3½ cups (438 grams) all-purpose flour
½   cup (100 grams) plus 1 tablespoon (12 grams) granulated sugar, divided, plus more for sprinkling
1¾ teaspoons (4.5 grams) kosher salt, divided
1   cup (227 grams) cold unsalted butter, cubed
¼   cup (57 grams) cold all-vegetable shortening, cubed
2   large eggs (100 grams), divided
⅓   cup (80 grams) ice water
1½ tablespoons (12 grams) cornstarch
2   cups (220 grams) chopped fresh figs
1½ cups (195 grams) fresh raspberries
3   tablespoons (45 grams) fresh orange juice
1   tablespoon (15 grams) balsamic vinegar
1   teaspoon (4 grams) vanilla extract

1. In a large bowl, stir together flour, 1 tablespoon (12 grams) sugar, and 1½ teaspoons (4.5 grams) salt. Using a pastry blender, cut in cold butter and cold shortening until mixture is crumbly.
2. In a small bowl, whisk together 1 egg (50 grams) and ⅓ cup (80 grams) ice water. Gradually add egg mixture to flour mixture, stirring with a fork just until dough begins to form a ball and pull away from sides of bowl. (Add more water, 1 tablespoon [15 grams] at a time, if needed.)
3. Divide dough into 12 portions, and shape each portion into a ball. On a lightly floured surface, flatten each ball, and roll into a 6-inch circle. Stack circles between layers of parchment paper. Wrap in plastic wrap, and refrigerate for at least 2 hours or up to 24 hours.
4. In a small saucepan, whisk together cornstarch and remaining ½ cup (100 grams) sugar. Stir in figs, raspberries, orange juice, vinegar, and remaining ¼ teaspoon salt. Cook over medium-low heat, stirring frequently, until mixture comes to a boil and is thickened, 5 to 7 minutes. Remove from heat, and stir in vanilla. Let cool completely.

5. Preheat oven to 425°F (220°C). Line 2 baking sheets with parchment paper.
6. In a small bowl, whisk remaining 1 egg (50 grams). Working with 1 circle at a time, brush edges of dough with egg wash. Spoon 2 rounded tablespoonfuls fig mixture onto center of each dough circle; fold dough over filling. Press edges together with a fork to seal. Trim rough edges with a pastry cutter. Place on prepared pans. Brush pies with egg wash, and sprinkle with additional sugar. Freeze for 20 minutes.
7. Bake until crust is golden brown, 22 to 25 minutes, rotating pans once. Let cool on a wire rack for 15 minutes before serving.

MAKE AHEAD
You can form the hand pies and freeze up to 3 days in advance. Just increase the bake time by a few minutes until crust is golden and filling is bubbly.

Photo by Matt Armendariz

TRIPLE CHOCOLATE PIE

Makes 1 (10-inch) deep-dish pie

Recipe by Kate Wood

Some days require chocolate; others call for triple chocolate. A crunchy, press-in crust is filled with a silky bittersweet chocolate custard and a fluffy, cocoa-scented Swiss meringue topping. It's a chocolate lover's dream, and I would know—I come from a long line of them.

2 cups (400 grams) granulated sugar, divided
6 tablespoons (48 grams) all-purpose flour
½ teaspoon (1.5 grams) kosher salt
3 cups (720 grams) whole milk
4 large egg yolks (74 grams), lightly beaten
6 ounces (175 grams) bittersweet chocolate, chopped
3 tablespoons (42 grams) unsalted butter
2½ teaspoons (10 grams) vanilla extract, divided
Chocolate Crust (recipe follows)
4 large egg whites (120 grams)
¼ teaspoon cream of tartar
2 tablespoons (10 grams) cocoa powder

1. In a medium saucepan, whisk together 1 cup (200 grams) sugar, flour, and salt. Slowly whisk in milk. Cook over medium heat, whisking constantly, until mixture is bubbly and thickened. Cook 2 minutes more.
2. Place egg yolks in a medium bowl. Slowly drizzle ½ cup hot milk mixture into egg yolks, whisking constantly. Whisk in remaining hot milk mixture. Return mixture to saucepan, and cook, stirring constantly, until mixture thickens, 5 to 10 minutes. Remove from heat; add chocolate, butter, and 1½ teaspoons (6 grams) vanilla, stirring until smooth. Pour filling into prepared Chocolate Crust. Cover with a piece of plastic wrap, pressing wrap directly onto surface of filling to prevent a skin from forming. Refrigerate overnight, or freeze for at least 3 hours.
3. In the top of a double boiler, whisk together egg whites, cream of tartar, remaining 1 cup (200 grams) sugar, and remaining 1 teaspoon (4 grams) vanilla. Cook over simmering water, stirring constantly with a spatula, until sugar is dissolved, about 6 minutes. Transfer mixture to the bowl of a stand mixer fitted with the whisk attachment; beat at high speed until medium-stiff peaks form, about 5

minutes. Fold in cocoa. Place large dollops of meringue on top of pie. Spread meringue just barely to edges of crust to prevent weeping. Using a kitchen torch, carefully brown meringue, or bake in a 500°F (260°C) oven until topping is browned, about 5 minutes. Serve immediately.

CHOCOLATE CRUST
Makes 1 (10-inch) deep-dish crust

1¼ cups (250 grams) granulated sugar
¾ cup (64 grams) dark cocoa powder
⅔ cup (83 grams) all-purpose flour
¼ teaspoon kosher salt
½ cup (113 grams) unsalted butter, melted

1. Preheat oven to 325°F (170°C).
2. In a medium bowl, whisk together sugar, cocoa, flour, and salt. Add melted butter, and stir with a spatula just until combined into large, moist clumps. Pat mixture into a tall-sided 10-inch fluted removable-bottom tart pan. Gently press mixture up sides first; pat remaining mixture into bottom.
3. Bake until set, 8 to 10 minutes. Let cool completely.

BLACK BOTTOM PEANUT BUTTER ICEBOX PIE

Makes 1 (9-inch) deep-dish pie

Recipe by Kate Wood

I've enjoyed my fair share of diner-style peanut butter pie, and this rich version pays homage to those early slices from my childhood. The brown sugar-pretzel crust really amps up the sweet and salty factor—always a plus in my book.

1½   cups (150 grams) finely crushed salted pretzels
¼   cup (55 grams) firmly packed light brown sugar
½   teaspoon (1.5 grams) kosher salt
½   cup (113 grams) unsalted butter, melted
5   ounces (150 grams) semisweet chocolate, chopped
2   cups plus 2 tablespoons (510 grams) heavy whipping cream, divided
8   ounces (225 grams) cream cheese, room temperature
1   cup (256 grams) creamy peanut butter
1   cup (120 grams) confectioners' sugar

1. Preheat oven to 350°F (180°C).
2. In a large bowl, stir together crushed pretzels, brown sugar, and salt. Add melted butter, and stir until mixture comes together in a wet sand consistency. Pat mixture into bottom of a 9-inch deep-dish pie plate.
3. Bake until set, 8 to 10 minutes. Let cool completely.
4. Place chocolate in a small heatproof bowl. In a medium saucepan, heat ½ cup plus 2 tablespoons (150 grams) cream over medium heat, stirring frequently, just until bubbles form around edges of pan. (Do not boil.) Pour hot cream over chocolate. Cover tightly with a piece of plastic wrap; let stand for 5 minutes. Uncover and whisk until smooth. If large pieces of chocolate remain, microwave on low in 15-second intervals, stirring between each, until smooth. Pour ganache into prepared crust, smoothing to edges. Freeze until firm, at least 2 hours.
5. In the bowl of a stand mixer fitted with the whisk attachment, beat remaining 1½ cups (360 grams) cream at low speed until stiff peaks form. Transfer to a medium bowl; set aside.
6. Clean bowl of stand mixer. Using the paddle attachment, beat cream cheese, peanut butter, and confectioners' sugar at medium-high speed until smooth and creamy. Add about ½ cup whipped cream, and beat to combine. Fold in remaining whipped cream. Spread filling onto ganache. Freeze until firm, at least 1 hour or until ready to serve. (This pie can also be served at room temperature, if desired.)

BRÛLÉED KEY LIME PIES

Makes 4 (4½-inch) pies

Recipe by Kate Wood

I made these mini pies for my dad on his birthday last year in honor of his two favorite desserts, crème brûlée and Key lime pie. The burnt sugar topping complements the tart pie filling and adds a touch of surprise to what is an otherwise simple dessert. For best results, make these pies ahead of time and brûlée them just before serving.

cup (130 grams) finely crushed graham crackers

3 tablespoons (42 grams) firmly packed light brown sugar

½ teaspoon (1.5 grams) kosher salt
¼ cup (57 grams) unsalted butter, melted
4 large egg yolks (74 grams)
1 (14-ounce) can (396 grams) sweetened condensed milk
1½ teaspoons (1.5 grams) Key lime zest
½ cup (120 grams) fresh Key lime juice
¼ cup (50 grams) granulated sugar

1. Preheat oven to 350°F (180°C). Butter and flour 4 (4½-inch) removable-bottom tart pans.

2. In the work bowl of a food processor, place crushed graham crackers, brown sugar, and salt; pulse until fine crumbs remain. Add melted butter, and pulse to combine. Divide mixture among prepared pans, pressing into bottoms and up sides. Place tart pans on a small baking sheet.

3. Bake until set, 8 to 10 minutes. Let cool slightly.

4. In a medium bowl, whisk egg yolks vigorously until slightly thickened and pale in color, 1 to 2 minutes. Add condensed milk and Key lime zest and juice, whisking to combine. Divide mixture among prepared crusts.

5. Bake until outer edges of pies have set, 11 to 12 minutes. Refrigerate until cold, 1 to 2 hours. Carefully unmold pies, and sprinkle tops with granulated sugar. Using a kitchen torch, carefully brûlée tops. Let stand for 3 to 4 minutes before serving.

BANANA COCONUT CREAM PIE

Makes 1 (9-inch) deep-dish pie

Recipe by Kate Wood

This Banana Coconut Cream Pie is perfect for the home baker who doesn't want to choose between two Southern favorites. I like this pie topped with a cloud of whipped cream and fresh banana slices, and a sprinkle of toasted coconut is great here as well.

1¼   cups (250 grams) granulated sugar, divided
6   tablespoons (48 grams) all-purpose flour
½   teaspoon (1.5 grams) kosher salt
2⅔   cups (640 grams) whole milk
4   large egg yolks (74 grams), lightly beaten
3   tablespoons (42 grams) unsalted butter
2½   teaspoons (10 grams) vanilla extract, divided
1   cup (60 grams) sweetened flaked coconut
2   large ripe bananas (248 grams), sliced
Vanilla-Coconut Crust (recipe follows)
1½   cups (360 grams) heavy whipping cream
Garnish: sliced banana

1. In a medium saucepan, whisk together 1 cup (200 grams) sugar, flour, and salt. Slowly whisk in milk. Cook over medium heat, whisking constantly, until mixture is bubbly and thickened. Cook 2 minutes more.
2. Place egg yolks in a small bowl. Slowly drizzle about 1 cup hot milk mixture into egg yolks, whisking constantly. Pour egg mixture into remaining hot milk mixture in saucepan, and cook for 1 to 2 minutes, stirring constantly. Add butter and 1½ teaspoons (6 grams) vanilla, stirring until combined. Stir in coconut. Let cool at room temperature for 10 minutes.
3. Layer banana slices in bottom of prepared Vanilla-Coconut Crust. Spoon filling over bananas. Cover with a piece of plastic wrap, pressing wrap directly onto surface of filling to prevent a skin from forming. Refrigerate for at least 4 hours. For best results, refrigerate overnight.
4. In the bowl of a stand mixer fitted with the whisk attachment, beat cream at medium speed until soft peaks form. Add remaining ¼ cup (50 grams) sugar and remaining 1 teaspoon (4 grams) vanilla, and beat until thickened and cloud-like. Spread whipped cream onto filling. Top with banana slices, if desired.

VANILLA-COCONUT CRUST

Makes 1 (9-inch) deep-dish crust

50   vanilla wafers (185 grams)
¾   cup (45 grams) sweetened flaked coconut
⅛   teaspoon kosher salt
6   tablespoons (84 grams) unsalted butter, melted

1. Preheat oven to 350°F (180°C). Line a 9-inch square baking dish with parchment paper, letting excess extend over sides of pan.
2. In the work bowl of a food processor, place vanilla wafers, coconut, and salt; pulse until fine crumbs remain. Add melted butter, and pulse to combine. Press mixture into bottom and halfway up sides of prepared pan.
3. Bake until set, about 8 minutes. Let cool completely. Using excess parchment as handles, gently remove crust.

Note: *I used a square baking dish, but this recipe will also work in a standard round deep-dish pie plate.*

HUMMINGBIRD PIE

Makes 1 (9-inch) pie

In this twist on the classic cake, billowy peaks of homemade Buttermilk Whipped Cream blanket a silky yellow custard.

- cup (240 grams) coconut milk, room temperature
- cup (240 grams) pineapple juice
- large egg yolks (74 grams), room temperature
- large egg (50 grams), room temperature
- ½ cup (100 grams) granulated sugar
- tablespoons (24 grams) cornstarch
- teaspoon (1.5 grams) kosher salt
- tablespoons (28 grams) unsalted butter, cubed
- tablespoons (30 grams) light rum
- medium bananas (282 grams), sliced ¼ inch thick

Pecan Piecrust (recipe follows)
Buttermilk Whipped Cream (recipe follows)

1. In a medium saucepan, heat coconut milk and pineapple juice over medium heat, stirring frequently, just until bubbles form around edges of pan. (Do not boil.) Remove from heat.

2. In a medium bowl, whisk together egg yolks, egg, sugar, cornstarch, and salt. Gradually add hot milk mixture to egg mixture, whisking constantly. Return mixture to saucepan, and cook, whisking constantly, until thickened. Pour through a fine-mesh sieve into a medium bowl, discarding solids. Stir in butter and rum until butter is melted. Cover with a piece of plastic wrap, pressing wrap directly onto surface of cream to prevent a skin from forming. Refrigerate overnight.

3. Place banana slices in two even layers in bottom of prepared Pecan Piecrust. Pour pineapple-coconut cream over banana slices, smoothing top with an offset spatula. Refrigerate for 1 to 2 hours. Top with Buttermilk Whipped Cream before serving.

PECAN PIECRUST

Makes 1 (9-inch) crust

- 1½ cups (188 grams) all-purpose flour
- ½ cup (57 grams) pecan halves
- 1½ teaspoons (6 grams) granulated sugar
- 1 teaspoon (2 grams) ground cinnamon
- ½ teaspoon (1.5 grams) kosher salt
- ½ teaspoon (1 gram) ground nutmeg
- ½ cup (113 grams) cold unsalted butter, cubed
- ¼ cup (60 grams) ice water

1. In the work bowl of a food processor, place flour, pecans, sugar, cinnamon, salt, and nutmeg; process until combined. Add cold butter, and pulse until mixture is crumbly. With processor running, add ¼ cup (60 grams) ice water in a slow, steady stream just until dough comes together. (Mixture may appear crumbly. It should be moist and hold together when pinched.) Shape dough into a disk, and wrap tightly in plastic wrap. Refrigerate for at least 30 minutes.

2. On a lightly floured surface, roll dough into a 12-inch circle. Transfer to a 9-inch pie plate, pressing into bottom and up sides. Trim excess dough to ½ inch beyond edge of plate. Fold edges under, and crimp as desired. Using a fork, prick bottom of crust. Freeze for 20 minutes.

3. Preheat oven to 350°F (180°C).

4. Top dough with a piece of parchment paper, letting ends extend over edges of plate. Add pie weights.

5. Bake until edges are set and golden, 15 to 20 minutes. Carefully remove paper and weights. Bake until bottom of crust is lightly golden, about 10 minutes more. Let cool completely.

BUTTERMILK WHIPPED CREAM

Makes about 1½ cups

- 1 cup (240 grams) heavy whipping cream, room temperature
- ½ cup (120 grams) whole buttermilk, room temperature
- 2 tablespoons (24 grams) granulated sugar
- ¼ teaspoon kosher salt

1. In the bowl of a stand mixer fitted with the whisk attachment, beat all ingredients at medium-high speed until stiff peaks form, 2 to 3 minutes. Use immediately.

Photo by Stephen DeVries

TARTS

With a base crust and a simple yet decadent filling, our tarts—featuring everything from pomegranate to treacle to creamy milk chocolate—imbue a singular elegance that brings effortless glamour to any and all occasions.

CUSTARD TART

Makes 1 (9-inch) tart

Recipe by Edd Kimber

When I was young, I lived in a small village called Thackley. When my family and I would pay the town bakery a visit, I would get the same thing every time: a custard tart. It is a love from childhood that has endured; a simple custard tart will always be a nostalgic pleasure for me. Just don't skimp on the nutmeg!

1¾ cups plus 1 tablespoon (226 grams) plain flour/cake flour
⅔ cup (150 grams) unsalted butter
¼ cup (50 grams) castor sugar
⅛ teaspoon kosher salt
1 large egg (50 grams)
1 large egg yolk (19 grams)
Custard Filling (recipe follows)
1 whole nutmeg

1. Place flour and butter in a large bowl. Using your fingertips, gently rub butter into flour until mixture is crumbly. Add sugar and salt, stirring to combine. Make a well in center of flour mixture; add egg. Using a fork, gently stir egg into flour mixture until dough starts to come together. Using your hands, gently knead dough until smooth. Wrap dough in cling film (plastic wrap), and refrigerate until firm, about 1 hour.
2. Lightly grease a 9-inch removable-bottom tart pan. Line a baking sheet with parchment paper.
3. On a lightly floured surface, roll dough into a 12-inch circle, ¼ inch thick. Transfer to prepared tart pan, pressing into bottom and up sides, letting excess drape over pan. Place on prepared baking sheet. Refrigerate until firm, about 30 minutes. (This will help the pastry keep its shape while baking.)
4. Preheat oven to 350°F (180°F).
5. Top dough with a piece of crumpled parchment paper, letting ends extend over edges of pan. Add pie weights.
6. Bake for 20 minutes. Carefully remove paper and weights. Bake until lightly browned, about 5 minutes more. Using a pastry brush, coat inside of crust with egg yolk. Bake until dried out, about 2 minutes more. (The egg yolk creates a nice seal so that the liquid in the filling can't make the pastry soggy.) Leave tart in oven. Reduce oven temperature to 265°F (129°C).
7. Carefully pour Custard Filling into prepared crust. Generously grate nutmeg over entire tart.
8. Bake until set around the edges but still slightly jiggly in center, 30 to 40 minutes. Let cool completely on a wire rack. Trim excess pastry, and remove from pan. Serve immediately.

CUSTARD FILLING
Makes about 3 cups

1½ cups (360 grams) single cream/half-and-half
Scant ½ cup (120 grams) whole milk
2 teaspoons (8 grams) vanilla extract or 1 vanilla pod/bean, split lengthwise, seeds scraped and reserved
8 large egg yolks (149 grams)
½ cup (100 grams) castor sugar

1. In a medium saucepan, heat half-and-half and milk over medium heat. Add vanilla extract or vanilla pod and reserved seeds, and bring to a simmer.
2. In a medium bowl, whisk together egg yolks and sugar. Pour hot cream mixture over yolks, whisking constantly. Remove vanilla pod before using.

Photo by Yuki Sugiura

YORKSHIRE CURD TART

Makes 1 (8-inch) tart

Recipe by Paul A. Young

I adapted my grandmother's recipe by introducing a buttery pastry and added melted butter to enrich the filling. I'm catapulted back to my childhood with every bite. To make the curds, you would traditionally leave milk out for one week, opening the lid of the bottle daily. Here, I use full-fat cottage cheese instead.

3½ cups (750 grams) full-fat cottage cheese

2 medium free-range eggs (94 grams)

½ cup (100 grams) plus ⅓ cup (67 grams) unrefined golden castor sugar, divided

½ teaspoon (1 gram) ground nutmeg

¼ teaspoon ground cinnamon

¼ teaspoon ground mace

½ cup (100 grams) currants

¼ cup (57 grams) unsalted butter, melted

¾ cup (170 grams) unsalted butter, softened

2 medium egg yolks (34 grams)

2 tablespoons (30 grams) warm water (105°F/41°C to 110°F/43°C)

2 cups (250 grams) plain flour/cake flour

Pinch ground nutmeg, for sprinkling

1. Place cottage cheese in a fine-mesh sieve. Run under cold water for about 1 minute to get as much liquid out of the curds as possible. Let curds strain in refrigerator overnight.

2. To make the filling, lightly whisk together eggs, ½ cup (100 grams) sugar, nutmeg, cinnamon, and mace. Add currants, and mix in ¼ cup (57 grams) melted butter and 2¼ cups (400 grams) curds. Place aside to let rest for 1 hour.

3. To make the pastry, cream together ¾ cup (170 grams) softened butter and remaining ⅓ cup (67 grams) sugar with a wooden spoon until light in color. Add yolks, and mix well. Gradually add 2 tablespoons (30 grams) warm water. Add flour, and mix until a soft paste is formed. It will be too soft to roll, so scoop out, and wrap in cling film (plastic wrap) and flatten, and refrigerate for 1 hour.

4. Unwrap dough, and on a lightly floured surface, roll out to ⅛-inch thickness. Transfer to an 8-inch tart ring, allowing pastry to hang over edge. Refrigerate for 20 minutes.

5. Preheat oven to 350°F (180°C).

6. Bake until golden, 20 to 25 minutes. (I use 4 layers of cling film [plastic wrap] layered into the lined tart and fill with

uncooked rice to bake blind.) Lift out baking beans/rice, and bake to dry out base and turn lightly golden in oven. If you see any small holes in base, use some leftover pastry to fill them in.

7. Mix curd filling, and pour into baked tart case. Sprinkle nutmeg over, and bake until golden and wobbly, 15 to 20 minutes. Trim off any excess pastry, and allow to cool until cold. Remove tart ring, and simply cut and serve. Allow tart to cool thoroughly. I find it tastes much better the next day, if you can wait that long. Serve at room temperature.

Note: *If you would like to get the curds for this tart using the traditional method, omit cottage cheese. In step 1, leave 6 cups (1,440 grams) whole milk (not homogenized, if you can get it) out for 1 week, opening lid of bottle daily. Strain through a fine-mesh sieve, leaving curds behind.*

Photo by Yuki Sugiura

EGGNOG CUSTARD TART

Makes 1 (9-inch) tart

Browned Butter lends nutty depth to the shortbread crust of this indulgent dessert. A dash of spiced rum gives the creamy eggnog custard a little kick. We'd remind you this is best enjoyed the da y of, but you won't be able to resist having a slice (or two or three) once it's out of the oven anyway.

Browned Butter (recipe follows), softened
⅓   cup (40 grams) confectioners' sugar
¾   teaspoon (3 grams) vanilla extract*
½   teaspoon (1.5 grams) kosher salt
1½ cups (188 grams) all-purpose flour
Eggnog Custard Filling (recipe follows)
Grated fresh nutmeg and grated fresh
     cinnamon, for dusting
Garnish: white chocolate curls (see Note)

1. In the bowl of a stand mixer fitted with the paddle attachment, beat Browned Butter at low speed until smooth, about 1 minute. Add confectioners' sugar, vanilla, and salt, beating until combined, stopping to scrape sides of bowl. Gradually add flour, beating until combined and dough comes together, 3 to 4 minutes.
2. Press dough into a 9-inch removable-bottom tart pan. Gently press dough into bottom and up sides of pan until smooth and even. Freeze for 30 minutes.
3. Preheat oven to 350°F (180°C). Line a baking sheet with parchment paper.
4. Remove tart pan from freezer. Place tart pan on prepared baking sheet.
5. Bake until light golden brown around the edges, 15 to 20 minutes. While crust is still warm, gently flatten any puffed areas with the back of a spoon. Let cool completely on a wire rack.
6. Pour warm Eggnog Custard Filling into prepared crust. Generously dust with nutmeg and cinnamon.
7. Bake until set around the edges but still slightly jiggly in center, 25 to 30 minutes. Let cool completely on a wire rack. Garnish with white chocolate curls, if desired. This tart is best enjoyed the day it is baked.

We used Heilala Vanilla Extract.

Note: *To create white chocolate curls, use a vegetable peeler to shave off thin pieces of a room temperature block of white chocolate. We used Callebaut White Chocolate.*

BROWNED BUTTER
Makes ¾ cup

¾   cup (170 grams) unsalted butter

1. In a medium saucepan, melt butter over medium heat. Cook, stirring constantly, until butter turns a medium-brown color and has a nutty aroma, 7 to 10 minutes. Immediately transfer to a small bowl; let cool completely. Refrigerate until ready to use.

EGGNOG CUSTARD FILLING
Makes 2 cups

1   cup (240 grams) half-and-half
½   cup (120 grams) whole milk
1   tablespoon (15 grams) dark spiced rum
2   teaspoons (8 grams) vanilla extract*
6   large egg yolks (112 grams)
⅓   cup (67 grams) castor sugar (see Note)

1. In a medium saucepan, heat half-and-half, milk, rum, and vanilla over medium heat, stirring frequently, just until bubbles form around edges of pan. (Do not boil.) Remove from heat.
2. In a medium bowl, whisk together egg yolks and sugar. Slowly pour in hot milk mixture, whisking constantly. Strain mixture through a fine-mesh sieve. Use immediately.

We used Heilala Vanilla Extract.

Note: *To make castor sugar, in the container of a blender or the work bowl of a food processor, blend or pulse ⅓ cup (67 grams) granulated sugar in short bursts, 2 to 3 times, until sugar becomes superfine. If sugar reaches a powdery consistency, you've gone too far.*

ASSAM TREACLE TART

Makes 1 (9-inch) tart

A standard of British baking, treacle tart is known for its simple but delicious bread crumb, golden syrup, and lemon-scented filling. In this aromatic twist on Harry Potter's favorite dessert, Assam-infused pastry balances the classic, gooey treacle filling.

Assam Tart Dough (recipe follows)
1   **large egg (50 grams)**
1   **tablespoon (15 grams) heavy whipping cream**
1¾ **cups (591 grams) golden syrup**
4¼ **cups (155 grams) fresh white bread crumbs**
¼   **cup (12 grams) lemon zest**
¼   **cup (60 grams) fresh lemon juice**

1. Preheat oven to 375°F (190°C). Butter and flour a 9-inch tart pan. Line a large plate with parchment paper.

2. On a lightly floured surface, roll two-thirds of Assam Tart Dough into a 12-inch circle. Transfer to prepared pan, pressing into bottom and up sides. Roll remaining dough to ⅛-inch thickness. Using a sharp knife, cut dough into 1x¼-inch rectangles. Place on prepared plate.
3. In a small bowl, whisk together egg and cream. Brush egg wash onto crust. Prick crust with a fork 6 times.
4. In a medium saucepan, heat golden syrup over medium-low heat until melted. (Do not boil.) Add bread crumbs and lemon zest and juice, stirring until combined. Pour filling into prepared crust. Top with rectangles in desired pattern. Brush egg wash onto rectangles.
5. Bake until crust is golden brown and filling is set, 30 to 35 minutes, covering with foil halfway through baking to prevent excess browning, if necessary. Serve warm or cold. Cover and refrigerate for up to 4 days.

ASSAM TART DOUGH
Makes 1 (9-inch) crust and lattice

3   **cups (375 grams) all-purpose flour**
1   **tablespoon (6 grams) Assam loose tea**
¾   **teaspoon (2.25 grams) kosher salt**
¾   **cup (170 grams) cold unsalted butter, cubed**
⅓   **cup (80 grams) ice water**

1. In the work bowl of a food processor, place flour, loose tea, and salt; pulse until combined. Add cold butter, and pulse until mixture is crumbly. With processor running, add ⅓ cup (80 grams) ice water in a slow, steady stream until dough comes together. Wrap in plastic wrap, and refrigerate for at least 30 minutes.

POMEGRANATE CRANBERRY CURD TART

Makes 1 (9-inch) tart

Velvety smooth cranberry curd finds the perfect complement in a Salty Peanut Crust. A halo of pomegranate arils adds another layer of tart, juicy flavor and a touch of glowing wintry charm.

2 cups (224 grams) frozen cranberries
1 cup (200 grams) granulated sugar
2½ tablespoons (7.5 grams) orange zest
⅓ cup (80 grams) fresh orange juice
¼ teaspoon kosher salt
½ cup (113 grams) unsalted butter, cubed and softened
2 large eggs (100 grams)
2 large egg yolks (37 grams)
Salty Peanut Crust (recipe follows)
¾ cup (125 grams) pomegranate arils

1. Preheat oven to 350°F (180°C).
2. In a medium saucepan, bring cranberries, sugar, orange zest and juice, and salt to a simmer over medium heat. Simmer until cranberries have softened and released their juices, about 10 minutes. Strain mixture through a fine-mesh sieve into a medium bowl, pressing on solids. Discard solids. Add butter to cranberry mixture, whisking until combined. Let cool for 3 minutes. Add eggs and egg yolks, whisking until well combined.
3. Return cranberry mixture to saucepan; cook over medium heat, whisking constantly, until thickened, 5 to 10 minutes. Let cool to room temperature. Pour cranberry mixture into prepared Salty Peanut Crust, smoothing top.
4. Bake until set, about 10 minutes. Let cool completely on a wire rack. Sprinkle with pomegranate arils. Store at room temperature for up to 2 days.

SALTY PEANUT CRUST
Makes 1 (9-inch) crust

1¼ cups (156 grams) all-purpose flour
1 cup (142 grams) unsalted roasted peanuts
¼ cup (27 grams) peanut butter powder
¾ teaspoon (2.25 grams) kosher salt
½ cup (113 grams) unsalted butter, cubed and softened
1 large egg yolk (19 grams)

1. Preheat oven to 350°F (180°C).
2. In the work bowl of a food processor, place flour, peanuts, peanut butter powder, and salt; pulse until finely ground. Add butter, and process until mixture is crumbly. Add egg yolk, and process until a crumbly dough forms. Shape dough into a disk, and wrap tightly in plastic wrap. Refrigerate for 10 minutes.
3. Transfer dough to a 9-inch removable-bottom tart pan, pressing into bottom and up sides. Freeze for 15 minutes.
4. Top dough with a piece of parchment paper, letting ends extend over edges of pan. Add pie weights.
5. Bake until edges are set, about 20 minutes. Carefully remove paper and weights. Bake until crust is golden brown, about 10 minutes more. Let cool completely on a wire rack.

REMOVE ARILS FROM YOUR POMEGRANATE

1. Fill a large bowl with cold water.
Roll pomegranate to loosen the seeds. Strike the hull with the tip of a knife, and gently crack open with your hands.
2. Use a sharp knife to slice into quarters. Submerge in cold water.
3. Pull apart quarters, releasing seeds with your hands. The pith will float, and the seeds will sink. Remove and discard pith, and drain the arils.
4. Place arils on paper towels to absorb excess moisture, being careful not to squeeze.

HONEY AND NUT ORANGE TARTS

Makes 2 (9-inch) tarts

Recipe by Mandy Dixon

These nut-filled tarts by Alaskan pastry chef Mandy Dixon are perfect for the winter pantry when there just isn't enough fresh fruit. Nut tarts hold up to field conditions when you need to pack a snack that won't be too difficult to eat on the trail.

2 cups (250 grams) all-purpose flour
3½ cups (396 grams) chopped mixed nuts (walnuts, cashews, and almonds), divided

1½ cups (340 grams) unsalted butter, divided
⅔ cup (80 grams) confectioners' sugar
½ cup (110 grams) firmly packed light brown sugar
½ cup (170 grams) honey
3 tablespoons (45 grams) heavy whipping cream
1 tablespoon (3 grams) orange zest

1. Preheat oven to 350°F (180°C). Grease 2 (9-inch) removable-bottom fluted tart pans.
2. In the work bowl of a food processor, place flour, 1 cup (113 grams) nuts, ¾ cup (170 grams) butter, and confectioners' sugar; pulse until finely ground and mixture begins to come together. Press mixture into bottom and up sides of prepared pans.
3. Bake until golden around the edges, 7 to 10 minutes.
4. In a medium saucepan, bring brown sugar, honey, cream, zest, remaining 2½ cups (283 grams) nuts, and remaining ¾ cup (170 grams) butter to a boil over medium-high heat; boil for 1 minute. Pour hot mixture into prepared tart shells. Let set until firm, about 2 hours.

HEIRLOOM TOMATO AND APRICOT

Makes 1 (9-inch) tart

With a buttery Pine Nut Crust; a rich ricotta, mozzarella, and basil filling; and an apricot-tomato layered topping, this savory tart brings seasonal treasures together.

¾ cup (180 grams) balsamic vinegar
1 cup (225 grams) ricotta cheese
4 large egg yolks (74 grams)
2 teaspoons (7 grams) minced garlic
1 teaspoon (3 grams) kosher salt
½ teaspoon (1 gram) ground black pepper
¾ cup (75 grams) shredded mozzarella cheese, divided
¼ cup (8 grams) chopped fresh basil
Pine Nut Crust (recipe follows)
2 heirloom tomatoes (638 grams), sliced ¼ inch thick and cut into thirds
6 fresh apricots (210 grams), sliced ¼ inch thick
Garnish: fresh basil leaves

1. Preheat oven to 350°F (180°C).
2. In a small saucepan, bring vinegar to a boil over medium heat. Cook until thickened and reduced by half, 15 to 20 minutes. Let cool completely.
3. In a medium bowl, whisk together ricotta, egg yolks, garlic, salt, and pepper. Add ½ cup (50 grams) mozzarella and basil, stirring to combine. Pour mixture into prepared Pine Nut Crust. Arrange tomato and apricot slices in desired pattern over ricotta mixture. Sprinkle with remaining ¼ cup (25 grams) mozzarella.
4. Bake until set, 45 to 60 minutes, covering with foil to prevent excess browning, if necessary. Let cool on a wire rack for 20 minutes. Remove tart from pan. Drizzle with balsamic reduction. Garnish with basil, if desired. Serve warm. Cover and refrigerate for up to 2 days.

PINE NUT CRUST

Makes 1 (9-inch) crust

1 cup (96 grams) ground toasted pine nuts
½ teaspoon (1.5 grams) kosher salt
½ teaspoon (1 gram) ground black pepper
1½ cups (188 grams) all-purpose flour
½ cup (113 grams) unsalted butter, softened
1 large egg yolk (19 grams)
1 teaspoon (5 grams) water

1. In the work bowl of a food processor, place pine nuts, salt, and pepper; pulse until combined. Add flour, and pulse until finely ground.
2. In the bowl of a stand mixer fitted with the paddle attachment, beat nut mixture, butter, egg yolk, and 1 teaspoon (5 grams) water at medium speed until combined. Wrap in plastic wrap, and refrigerate for at least 10 minutes.
3. Press dough into bottom and up sides of a 9-inch removable-bottom tart pan. Freeze for 20 minutes.

CHOCOLATE LEMON TART

Makes 1 (9-inch) tart

Balancing acidic tang with sweet cocoa notes, this sunny spring tart has a hidden layer of milk chocolate ganache running under a silky lemon curd filling.

Tart Dough (recipe follows)
Chocolate Ganache (recipe follows)
1   cup (200 grams) granulated sugar
4   large eggs (200 grams), room temperature
⅔   cup (150 grams) unsalted butter, cubed and softened
¼   cup (12 grams) lemon zest
½   cup (120 grams) fresh lemon juice

1. Preheat oven to 350°F (180°C).
2. On a lightly floured surface, roll Tart Dough into a 12-inch circle. Transfer to a 9-inch tart pan, pressing into bottom and up sides. Trim excess dough. Using a fork, prick bottom of tart shell. Freeze for 15 minutes.
3. Top dough with a piece of parchment paper, letting ends extend over edges of pan. Add pie weights.
4. Bake until edges are set, about 20 minutes. Carefully remove paper and weights. Bake until crust is golden brown, about 10 minutes more. Let cool completely on a wire rack.
5. Pour two-thirds of Chocolate Ganache into prepared crust, and spread to edges. Freeze for 45 minutes.
6. In the top of a double boiler, whisk together sugar, eggs, butter, and lemon zest and juice. Cook over simmering water, stirring constantly, until thickened, about 10 minutes. Strain mixture, discarding solids. Cover and refrigerate for 30 minutes.
7. Pour lemon curd over Chocolate Ganache in pan. Refrigerate until set, about 2 hours. Just before serving, drizzle with remaining Chocolate Ganache.

Tart Dough
Makes 1 (9-inch) crust

1⅓ cups (167 grams) all-purpose flour
⅓   cup (40 grams) confectioners' sugar
¾   teaspoon (2.25 grams) kosher salt
½   cup (113 grams) cold unsalted butter, cubed
1   large egg yolk (19 grams)
2   tablespoons (30 grams) ice water

1. In the work bowl of a food processor, place flour, confectioners' sugar, and salt; pulse until combined. Add cold butter, and pulse until mixture is crumbly. With processor running, add egg yolk and 2 tablespoons (30 grams) ice water, pulsing until dough comes together. Shape dough into a disk, and wrap in plastic wrap. Refrigerate for at least 30 minutes or up to 24 hours.

Chocolate Ganache
Makes about 1 cup

6   ounces (175 grams) 45% cacao milk chocolate*, chopped
3   tablespoons (45 grams) heavy whipping cream
3   tablespoons (42 grams) unsalted butter

1. Place chocolate in a medium heatproof bowl.
2. In a medium saucepan, heat cream and butter over medium heat, stirring frequently, just until bubbles form around edges of pan. (Do not boil.) Remove from heat; pour hot cream mixture over chocolate. Let stand for 5 minutes; stir until chocolate is melted and mixture is smooth. Use immediately.

We used Guittard 45% Cacao Soleil D'Automne Milk Chocolate.

BOOZY FIG & MUSCADINE TARTLETS

Makes 8 tartlets

Recipe by Marian Cooper Cairns

A spicy gingersnap crust, a bourbon-spiked custard filling, and a sweet fig and muscadine topping make these tartlets a medley of fall flavors.

30 gingersnap cookies* (214 grams), broken into pieces
5 tablespoons (70 grams) unsalted butter, melted
1⅛ teaspoons (3 grams) kosher salt, divided
¼ cup (31 grams) cake flour
½ cup (100 grams) granulated sugar
1½ cups (360 grams) whole milk
4 large egg yolks (74 grams)
2 tablespoons (30 grams) bourbon
1 tablespoon (14 grams) cold unsalted butter
2 teaspoons (8 grams) vanilla extract
½ cup (57 grams) finely diced muscadines or grapes
3 tablespoons (61 grams) fig preserves

1½ teaspoons (7.5 grams) fresh lemon juice
1 teaspoon minced fresh rosemary
2½ cups (275 grams) assorted fig wedges
Garnish: fresh rosemary sprigs

1. Preheat oven to 325°F (170°C).
2. In the work bowl of a food processor, process gingersnaps until fine crumbs form. Add melted butter and ½ teaspoon (1.5 grams) salt; process until well combined. Press mixture into bottoms and up sides of 8 (4-inch) removable-bottom tart pans. Place on a baking sheet.
3. Bake until set, 10 to 12 minutes. Let cool completely.
4. In a small saucepan, whisk together flour, sugar, and ½ teaspoon (1.5 grams) salt. Whisk in milk, egg yolks, and bourbon. Cook over medium-low heat, whisking constantly, until thickened, 4 to 5 minutes. Whisk in cold butter and vanilla until butter is melted. Transfer to a bowl. Cover with a piece of plastic wrap, pressing wrap directly onto surface of warm custard to prevent a skin from forming. Refrigerate until cold, about 3 hours.

5. In a medium bowl, toss together muscadines, fig preserves, lemon juice, rosemary, and remaining ⅛ teaspoon salt until well combined. Fold in figs.
6. Spoon custard into prepared tart shells, and top with muscadine-fig mixture. Serve immediately, or refrigerate for up to 2 hours. Garnish with rosemary, if desired.

We used Nabisco Ginger Snaps.

MAKE AHEAD
This dessert is easily prepped up to 2 days in advance of assembly. Store cooled crusts in an airtight container, and whisk up the boozy pastry cream up to 2 days ahead. Just be sure to chill it with plastic wrap directly on the surface of the pudding.

Photo by Matt Armendariz

GINGER PEAR AND WALNUT TART

Makes 1 (14x4-inch) tart

Recipe by Kelsey Siemens

There's something about the way the light streams through my family's pear trees that makes it one of the most beautiful spots in our British Columbian orchard. We grow five different types of pears, and everyone in my family has their own favorite. For me, it's the Bosc pear, the star of this Ginger Pear and Walnut Tart, as I love its rustic golden skin and, more importantly, the way it holds its shape when baked. Ginger complements the pear flavor so well, and the poached pears are nestled into a deliciously buttery filling and surrounded by a flaky crust.

1½ cups (188 grams) all-purpose flour
⅓ cup (40 grams) confectioners' sugar
2 tablespoons (12 grams) ground walnuts
¼ teaspoon kosher salt
½ cup (113 grams) cold unsalted butter, cubed
1 large egg yolk (19 grams)
1 teaspoon (4 grams) vanilla extract
Walnut Tart Filling (recipe follows)
Poached Ginger Pears (recipe follows)

1. In the bowl of a stand mixer fitted with the paddle attachment, beat flour, confectioners' sugar, walnuts, and salt at low speed until combined. With mixer on medium speed, add cold butter, beating until mixture is crumbly. Add egg yolk and vanilla, beating just until combined. (If dough seems a bit dry and is not coming together, add 1 to 2 tablespoons [15 to 30 grams] very cold water.)
2. Turn out dough onto a lightly floured surface, and gently press into a rough rectangle about the size of your hand. Wrap in plastic wrap, and refrigerate for at least 30 minutes or up to 1 hour.
3. Preheat oven to 375°F (190°C).
4. Turn out dough onto a lightly floured surface, and lightly dust with flour. Roll dough into a 16x6-inch rectangle, about ⅛ inch thick. Transfer to a 14x4-inch removable-bottom tart pan, pressing into bottom and up sides and into corners of pan. Trim excess dough. Prick bottom of dough with a fork several times. Place parchment over dough, and add pie weights.
5. Bake until lightly browned, 15 to 20 minutes. Pour Walnut Tart Filling into prepared crust. Use an offset spatula to adjust walnuts to they are evenly dispersed throughout tart. Gently

slice Poached Ginger Pears, and arrange on top of filling. Bake until crust is golden and filling is bubbly, about 15 minutes more. Let cool for 5 to 10 minutes. This tart is best the first day, but will keep refrigerated in an airtight container for up to 3 days.

WALNUT TART FILLING
Makes 1½ cups

2 large eggs (100 grams)
1 cup (220 grams) firmly packed dark brown sugar
⅓ cup (76 grams) unsalted butter
¼ cup (60 grams) heavy whipping cream
1 teaspoon (4 grams) vanilla extract
½ cup (57 grams) chopped walnuts

1. In a large saucepan, whisk eggs until frothy. Place over medium heat, and immediately add brown sugar, butter, cream, and vanilla, stirring to combine. Bring to a boil over medium-high heat; reduce heat to medium, and cook, whisking constantly, until thickened, about 7 minutes. Remove from heat, and stir in walnuts.

POACHED GINGER PEARS
Makes 4 cups

4 cups (960 grams) water
½ cup (170 grams) honey
1 (1-inch) piece fresh ginger, peeled and thinly sliced
4 medium Bosc pears (768 grams)

1. In a large heavy-bottomed stockpot, bring 4 cups (960 grams) water to a boil. Stir in honey until dissolved; add ginger.
2. Peel pears, and cut in half. Using a spoon or small paring knife, carefully core each pear half. Slip pear halves into boiling liquid. Reduce heat to a gentle simmer. Cover and cook until a fork can pierce pears, about 30 minutes. (Overcooking may cause the pears to fall apart, especially if they're on the riper side.) Use immediately, or make the day before, and refrigerate in an airtight container in its liquid for a stronger flavor.

Photo by Kelsey Siemens

BOURBON-PINEAPPLE POUND TART

Makes 1 (10-inch) tart

Recipe by Ben Mims

Pound cakes have long been relegated to large, deep pans, and for good reason: The heaviness of the cakes means they don't rise much and need to "settle" into pans that already have structure in order to bake up well. But for this cake, I went with a large, deep tart pan to produce a sleek, slim wedge of cake that eats like a tart, complete with fluted edge and chunks of fresh fruit on top.

¾ cup (170 grams) unsalted butter, softened
1½ cups (300 grams) granulated sugar
2 tablespoons plus 1 teaspoon (35 grams) bourbon, divided
1 teaspoon (3 grams) kosher salt
1 teaspoon (4 grams) vanilla extract
½ teaspoon (2.5 grams) baking powder
3 large eggs (150 grams), room temperature
1½ cups (187 grams) cake flour
8 ounces (225 grams) peeled and cored fresh pineapple, cut into ½-inch chunks
2 cups (240 grams) confectioners' sugar
2 tablespoons (28 grams) fresh pineapple juice
1 ring candied pineapple

1. Preheat oven to 325°F (170°C). Butter and flour a 10-inch removable-bottom fluted tart pan.
2. In the bowl of a stand mixer fitted with the paddle attachment, beat butter, granulated sugar, 1 tablespoon (15 grams) bourbon, salt, vanilla, and baking powder at medium speed until fluffy and pale, at least 6 minutes. Add eggs, one at a time, beating until there are no streaks of yolk left after each addition, about 15 seconds. Scrape bottom and sides of bowl with a rubber spatula. With mixer on medium-high speed, beat until superlight and airy, at least 3 minutes. Add flour, and stir with a rubber spatula just until combined. Spoon batter into prepared pan, and smooth top.
3. Place pineapple chunks on a layer of paper towels to dry thoroughly; scatter pineapple over batter.
4. Bake until golden brown and a wooden pick inserted in center comes out clean, 1 hour and 15 minutes to 1 hour and 30 minutes. Let cool in pan for 30 minutes. Carefully loosen edges of pan from tart. Lift bottom of pan to unmold it from outer ring. Loosen bottom of pan from tart, and slide tart onto a wire rack.
5. In a medium bowl, whisk together confectioners' sugar, pineapple juice, and remaining 1 tablespoon plus 1 teaspoon (20 grams) bourbon.
6. Using a fork, drizzle pineapple glaze back and forth over top of tart, letting it fall over sides. Thinly slice candied pineapple ring into matchsticks, and sprinkle over top of tart while glaze is still wet. Let stand for at least 10 minutes to let icing set before serving.

PEACH BLACKBERRY BOURBON CROSTATA

Makes 1 (9-inch) crostata

The crostata, an Italian rustic tart, may seem an unlikely vessel for juicy peaches. But take one bite of this richly crusted treat, and you'll find a uniquely Southern combination of jammy peach and blackberry filling with a warm splash of bourbon.

4 cups (900 grams) sliced peeled fresh peaches (about 5 medium peaches)
½ cup (110 grams) firmly packed light brown sugar
2 tablespoons (16 grams) all-purpose flour
2 tablespoons (16 grams) cornstarch
3 tablespoons (45 grams) bourbon, divided
⅛ teaspoon kosher salt
Crostata Dough (recipe follows)
½ cup (85 grams) fresh blackberries, sliced
1 large egg (50 grams)
1 teaspoon (5 grams) water
1 tablespoon (12 grams) turbinado sugar

1. Preheat oven to 375°F (190°C). Line a large rimmed baking sheet with parchment paper.
2. In a large bowl, toss together peaches, brown sugar, flour, cornstarch, 2 tablespoons (30 grams) bourbon, and salt.
3. On a lightly floured surface, roll Crostata Dough into a 12-inch circle. Transfer to prepared pan. Pour peach mixture onto center of Crostata Dough. Sprinkle with blackberries. Fold edges of dough up and over to encase filling.
4. In a small bowl, whisk together egg and 1 teaspoon (5 grams) water. Brush dough with egg wash, and sprinkle with turbinado sugar.
5. Bake for 20 minutes. Cover filling with foil, and bake until crust is deep golden brown, about 25 minutes more. Let cool for 20 minutes. Brush filling with remaining 1 tablespoon (15 grams) bourbon just before serving.

CROSTATA DOUGH
Makes 1 (9-inch) crust

1¼ cups (156 grams) all-purpose flour
2 teaspoons (8 grams) granulated sugar
1 teaspoon (3 grams) kosher salt
½ cup plus 1 tablespoon (127 grams) cold unsalted butter, cubed
6 tablespoons (90 grams) ice water, divided

1. In a medium bowl, stir together flour, sugar, and salt. Add cold butter, and use both hands to turn mixture over in a snapping motion to incorporate butter with flour mixture.
2. Transfer to the work bowl of a food processor, and pulse until mixture is crumbly. With processor running, add 5 tablespoons (75 grams) ice water in a slow, steady stream, just until dough comes together. Add remaining 1 tablespoon (15 grams) ice water if needed.
3. Turn out dough, and shape into a disk. Wrap in plastic wrap, and refrigerate for at least 1 hour.

PASTRIES

TRADITIONAL CORNISH PASTIES

Makes 6 pasties

Recipe by Edd Kimber

When I was little, we spent many summer holidays in Devon and Cornwall, and I found a love for the Cornish pasty, a traditional dish from Cornwall often associated with the local miners. The story goes that the pasty made for a great portable lunch they could take down in the mines. To keep soot from contaminating the miners' meal, the rim of the pasty was made thick so that it could be used as a handle and discarded after the remainder of the pasty was eaten. These days, we absolutely eat the whole thing.

1   pound (455 grams) skirt steak, diced
2   cups (350 grams) diced potato
1   cup (200 grams) diced swede,
     rutabaga, or turnip
1   cup (150 grams) diced onion
1   tablespoon (9 grams) sea salt
2   teaspoons (4 grams) dry mustard
1½   teaspoons (3 grams) ground black pepper
Leaves from 3 sprigs fresh thyme (3 grams)
Cornish Pasty Dough (recipe follows)
4   large egg yolks (74 grams), lightly beaten

1. Preheat oven to 375°F (190°C). Line 2 baking sheets with parchment paper.
2. In a large bowl, toss together steak, potato, swede, onion, salt, mustard, pepper, and thyme.
3. Divide Cornish Pasty Dough into 6 equal pieces. Roll each piece into an 8- to 10-inch circle. Place about 1¼ cups filling in center of each round.
4. Brush edges with water, and stretch and fold dough over filling, pressing edges to seal. Use thumb and forefinger to twist dough over and crimp along edge. Carefully place pasties on prepared pans, and brush with egg yolks.
5. Bake until deep golden brown, about 45 minutes. Let cool slightly on wire racks. Serve warm.

CORNISH PASTY DOUGH
Makes dough for 6 to 12 pasties

4¼   cups (540 grams) bread flour, divided
1   teaspoon (3 grams) kosher salt
⅔   cup (150 grams) cold lard, cubed
⅔   cup (150 grams) cold unsalted butter,
     cubed
½   cup (120 grams) water

1. In a large bowl, combine 4 cups (508 grams) flour and salt. Add cold lard and cold butter, tossing to coat in flour. Using your hands or a pastry blender, cut in lard and butter until mixture is crumbly. Stir in ½ cup (120 grams) water, mixing until dough starts to pull together. Using your hands, lightly knead dough until it becomes smooth and slightly elastic. Knead in remaining ¼ cup (32 grams) flour as needed until dough reaches desired consistency. (This dough works brilliantly in a food processor, pulsing in the water until the dough forms and allowing the processor to run for 1 minute or so extra to get the elasticity into the dough.)
2. Shape dough into a disk, and wrap in cling film (plastic wrap). Refrigerate for at least 3 to 4 hours before using. It will keep refrigerated for up to 3 days, but let it stand at room temperature for about 10 minutes when ready to bake.

CHEDDAR-CARAMEL APPLE PASTIES

Makes 12 pasties

If an American apple pie met a British pasty, this hybrid treat would be the result. With a little help from a crunchy turbinado sugar topping, this warm pasty brimming with cinnamon, white Cheddar, and apple hits just the right sweet and savory notes.

cups (740 grams) cubed peeled apple
cup (55 grams) firmly packed light brown sugar
tablespoons (12 grams) ground cinnamon
Cornish Pasty Dough (recipe follows)
½ cups (150 grams) shredded English Cheddar cheese*
large egg yolks (74 grams), lightly beaten
Turbinado sugar, for sprinkling

1. Preheat oven to 375°F (190°C). Line baking sheets with parchment paper.
2. In a large bowl, combine apple, brown sugar, and cinnamon.
3. Divide Cornish Pasty Dough into 2 equal pieces. Divide each piece in half, and shape each half into a ball. Roll each ball into a 4-inch circle. Place about ¼ cup apple mixture in center of half of rounds. Sprinkle 2 tablespoons cheese over apple mixture on each round.
4. Cut an "X" in center of each remaining round, and place over filling. Brush edges with water, and press to seal. Use thumb and forefinger to twist dough over and crimp along edge. Carefully place pasties on prepared pans. Brush with egg yolks, and sprinkle with turbinado sugar.
5. Bake until deep golden brown, about 45 minutes. Let cool slightly on wire racks. Serve warm.

*We used Neal's Yard Dairy Montgomery's Cheddar.

CORNISH PASTY DOUGH
Makes dough for 6 to 12 pasties

Recipe by Edd Kimber

4¼ cups (540 grams) bread flour, divided
1 teaspoon (3 grams) kosher salt
⅔ cup (150 grams) cold lard, cubed
⅔ cup (150 grams) cold unsalted butter, cubed
½ cup (120 grams) water

1. In a large bowl, combine 4 cups (508 grams) flour and salt. Add cold lard and cold butter, tossing to coat in flour. Using your hands or a pastry blender, cut in lard and butter until mixture is crumbly. Stir in ½ cup (120 grams) water, mixing until dough starts to pull together. Using your hands, lightly knead dough until it becomes smooth and slightly elastic. Knead in remaining ¼ cup (32 grams) flour as needed until dough reaches desired consistency. (This dough works brilliantly in a food processor, pulsing in the water until the dough forms and allowing the processor to run for 1 minute or so extra to get the elasticity into the dough.)
2. Shape dough into a disk, and wrap in cling film (plastic wrap). Refrigerate for at least 3 to 4 hours before using. It will keep refrigerated for up to 3 days, but let it stand at room temperature for about 10 minutes when ready to bake.

ENGLISH BREAKFAST PASTIES

Makes 6 pasties

Rise and shine with a hearty, handheld breakfast. We took the components of a classic English breakfast—eggs, sausage, baked beans, and tomatoes—and wrapped them into one pasty. Enjoy the leftover beans the British way over toast!

Cornish Pasty Dough (recipe follows)
1½ cups (390 grams) English-Style Baked Beans (recipe follows)
2   cups (140 grams) white mushrooms, sliced
3   links (227 grams) English or bratwurst sausage, quartered, or 6 links breakfast or banger sausage, halved lengthwise
6   large eggs (300 grams), soft-cooked and halved lengthwise
2   small tomatoes (60 grams), thinly sliced
4   large egg yolks (74 grams), lightly beaten

1. Preheat oven to 375°F (190°C). Line 2 baking sheets with parchment paper.
2. Divide Cornish Pasty Dough into 6 equal pieces. Roll each piece into an 8- to 10-inch circle. Place ¼ cup English-Style Baked Beans on bottom half of each round, leaving a 1½-inch border. Top with ¼ cup mushrooms. Place 1 sausage piece on outside edge and 1 on inside, forming a barrier. Place 2 egg halves in center. Place 2 slices tomato on top.
3. Brush edges with water, and stretch and fold dough over filling, pressing edges to seal. Use thumb and forefinger to twist dough over and crimp along edge. Carefully place pasties on prepared pans, and brush with egg yolks. Cut 3 vents in top of dough to release steam.
4. Bake until deep golden brown, about 45 minutes. Let cool slightly on wire racks. Serve warm.

CORNISH PASTY DOUGH
Makes dough for 6 to 12 pasties

Recipe by Edd Kimber

4¼ cups (540 grams) bread flour, divided
1   teaspoon (3 grams) kosher salt
⅔   cup (150 grams) cold lard, cubed
⅔   cup (150 grams) cold unsalted butter, cubed
½   cup (120 grams) water

1. In a large bowl, combine 4 cups (508 grams) flour and salt. Add cold lard and cold butter, tossing to coat in flour. Using your hands or a pastry blender, cut in lard and butter until mixture is crumbly. Stir in ½ cup (120 grams) water, mixing until dough starts to pull together. Using your hands, lightly knead dough until it becomes smooth and slightly elastic. Knead in remaining ¼ cup (32 grams) flour as needed until dough reaches desired consistency. (This dough works brilliantly in a food processor, pulsing in the water until the dough forms and allowing the processor to run for 1 minute or so extra to get the elasticity into the dough.)
2. Shape dough into a disk, and wrap in cling film (plastic wrap). Refrigerate for at least 3 to 4 hours before using. It will keep refrigerated for up to 3 days, but let it stand at room temperature for about 10 minutes when ready to bake.

ENGLISH-STYLE BAKED BEANS
Makes 1 quart

½   pound (228 grams) dry navy beans
1   tablespoon (14 grams) vegetable oil
½   medium onion (75 grams), finely chopped
1   large clove garlic (5 grams), finely chopped

1½ teaspoons (4.5 grams) kosher salt
½   teaspoon (1 gram) ground black pepper
2   cups (480 grams) chicken broth
1   (15-ounce) can (425 grams) tomato sauce
¼   cup (55 grams) firmly packed dark brown sugar
1½ tablespoons (22.5 grams) apple cider vinegar
1½ tablespoons (20 grams) Worcestershire sauce
1   tablespoon (13 grams) tomato paste
1   bay leaf

1. In a large Dutch oven, combine beans and water to cover by 2 inches. Let stand for 8 hours. Drain.
2. In a large Dutch oven, heat oil over medium-high heat until shimmering. Add onion, garlic, salt, and pepper; cook, stirring frequently, until softened but not browned, about 4 minutes.
3. Add beans, broth, tomato sauce, brown sugar, vinegar, Worcestershire, tomato paste, and bay leaf; bring to a simmer. Reduce heat to low; cover and cook for 4 to 5 hours, stirring occasionally. Remove bay leaf. Let cool completely. Refrigerate for up to 1 week, or freeze for up to 6 months.

MINCEMEAT PASTIES

Makes 12 pasties

It's best to let mincemeat stand for at least several days before using. This gives the traditional English filling's dried fruit time to tenderize, soaking in the spices and spirits. The leftover mincemeat will keep in the refrigerator for up to 6 months and get better with age. It is wonderful stuffed in a pork loin.

½   cup (113 grams) unsalted butter, cubed
1¾ cups (224 grams) dark raisins
1¾ cups (224 grams) golden raisins
1   cup (220 grams) firmly packed muscovado sugar
1   large firm apple (185 grams), diced
½   cup (64 grams) currants
½   cup (55 grams) candied lemon peel, chopped
1   tablespoon (3 grams) lemon zest
¼   cup (60 grams) fresh lemon juice
1   tablespoon (3 grams) orange zest
¼   cup (60 grams) fresh orange juice
½   teaspoon (1 gram) ground cinnamon
½   teaspoon (1 gram) ground nutmeg
¼   teaspoon ground cloves
¼   teaspoon ground cardamom
¼   teaspoon ground allspice
3   tablespoons (45 grams) brandy, rum, or sherry
1   tablespoon (15 grams) Grand Marnier
Cornish Pasty Dough (recipe follows)
4   large egg yolks (74 grams), lightly beaten

1. In a large saucepan, melt butter over medium-high heat. Add raisins, muscovado sugar, apple, currants, candied lemon peel, lemon zest and juice, orange zest and juice, cinnamon, nutmeg, cloves, cardamom, and allspice; reduce heat to medium. Cook, stirring occasionally, until mixture is heated through, about 10 minutes. Remove from heat; let cool completely. Stir in brandy and Grand Marnier. Place mixture in a jar, and seal. Refrigerate for at least 3 days before using.
2. Preheat oven to 375°F (190°C). Line 2 baking sheets with parchment paper.
3. Divide Cornish Pasty Dough into 12 equal pieces. Roll each piece into a 6-inch circle. Place ⅓ cup filling in center of each round.
4. Brush edges with water, and stretch and fold dough over filling, pressing edges to seal. Use thumb and forefinger to twist dough over and crimp along edge. Carefully

place pasties on prepared pans, and brush with egg yolks. Cut 3 vents in top of dough to release steam.
5. Bake until deep golden brown, about 45 minutes. Let cool slightly on wire racks. Serve warm.

CORNISH PASTY DOUGH
Makes dough for 6 to 12 pasties

Recipe by Edd Kimber

4¼ cups (540 grams) bread flour, divided
1   teaspoon (3 grams) kosher salt
⅔   cup (150 grams) cold lard, cubed
⅔   cup (150 grams) cold unsalted butter, cubed
½   cup (120 grams) water

1. In a large bowl, combine 4 cups (508 grams) flour and salt. Add cold lard and cold butter, tossing to coat in flour. Using your hands or a pastry blender, cut in lard and butter until mixture is crumbly. Stir in ½ cup (120 grams) water, mixing until dough starts to pull together. Using your hands, lightly knead dough until it becomes smooth and slightly elastic. Knead in remaining ¼ cup (32 grams) flour as needed until dough reaches desired consistency. (This dough works brilliantly in a food processor, pulsing in the water until the dough forms and allowing the processor to run for 1 minute or so extra to get the elasticity into the dough.)
2. Shape dough into a disk, and wrap in cling film (plastic wrap). Refrigerate for at least 3 to 4 hours before using. It will keep refrigerated for up to 3 days, but let it stand at room temperature for about 10 minutes when ready to bake.

SHEPHERD'S PIE PASTIES

Makes 6 pasties

Merging the pasty with another British standard, this no-fuss version of shepherd's pie brings all the meat, potatoes, and veggie-filled comfort with half the labor.

½   **cup (104 grams) tomato paste**
3   **tablespoons (39 grams) Worcestershire sauce**
2   **tablespoons (4 grams) chopped fresh rosemary**
2   **tablespoons (4 grams) chopped fresh thyme**
1   **teaspoon (3 grams) kosher salt**
½   **teaspoon (1 gram) ground black pepper**
1½   **pounds (680 grams) ground lamb**
2   **cups (350 grams) diced potato**
1⅓   **cups (200 grams) diced yellow onion**
1   **cup (130 grams) thinly sliced carrot**
2   **cloves garlic (10 grams), minced**
Cornish Pasty Dough (recipe follows)
4   **large egg yolks (74 grams), lightly beaten**

1. Preheat oven to 375°F (190°C). Line 2 baking sheets with parchment paper.

2. In a large bowl, combine tomato paste, Worcestershire, rosemary, thyme, salt, and pepper. Add lamb, potato, onion, carrot, and garlic, stirring to combine.
3. Divide Cornish Pasty Dough into 6 equal pieces. Roll each piece into an 8- to 10-inch circle. Place about 1½ cups filling in center of each round. Bring outside edges together up over filling, pressing edges to seal. Use thumb and forefinger to twist dough over and crimp along edge. Carefully place pasties on prepared pans, and brush with egg yolks.
4. Bake until deep golden brown, about 45 minutes. Let cool slightly on wire racks. Serve warm.

CORNISH PASTY DOUGH
Makes dough for 6 to 12 pasties

Recipe by Edd Kimber

4¼   **cups (540 grams) bread flour, divided**
1   **teaspoon (3 grams) kosher salt**
⅔   **cup (150 grams) cold lard, cubed**
⅔   **cup (150 grams) cold unsalted butter, cubed**
½   **cup (120 grams) water**

1. In a large bowl, combine 4 cups (508 grams) flour and salt. Add cold lard and cold butter, tossing to coat in flour. Using your hands or a pastry blender, cut in lard and butter until mixture is crumbly. Stir in ½ cup (120 grams) water, mixing until dough starts to pull together. Using your hands, lightly knead dough until it becomes smooth and slightly elastic. Knead in remaining ¼ cup (32 grams) flour as needed until dough reaches desired consistency. (This dough works brilliantly in a food processor, pulsing in the water until the dough forms and allowing the processor to run for 1 minute or so extra to get the elasticity into the dough.)
2. Shape dough into a disk, and wrap in cling film (plastic wrap). Refrigerate for at least 3 to 4 hours before using. It will keep refrigerated for up to 3 days, but let it stand at room temperature for about 10 minutes when ready to bake.

ROSEMARY-TALEGGIO KNISH

Makes 9 knishes

Recipe by Erin Jeanne McDowell

This is not your bubbie's knish, but it will conquer the craving and then some. Traditional knish dough is rather soft and can be manipulated to be very thin; this dough is on the flakier side. The dough is simply patted out with your hands, then filled with a decadent combination of herby mashed potatoes and a fat wedge of Taleggio.

3   cups (375 grams) all-purpose flour
½   cup (112 grams) vegetable oil
⅓   cup (80 grams) cool water (60°F/15°C)
¼   cup (57 grams) unsalted butter, melted
2   large eggs (100 grams), divided
1   large egg yolk (19 grams)
1¼   teaspoons (6.25 grams) baking powder
½   teaspoon (1.5 grams) fine sea salt
2   pounds (910 grams) russet potatoes, peeled and diced
5   tablespoons (70 grams) unsalted butter
1   medium sweet onion (175 grams), diced
2   tablespoons (4 grams) chopped fresh rosemary
4   ounces (115 grams) cream cheese
⅓   cup (80 grams) sour cream

Kosher salt and ground black pepper, to taste
9   ounces (250 grams) Taleggio cheese (rind trimmed), cut into 9 cubes
1   tablespoon (15 grams) water

1. In the bowl of a stand mixer fitted with the paddle attachment, beat flour, oil, ⅓ cup (80 grams) cool water, melted butter, 1 egg (50 grams), egg yolk, baking powder, and sea salt at medium speed until combined, about 2 minutes. Cover dough with plastic wrap, and refrigerate for at least 2 hours or overnight.

2. In a medium stockpot, bring potatoes and water to cover by at least 1 inch to a boil over medium-high heat. Reduce heat, and simmer until fork-tender, 15 to 18 minutes. Drain, and transfer to a medium bowl. Using a potato masher or a fork, mash potatoes. Set aside.

3. In a medium sauté pan, melt butter over medium heat. Add onion; sauté until lightly golden, 5 to 6 minutes. Add rosemary; sauté for 1 minute. Add onion mixture, cream cheese, and sour cream to potatoes, stirring until well combined. Season with salt and pepper. Let cool completely.

4. Preheat oven to 400°F (200°C). Line a baking sheet with parchment paper.

5. Divide dough into 9 (143-gram) pieces, and roll each piece into a ball. (If surface of dough feels too oily, gently knead several times to reincorporate oil.) Working with one ball at a time, use your hands to flatten dough into a 4-inch round, about ¼ inch thick. Scoop ¼ cup potato mixture into center of each round. Press a cube of Taleggio into center of potato mixture. Top with another 2 tablespoons potato mixture. Gently fold edges of dough up and over to encase filling. (It will be pretty rustic, but you can work it as much as you like to get it to look even.) Place on prepared pan. Repeat with remaining dough, potato mixture, and Taleggio.

6. In a small bowl, whisk together 1 tablespoon (15 grams) water and remaining 1 egg (50 grams). Brush egg wash onto dough.

7. Bake until dough is golden brown, 15 to 17 minutes. Let cool for at least 10 minutes before serving.

Photo by Mark Weinberg

CROISSANTS

Makes 8 croissants

Recipe by Cenk Sönmezsoy

A croissant is the beautiful fusion of a puff pastry and bread. The dough has milk and yeast in it, which increase the rise and richness. The lamination process gives this pastry its signature flaky layers. Self-taught baker and award-winning cookbook author Cenk Sönmezsoy takes on the ultimate pastry with a recipe adapted from his cookbook The Artful Baker: Extraordinary Desserts From an Obsessive Home Baker.

4   cups (500 grams) all-purpose flour
3   tablespoons (36 grams) granulated sugar
3¼ teaspoons (10 grams) instant yeast
2   teaspoons (16 grams) plus ⅛ teaspoon fine sea salt, divided
1¼ cups (300 grams) plus 1 tablespoon (15 grams) whole
    milk, room temperature and divided
5   tablespoons (70 grams) unsalted butter, melted and
    cooled
Butter Block (recipe follows)
1   large egg (50 grams)

1. In a large bowl, stir together flour, sugar, yeast, and 2 teaspoons (16 grams) salt. Add 1¼ cups (300 grams) milk and melted butter, stirring until flour is completely absorbed. Turn out mixture onto an unfloured surface, and knead until a rough, slightly sticky dough forms, about 4 minutes. (Avoid adding more flour; the dough will become easier to handle as you knead.) Shape dough into a ball. Wrap in plastic wrap, and let rest at room temperature until dough puffs up slightly, about 45 minutes.

2. Place dough in a generously buttered medium bowl, turning to coat with butter completely. Cover tightly with plastic wrap, and refrigerate overnight.

3. Turn out dough onto a lightly floured surface, and roughly shape into a small rectangle with your hands. Lightly flour dough, and roll into a 15¾x9-inch rectangle, about ⅜ inch thick. Gently stretch out rounded corners occasionally to make a neat rectangle, taking care not to tear dough. Place dough on a baking sheet lined with parchment paper. Cover with plastic wrap, and freeze for 10 minutes.

4. (For a visual tutorial of the lamination process in steps 4 through 8, turn to page 248.) For the first turn, place chilled dough on a lightly floured surface with one short side facing you. Unfold chilled butter envelope, peel away parchment, and center Butter Block on dough. Fold top and bottom sides of dough over Butter Block so ends meet in middle. Pinch seam closed. Pinch closed right and left open sides of dough to fully enclose Butter Block in a neatly sealed square.

5. Turn dough 90 degrees so that sealed center seam is perpendicular to you. Working from center outward on both sides, roll dough into a 15¾x9½-inch rectangle, about ⅝ inch thick. Lightly flour work surface and dough as needed, brushing off excess flour between turns.

6. Fold top third of dough down over center, and fold bottom third of dough up over top to make a 9½x6-inch rectangle. Transfer dough to a baking sheet lined with parchment paper, and cover tightly with plastic wrap. Refrigerate for 1 hour, and then freeze for 20 minutes. If your kitchen is cool (68°F/20°C or under), you can forgo the resting stage in the freezer and continue with the next turn after refrigerating the dough for 1 hour.

7. For the second turn, repeat steps 5 and 6.

8. For the final turn, place dough on work surface with one short side facing you, and roll into a 15¾x9½-inch rectangle. This time, fold top and bottom sides of dough almost to center, leaving about a ¾-inch gap in middle. Fold bottom up over top as if you were closing a book. You should have a 9½x4-inch rectangle. Return dough to lined baking sheet, and cover tightly with plastic wrap. Refrigerate for 1 hour, and then freeze for 20 minutes.

9. Place dough on work surface with one long side facing you. Roll dough into a 20½x9¾-inch rectangle, about ½ inch thick, lightly flouring work surface and dough as needed. Trim dough into a neat 20x9½-inch rectangle.

10. Using the tip of a paring knife, mark top edge of dough every 5 inches. Starting 2½ inches from left, mark bottom edge of dough every 5 inches. Position a ruler to connect top left corner with first mark on bottom, and cut dough along that line. Pivot ruler to connect end of bottom cut with next mark along top, and cut dough along that line. Continue to pivot and connect each ending point to next point on opposite side of dough, making 8 cuts in all. Place two smaller end pieces with their straight edges together, and pinch seams together to make a triangle matching the others. Turn over, and pinch seam on reverse to seal pieces together. You will now have 8 matching triangles. Transfer triangles to lined baking sheet, and cover tightly with plastic wrap. Freeze until firm, about 15 minutes. Line a baking sheet with parchment paper.

11. Place a partially frozen triangle on a lightly floured surface with base facing you. Roll to lengthen triangle until it is 12½ inches long and about ¼ inch thick. Fold corners of base upward and inward about 1 inch. Roll triangle from base to last 1½ inches of tip. While holding dough in place with one hand, stretch tip of dough slightly with your other hand to reach it up and tuck it under front of roll. (Roll dough up tightly so that it does not fall apart.) Repeat with remaining triangles, arranging them, tucked ends down, 2 inches apart on prepared pan. Cover loosely with plastic wrap, and let rise at room temperature until 1½ times their volume, 2½ to 3 hours, and then freeze for 20 minutes.

12. Preheat oven to 350°F (180°C). Line a baking sheet with parchment paper.

13. Arrange half of partially frozen croissants 4 inches apart on prepared pan. Keep remaining croissants in refrigerator.

14. In a small bowl, whisk together egg, remaining 1 tablespoon (15 grams) milk, and remaining ⅛ teaspoon salt with a fork until frothy. Using a pastry brush, gently apply a thin coating of egg wash onto croissants, taking care not to deflate them.

15. Bake until tops are golden brown, 35 to 40 minutes. Let cool on a wire rack for 15 minutes. Repeat with remaining croissants. Serve warm. The croissants are best shortly after they are made, but they will keep wrapped tightly in plastic wrap at room temperature for up to 24 hours. Reheat in a 350°F (180°C) oven until warmed through, about 8 minutes.

BUTTER BLOCK
Makes 1 (8-inch) square

1½ cups (340 grams) cold unsalted butter, cubed
¼ cup (31 grams) all-purpose flour

1. Cut a 20-inch-long sheet of parchment paper. Fold parchment in half lengthwise, and then fold over the three open sides to create an 8-inch square envelope.

2. In the bowl of a stand mixer fitted with the paddle attachment, beat butter and flour at medium speed until combined, about 1 minute.

3. Unfold envelope, and scrape butter mixture into center of square. Using an offset spatula, spread butter mixture onto square, leaving a ½-inch border on all sides. Fold envelope, creasing it firmly, and turn it so open sides are secured. Roll butter mixture from center to edges to create an 8-inch even slab, about ¼ inch thick. Transfer wrapped Butter Block to a baking sheet, and refrigerate until firm enough to leave just a slight indentation when you press your finger into it, about 20 minutes.

Photo by Cenk Sönmezsoy

Laminate the Dough: In steps 4 through 8 of the croissant recipe, you laminate the dough by repeatedly rolling and folding it with a slab of butter (a.k.a. a "turn") to create many thin alternating layers. This is a breakdown of how the first, second, and final turns should look.

Roll out Butter Block in an envelope made from a folded sheet of parchment paper to get an even slab.

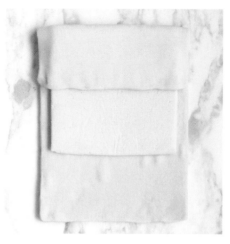

For the first turn, place chilled dough on a lightly floured surface. Place Butter Block in the center of the dough, and fold top of dough over it.

Fold bottom of dough over Butter Block so ends meet in middle.

Pinch seam closed. Pinch open sides of dough to fully enclose Butter Block in a sealed square.

Turn dough 90 degrees so that sealed center seam is perpendicular to you. Roll dough into a 15¾x9½-inch rectangle. Fold top third of rectangle down over center.

Fold bottom third of rectangle up over top fold to make another rectangle. Refrigerate for 1 hour, and then freeze for 20 minutes.

For the second turn, repeat the two previous steps.

For the final turn, place dough with one short side facing you, and roll into a 15¾x9½-inch rectangle. Fold top and bottom sides of dough almost to center, leaving about a ¾-inch gap in middle.

Fold bottom up over top as if you were closing a book. You should have a 9½x4-inch rectangle.

Photos by Cenk Sönmezsoy

PASTÉIS DE NATA

Makes 16 pastéis de natas

Portugal's most famous contribution to pastry is a simultaneously crisp and creamy mini tart. In our warmly spiced version, we spike our vanilla bean-speckled egg custard with cinnamon and cardamom. For that iconic spot-blistered top, high heat and a final sear under the broiler help you bring the quality of the Portuguese pastelerias to your home oven.

1⅓	cups (167 grams) all-purpose flour
1½	teaspoons (4.5 grams) kosher salt
1	cup (227 grams) unsalted butter, frozen
4	tablespoons (60 grams) ice water, divided
2	cups (480 grams) heavy whipping cream
1½	cups (360 grams) whole milk
1	vanilla bean, split lengthwise, seeds scraped and reserved
2	green cardamom pods*, cracked open
1	cinnamon stick
1	cup plus 2 tablespoons (224 grams) granulated sugar
¼	cup (32 grams) cornstarch
2	large eggs (100 grams)
4	large egg yolks (74 grams)

1. In a medium bowl, whisk together flour and salt. Using a cheese grater, gradually grate frozen butter into flour mixture, tossing and coating with flour as you go. (If you grate too much butter at once, it will clump up and not mix well with flour.) Drizzle 2 tablespoons (30 grams) ice water over flour mixture; toss with flour until fully absorbed. Add remaining 2 tablespoons (30 grams) ice water, and knead a few times to work it all together. Turn out dough onto a lightly floured surface, and shape into a disk. Wrap in plastic wrap, and refrigerate overnight.

2. In a medium saucepan, heat cream, milk, vanilla bean and reserved seeds, cardamom pods, and cinnamon stick over medium heat for 10 minutes.

3. In a medium bowl, whisk together sugar and cornstarch; whisk in eggs and egg yolks. Add about ½ cup hot milk mixture to egg mixture, whisking constantly. Add egg mixture to remaining hot milk mixture in pan, whisking to combine. Cook, whisking constantly, until mixture is thickened, about 10 minutes. (A good indicator for thickness: Once you stop whisking, the custard immediately stops moving as well.) Strain custard through a fine-mesh sieve into a medium bowl. Cover with plastic wrap, pressing wrap directly onto surface of custard to prevent a skin from forming. Refrigerate overnight.

4. Preheat oven to 450°F (230°C). Line 16 muffin cups with 2 (1-inch) strips of parchment paper.

5. On a lightly floured surface, divide dough in half. Roll half of dough into a 10x8-inch rectangle. Sprinkle with water, and roll up dough, jelly roll style. Cut dough into 8 (1-inch) rounds. On a lightly floured surface, roll each round into a 4-inch circle. Transfer circles to prepared muffin cups, pressing into bottoms and up sides. Repeat with remaining dough. Pour custard into prepared crusts, filling three-fourths full.

6. Bake for 13 minutes. Increase oven temperature to broil. Broil until desired level of brownness is achieved, about 10 minutes. (For more browning, place on a higher rack during broil.) Alternatively, brown with a kitchen torch. Serve warm. Store in an airtight container for up to 3 days.

*If you're a cardamom fan, feel free to add a third pod.

Note: *Dough can be made in a food processor; however, it will result in a much less flaky dough.*

BLACK COCOA KOUIGN AMANN

Makes 12 kouignoù amann

The buttered, sugared, and laminated Breton pastry, now in your favorite shade of cocoa. Little can be improved upon the kouign amann, but here, the deep chocolate flavor layered within the caramelized crunch surpasses all expectations.

3	cups (381 grams) bread flour
2	cups (400 grams) plus 3 tablespoons (36 grams) granulated sugar, divided
2½	tablespoons (12.5 grams) black cocoa powder
1	tablespoon (9 grams) kosher salt
1½	cups (340 grams) plus 1 tablespoon (14 grams) unsalted butter, softened and divided
2	teaspoons (6 grams) instant yeast
1	cup plus 2 tablespoons (270 grams) cold water

1. In the bowl of a stand mixer fitted with the dough hook attachment, place flour, 3 tablespoons (36 grams) sugar, black cocoa, salt, 1 tablespoon (14 grams) butter, and yeast. Add 1 cup plus 2 tablespoons (270 grams) cold water, and beat at low speed until moistened, about 2 minutes. Increase mixer speed to medium-high, and beat until a smooth and elastic dough forms, 8 to 10 minutes. Cover with plastic wrap, and let rise at room temperature for 1 hour.

2. Punch down dough, and roll into a 10-inch square. Wrap dough in plastic wrap, and freeze for 30 minutes, turning halfway through.

3. On a sheet of parchment paper, draw a 6½-inch square. Turn parchment over; place remaining 1½ cups (340 grams) butter onto drawn square. Shape butter into a square, and wrap in parchment. Refrigerate for 10 to 15 minutes.

4. On a lightly floured surface, place chilled dough. Unwrap butter block, and place in center of square, one corner toward you. Fold dough edges over to enclose butter block, pinching seams. Roll dough into a 24x10-inch rectangle. Fold dough into thirds, like a letter. Repeat this rolling and folding process two more times. Wrap in plastic wrap, and refrigerate for 45 minutes.

5. Coat a work surface with ½ cup (50 grams) sugar. Transfer dough to work surface, and roll into a 24x10-inch rectangle. Sprinkle dough with ½ cup (50 grams) sugar, and fold into thirds, like a letter. Sprinkle work surface with another ½ cup (50 grams) sugar. Roll dough into a 24x10-inch rectangle again, and sprinkle with remaining ½ cup (50 grams) sugar. Cut dough into 4-inch squares, discarding scraps. Fold in corners of each square to center, pressing center firmly.

6. Preheat oven to 365°F (185°C). Place a rimmed baking sheet in oven to catch any butter drips. Generously butter a 12-cup muffin pan.

7. Transfer folded squares to prepared muffin cups. Cover with plastic wrap, and let rise at room temperature for 20 minutes.

8. Place muffin pan on baking sheet in oven. Bake until sugar starts to turn golden, about 30 minutes. Immediately remove from pan, and let cool on a wire rack for 20 minutes. Kouign amanns are best enjoyed the day they are baked.

PRO TIP
If dough becomes too difficult to work with at any time, refrigerate for 15 to 20 minutes before proceeding with recipe.

CARAMELIZED WHITE CHOCOLATE CHOUX PUFFS

Makes about 24 puffs

Recipe by Jesse Szewczyk

This recipe uses the same technique as choux au craquelin, the adorable cream puffs topped with crunchy sugar. The crackled topping accentuates the thick layer of silky Whipped Caramelized White Chocolate Ganache perfectly. Pastry can be complicated, but these are relatively easy and all of the steps are fairly forgiving. (If you've made pâte à choux and sugar cookie dough before, this will be a breeze.)

    cup (227 grams) unsalted butter, softened and divided
½   cup (110 grams) firmly packed light brown sugar
2¼ cups (281 grams) all-purpose flour, divided
    cup (240 grams) water
    teaspoon (4 grams) granulated sugar
¼ teaspoon kosher salt
4   large eggs (200 grams)
½ recipe Whipped Caramelized White Chocolate Ganache (recipe on page 37)

1. In the bowl of a stand mixer fitted with the paddle attachment, beat ½ cup (113.5 grams) butter and brown sugar at medium speed until creamy, 3 to 4 minutes, stopping to scrape sides of bowl. With mixer on low speed, gradually add 1 cup (125 grams) flour, beating until smooth, about 2 minutes. Shape dough into a disk, and wrap in plastic wrap. Refrigerate for 30 minutes.

2. Preheat oven to 375°F (190°C). Line 2 sheet trays with parchment paper. Using a 1½-inch round cutter, trace 24 circles onto parchment; turn parchment over.

3. In a small saucepan, bring 1 cup (240 grams) water, granulated sugar, salt, and remaining ½ cup (113.5 grams) butter to a boil over medium heat. Add remaining 1¼ cups (156 grams) flour, and stir with a wooden spoon until completely homogenous. Cook, stirring constantly, until a thin film coats bottom of pan, about 3 minutes.

4. Transfer mixture to the bowl of a stand mixer fitted with the paddle attachment, and beat at medium speed until slightly cooled, about 2 minutes. Add eggs, one at a time, beating well after each addition. Transfer batter to a piping bag fitted with a straight tip. With a ½-inch distance between piping tip and parchment, pipe batter onto drawn circles on prepared pans, smoothing tops with a wet finger.

5. Between 2 sheets of parchment paper, roll dough to ¼-inch thickness. Using a 1½-inch round cutter, cut 24 rounds from dough, and place on top of piped batter circles.

6. Bake until puffed and golden, 30 to 35 minutes. Let cool completely. Cut puffs in half horizontally. Using a pastry bag fitted with a star tip, fill each puff with Whipped Caramelized White Chocolate Ganache. Serve immediately, or store in an airtight container at room temperature for up to 2 days. (Do not refrigerate after assembling. The whipped filling will set and become too firm.)

MAKE AHEAD
You can make the puffs (unfilled) up to 3 days in advance and leave them at room temperature. When ready to assemble, bake at 375°F (190°C) for about 5 minutes to crisp them back up.

Photo by Mark Weinberg

HAZELNUT FINANCIERS

Makes 16 financiers

Financiers are always an elegant affair—but baked into fluted barquette molds, they take on a new dimension of elegance. Our tender Hazelnut Financiers are sweetened with a touch of honey, but the real showstopper is its literal crowning glory: crunchy, salty Candied Hazelnuts.

½ cup plus 4 tablespoons (169 grams) unsalted butter, softened and divided
2 tablespoons (42 grams) honey
1½ cups (144 grams) hazelnut flour
¾ cup plus 2 tablespoons (174 grams) granulated sugar
½ cup (63 grams) all-purpose flour
¼ teaspoon kosher salt
3 large egg whites (90 grams), room temperature
1 tablespoon (18 grams) vanilla bean paste
Candied Hazelnuts (recipe follows)

1. Preheat oven to 400°F (200°C). Using 2 tablespoons (28 grams) butter, heavily grease 16 (5-inch) barquette molds* (or a 24-cup mini muffin pan). Place molds on a sheet pan, and freeze while preparing batter.
2. In a medium saucepan, melt remaining ½ cup plus 2 tablespoons (141 grams) butter over medium heat. Cook until butter turns a medium-brown color and has a nutty aroma, about 10 minutes. Remove from heat; stir in honey. Let cool slightly.
3. In a large bowl, whisk together hazelnut flour, sugar, all-purpose flour, and salt. Add egg whites and vanilla bean paste, whisking until smooth. Slowly whisk in browned butter mixture just until incorporated. Spoon batter into prepared molds or muffin cups, filling three-fourths full. Tap molds to level batter. (If you do not have 16 molds and need to bake in batches, the batter will keep in the refrigerator. You do not have to let it come to room temperature before baking, but do not

stir the batter.) With molds still on sheet pan, place in oven, and immediately reduce oven temperature to 375°F (190°C).
4. Bake until a wooden pick inserted in center comes out clean, about 15 minutes, rotating pan halfway through baking. (Bake mini muffins for 13 to 14 minutes.) Let cool completely in molds. Unmold financiers, using a knife if needed. Top with Candied Hazelnuts before serving. Financiers (without Candied Hazelnuts) can be stored in an airtight container at room temperature for up to 1 week.

*We used Gobel Nonstick Fluted Barquette Molds, available on surlatable.com.

CANDIED HAZELNUTS
Makes about 1 cup

½ cup (100 grams) granulated sugar
1½ tablespoons (22.5 grams) water
½ cup (71 grams) dry roasted unsalted hazelnuts, halved
½ teaspoon (1.5 grams) flaked sea salt

1. Line a sheet pan with a nonstick baking mat.
2. In a small saucepan, heat sugar and 1½ tablespoons (22.5 grams) water over high heat. (It should look like wet sand.) Using a pastry brush, brush down sides of pan using water. Cook, stirring gently, until sugar is dissolved and mixture is light amber colored. (Do not stir after mixture starts to boil.) Immediately remove from heat, and quickly stir in hazelnuts; pour onto prepared pan. Using a heatproof spatula, spread hazelnuts in a single layer; sprinkle with salt. Let cool completely.
3. Gently tap hazelnuts on sheet pan to break into smaller pieces, and chop using a chef's knife. Use the same day. Keep uncovered until ready to use.

COOKIES AND BARS

COOKIES

Featuring modern takes on the classic snickerdoodle and a
nostalgic black cocoa throwback, our cookies will get you
through your parties, picnics, holiday meals, and every
celebration in between.

STRAWBERRY AND ROSEMARY SHORTBREAD

Makes 8 to 10 servings

This herbal, crumbly shortbread turns a blush pink with a final dusting of Strawberry Sugar.

1   cup (227 grams) unsalted butter, softened
½   cup (100 grams) granulated sugar
1½   cups (188 grams) all-purpose flour
½   cup (64 grams) cornstarch
⅓   cup (5 grams) freeze-dried strawberries, powdered (see PRO TIP)
½   teaspoon (1.5 grams) kosher salt
1   tablespoon (2 grams) chopped fresh rosemary
⅓   cup (49 grams) diced fresh strawberries
Strawberry Sugar (recipe follows)

1. Preheat oven to 350°F (180°C). Butter and flour a 9-inch square baking dish.
2. In the bowl of a stand mixer fitted with the paddle attachment, beat butter and granulated sugar at medium speed until creamy, 3 to 4 minutes, stopping to scrape sides of bowl.
3. In a medium bowl, sift together flour, cornstarch, freeze-dried strawberries, and salt. Stir in rosemary. With mixer on low speed, gradually add flour mixture to butter mixture, beating until almost combined. Add fresh strawberries, beating until combined.
4. Turn out dough onto a heavily floured surface. Using well-floured hands, knead dough 5 to 10 times, about 1 minute. Press dough into prepared pan.
5. Bake until lightly golden, 30 to 35 minutes. Let cool completely on a wire rack. Sprinkle with Strawberry Sugar.

STRAWBERRY SUGAR
Makes about ½ cup

½   cup (8 grams) freeze-dried strawberries
⅓   cup (67 grams) granulated sugar

1. In the work bowl of a food processor, place freeze-dried strawberries and sugar; process until a fine pink sugar forms, about 2 minutes.

PRO TIP
To make powdered freeze-dried strawberries, place freeze-dried strawberries in the bowl of a food processor; pulse until reduced to a powder.

CHOCOLATE-COVERED GINGER COOKIES WITH STRAWBERRY MARSHMALLOW

Makes 12 cookies

The retro Nabisco Mallomars, now in millennial pink. Our rendition pairs a gingersnap cookie with a chocolate-capped peak of marshmallow.

Strawberry Marshmallow (recipe on page 362)
12 Strawberry Gingersnaps (recipe follows)
10 ounces (300 grams) dark chocolate melting wafers

1. Place a wire rack on a rimmed baking sheet.
2. Spoon Strawberry Marshmallow into a pastry bag fitted with a Wilton #2A round piping tip. Using even pressure, pipe a "kiss" shape onto each Strawberry Gingersnap. Let marshmallow set, about 20 minutes.
3. In a medium microwave-safe bowl, microwave chocolate wafers on high in 30-second intervals, stirring between each, until melted and smooth. Dip marshmallow-topped gingersnaps in melted chocolate, and place on prepared rack. (Melted chocolate can also be spooned over marshmallow if bowl is too shallow for dipping.) Let chocolate set. Store in an airtight container at room temperature for up to 5 days.

STRAWBERRY GINGERSNAPS
Makes about 60

1   cup (227 grams) unsalted butter, softened
1⅓ cups (267 grams) granulated sugar
1   large egg (50 grams), room temperature
1   large egg yolk (19 grams), room temperature
½   teaspoon (2 grams) vanilla extract
⅓   cup (113 grams) molasses
3   cups (375 grams) all-purpose flour
½   cup (8 grams) freeze-dried strawberries, powdered (see PRO TIP on page 260)
2½ teaspoons (12.5 grams) baking soda
2½ teaspoons (5 grams) ground cinnamon
2½ teaspoons (5 grams) ground ginger
¾   teaspoon (2.25 grams) kosher salt
¼   teaspoon ground black pepper
½   cup (48 grams) chopped Candied Strawberries (recipe follows)
¼   cup (43 grams) diced crystallized ginger

1. In the bowl of stand mixer fitted with the paddle attachment, beat butter and sugar at medium speed until fluffy, 3 to 4 minutes, stopping to scrape sides of bowl. Add egg, egg yolk, and vanilla, beating just until combined. Beat in molasses.
2. In a medium bowl, whisk together flour, freeze-dried strawberries, baking soda, cinnamon, ground ginger, salt, and pepper. With mixer on low speed, gradually add flour mixture to butter mixture, beating just until combined. Add chopped Candied Strawberries and crystallized ginger, beating until combined.
3. On a heavily floured surface, divide dough in half. Shape each half into a 2-inch-wide log. Wrap tightly in plastic wrap, and freeze until firm, at least 1 hour.
4. Preheat oven to 325°F (170°C). Line 3 baking sheets with parchment paper.
5. Working with one log at a time, slice into ¼-inch-thick slices. Place on prepared pans.
6. Bake until edges are browned, 10 to 14 minutes. Let cool completely.

CANDIED STRAWBERRIES
Makes 1 cup

1   cup (200 grams) granulated sugar
½   cup (120 grams) water
½   cup (120 grams) fresh lemon juice
4   cups (680 grams) (⅛-inch-thick*) sliced fresh strawberries

1. In a small saucepan, bring sugar, ½ cup (120 grams) water, and lemon juice to a boil over medium heat; cook until sugar is dissolved. Remove from heat, and let cool completely.
2. Preheat oven to 200°F (93°C). Line 2 rimmed baking sheets with nonstick baking mats.
3. In a medium bowl, toss together sugar mixture and strawberries. Strain strawberries through a fine-mesh sieve. Place in a single layer on prepared pans. Gently pat strawberries with a paper towel to remove excess liquid.
4. Bake until dry but tacky, 2½ to 3 hours. Let cool completely. Cover and refrigerate for up to 1 week.

We used a mandoline to slice.

MILK CHOCOLATE EGG COOKIES

Makes about 30 cookies

A nostalgic ode to Easter candy, this Cadbury egg-studded cookie is all about the texture. Crispy on the outside, chewy on the inside, and with a boost of crunch from the candy-coated chocolate eggs, it's a new and improved way to indulge in the iconic Easter treat.

½ cup (113 grams) unsalted butter, melted
1 cup (200 grams) granulated sugar
½ cup (110 grams) firmly packed light brown sugar
4 ounces (115 grams) 45% cacao milk chocolate, melted
2 large eggs (100 grams), room temperature
1 teaspoon (4 grams) almond extract
½ teaspoon (2 grams) vanilla extract
1 cup (125 grams) all-purpose flour
½ cup (43 grams) unsweetened cocoa powder
¾ teaspoon (2.25 grams) kosher salt
½ teaspoon (2.5 grams) baking soda
½ teaspoon (2.5 grams) baking powder
2½ cups (450 grams) crushed candy-coated milk chocolate eggs, divided
½ cup (85 grams) 38% cacao milk chocolate chunks*

1. In the bowl of a stand mixer fitted with the paddle attachment, beat melted butter, sugars, melted chocolate, eggs, and extracts at medium speed until well combined.
2. In a medium bowl, sift together flour, cocoa, salt, baking soda, and baking powder. With mixer on low speed, gradually add flour mixture to butter mixture, beating until combined. Add ½ cup (90 grams) crushed chocolate eggs and chocolate chunks, beating just until combined. Cover and refrigerate for at least 1 hour or overnight.
3. Preheat oven to 325°F (170°C). Line 3 baking sheets with parchment paper.
4. Using a 1-ounce spring-loaded scoop, scoop dough, and shape into ½-inch-thick disks. Place remaining 2 cups (360 grams) crushed chocolate eggs in a small bowl. Press each disk into candy eggs, coating well. Place 1½ inches apart on prepared pans.
5. Bake until set, 12 to 15 minutes. Let cool completely.

We used Guittard Milk Chocolate Organic Wafers 38% Cacao.

SNICKERDOODLE SABLÉS

Makes about 24 cookies

Recipe by Marian Cooper Cairns

A sophisticated spin on the classic American cookie, this recipe delivers the buttery cinnamon flavor you love in a crumbly French shortbread. Instead of just rolling the dough in cinnamon and sugar like the standard snickerdoodle recipe requires, we incorporate the ingredients into the dough, brush with egg yolk, and dip them in cinnamon and sugar again before baking.

⅓ cup (133 grams) granulated sugar
2 teaspoons (4 grams) ground cinnamon
1 cup (227 grams) unsalted butter, softened
⅓ cup (40 grams) confectioners' sugar
½ teaspoon (1.5 grams) fine sea salt
2 large egg yolks (37 grams), divided
1 teaspoon (4 grams) vanilla extract
2 cups (250 grams) all-purpose flour

1. In a small bowl, combine granulated sugar and cinnamon.

2. In the bowl of stand mixer fitted with the paddle attachment, beat butter at medium speed just until creamy. Add ⅓ cup cinnamon sugar, confectioners' sugar, and sea salt, and beat until smooth, about 1 minute, stopping to scrape sides of bowl. Add 1 egg yolk (18.5 grams) and vanilla, and beat for 1 minute. With mixer on low speed, gradually add flour, beating just until combined.

3. Turn out dough onto a lightly floured surface. Press and knead until dough comes together. Divide dough in half, and roll each half into a 7-inch log. Wrap logs in plastic wrap, and refrigerate for at least 4 hours or up to 2 days.

4. Preheat oven to 350°F (180°C). Line 2 baking sheets with parchment paper.

5. Using a sharp knife, cut dough into ½-inch-thick rounds. Brush top of rounds with remaining 1 egg yolk (18.5 grams), and dip in remaining cinnamon sugar. Place rounds 2 inches apart on prepared pans.

6. Bake until golden, 18 to 22 minutes, rotating pans once. Let cool on pans for 5 minutes. Remove from pans, and let cool completely on wire racks.

Photo by Matt Armendariz

BLACK COCOA SANDWICH COOKIES

Just like the Oreo® sandwich cookies of your childhood—only bigger, better, and baked completely from scratch.

¼   cup plus 3 tablespoons (36 grams) black cocoa powder, plus more for dusting
2   tablespoons (28 grams) unsalted butter, melted
5   tablespoons (70 grams) unsalted butter, softened
½   cup (110 grams) firmly packed light brown sugar
¼   teaspoon kosher salt
1   large egg (50 grams)
1   teaspoon (4 grams) vanilla extract
1½   cups (188 grams) all-purpose flour
Vanilla Filling (recipe follows)

1. In a small bowl, whisk together black cocoa and melted butter. Let cool slightly.
2. In the bowl of a stand mixer fitted with the paddle attachment, beat softened butter, brown sugar, and salt at medium speed until fluffy, 3 to 4 minutes, stopping to scrape sides of bowl. Beat in cocoa mixture. Add egg and vanilla, beating until well combined. Add flour, and beat until fully incorporated and a smooth dough forms.
3. Between 2 sheets of parchment paper, roll dough to ⅛-inch thickness. Transfer dough between parchment to freezer. Freeze until set, about 30 minutes.
4. Preheat oven to 325°F (170°C). Line a baking sheet with parchment paper.
5. Dip a 3-inch fluted round cutter in black cocoa to prevent cutter from sticking to dough. Cut dough, and place cookies about ½ inch apart on prepared pan. (Reroll scraps between

2 sheets of parchment as necessary. Freeze rerolled dough at least 15 minutes or until ready to cut cookies and bake.)
6. Bake until a slight indentation is left when pressed with a finger, about 10 to 12 minutes. Let cool completely on pan.
7. Place Vanilla Filling in a pastry bag fitted with a round piping tip. Pipe Vanilla Filling on flat side of half of cookies. Place remaining cookies, flat side down, on top of filling.

VANILLA FILLING
Makes about 2 cups

1   cup (227 grams) unsalted butter, softened
4   cups (480 grams) confectioners' sugar
1   teaspoon (6 grams) vanilla bean paste
⅛   teaspoon kosher salt

1. In the bowl of a stand mixer fitted with the paddle attachment, beat butter at medium speed until creamy, 5 to 6 minutes. Gradually add confectioners' sugar, beating until combined. Add vanilla bean paste and salt, beating until smooth.

SPICE IT UP
Black cocoa pairs well with spice, neither bowing to nor overpowering the warm, aromatic flavor. For a spicy update on the sandwich cookie, consider adding ¼ teaspoon to ½ teaspoon (1 gram) ground cardamom, cinnamon, or even cayenne to the cookie dough (after beating in the vanilla in step 2).

S'MORES CHOCOLATE CHUNK COOKIES

Makes about 30 cookies

Recipe by Marian Cooper Cairns

We fused all the flavors of the classic campfire treat into one dough. In the mood for ice cream sandwiches? Vanilla bean, rocky road, and fudge will all be delicious sandwiched between these chewy yet crispy-in-the-right-places cookies.

¾   cup (170 grams) unsalted butter, softened
1   cup (220 grams) firmly packed dark brown sugar
⅓   cup (67 grams) granulated sugar
2   large eggs (100 grams)
2   teaspoons (8 grams) vanilla extract
2   cups (250 grams) all-purpose flour
1   cup (130 grams) graham cracker crumbs
1   teaspoon (5 grams) baking soda
1   teaspoon (3 grams) kosher salt
1½   (12-ounce) packages (408 grams) chocolate chunks (about 2⅓ cups)
1   cup (51 grams) miniature marshmallows bits*

1. Preheat oven to 350°F (180°C). Line 2 baking sheets with parchment paper.
2. In the bowl of a stand mixer fitted with the paddle attachment, beat butter and sugars at medium speed until fluffy, 3 to 4 minutes, stopping to scrape sides of bowl. Add eggs and vanilla, beating until combined.
3. In a medium bowl, whisk together flour, graham cracker crumbs, baking soda, and salt. With mixer on low speed, gradually add flour mixture to butter mixture, beating just until combined. Beat in chocolate chunks and marshmallow bits just until combined. Working in 2 batches, drop dough by 2 tablespoonfuls 2 inches apart onto prepared pans.

4. Bake until desired degree of doneness, 10 to 14 minutes. Let cool on pans for 5 minutes. Remove from pans, and let cool completely on wire racks.

We used Jet-Puffed Mallow Bits, a smaller, more dehydrated marshmallow product than regular miniature marshmallows. Do not use regular miniature marshmallows in this recipe. They will melt and burn.

> **PRO TIP**
> To get photo-worthy cookies like the ones shown, press a few chocolate chunks and marshmallow bits onto the exterior of each dough ball right before popping them in the oven.

Photo by Matt Armendariz

CHOCOLATE PEPPERMINT COOKIES

Makes about 45 cookies

These addictive cookies get a creamy boost from milk chocolate chips and a hint of crisp mint from peppermint extract. Crushed candy canes speckle the top for a traditional wintry finish.

1½ cups (340 grams) unsalted butter, softened
1¼ cups (275 grams) firmly packed light brown sugar
½   cup (100 grams) granulated sugar
3   large eggs (150 grams)
2   teaspoons (8 grams) vanilla extract
½   teaspoon (2 grams) peppermint extract
3¼ cups (406 grams) all-purpose flour
1   cup (85 grams) Dutch process cocoa powder
1½ teaspoons (4.5 grams) kosher salt
1   teaspoon (5 grams) baking soda
2½ cups (425 grams) milk chocolate chips
½   cup (75 grams) candy cane pieces

1. In the bowl of a stand mixer fitted with the paddle attachment, beat butter and sugars at medium speed until fluffy, 2 to 3 minutes, stopping to scrape sides of bowl. Reduce mixer speed to medium-low. Add eggs, one at a time, beating well after each addition. Beat in extracts.
2. In a large bowl, whisk together flour, cocoa, salt, and baking soda. With mixer on low speed, gradually add flour mixture to butter mixture, beating just until combined. (Do not overmix.) Gently stir in chocolate chips. Refrigerate for 30 minutes.
3. Preheat oven to 350°F (180°C). Line rimmed baking sheets with parchment paper.
4. Using a 2-tablespoon scoop, drop dough at least 2 inches apart onto prepared pans.
5. Bake, one batch at a time, for 16 minutes, rotating pan halfway through baking. Remove from oven, and immediately sprinkle ½ teaspoon candy cane pieces on top of each cookie. Let cool on pans for 5 minutes. Using a thin spatula, remove from pans, and let cool completely on wire racks. Store in an airtight container at room temperature for up to 5 days.

SPICED CHOCOLATE CHUNK OATMEAL COOKIES

Makes 24 to 30 cookies

Recipe by Thalia Ho

Filled with comforting spice, a drop of warmth from rum, notes of herbaceous rosemary, and molten bursts of dark chocolate, these cookies are stellar.

¾ cup plus 2 tablespoons (198 grams) unsalted butter, softened
¾ cup plus 2 tablespoons (174 grams) granulated sugar
¾ cup plus 1 tablespoon (179 grams) firmly packed light brown sugar
2 large eggs (100 grams), room temperature
1 tablespoon (14 grams) rum (optional)
1 teaspoon (4 grams) vanilla extract
1⅓ cups (167 grams) all-purpose flour
¾ teaspoon (3.75 grams) baking powder
¾ teaspoon (3.75 grams) baking soda
¾ teaspoon (1.5 grams) ground cinnamon
½ teaspoon (1 gram) ground ginger
¼ teaspoon kosher salt
¼ teaspoon ground cardamom
¼ teaspoon ground cloves
¼ teaspoon ground nutmeg
¼ teaspoon dried rosemary
2¼ cups (203 grams) old-fashioned oats
¾ cup (112 grams) very roughly chopped dark chocolate
½ cup (50 grams) rye flakes*
½ cup (57 grams) toasted chopped walnuts
Flaked salt, for finishing

1. In the bowl of a stand mixer fitted with the paddle attachment, beat butter and sugars at medium speed until fluffy, 2 to 3 minutes, stopping to scrape sides of bowl. Add eggs, one at a time, beating well after each addition. Beat in rum (if using) and vanilla.
2. In a medium bowl, whisk together flour, baking powder, baking soda, cinnamon, ginger, kosher salt, cardamom, cloves, nutmeg, and rosemary. With mixer on low speed, gradually add flour mixture to butter mixture, beating just until combined, about 1 minute. (Some dry floury pockets may remain in dough.) Using a large wooden spoon, gently fold in oats, chocolate, rye flakes, and walnuts. Cover and refrigerate for at least 1 hour.
3. Preheat oven to 350°F (180°C). Line baking sheets with parchment paper.
4. Scoop dough by heaping tablespoonfuls (about 45 grams), and roll into balls. Place 2 inches apart on prepared pans.
5. Bake for 12 to 15 minutes, rotating pans halfway through baking, raising pans a few inches above oven rack, and tapping pans firmly against rack to slightly deflate, spread and help disperse melted chocolate into cookies. Repeat procedure every 2 minutes until cookies are just golden brown, firm around the edges and slightly soft in center, and have molten pockets of chocolate running throughout them.
6. Remove from oven; immediately sprinkle cookies with flaked salt. Let cool on pans for 5 minutes. Remove from pans, and let cool completely on wire racks. Best served warm on the day of baking but can be stored in an airtight container at room temperature for up to 5 days.

Rye flakes are available at health food stores or online. You can also use ½ cup (45 grams) old-fashioned oats instead.

Photo by Thalia Ho

GLAZED CAMPARI & STRAWBERRY COOKIES

Makes about 30 cookies

Recipe by Marian Cooper Cairns

If you love a Negroni (the ultimate stiff summer cocktail), this will be your signature summer cookie.

- 1 cup (227 grams) unsalted butter, softened
- 1 cup (200 grams) granulated sugar
- 2 large egg whites (60 grams)
- 2 tablespoons (30 grams) plus 2 teaspoons (10 grams) heavy whipping cream, divided
- 1 tablespoon (3 grams) grapefruit zest
- 1 teaspoon (4 grams) vanilla extract
- 2¾ cups (344 grams) cake flour
- 2 teaspoons (10 grams) baking powder
- 1¼ teaspoons (3.75 grams) kosher salt
- 1 (0.8-ounce) package (16 grams) freeze-dried strawberries, chopped (about 1 cup)
- 1 to 1¼ cups (120 to 150 grams) confectioners' sugar
- 2 tablespoons (30 grams) Campari

1. Preheat oven to 350°F (180°C). Line 2 baking sheets with parchment paper.
2. In the bowl of a stand mixer fitted with the paddle attachment, beat butter and granulated sugar at medium speed until creamy, about 2 minutes, stopping to scrape sides of bowl. Add egg whites, 2 tablespoons (30 grams) cream, zest, and vanilla, beating until well combined.
3. In a medium bowl, stir together flour, baking powder, and salt. With mixer on low speed, gradually add flour mixture to butter mixture, beating just until combined. Stir in freeze-dried strawberries until combined. Using a 2-tablespoon scoop, scoop dough into rounds, and place about 2½ inches apart on prepared pans.
4. Bake until puffed and pale golden, 14 to 16 minutes, rotating pans once. Let cool completely on pans.
5. In a small bowl, whisk together 1 cup (120 grams) confectioners' sugar, Campari, and remaining 2 teaspoons (10 grams) cream until smooth. Add remaining ¼ cup (30 grams) confectioners' sugar, if needed. Dip or drizzle glaze over top of cooled cookies. Let stand until set, about 30 minutes.

Photo by Matt Armendariz

OATMEAL CHERRY WALNUT COOKIES

Makes about 24 cookies

Recipe by Marian Cooper Cairns

Who needs raisins when you can have a much bigger, even sweeter flavor impact with plump dried cherries? If walnuts are not your jam, pecans or hazelnuts are great substitutes. Be sure to toast the nuts for optimal flavor. Baking at 350°F (180°C) until the nuts smell slightly fragrant, about 8 minutes, will do the trick.

1 cup (227 grams) unsalted butter, softened
1 cup (200 grams) granulated sugar
1 cup (220 grams) firmly packed dark brown sugar
2 large eggs (100 grams)
2 teaspoons (8 grams) vanilla extract

2 cups (250 grams) all-purpose flour
1 teaspoon (5 grams) baking soda
1 teaspoon (5 grams) baking powder
1 teaspoon (3 grams) kosher salt
¾ teaspoon (1.5 grams) ground cinnamon
½ teaspoon (1 gram) ground nutmeg
3 cups (240 grams) old-fashioned oats
1½ cups (192 grams) dried cherries, coarsely chopped
1½ cups (170 grams) coarsely chopped toasted walnuts

1. Preheat oven to 350°F (180°C). Line 2 baking sheets with parchment paper.
2. In the bowl of a stand mixer fitted with the paddle attachment, beat butter and sugars at medium speed until fluffy, about 2 minutes, stopping to scrape sides of bowl. Add eggs and vanilla, beating until combined.

3. In a medium bowl, stir together flour, baking soda, baking powder, salt, cinnamon, and nutmeg. With mixer on low speed, gradually add flour mixture to butter mixture, beating just until combined. Beat in oats, cherries, and walnuts. Working in 2 batches, drop dough by 3 tablespoonfuls 2 inches apart onto prepared pans. (For picture-perfect cookies, press a few walnuts and cherries onto exterior of each dough ball.)
4. Bake until golden but still slightly soft in center, 15 to 18 minutes, rotating pans once Let cool on pans for 3 minutes. Remove from pans, and let cool completely on wire racks.

Photo by Matt Armendariz

SPICED CRANBERRY BARK COOKIES

Makes 36 cookies

Recipe by Rebecca Firth

Picture the very yummiest chocolate chip cookie, and then swap out the usual chocolate chips for a homemade chocolate bark that's loaded with toasted hazelnuts, fresh cranberries, holiday spices, and sea salt flakes. And don't be intimidated by the extra step of making the bark. This would be a great recipe to experiment with and swap in some other favorite fruit and nut combinations.

10 tablespoons (140 grams) unsalted butter, softened
1¼ cups (275 grams) firmly packed light brown sugar
½ cup (100 grams) granulated sugar
⅓ cup (75 grams) sunflower seed oil or other neutral oil
2 large eggs (100 grams), room temperature
2 tablespoons (30 grams) milk, room temperature
1 tablespoon (13 grams) vanilla extract
2 cups (260 grams) all-purpose flour
1 cup (127 grams) bread flour
2 teaspoons (10 grams) baking powder
1 teaspoon (5 grams) baking soda
1 teaspoon (3 grams) sea salt
1 teaspoon (2 grams) ground cinnamon
½ teaspoon (1 gram) ground nutmeg
Cranberry Bark (recipe follows), coarsely chopped
Flaked sea salt, for sprinkling

1. Preheat oven to 350°F (180°C). Line several baking sheets with parchment paper.
2. In the bowl of a stand mixer fitted with the paddle attachment, beat butter, sugars, and oil at medium speed until fluffy, 2 to 3 minutes, stopping to scrape sides of bowl. Add eggs, one at a time, beating well after each addition. With mixer on low speed, add milk and vanilla, beating until well combined, about 1 minute.
3. In a medium bowl, whisk together flours, baking powder, baking soda, sea salt, cinnamon, and nutmeg. Gradually add flour mixture to butter mixture, beating just until combined. (You still want some streaks of flour.) Fold Cranberry Bark into dough until evenly distributed. Let dough stand at room temperature for 15 minutes.
4. Scoop dough by 2 tablespoonfuls, and roll into balls. Place about 2 inches apart on prepared pans.

5. Bake for 11 to 12 minutes. Tap pans on counter once, and sprinkle with flaked salt. Let cool on pans for 10 minutes. Remove from pans, and let cool completely on wire racks. Store in an airtight container for up to 3 days.

CRANBERRY BARK

Makes 4 cups

10 ounces (300 grams) dark chocolate, finely chopped
½ teaspoon (1 gram) ground cinnamon
½ teaspoon (1 gram) ground allspice
¼ teaspoon ground cloves
1 cup (100 grams) fresh cranberries, room temperature, some chopped and some left whole
¼ cup (28 grams) chopped toasted hazelnuts
1 teaspoon (3 grams) flaked sea salt

1. Line a baking sheet with parchment paper.
2. In the top of a double boiler, combine chocolate, cinnamon, allspice, and cloves. Cook over simmering water, stirring frequently, until chocolate is melted.
3. Pour melted chocolate onto prepared pan. Using a spatula, spread to ⅛- to ¼-inch thickness. Immediately sprinkle with cranberries and hazelnuts, and gently press into chocolate. Sprinkle with flaked salt. Refrigerate or freeze until ready to use.

Photo by Rebecca Firth

VANILLA CHAI PINWHEEL COOKIES

Makes 40 cookies

Recipe by Becky Sue Wilberding

Vanilla and chai-spiced cookie doughs are swirled together in a hypnotizing spiral of simple sweetness and aromatic spice with festive sparkling sugar edges.

2¾   cups (344 grams) all-purpose flour, divided
2   teaspoons (4 grams) ground cinnamon
1   teaspoon (2 grams) ground cardamom
¾   teaspoon (1.5 grams) ground ginger
1   teaspoon (5 grams) baking powder, divided
1   teaspoon (3 grams) kosher salt, divided
¼   teaspoon ground allspice
¼   teaspoon ground white pepper
½   cup (113 grams) pecan halves
1   cup (227 grams) unsalted butter, softened and divided
½   cup (110 grams) firmly packed light brown sugar
3   large eggs (150 grams), divided
2½   teaspoons (10 grams) vanilla extract, divided
½   cup (100 grams) granulated sugar
¼   cup (50 grams) sparkling or turbinado sugar

1. Preheat oven to 350°F (180°C).
2. In a medium bowl, whisk together 1¼ cups (156 grams) flour, cinnamon, cardamom, ginger, ½ teaspoon (2.5 grams) baking powder, ½ teaspoon (1.5 grams) salt, allspice, and white pepper. Set aside.
3. Arrange pecans on a baking sheet, and toast until they start to deepen in color, about 8 minutes. Let cool slightly. Transfer to the work bowl of a food processor. Add 2 tablespoons flour mixture, and pulse until pecans are finely ground. (The flour will absorb the oils from the nuts and will prevent a nut butter from forming in the food processor.) Add pecan mixture to remaining flour mixture, whisking to combine.
4. In the bowl of a stand mixer fitted with the paddle attachment, beat ½ cup (113.5 grams) butter and brown sugar at medium speed until creamy, 2 to 3 minutes, stopping to scrape sides of bowl. Add 1 egg (50 grams) and 1 teaspoon (4 grams) vanilla, beating until combined. With mixer on low speed, gradually add flour mixture, beating until combined. Turn out dough onto a lightly floured surface, and shape into a disk. Wrap in plastic wrap, and refrigerate for at least 1 hour.
5. In the bowl of a stand mixer fitted with the paddle attachment, beat granulated sugar and remaining ½ cup (113.5 grams) butter at medium speed until creamy, 2 to 3 minutes, stopping to scrape sides of bowl. Add 1 egg (50 grams) and remaining 1½ teaspoons (6 grams) vanilla, beating until combined.

6. In a medium bowl, whisk together remaining 1½ cups (188 grams) flour, remaining ½ teaspoon (2.5 grams) baking powder, and remaining ½ teaspoon (1.5 grams) salt. With mixer on low speed, gradually add flour mixture to butter mixture, beating until combined. Turn out dough onto a lightly floured surface, and shape into a disk. Wrap in plastic wrap, and refrigerate for at least 1 hour.
7. Let doughs stand at room temperature until slightly softened, about 5 minutes. On a lightly floured sheet of parchment paper, roll vanilla cookie dough into a 16x12-inch rectangle, ⅛ inch thick. Transfer dough on parchment to a baking sheet. Refrigerate for 15 minutes. Repeat procedure with chai cookie dough.
8. Transfer vanilla cookie dough on parchment to a flat surface. Carefully invert chai cookie dough on top of vanilla cookie dough. Between sheets of parchment, gently roll over doughs a few times to press together. Peel away top sheet of parchment.
9. Starting at one long side, roll dough into a log, using bottom sheet of parchment to help lift and roll. (If dough cracks, stop rolling, and let stand for a few minutes until pliable.) Be sure to roll doughs together as tight as possible to avoid gaps. Tightly wrap in parchment paper, twisting ends to seal. Transfer to a baking sheet, seam side down. Refrigerate for at least 2 hours, or freeze until ready to use.
10. Preheat oven to 350°F (180°C). Line 2 baking sheets with parchment paper.
11. In a small bowl, whisk remaining 1 egg (50 grams). Brush log with egg wash, and sprinkle with sparkling or turbinado sugar. Roll back and forth a few times so sugar sticks to log. Using a sharp knife, cut into ¼-inch-thick slices. Place about 1 inch apart on prepared pans.
12. Bake on upper and middle racks of oven until edges are just beginning to turn golden, 12 to 15 minutes, rotating pans halfway through baking. Let cool completely on pans. Store in an airtight container for up to 2 weeks.

Note: *Dough can be refrigerated for up to 3 days or frozen for up to 1 month.*

PRO TIP
Use 1 to 2 paper towel rolls sliced lengthwise to keep the dough log from flattening on one side.

Photo by Becky Sue Wilberding

ROSEMARY SHORTBREAD SANDWICH COOKIES WITH CONCORD GRAPE JAM

Makes about 12 cookies

Recipe by Laura Kasavan

Buttery shortbread rounds infused with rosemary offer a lovely, herbaceous counterpoint to Concord Grape Jam. A final sprinkle of granulated sugar makes these sandwich cookies sparkle.

¾ cup (170 grams) unsalted butter, softened
⅔ cup (133 grams) plus 2 tablespoons (24 grams) granulated sugar, divided
½ teaspoon finely chopped fresh rosemary
½ teaspoon (2 grams) vanilla extract
⅛ teaspoon kosher salt
1¾ cups (219 grams) all-purpose flour
Fresh rosemary leaves (optional)
Concord Grape Jam* (recipe on page 347)

1. In the bowl of a stand mixer fitted with the paddle attachment, beat butter, ⅔ cup (133 grams) sugar, and chopped rosemary at medium speed until creamy, 3 to 4 minutes, stopping to scrape sides of bowl. With mixer on medium-low speed, add vanilla and salt, beating until combined. With mixer on low speed, add flour, beating until combined and dough starts to come together. Turn out dough, and shape into a disk. Wrap tightly in plastic wrap, and refrigerate until firm, about 45 minutes.
2. Preheat oven to 350°F (180°C). Line 2 baking sheets with parchment paper.
3. On a lightly floured surface, roll dough to ¼-inch thickness. Using a 2-inch fluted round cutter dipped in flour, cut dough, rerolling scraps as necessary. Place on prepared pans, and sprinkle with remaining 2 tablespoons (24 grams) sugar. Top half of cookies with rosemary leaves, if desired. Refrigerate for 20 minutes.
4. Bake until lightly golden and tops and edges are set, 14 to 16 minutes, rotating pans halfway through baking. Let cool on pans for 5 minutes. Remove from pans, and let cool completely on wire racks.
5. Place a spoonful of Concord Grape Jam on flat side of plain cookies. Place rosemary-topped cookies, flat side down, on top of jam.

*When making Concord Grape Jam, omit cloves. At the end of step 2, remove mixture from heat. Pour into a glass bowl, and let cool before using.

> **PRO TIP**
> If fresh Concord grapes are not available, you can substitute high-quality store-bought Concord grape jam for the homemade jam. We suggest using Stonewall Kitchen Concord Grape Jelly, available at stonewallkitchen.com.

Photo by Laura Kasavan

FIG, WALNUT, AND DARK CHOCOLATE CHUNK COOKIES

Makes about 33 cookies

Recipe by Marian Cooper Cairns

We gave the chocolate chip cookie a killer autumn update: dried figs, rich dark chocolate, and toasted walnuts. One last sprinkle of flaked sea salt turns these cookies into an instant classic.

1¼ cups (284 grams) unsalted butter*, softened
2¼ cups (495 grams) firmly packed dark brown sugar
2 large eggs (100 grams)
1 tablespoon (13 grams) vanilla extract
3⅔ cups (458 grams) all-purpose flour
1½ teaspoons (7.5 grams) baking powder
1¼ teaspoons (6.25 grams) baking soda
1 teaspoon (3 grams) kosher salt

2 cups (340 grams) dark chocolate chunks
1½ cups (235 grams) chopped dried mission figs
1½ cups (170 grams) chopped toasted walnuts
Flaked sea salt, for sprinkling

1. In the bowl of a stand mixer fitted with the paddle attachment, beat butter and brown sugar at medium speed until fluffy, 3 to 4 minutes, stopping to scrape sides of bowl. Add eggs, one at a time, beating well after each addition. Beat in vanilla.
2. In a medium bowl, whisk together flour, baking powder, baking soda, and salt. With mixer on low speed, gradually add flour mixture to butter mixture, beating just until combined, about 10 seconds. Add chocolate, figs, and walnuts, beating just until combined. Cover and refrigerate for at least 24 hours.
3. Preheat oven to 425°F (220°C). Line baking sheets with parchment paper.
4. Let dough come to room temperature. Using a 3-tablespoon scoop, scoop dough, and roll into balls. Gently flatten each ball into a 2-inch circle. Place about 3 inches apart on prepared pans. Sprinkle with sea salt.
5. Bake, in batches, until edges are just beginning to brown and centers still look soft, 8 to 9 minutes. Let cool on pans for 5 minutes. Remove from pans, and let cool completely on wire racks.

*For best results, do not use European-style butter.

Photo by Matt Armendariz

CRÈME FRAÎCHE APRICOT COOKIES

Makes about 24 cookies

This decadent cookie fuses warm and golden brandy, jewel-like dried apricots, crunchy pearl sugar, and a dose of silky crème fraîche.

⅔ cup (85 grams) diced dried apricots
½ cup (120 grams) brandy
⅓ cup (76 grams) unsalted butter, softened
¾ cup (150 grams) granulated sugar
2 large egg yolks (37 grams)
1 large egg (50 grams)
½ cup (120 grams) crème fraîche
2½ cups (313 grams) all-purpose flour
½ teaspoon (2.5 grams) baking powder
¼ teaspoon (1.25 grams) baking soda
¼ teaspoon kosher salt
1 cup (200 grams) pearl sugar*

1. In a small saucepan, bring apricots and brandy just to a boil. Reduce heat, and simmer, stirring occasionally, until almost all liquid is evaporated, 8 to 10 minutes. Remove from heat, and let cool completely.
2. In the bowl of a stand mixer fitted with the paddle attachment, beat butter and granulated sugar at medium speed just until combined, 1 to 2 minutes. Beat in egg yolks and egg. Add crème fraîche, beating until combined.
3. In a medium bowl, whisk together flour, baking powder, baking soda, and salt. With mixer on low speed, gradually add flour mixture to butter mixture, beating until combined. Gently stir in cooled apricots. (Dough will be sticky.) Refrigerate for 30 minutes.
4. Preheat oven to 350°F (180°C). Line 3 rimmed baking sheets with parchment paper.

5. Place pearl sugar in a small bowl. Using a 1½-tablespoon scoop, scoop dough, and roll into balls. (If dough is sticky, you can dampen your hands with water to roll into balls.) Roll balls in pearl sugar, and place 2 inches apart on prepared pans. Flatten slightly with the palm of your hand.
6. Bake, one batch at a time, until cookies are set but not browned, 10 to 12 minutes. Let cool on pans for 5 minutes. Remove from pans, and let cool completely on wire racks.

We used Lars Own Swedish Pearl Sugar.

FIVE-SPICE GINGERBREAD COOKIES

Makes 35 to 65 cookies

Recipe by Rebecca Firth

Chinese five-spice powder is one of my favorite go-to holiday spice blends. It has all of the usual holiday flavors, such as cinnamon and cloves, but also typically has Sichuan peppercorns for an added kick and fennel and star anise to keep things interesting. The five-spice is subtle in these, but feel free to add up to ½ teaspoon (1 gram) more to give these mega jazz hands.

¾ cup (170 grams) unsalted butter, softened
¾ cup (165 grams) firmly packed dark brown sugar
¾ cup (255 grams) unsulphured molasses
1 large egg (50 grams), room temperature
2 teaspoons (8 grams) vanilla extract
3⅔ cups (484 grams) bread flour
1 tablespoon (6 grams) ground ginger
2 teaspoons (4 grams) Chinese five-spice powder
1 teaspoon (3 grams) sea salt
½ teaspoon (1 gram) ground cinnamon
1½ cups (180 grams) confectioners' sugar

3 to 4 tablespoons (45 to 60 grams) whole milk
½ vanilla bean, split lengthwise, seeds scraped and reserved
Garnish: gold sprinkles

1. In the bowl of a stand mixer fitted with the paddle attachment, beat butter and brown sugar at medium speed until creamy, 2 to 3 minutes, stopping to scrape sides of bowl. With mixer on low speed, add molasses, and beat until well combined, about 1 minute. Add egg and vanilla, and beat for 1 minute.
2. In a medium bowl, whisk together flour, ginger, five-spice powder, salt, and cinnamon. Gradually add flour mixture to butter mixture, beating just until combined, about 1 minute. Using a spatula, scrape sides and bottom of bowl to ensure everything is incorporated. Shape dough into a disk, and wrap tightly in plastic wrap. Refrigerate for 15 minutes. (You want dough chilled but not so cold that it cracks when rolled out. If you refrigerate longer, let come closer to room temperature before rolling.)
3. Line a baking sheet with parchment paper.
4. On a lightly floured surface, roll dough to

¼- to ½-inch thickness. Add more flour as needed, and turn dough 90 degrees after each roll to keep sticking at bay. Place dough on prepared pan. Freeze for 10 minutes, or refrigerate for 20 minutes.
5. Position oven rack in top third of oven, no less than 6 inches from heat. Preheat oven to 350°F (180°C). Line several baking sheets with parchment paper.
6. Using a 1½-inch round cutter, cut dough, rerolling scraps as necessary. Place 1 inch apart on prepared pans. Freeze for 10 minutes, or refrigerate for 20 minutes.
7. Bake in top third of oven for 8 minutes. Let cool on pans for 5 minutes. Remove from pans, and let cool completely on wire racks.
8. In a small bowl, whisk together confectioners' sugar, milk, and vanilla bean seeds until smooth. Dip top of cooled cookies in glaze, letting excess drip off. Place cookies on wire rack, and immediately garnish with sprinkles, if desired. Let glaze set before serving. Store in an airtight container for up to 3 days.

Photo by Rebecca Firth

CHOCOLATE PEPPERMINT CRINKLE COOKIES

Makes 20 cookies

Recipe by Edd Kimber

My favorite holiday combo is always chocolate and peppermint. If you like your cookies soft and fudgy, these are for you.

7	ounces (200 grams) 70% cacao dark chocolate, roughly chopped
½	cup plus 1 tablespoon (127 grams) unsalted butter, cubed
1	teaspoon (4 grams) peppermint extract*
1	cup (200 grams) castor sugar
¼	cup (55 grams) firmly packed light brown sugar
2	large eggs (100 grams)
1	cup (125 grams) all-purpose flour
3	tablespoons (15 grams) black cocoa powder
1	teaspoon (5 grams) baking powder
¼	teaspoon kosher salt
½	cup (60 grams) confectioners' sugar

1. In the top of a double boiler, combine chocolate and butter. Cook over simmering water, stirring occasionally, until chocolate is melted and mixture is smooth. Remove from heat; add peppermint extract, stirring until combined. Let cool to room temperature, about 30 minutes.

2. In the bowl of a stand mixer fitted with the whisk attachment, beat castor sugar, brown sugar, and eggs at high speed until sugars are dissolved, about 1 minute. Add chocolate mixture, beating just until combined.

3. In a medium bowl, whisk together flour, black cocoa, baking powder, and salt. Fold flour mixture into chocolate mixture just until combined. Cover bowl with plastic wrap, and refrigerate for 1 hour.

4. Preheat oven to 350°F (180°C). Line 2 half sheet pans with parchment paper.

5. Using a 3-tablespoon scoop, scoop dough, and roll into balls. Roll balls in confectioners' sugar. (When rolling, you will want to compact the sugar onto the outside of the cookie because some of the sugar will absorb into the dough as they bake. If you don't add enough, you will lose the decorative look of the sugar. With only a thin layer of sugar, the beautiful cracking will be less pronounced.) Place on prepared pans.

6. Bake until lightly puffed and just slightly set around the edges, 11 to 12 minutes. Let cool completely on pans. Store in an airtight container for up to 4 days.

*I used Nielsen-Massey Pure Peppermint Extract.

Photo by Edd Kimber

SLICE-AND-BAKE MATCHA CHRISTMAS TREE COOKIES

Makes about 30 cookies

Recipe by Sarah Brunella

With a subtle, earthy sweetness, these rustic slice-and-bake cookies will be your go-to make-ahead cookies this holiday season. Prepare and freeze the dough logs ahead of time so all you have to do is slice and bake when you're ready.

3¼ cups (406 grams) all-purpose flour, sifted
¾   cup (170 grams) cold unsalted butter, cubed
¾   cup (150 grams) granulated sugar
1   teaspoon (3 grams) kosher salt
2   large eggs (100 grams), room temperature
1   teaspoon (4 grams) vanilla extract
1   tablespoon (6 grams) matcha powder
Green food coloring (optional)
Sprinkles

1. In the bowl of a stand mixer fitted with the paddle attachment, beat flour, cold butter, sugar, and salt at medium speed until crumbly. Add eggs and vanilla, and beat until a dough forms. Remove two-thirds of dough, and shape into a log. Wrap in plastic wrap, and refrigerate.

2. Add matcha and food coloring (if using) to remaining dough, and beat until dough is green. Roll green dough to about ½-inch thickness. Wrap in plastic wrap, and freeze for 10 to 15 minutes.

3. Using a 1½-inch tree-shaped cutter, cut as many trees from green dough as you can. Combine scraps, and roll again. Freeze, and cut more trees. Repeat until all green dough is used. Freeze trees for 10 minutes.

4. Stack trees, using a bit of water to help them adhere. Make 3 stacks of trees, and freeze until solid, 30 to 40 minutes.

5. Divide plain dough into thirds. Divide each third into smaller pieces, and roll each piece into a narrow rope. Wrap ropes around outline of trees. You will end up with 3 logs

of dough. Roll each log in sprinkles. Wrap in plastic wrap, and refrigerate for at least 6 hours or overnight.

6. Preheat oven to 350°F (180°C). Line baking sheets with parchment paper.

7. Cut logs into ¼-inch-thick slices. Place 2 inches apart on prepared pans.

8. Bake for 10 to 12 minutes. Let cool slightly. Serve immediately, or store in an airtight container for up to 1 week. They will also freeze well for longer life.

PRO TIP
If you want your tree with sharp edges and your cookies not to spread too much, let them fully chill in the freezer and refrigerator. The dough (especially the green one) has to be very cold; if not, the tree will spread.

Photo by Sarah Brunella

MOLASSES, GINGER, AND CARDAMOM SPICE COOKIES

Makes 18 cookies

Recipe by Edd Kimber

Toasty and gently spiced with a unique molasses flavor, these cookies epitomize all a holiday cookie should be. With the addition of fresh ginger and a heavy dose of cardamom, they have a little more depth than the traditional spice cookie.

1 cup (227 grams) unsalted butter, softened

1⅓ cups (293 grams) firmly packed light brown sugar

¼ cup (85 grams) molasses

2 tablespoons (35 grams) grated fresh ginger

1 large egg (50 grams)

1 teaspoon (4 grams) vanilla extract

3¼ cups (406 grams) all-purpose flour

2 teaspoons (10 grams) baking soda

2 teaspoons (4 grams) freshly ground cardamom

1 teaspoon (2 grams) ground ginger

½ teaspoon (1.5 grams) kosher salt

½ teaspoon (1 gram) ground cinnamon

½ cup (100 grams) granulated sugar

1. Preheat oven to 350°F (180°C). Line 2 half sheet pans with parchment paper.

2. In the bowl of a stand mixer fitted with the paddle attachment, beat butter, brown sugar, molasses, and grated ginger at medium speed until fluffy, 2 to 3 minutes, stopping to scrape sides of bowl. Add egg and vanilla, beating until combined.

3. In a medium bowl, whisk together flour, baking soda, cardamom, ground ginger, salt, and cinnamon. With mixer on low speed, gradually add flour mixture to butter mixture, beating just until combined. Cover bowl with plastic wrap, and refrigerate for 1 hour. (Baking straight away will make the cookies spread a little too much.)

4. Using a ¼-cup scoop, scoop dough, and roll into balls. Roll balls in granulated sugar, coating completely. Place 2 inches apart on prepared pans.

5. Bake until slightly puffed and cracked all over, 13 to 14 minutes. Remove from oven, and tap pan sharply on a work surface to slightly collapse cookies. (This will give the center of the cookies a nice, soft texture and the outside a slight chew.) Let cool on pans for 5 minutes. Remove from pans, and let cool completely on wire racks. Store in an airtight container for up to 5 days.

Photo by Edd Kimber

SALTED CARAMEL SNICKERDOODLES

Makes about 46 cookies

Recipe by Erin Clarkson

This recipe is inspired by one of my favourite cookies in the town where I went to university—a giant cookie with melty pockets of salted caramel studded throughout. I've added a holiday snickerdoodle spin on this, adding crushed caramel into the dough for extra chew, and rolling it in cinnamon sugar for a classic snickerdoodle taste.

Salted Caramel (recipe follows)
1	**cup (227 grams) unsalted butter, softened**
¾	**cup (150 grams) granulated sugar, divided**
¼	**cup (55 grams) firmly packed dark brown sugar**
1	**large egg (50 grams)**
1	**teaspoon (4 grams) vanilla extract**
2¾	**cups plus 2 teaspoons (350 grams) all-purpose flour**
½	**teaspoon (2.5 grams) baking soda**
½	**teaspoon (1.5 grams) kosher salt**
½	**teaspoon (1 gram) ground cinnamon**

Flaked sea salt, for finishing

1. Prepare Salted Caramel. Break into large chunks, and weigh out 1 cup (200 grams) caramel. Place into a resealable plastic bag, and break with a rolling pin until it forms small chunks. Set aside.

2. Place remaining Salted Caramel in the work bowl of a food processor; pulse until finely ground. Weigh out ¾ cup (150 grams) ground caramel. (The caramel, once ground, will pull moisture out of the environment very quickly and start to clump, so use the ground caramel fresh out of the food processor.)

3. Preheat oven to 350°F (180°C). Line several baking sheets with parchment paper.

4. In the bowl of a stand mixer fitted with the paddle attachment, beat ¾ cup (150 grams) ground caramel, butter, ½ cup (100 grams) granulated sugar, and brown sugar at high speed until creamy, 2 to 3 minutes, stopping to scrape sides of bowl. With mixer on medium speed, add egg and vanilla, beating until combined.

5. In a medium bowl, sift together flour, baking soda, and salt. With mixer on low speed, gradually add flour mixture to butter mixture, beating just until combined. Stir in 1 cup (200 grams) caramel chunks until evenly distributed.

6. In a small bowl, stir together cinnamon and remaining ¼ cup (50 grams) granulated sugar. Using a 1-tablespoon scoop, scoop dough, and roll into balls. Roll balls in cinnamon sugar mixture. Place 2 inches apart on prepared pans. Freeze for 5 minutes.

7. Bake, one batch at a time, until golden brown and puffed up, 11 to 12 minutes. Let cool completely on pans. Sprinkle with sea salt. Store in an airtight container.

Note: *If you do not want to bake all of these cookies at once, the dough, once rolled in the cinnamon sugar, can be stored in a resealable plastic bag in the freezer. Freeze until solid on a baking sheet before transferring to a bag.*

SALTED CARAMEL
Makes about 2 cups

2	**cups (400 grams) granulated sugar**
1	**teaspoon (3 grams) kosher salt**

1. Line a half sheet pan with a nonstick baking mat.

2. In a medium saucepan, heat sugar over medium heat, whisking occasionally, until sugar is dissolved. (Sugar will clump as you heat, but continue to stir, and it will soon smooth out.) Cook until sugar turns amber colored and is just beginning to smoke slightly. Immediately pour onto prepared pan, and sprinkle with salt. Let cool completely.

> **PRO TIP**
> Have everything ready to go for the Salted Caramel. There are a few seconds between a toasty caramel and a burnt sugar, so you want to be able to pour out the caramel as soon as it is ready.

Photo by Erin Clarkson

EGGNOG SUGAR COOKIES

Makes about 14 cookies

Recipe by Sarah Kieffer

Delicate, buttery, nutmeg-scented cookies receive a frosty coat of bourbon and eggnog-infused icing for the perfect nod to my favorite holiday quaff.

1⅛ cups (140 grams) all-purpose flour
⅓ cup (40 grams) confectioners' sugar
½ teaspoon (1.5 grams) fine sea salt
½ teaspoon (1 gram) freshly ground nutmeg
½ cup (113 grams) unsalted butter, cubed and softened
Eggnog Icing (recipe follows)

1. Preheat oven to 350°F (180°C). Line a baking sheet with parchment paper.

2. In the bowl of a stand mixer fitted with the paddle attachment, beat flour, confectioners' sugar, sea salt, and nutmeg at low speed until combined. With mixer on medium speed, add butter, one piece at a time, beating until incorporated and dough starts to form a ball. Turn out dough onto a lightly floured surface, and shape into a disk. Wrap in plastic wrap, and refrigerate for 30 minutes.

3. On a lightly floured surface, roll dough to ⅛-inch thickness. Using a 2-inch round cutter, cut dough. Using a metal spatula, gently place cookies on prepared pan. (Refrigerate dough scraps for 30 minutes, and repeat.)

4. Bake until edges begin to brown, 15 to 17 minutes. Let cool completely on pans. Spread Eggnog Icing onto cooled cookies. Let icing set before serving. Store in an airtight container for up to 3 days.

EGGNOG ICING

Makes 1 cup

2 cups (240 grams) confectioners' sugar
4 to 6 tablespoons (60 to 90 grams) prepared eggnog
1 tablespoon (15 grams) bourbon (optional)

1. In a small bowl, whisk together confectioners' sugar and eggnog, 1 tablespoon (15 grams) at a time, until a thin glaze consistency is reached. Add bourbon (if using) along with eggnog, whisking to combine. Use immediately.

Photo by Sarah Kieffer

FINNISH PINWHEEL COOKIES (JOULUTORTTU)

Makes about 24 cookies

Walking the fine line between a cookie and a tart, the joulutorttu is a favorite holiday treat found in bakeries and homes across Finland. The traditional recipe calls for a prune preserve filling, but we opted for a bright, boozy cranberry and ruby port reduction.

3   cups (375 grams) all-purpose flour
1   cup (227 grams) cold unsalted butter, cubed
1   teaspoon (3 grams) kosher salt
1   cup (225 grams) ricotta cheese
¼   cup (60 grams) whole milk
Cranberry Port Preserves (recipe follows)
Garnish: confectioners' sugar

1. In the work bowl of a food processor, place flour, cold butter, and salt; pulse until mixture is crumbly. Add ricotta and milk, and pulse until dough comes together. Divide dough into 3 equal portions. Shape each portion into a disk, and wrap in plastic wrap. Refrigerate overnight.
2. Preheat oven to 400°F (200°C). Line 3 rimmed baking sheets with parchment paper.
3. Working with one disk of dough at a time, roll dough to ⅛-inch thickness on a lightly floured surface. Using a 3-inch square cutter, cut dough, and place on prepared pans. On each square, make 4 (1-inch) cuts at corners diagonally toward center. Place 1 teaspoon (7 grams) Cranberry Port Preserves in center of each cookie. Fold every other tip over toward center, forming a pinwheel. Dab ends of tips with water to help adhere and prevent separation during baking.
4. Bake until edges are just barely golden brown, 11 to 12 minutes. Let cool completely on pans. Dust with confectioners' sugar, if desired.

CRANBERRY PORT PRESERVES

Makes about 1 cup

2   cups (210 grams) frozen cranberries, thawed
¼   cup (55 grams) firmly packed light brown sugar
¼   cup (60 grams) water
¼   cup (60 grams) ruby port wine

1. In a medium saucepan, bring all ingredients to a boil over medium-high heat. Mash cranberries, and reduce heat to low; simmer for 10 minutes. Pour mixture into a jar with a tight-fitting lid, and let cool completely. Refrigerate any leftover cranberry preserves for up to 2 weeks. (Leftover hot preserves can be transferred to sterilized jars, water bath processed for 10 minutes, and stored for up to 6 months.)

BROWNED BUTTER GINGERBREAD LACE COOKIES

Makes about 26 cookies

Recipe by Thalia Ho

These delicate cookies are an elevated take on the traditional gingerbread, with nutty browned butter creating an unmistakable undertone of depth, complexity, and richness. The result is a character-filled cookie adorned with a dusting of confectioners' sugar.

½ cup plus 1 tablespoon (127 grams) unsalted butter, cubed
½ cup (110 grams) firmly packed dark brown sugar
⅓ cup plus 1 tablespoon (134 grams) molasses
1 large egg (50 grams)
1 teaspoon (4 grams) vanilla extract
2⅓ cups plus 1 tablespoon (300 grams) all-purpose flour
1 tablespoon (5 grams) Dutch process cocoa powder
1 tablespoon (6 grams) ground ginger
2 teaspoons (4 grams) ground cinnamon
½ teaspoon (2.5 grams) baking soda
½ teaspoon (3 grams) table salt
½ teaspoon (1 gram) ground nutmeg
½ teaspoon (1 gram) ground cloves
¼ teaspoon ground anise
⅛ teaspoon ground black pepper
1¼ cups (150 grams) confectioners' sugar

1. In a small saucepan, melt butter over medium heat. Cook, stirring frequently, until butter turns a medium-brown color and has a nutty aroma. Remove from heat, and pour into a small heatproof bowl. Refrigerate until softened, about 1 hour.
2. Remove malleable browned butter from refrigerator, and reweigh it. Some butter solids will have reduced during the browning process, so add a little more unsalted butter to make up original volume, if necessary.
3. In the bowl of a stand mixer fitted with the paddle attachment, beat browned butter and brown sugar at medium speed until creamy, 2 to 3 minutes, stopping to scrape sides of bowl. Add molasses, egg, and vanilla, beating until well combined.
4. In a medium bowl, whisk together flour, cocoa, ginger, cinnamon, baking soda, salt, nutmeg, cloves, anise, and pepper. With mixer on low speed, gradually add flour mixture to butter mixture, beating just until combined. Using a large wooden spoon, finish mixing by hand. Shape dough into a disk, and wrap in plastic wrap. Refrigerate for at least 1 hour or overnight.
5. Preheat oven to 350°F (180°C). Line 2 large baking sheets with parchment paper.
6. Turn out dough onto a lightly floured surface, and lightly dust top with flour. Roll dough to ¼-inch thickness. Using a 2½-inch round cutter, cut dough, rerolling scraps as necessary. Place 3 inches apart on prepared pans.
7. Bake until edges are just firm and beginning to brown, 8 to 10 minutes. Let cool on pans for 3 minutes. Remove from pans, and let cool completely on wire racks.
8. To decorate, place a small piece of lace or a doily over top of a cookie. Using a fine-mesh sieve, sift confectioners' sugar over top. Carefully remove lace or doily to reveal intricate pattern. Repeat with remaining cookies. These are best eaten on the day of baking, but they can be stored in an airtight container in a cool, dark place for up to 2 weeks.

Photo by Thalia Ho

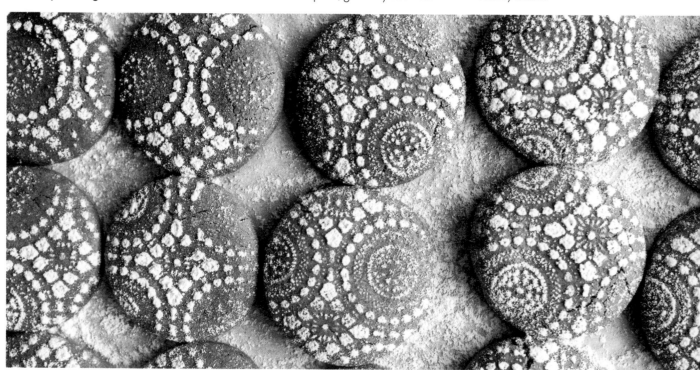

CARAMELIZED WHITE CHOCOLATE SABLÉS WITH SEA SALT

Makes about 48 cookies

Recipe by Zoë François

White chocolate often leaves me wanting more flavor, so caramelizing it before adding it to the cookie batter gives it the toasty notes of butterscotch with the richness of chocolate. It may go through an awkward phase as you caramelize it, but don't worry, it'll turn into a golden delight by the end.

1½ cups (255 grams) chopped white chocolate
1 cup (227 grams) unsalted butter, softened
¾ cup (150 grams) granulated sugar
1 large egg yolk (19 grams)
1 teaspoon (4 grams) vanilla extract
2 cups (250 grams) all-purpose flour
¼ teaspoon kosher salt
3 to 4 tablespoons (45 to 60 grams) heavy whipping cream, warmed
Sea salt, for sprinkling

1. Preheat oven to 300°F (150°C). Line a baking sheet with a nonstick baking mat.
2. Spread white chocolate on prepared pan.
3. Bake until chocolate starts to melt, about 10 minutes. Using a spatula, spread chocolate into a thin layer. Bake 10 minutes more. Stir, and repeat procedure until chocolate is caramel colored. The chocolate may liquefy, or it may become granular. If chocolate is grainy, place it in a coffee grinder or blender to smooth it out. It doesn't need to be perfectly smooth at this point. Let cool slightly. If you make this ahead, warm it slightly in microwave for 10 to 20 seconds before proceeding.
4. In the bowl of a stand mixer fitted with the paddle attachment, beat butter and sugar at medium speed until creamy, 2 to 3 minutes, stopping to scrape sides of bowl. Add egg yolk and vanilla, and beat for 1 minute. Add 3 tablespoons (57 grams) softened caramelized white chocolate, beating until combined. With mixer on low speed, gradually add flour and salt, beating just until combined.
5. Divide dough in half, and shape each half into a 1½-inch-wide log. Wrap logs in plastic wrap, and refrigerate for at least 1 hour or overnight.
6. Preheat oven to 350°F (180°C). Line a baking sheet with parchment paper.
7. Cut logs into ¼-inch-thick slices, and place on prepared pan.
8. Bake until edges are golden, 8 to 10 minutes. Let cool completely on wire racks.
9. In a microwave-safe bowl, microwave remaining caramelized white chocolate to soften. Add warm cream, 1 teaspoon (5 grams) at a time, stirring until white chocolate is thin enough to spread but not too liquidy. Spread 1 teaspoon ganache onto each cookie, and sprinkle with sea salt. Serve the same day, or cookies will soften.

Photo by Zoë François

PAN-BANGING MOLASSES ESPRESSO COOKIES WITH CHOCOLATE

Makes 10 cookies

Recipe by Sarah Kieffer

The Pan-Banging Cookie has a devoted, wonderful fanbase. I decided to recreate a holiday version as a present from me to the fans. Spiked with espresso and molasses, this cookie packs a bigger punch than my normal chocolate chip version.

¾   cup (170 grams) unsalted butter, softened
1½   cups (300 grams) granulated sugar
2   tablespoons (42 grams) mild molasses
1   large egg (50 grams)
1   teaspoon (4 grams) vanilla extract
2   cups (250 grams) all-purpose flour
1   tablespoon (6 grams) ground espresso
¾   teaspoon (2.25 grams) fine sea salt
½   teaspoon (2.5 grams) baking soda
4   ounces (113 grams) bittersweet or semisweet chocolate, chopped

1. Preheat oven to 350°F (180°C). Line 3 baking sheets with foil, dull side up.
2. In the bowl of a stand mixer fitted with the paddle attachment, beat butter at medium speed until creamy. Add sugar, and beat until fluffy, 2 to 3 minutes. With mixer on low speed, add molasses, egg, and vanilla, beating to combine.
3. In a medium bowl, whisk together flour, espresso, sea salt, and baking soda. Gradually add flour mixture to butter mixture, beating until combined. Using a spatula, make sure molasses is completely combined into dough and that dough is a uniform color. Add chocolate, and stir to combine. Shape dough into 10 (3-ounce) balls, and place an equal distance apart on prepared pans. Freeze for 15 minutes.
4. Bake, one batch at a time, until cookies are slightly puffed in center, about 7 minutes. Lift side of baking sheet up about 4 inches, and gently let it drop down against oven rack so edges of cookies set and insides fall back down. (This will feel wrong, but trust me.) After cookies puff up again in about 1 minute, repeat lifting and dropping pan. Repeat 3 to 4 more times to create ridges around edges of cookies. Bake until cookies have spread out and edges are golden brown but centers are much lighter and not fully cooked, 14 to 15 minutes total. Let cool completely on pans. Refrigerate in an airtight container for up to 3 days.

Photo by Sarah Kieffer

SALTED CARAMEL THUMBPRINT COOKIES

Makes about 20 cookies

Recipe by Laura Kasavan

These bourbon-pecan thumbprint cookies are rolled in sparkling sugar and filled with Salted Caramel Sauce.

½   cup (57 grams) chopped toasted pecans
⅔   cup (133 grams) granulated sugar
¾   cup (170 grams) unsalted butter, softened
2   tablespoons (30 grams) bourbon
½   teaspoon (2 grams) vanilla extract
⅛   teaspoon kosher salt
1¾   cups (219 grams) all-purpose flour
¼   cup (50 grams) turbinado sugar
Salted Caramel Sauce (recipe follows)
Garnish: flaked sea salt

1. In the work bowl of a food processor, place pecans and granulated sugar; process until combined.
2. In the bowl of a stand mixer fitted with the paddle attachment, beat pecan sugar and butter at medium speed until fluffy, 2 to 3 minutes, stopping to scrape sides of bowl. With mixer on medium-low speed, add bourbon, vanilla, and kosher salt, beating

until combined. With mixer on low speed, add flour, beating until combined and dough starts to come together. Turn out dough, and shape into a disk. Wrap tightly in plastic wrap, and refrigerate until firm, about 2 hours.
3. Preheat oven to 350°F (180°C). Line 2 rimmed baking sheets with parchment paper.
4. Place turbinado sugar in a shallow bowl. Shape dough into 1¼-inch balls, and roll in sugar to coat. Place on prepared pans. Freeze for 15 minutes. Using your thumb or the back of a spoon, gently make an indentation in center of each ball.
5. Bake until lightly golden and tops and edges are set, 14 to 16 minutes, rotating pans after 8 minutes of baking. Remove from oven, and press down centers again. Let cool on pans for 10 minutes. Remove from pans, and let cool completely on wire racks.
6. Pipe or spoon about 1 teaspoon Salted Caramel Sauce in center of each cookie. Garnish with sea salt, if desired.

SALTED CARAMEL SAUCE
Makes about 1 cup

1   cup (200 grams) granulated sugar
¼   cup (57 grams) unsalted butter, cubed and softened

½   cup (120 grams) heavy whipping cream, room temperature
½   teaspoon (2 grams) vanilla extract
¼   teaspoon kosher salt

1. In a medium heavy-bottomed saucepan, heat sugar over medium heat, stirring constantly with a heat-resistant spatula. Cook until sugar forms clumps and melts into a light amber-colored liquid, 4 to 5 minutes.
2. Once sugar is completely melted, carefully add butter, a few pieces at a time, whisking constantly until fully incorporated.
3. Slowly drizzle in cream, whisking constantly; boil for 1 minute. Remove from heat, and pour into a glass bowl or measuring cup. Stir in vanilla and salt. Let cool completely before using, about 2 hours. If caramel seems too runny once fully cooled, refrigerate for 15 to 30 minutes before filling cookies.

Note: *Salted Caramel Sauce can be made in advance and refrigerated for up to 2 weeks in an airtight container. Warm briefly before using.*

Photo by Laura Kasavan

SALTED VANILLA BEAN SUGAR COOKIES

Makes 15 to 20 cookies

Recipe by Joshua Weissman

These iced sugar cookies are just as effortlessly beautiful as real snowflakes. I love how the tiny flecks of vanilla are visible in the icing. In this case, the salted butter mellows out the cookies' sweetness.

1	cup plus 2 tablespoons (255 grams) salted butter
1	cup (200 grams) granulated sugar
1	large egg (50 grams)
1	large egg yolk (19 grams)
1½	teaspoons (6 grams) vanilla extract
3	cups (375 grams) all-purpose flour
¼	teaspoon kosher salt
3	cups (360 grams) confectioners' sugar
3	tablespoons (45 grams) whole milk
1	vanilla bean, split lengthwise, seeds scraped and reserved

1. In the bowl of a stand mixer fitted with the paddle attachment, beat butter and granulated sugar at medium speed until creamy, 2 to 3 minutes, stopping to scrape sides of bowl. Add egg, egg yolk, and vanilla, beating until combined.

2. With mixer on low speed, gradually add flour and salt, beating until a cohesive dough forms. Turn out dough onto a heavily floured surface, and knead until completely combined with no dry clumps of flour. Shape into a disk, and wrap in plastic wrap. Refrigerate for at least 1 hour or up to 2 days.

3. Preheat oven to 375°F (190°C). Line a baking sheet with parchment paper or a nonstick baking mat.

4. Roll dough to ¼-inch thickness. Using a 3¾-inch snowflake-shaped cutter, cut dough, and place on prepared pan.

5. Bake until set and edges are just beginning to brown, 7 to 10 minutes. Let cool completely on a wire rack.

6. In a medium bowl, whisk together confectioners' sugar and milk, 1 tablespoon (15 grams) at a time, until desired consistency is reached. (It should be runny enough that it runs off whisk but thick enough that when running whisk through it, it leaves a trail that eventually closes up and shows no trace of whisk marks left behind.)

7. Place a sheet of parchment paper under wire rack. Dip top of cookies into icing, letting excess drip off. Place cookies, icing side up, on wire rack. Using a flicking motion, fleck vanilla bean seeds onto icing. Let stand until icing is set. Store in an airtight container.

Photo by Joshua Weissman

EARL GREY ROLLOUT COOKIES WITH LEMON ROYAL ICING

Makes about 30 cookies

Recipe by Erin Clarkson

These are a wee twist on the traditional rollout cookie. I added some Earl Grey tea and bergamot extract, then made the royal icing with lemon juice, which elevates the tea taste in the cookies.

1   cup (227 grams) unsalted butter, softened
¾   cup (150 grams) granulated sugar
¼   cup (55 grams) firmly packed light brown sugar
3   tablespoons (25 grams) loose-leaf Earl Grey tea, finely ground
1   teaspoon (6 grams) vanilla bean paste
½   teaspoon (1.5 grams) kosher salt
½   teaspoon (2 grams) bergamot extract
1   large egg (50 grams)
3¼   cups (406 grams) all-purpose flour
½   teaspoon (2.5 grams) baking powder
Lemon Royal Icing (recipe follows)

1. In the bowl of a stand mixer fitted with the paddle attachment, beat butter, sugars, tea, vanilla bean paste, salt, and bergamot extract at medium speed until creamy, 2 to 3 minutes, stopping to scrape sides of bowl. Add egg, beating well. Sift in flour and baking powder, and beat at low speed just until combined. Divide dough in half, and shape each half into a disk. Wrap tightly in plastic wrap, and refrigerate overnight.
2. Preheat oven to 350°F (180°C). Line several baking sheets with parchment paper.
3. Working with one piece of dough at a time, place between 2 sheets of parchment paper, and roll to ¼-inch thickness. Freeze for 10 minutes. Remove top sheet of parchment. Using desired cutters, cut dough, rerolling scraps as necessary. Place on prepared pans, leaving a little room between each. Repeat with remaining dough.
4. Bake, one batch at a time, until set and barely golden, 9 to 10 minutes. Let cool on pans for 10 minutes. Remove from pans, and let cool completely on wire racks. Place Lemon Royal Icing in a small piping bag fitted with a very small round tip, such as a Wilton #1 tip. Pipe icing onto cooled cookies as desired.

LEMON ROYAL ICING
Makes about 2 cups

¼   cup (60 grams) fresh lemon juice, plus more to thin as needed
1½   tablespoons (15 grams) meringue powder*
2¾   cups (330 grams) confectioners' sugar, sifted
½   teaspoon (3 grams) vanilla bean paste

1. In the bowl of a stand mixer fitted with the paddle attachment, whisk together lemon juice and meringue powder by hand. Add confectioners' sugar and vanilla bean paste, and beat at low speed until very thick, 8 to 10 minutes.
2. Transfer about 1 cup royal icing to a small bowl. Thin down with more lemon juice, adding 1 teaspoon (5 grams) at a time, until a pipable consistency is reached. Only thin out as much of the icing as you need to pipe the cookies—you can always thin out more as you go. (If thinned out too much, add more of the thicker icing to thicken rather than adding more confectioners' sugar.) Leftover icing can be refrigerated in an airtight container. Cover with a piece of plastic wrap, pressing wrap directly onto surface of icing to prevent a skin from forming.

Meringue powder is available at Michaels or online.

Photo by Erin Clarkson

CHOCOLATE GINGER SUGAR COOKIES

Makes 12 cookies

Recipe by Sarah Kieffer

Sugar cookies are great on their own, but add cocoa powder, crystallized ginger, dark chocolate, and more butter, and they become an incredible and unique addition to any holiday table.

1　cup (227 grams) unsalted butter, softened
2¼　cups (450 grams) granulated sugar, divided
1　large egg (50 grams)
1　teaspoon (4 grams) vanilla extract
2　cups (250 grams) all-purpose flour
½　cup (43 grams) natural cocoa powder or a combination cocoa powder*

1　teaspoon (2 grams) ground ginger
¾　teaspoon (3.75 grams) baking soda
½　teaspoon (1.5 grams) kosher salt
4　ounces (115 grams) semisweet chocolate, chopped
¼　cup (41 grams) chopped crystallized ginger

1. Preheat oven to 350°F (180°C). Line 2 baking sheets with parchment paper.
2. In the bowl of a stand mixer fitted with the paddle attachment, beat butter at medium speed until smooth. Add 1¾ cups (350 grams) sugar, and beat until fluffy, 2 to 3 minutes. Add egg and vanilla, and beat until combined.
3. In a medium bowl, combine flour, cocoa, ground ginger, baking soda, and salt. With mixer on low speed, gradually add flour mixture to butter mixture, beating just until combined. Stir in chopped chocolate and crystallized ginger.
4. Place remaining ½ cup (100 grams) sugar in a medium bowl. Shape dough into 12 (85-gram) balls (a scant ⅓ cup each). Roll each ball in sugar, and place 6 cookies, 2 inches apart, on each prepared pan.
5. Bake, one batch at a time, until edges are set and centers are puffed and starting to crackle, 11 to 14 minutes. Let cool completely on pans. Refrigerate in an airtight container for up to 3 days.

*I used Hershey's Special Dark Cocoa.

Photo by Sarah Kieffer

CRANBERRY PECAN MAPLE SHORTBREAD

Makes about 30 cookies

Recipe by Rebecca Firth

Calling all one-bowl baking lovers! This little gem is a one-bowl wonder that comes together in a snap, rolls like a dream, and is a real stunner. Although the finished cookies will look different, you could use regular dried cranberries in a pinch.

1	cup (227 grams) unsalted butter, softened
¾	cup (90 grams) confectioners' sugar
2	large eggs (100 grams), room temperature
2	tablespoons (42 grams) pure maple syrup
1½	teaspoons (6 grams) vanilla extract
½	teaspoon (2 grams) maple extract
½	teaspoon (1.5 grams) sea salt
½	teaspoon (1 gram) ground cinnamon
2½	cups (324 grams) all-purpose flour
¼	cup (4 grams) freeze-dried cranberries
3	tablespoons (21 grams) finely chopped toasted pecans

1. In the bowl of a stand mixer fitted with the paddle attachment, beat butter and confectioners' sugar at medium speed until creamy, 2 to 3 minutes, stopping to scrape sides of bowl. Add eggs, one at a time, beating well after each addition. Add maple syrup, extracts, sea salt, and cinnamon, and beat for 1 minute.

2. With mixer on low speed, gradually add flour, beating just until combined, about 1 minute. Using a spatula, scrape sides and bottom of bowl to ensure everything is incorporated. Shape dough into a disk, and wrap tightly in plastic wrap. Refrigerate for 15 minutes. (You want dough chilled but not so cold that it cracks when rolled out. If you refrigerate longer, let come closer to room temperature before rolling.)

3. Line a baking sheet with parchment paper.

4. On a lightly floured surface, roll dough to ¼- to ½-inch thickness. Add more flour as needed, and turn dough 90 degrees after each roll to keep sticking at bay. In the work bowl of a food processor, process freeze-dried cranberries to a fine powder. Sprinkle dough with cranberry powder and pecans. Roll dough one more time, gently pressing cranberries and pecans into dough. Place dough on prepared pan. Freeze for 10 minutes, or refrigerate for 20 minutes.

5. Position oven rack in top third of oven, no less than 6 inches from heat. Preheat oven to 350°F (180°C). Line several baking sheets with parchment paper.

6. Using a 2½x1½-inch fluted rectangle cutter, cut dough, rerolling scraps as necessary. Place on prepared pans. Freeze for 10 minutes, or refrigerate for 20 minutes.

7. Bake in top third of oven for 8 minutes. Let cool on pans for 5 minutes. Remove from pans, and let cool completely on wire racks. Store in an airtight container for up to 5 days.

Photo by Rebecca Firth

DANISH BUTTER COOKIES

Makes 15 to 20 cookies

Recipe by Joshua Weissman

This is a homemade rendition of the classic Royal Dansk cookies that are ubiquitous during the holidays. The crisp cookies come in all sorts of shapes and textures in a round blue tin. With a snappy crunch and buttery background flavor, this from-scratch version has even better flavor and richness.

¾ cup plus 1 tablespoon (184 grams) unsalted butter, softened
¾ cup (150 grams) granulated sugar
2 tablespoons (26 grams) vanilla extract
3 large eggs (150 grams), divided
1¾ cups (219 grams) all-purpose flour*
1 teaspoon (3 grams) kosher salt
Edible gold sparkling sugar, for sprinkling

1. In the bowl of a stand mixer fitted with the paddle attachment, beat butter, granulated sugar, and vanilla at medium speed until creamy, 2 to 3 minutes, stopping to scrape sides of bowl. Add 2 eggs (100 grams), one at a time, beating well after each addition.
2. With mixer on low speed, gradually add flour and salt, beating until a cohesive dough forms. Turn out dough, and use a bench scraper to divide into thirds. Shape each piece into a disk, and wrap in plastic wrap. Refrigerate until firm, about 2½ hours.
3. Preheat oven to 350°F (180°C). Line baking sheets with parchment paper.
4. Remove one disk of dough from refrigerator, and let stand at room temperature until slightly softened, about 5 minutes. Between 2 sheets of lightly floured parchment paper, roll dough to ¼-inch thickness. Remove top sheet of parchment. Using a 2¾-inch round cutter, cut dough, and place on prepared pans. Using a 1-inch round cutter, cut centers from cookies. Repeat with remaining dough.
5. In a small bowl, lightly whisk remaining 1 egg (50 grams). Brush egg wash onto cookies, and sprinkle with sparkling sugar. Freeze until firm, about 12 minutes.
6. Bake until edges are just beginning to brown, 10 to 15 minutes. Let cool completely on wire racks. Store in an airtight container.

I used Bob's Red Mill All-Purpose Flour.

Photo by Joshua Weissman

FRENCH BUTTER COOKIES

Makes 36 cookies

Recipe by Sarah Kieffer

Butter cookies, also known as sablés, are traditionally French, and there are many ways to make them. This cookie falls along the lines of shortbread with extra butter and egg yolks, making for a rich, crisp bite. A final dusting of sanding sugar dresses them up and adds a pleasant crunch.

- **1 cup plus 2 tablespoons (255 grams) unsalted butter, softened**
- **1 cup (200 grams) granulated sugar**
- **½ teaspoon (1.5 grams) fine sea salt**
- **3 large egg yolks (56 grams)**
- **1 teaspoon (4 grams) vanilla extract**
- **2½ cups plus 1 tablespoon (321 grams) all-purpose flour**
- **Sanding sugar, for sprinkling**

1. In the bowl of a stand mixer fitted with the paddle attachment, beat butter, granulated sugar, and sea salt at medium speed until creamy, 2 to 3 minutes, stopping to scrape sides of bowl. Add egg yolks and vanilla, and beat until combined. With mixer on low speed, gradually add flour, beating until dough starts to form a ball. Turn out dough onto a lightly floured surface, and shape into a disk. Wrap in plastic wrap, and refrigerate for 30 minutes.

2. Preheat oven to 350°F (180°C). Line 3 baking sheets with parchment paper.

3. On a lightly floured surface, roll dough to ¼-inch thickness. Using a 2-inch round cutter, cut dough. Using a metal spatula, gently place 12 cookies on each prepared pan. (Any dough scraps can be rewrapped and refrigerated while cookies are baking.) Sprinkle generously with sanding sugar.

4. Bake, one batch at a time, until edges begin to brown, 14 to 16 minutes. Let cool completely on pans. Store in an airtight container for up to 3 days.

Photo by Sarah Kieffer

STOLLEN MARZIPAN SHORTBREAD

Makes 24 cookies

Stollen, a classic German Christmas treat, packs booze-saturated fruit, ropes of marzipan, and warm, aromatic spices into a sweetened, yeasted bread loaf. This shortbread is a scaled-down affair, with rich, chewy Marzipan mixed directly into the dough and a buttery drizzle of Rum Glaze topping it off.

⅔   cup (150 grams) unsalted butter, softened
¼   cup (50 grams) granulated sugar
⅓   cup (100 grams) Marzipan (recipe follows)
1   large egg yolk (19 grams)
2   teaspoons (2 grams) orange zest
1   vanilla bean, split lengthwise, seeds scraped and reserved
2   cups (250 grams) all-purpose flour
¼   teaspoon kosher salt
⅛   teaspoon ground nutmeg
⅛   teaspoon ground ginger
Rum-Soaked Fruit (recipe follows)
Rum Glaze (recipe follows)

1. In the bowl of a stand mixer fitted with the paddle attachment, beat butter and sugar at medium speed until creamy, 3 to 4 minutes, stopping to scrape sides of bowl. Add Marzipan, and beat until well combined. Beat in egg yolk. Beat in zest and vanilla bean seeds.

2. In a medium bowl, sift together flour, salt, nutmeg, and ginger. With mixer on low speed, add flour mixture to butter mixture in 2 additions, letting first addition fully incorporate before adding the second. Stir in Rum-Soaked Fruit. Turn out dough, and shape into a 7-inch square. Wrap in plastic wrap, and refrigerate for 30 minutes.

3. Preheat oven to 325°F (170°C). Line a baking sheet with parchment paper.

4. Between 2 sheets of parchment paper, roll dough into a 9-inch square. Freeze for 15 minutes. Using a sharp knife, cut dough into 2¼x1½-inch rectangles. Place 1 inch apart on prepared pan. (If dough starts to soften, place back in freezer until firm again.)

5. Bake until lightly browned, 15 to 17 minutes. Let cool on pans for 3 minutes. Remove from pans, and let cool completely on wire racks. Pipe Rum Glaze over cooled cookies.

MARZIPAN

Makes about 1 cup

2¼   cups (216 grams) blanched almond flour
1½   cups (180 grams) confectioners' sugar
1   large egg white (30 grams)
2   teaspoons (8 grams) vanilla extract
2   teaspoons (8 grams) almond extract

1. In the work bowl of a food processor, place almond flour and confectioners' sugar; pulse until combined. Add egg white and extracts; process until mixture holds together. If mixture is too dry, add water, 1 teaspoon (5 grams) at a time. Wrap tightly in plastic wrap, and refrigerate for up to 1 month.

RUM-SOAKED FRUIT

Makes ¾ cup

¼   cup (32 grams) diced dried apricots
¼   cup (32 grams) dried cherries, halved
3   tablespoons (45 grams) dark spiced rum
2   tablespoons (24 grams) raisins
2   tablespoons (24 grams) golden raisins

1. In a small bowl, toss together all ingredients. Cover and let stand at room temperature overnight.

RUM GLAZE

Makes about ¾ cup

2   cups (240 grams) confectioners' sugar
3   tablespoons (45 grams) whole milk
2   tablespoons (30 grams) dark spiced rum

1. In a small bowl, stir together all ingredients until smooth. Use immediately.

ORANGE BUTTER COOKIES

Makes 24 cookies

There are so many things to love about this cookie. The dough doesn't need refrigerating, holds an impressive cookie stamp imprint, and combines citrusy orange with smooth bittersweet chocolate. Bake it for 6 minutes for a nice soft cookie, or let it bake a few minutes more for those satisfyingly crisp, golden-brown edges.

1 cup (227 grams) unsalted butter, softened
2 cups (240 grams) confectioners' sugar
1 large egg (50 grams)
2 tablespoons (6 grams) orange zest
1 teaspoon (4 grams) vanilla extract
3 cups (375 grams) all-purpose flour
2 teaspoons (10 grams) baking powder
1 teaspoon (3 grams) kosher salt
1 cup (200 grams) granulated sugar
6 ounces (175 grams) 60% cacao bittersweet chocolate, chopped

1. Preheat oven to 425°F (220°C). Line 2 rimmed baking sheets with parchment paper.
2. In the bowl of a stand mixer fitted with the paddle attachment, beat butter and confectioners' sugar at medium speed until fluffy, 3 to 4 minutes, stopping to scrape sides of bowl. Add egg, zest, and vanilla, beating until combined.
3. In a medium bowl, whisk together flour, baking powder, and salt. With mixer on low speed, gradually add flour mixture to butter mixture, beating until a dough forms.
4. Using a 2-tablespoon scoop, scoop dough, and roll into balls. Roll balls in granulated sugar, coating completely. Place on prepared pans. Using a cookie stamp*, gently press down on dough balls. (Dough should just barely meet edge of cookie stamp.) Cookies should be 2 inches apart on pans.

5. Bake until golden brown, 6 to 8 minutes. Let cool on pans for 2 minutes. Remove from pans, and let cool completely on wire racks.
6. In the top of a double boiler, place chocolate. Cook over simmering water, stirring constantly, until melted. Remove from heat. Dip bottom of each cookie in melted chocolate, gently scraping bottom of cookie along edge of bowl to remove excess. Place on parchment paper, and let stand until chocolate is set. Store in an airtight container for up to 2 weeks.

We used Nordic Ware Geo Cast Cookie Stamps, available on nordicware.com.

MILANESINI

Makes 50 to 60 cookies

Recipe by Sarah Brunella

Originating at the end of the 18th century, Milanesini are one of the most beloved Christmas cookies in Switzerland, where you can purchase them by the bag in various shapes. The citrusy, crunchy cookies taste even better when made from scratch.

1	**cup (227 grams) unsalted butter, softened**
1	**cup (200 grams) granulated sugar**
2	**large eggs (100 grams), room temperature**
½	**teaspoon (1.5 grams) kosher salt**
4	**cups (500 grams) all-purpose flour**
2	**teaspoons (2 grams) lemon zest**
	Lemon Glaze (recipe follows)

1. In the bowl of a stand mixer fitted with the paddle attachment, beat butter, sugar, eggs, and salt at low speed until well combined, about 30 seconds. With mixer on medium-low speed, gradually add flour and zest, beating until a dough starts to form. Turn out dough, and knead for a few seconds. Shape into a ball, and wrap in plastic wrap. Refrigerate until firm, about 1 hour.
2. Preheat oven to 400°F (200°C). Line baking sheets with parchment paper.
3. On a heavily floured surface, roll dough to ⅛-inch thickness. Using various star-shaped cutters, cut dough, and place on prepared pans. Refrigerate for at least 15 minutes.
4. Bake for 10 to 12 minutes. Let cool on pans for 10 minutes. Dip cookies in Lemon Glaze, and let cool completely on wire racks.

Lemon Glaze

Makes ⅔ cup

1½	**cups (180 grams) confectioners' sugar**
3	**tablespoons (45 grams) fresh lemon juice**
	Yellow gel paste food coloring

1. In a small bowl, stir together confectioners' sugar and lemon juice with a fork until smooth. Add food coloring, stirring to combine.

PRO TIP

When chilling the dough, instead of using plastic wrap, place in a resealable plastic bag and flatten it by rolling it. It will take less time to firm up and will be easier to roll to get the right thickness. Plus, using more than 1 plastic bag allows you to take a smaller amount of dough out of the fridge at a time, leaving the rest of the dough to chill until the very last moment, which is always a good idea when working with shortbread.

Photo by Sarah Brunella

ORANGE JAM COOKIES WITH DARK CHOCOLATE GANACHE

Makes 35 to 40 cookies

Recipe by Sarah Brunella

With crisp citrus cookies, rich Dark Chocolate Ganache, and sweet orange jam, these sandwich cookies are a triple threat. The best part is the unexpected crunch from the chopped almonds hidden underneath the jam.

3¼ cups (406 grams) all-purpose flour, sifted
1½ cups (144 grams) almond flour, sifted
⅔ cup (133 grams) granulated sugar
½ teaspoon (1.5 grams) kosher salt
1 cup (227 grams) cold unsalted butter, cubed
1 tablespoon (3 grams) orange zest
1 large egg (50 grams), room temperature
1 tablespoon (15 grams) heavy whipping cream, room temperature
1 cup (170 grams) 60% cacao chocolate chips, melted
Dark Chocolate Ganache (recipe follows)
¾ cup (106 grams) blanched almonds, toasted and roughly chopped
1 cup (320 grams) orange jam
Garnish: confectioners' sugar

1. In the bowl of a stand mixer fitted with the paddle attachment, beat flours, granulated sugar, and salt at low speed for 3 to 4 seconds. Add cold butter and zest, beating until mixture is crumbly. With mixer on medium-low speed, add egg and cream, beating until a dough starts to form. Turn out mixture, and knead until a smooth dough forms. Wrap in plastic wrap, and refrigerate until firm, about 1 hour.

2. Preheat oven to 350°F (180°C). Line baking sheets with parchment paper.

3. On a floured surface, roll dough to ¼-inch thickness. Using a 2-inch fluted round cutter, cut dough, and place on prepared pans. Using a 1-inch heart-shaped cutter, cut centers from half of cookies.

4. Bake for 10 to 12 minutes. Let cool on pans for 5 minutes. Remove from pans, and let cool completely on wire racks. Dip cookies with cutouts in melted chocolate; let set.

5. Place Dark Chocolate Ganache in a piping bag fitted with a star-shaped piping tip*. Pipe Dark Chocolate Ganache around edges of all solid cookies. Place 1 teaspoon (2 grams) toasted almonds in center, and top with 1 teaspoon (7 grams) orange jam. Dust cookies with cutouts with confectioners' sugar, if desired, and place on top of solid cookies.

*I used Wilton No. 21 Open Star Decorating Tip.

DARK CHOCOLATE GANACHE
Makes about 1¼ cups

8 ounces (225 grams) 60% cacao dark chocolate, chopped
½ cup (120 grams) heavy whipping cream

1. Place chocolate in a microwave-safe bowl.

2. In a small saucepan, heat cream over medium heat, stirring frequently, just until bubbles form around edges of pan. (Do not boil.) Remove from heat. Pour hot cream over chocolate. Let stand for 1 minute; stir until melted. (If chocolate does not melt completely, microwave on medium in 5-second intervals, stirring between each, until smooth and silky.) Refrigerate for 30 minutes.

3. Place ganache in the bowl of a stand mixer fitted with the whisk attachment, and beat until fluffy. Use immediately. Leftover Dark Chocolate Ganache can be refrigerated for up to 5 days or used for icing cakes.

Photo by Sarah Brunella

CRANBERRY PISTACHIO SHORTBREAD COOKIES

Makes 12 cookies

Recipe by Laura Kasavan

These vanilla shortbread cookies studded with jeweled cranberries and dipped in white chocolate make a festive addition to any cookie platter. To make chopping the dried fruit easier, spray your knife with cooking spray.

- ¾ cup (170 grams) unsalted butter, softened
- ⅔ cup (133 grams) plus 1 tablespoon (12 grams) granulated sugar, divided
- ½ teaspoon (2 grams) vanilla extract
- ⅛ teaspoon kosher salt
- 1¾ cups (219 grams) all-purpose flour
- ½ cup (64 grams) dried cranberries, chopped
- ½ cup (57 grams) finely chopped roasted salted pistachios
- 8 ounces (225 grams) white chocolate, chopped

Garnish: holiday sprinkles

1. Spray a 9-inch removable-bottom tart pan with cooking spray.

2. In the bowl of a stand mixer fitted with the paddle attachment, beat butter and ⅔ cup (133 grams) sugar at medium speed until creamy, 2 to 3 minutes, stopping to scrape sides of bowl. With mixer on medium-low speed, add vanilla and salt, beating until combined. With mixer on low speed, add flour, beating until combined and dough starts to come together. Add cranberries and pistachios, beating just until combined. Transfer dough to prepared pan, pressing into bottom and up sides. Cover and refrigerate until firm, about 1 hour.

3. Preheat oven to 350°F (180°C).

4. Using a sharp knife, score dough into 12 wedges, and prick all over with a wooden skewer. Sprinkle with remaining 1 tablespoon (12 grams) sugar. Place tart pan on a rimmed baking sheet to catch any butter that may drip out while baking.

5. Bake until top is light golden and center is set, 28 to 32 minutes. Using a sharp knife, recut shortbread into wedges, and let cool completely in pan.

6. Line a rimmed baking sheet with parchment paper.

7. In the top of a double boiler, place white chocolate. Cook over simmering water, stirring occasionally, until glossy and smooth. One by one, dip widest end of each cookie triangle in melted chocolate, and place on prepared pan. Garnish with holiday sprinkles, if desired. Refrigerate until chocolate is set, about 20 minutes.

MAKE AHEAD
Shortbread dough can be made up to 1 month in advance. After refrigerating dough for 1 hour, score dough into wedges, and prick all over with a wooden skewer. Wrap tart pan in foil, and place in a large resealable plastic bag to freeze. When you're ready to bake, you can bake the shortbread directly from the freezer, adding 2 or 3 minutes to baking time.

Photo by Laura Kasavan

PINKY BAR COOKIES

Makes about 16 cookies

Recipe by Erin Clarkson

This is a cookie version of a classic New Zealand candy bar my grandfather always gave us at Christmastime when I was growing up. The Cadbury Pinky bar is made up of a fluffy pink marshmallow, a thin layer of caramel, and a coating of milk chocolate. I added freeze-dried raspberry powder into the marshmallow.

1	cup plus 1½ tablespoons (248 grams) unsalted butter, softened
¾	cup plus 4 teaspoons (98 grams) confectioners' sugar, sifted
½	teaspoon (2 grams) vanilla extract
¼	teaspoon kosher salt
2⅛	cups (265 grams) all-purpose flour
⅔	cup plus 1 tablespoon (55 grams) Dutch process cocoa powder

Salted Caramel Sauce (recipe follows)
Raspberry Marshmallow (recipe follows)

1. In the bowl of a stand mixer fitted with the paddle attachment, beat butter, confectioners' sugar, vanilla, and salt at medium speed until creamy, 2 to 3 minutes, stopping to scrape sides of bowl. With mixer on low speed, add flour and cocoa, beating just until combined.

2. Cut 2 (18x13-inch) sheets of parchment paper. Turn out dough onto one sheet of parchment, and flatten into a rough rectangle. Top with second sheet of parchment, smoothing down well. Roll to ¼-inch thickness. (Remove top sheet, and smooth down again if you are getting wrinkles.) Transfer dough between parchment to a half sheet pan. Freeze until completely solid, 20 to 30 minutes.

3. Preheat oven to 350°F (180°C). Line 2 baking sheets with parchment paper.

4. Remove dough from freezer, and remove top sheet of parchment. Using a 2¼-inch round cutter, cut dough, and carefully place on prepared pans, leaving a little room between each. (They do not spread much.) If at any point your dough gets hard to work with or gets too soft, place in freezer again for 5 minutes to firm up. Reroll any scraps, refreeze, and cut out more rounds. Repeat until you have used all dough.

5. Bake, one batch at a time, until set, 11 to 12 minutes. Let cool on pans for 15 minutes. Remove from pans, and let cool completely on wire racks.

6. Generously spread Salted Caramel Sauce onto flat side of half of cookies. Freeze until caramel firms up, about 5 minutes. Place Raspberry Marshmallow in a large piping bag fitted with a large round tip, such as an Ateco #807. Holding piping bag straight up and down about 1 inch from cookie, pipe a blob of Raspberry Marshmallow wide enough to cover caramel, bearing in mind that when you sandwich it, it will spread out slightly. Place remaining cookies, flat side down, on top of marshmallow. (Do one to start to test the amount of marshmallow you are piping on to make sure you are happy with it.) Repeat piping process with remaining cookies. Let stand until marshmallow is set, 1 to 2 hours. Refrigerate in an airtight container. These cookies are best eaten on the day they are made.

Note: *Chocolate shortbread dough can be made ahead of time and stored rolled out in freezer until you are ready to use.*

SALTED CARAMEL SAUCE
Makes 1¼ cups

½	cup (120 grams) heavy whipping cream
1	cup (200 grams) granulated sugar
6	tablespoons (84 grams) unsalted butter, cubed and softened
1	teaspoon (3 grams) kosher salt

1. In a small saucepan, heat cream over low heat, watching carefully to ensure it warms but does not burn.

2. In a medium heavy-bottomed saucepan, heat sugar over medium heat, stirring constantly. (Sugar will clump as you heat, but continue to stir, and it will soon smooth out.) Cook until sugar turns amber colored; remove from heat, and immediately add butter. (Use caution as it may bubble.) Whisk vigorously until all butter is incorporated; add hot cream, and whisk until well combined and emulsified. Stir in salt. Transfer to a jar or other container, and let cool to room temperature. Refrigerate until ready to use.

> **PRO TIP**
> For Salted Caramel Sauce, have everything ready to go because things move quickly once the sugar is ready. Salted Caramel Sauce needs time to cool, so ensure that you allow enough time for this.

RASPBERRY MARSHMALLOW

Makes about 5 cups

½   cup plus 2 tablespoons (150 grams) cold water, divided
3½   teaspoons (14 grams) unflavored gelatin
2¼   cups plus 1½ tablespoons (468 grams) granulated sugar
¼   cup plus 1 tablespoon (106 grams) light corn syrup
2   tablespoons (18 grams) freeze-dried raspberry powder
1   tablespoon (18 grams) vanilla bean paste or 1 vanilla bean,
     split lengthwise, seeds scraped and reserved
1   tablespoon (15 grams) liquid red food coloring

1. In the bowl of a stand mixer fitted with the whisk attachment, stir together ¼ cup plus 1 tablespoon (75 grams) cold water and gelatin by hand. Let stand until softened, about 5 minutes.

2. In a medium heavy-bottomed saucepan, heat sugar, corn syrup, raspberry powder, vanilla bean paste, and remaining ¼ cup plus 1 tablespoon (75 grams) cold water over medium heat. Cook, stirring occasionally, until a candy thermometer registers 240°F (116°C). Remove from heat, and let cool to 210°F (99°C).

3. With mixer on medium speed, break up gelatin slightly. Add sugar syrup mixture in a slow, steady stream. Increase mixer speed to high, and beat until marshmallow is doubled in size, holds a small peak, and is fluffy, 5 to 7 minutes, adding food coloring during last 1 minute. Use immediately. Leftovers can be piped into a greased dish and allowed to cure to be used for Raspberry Marshmallows.

Note: *It is especially important to make this marshmallow recipe using grams—with all the sticky ingredients, such as corn syrup, it is much easier to weigh them all directly into the saucepan and mixing bowl.*

Photo by Erin Clarkson

GINGER BOMBS

Makes 22 cookies

Recipe by Rebecca Firth

Come holiday season, I want everything all ginger, molasses, mistletoe, and sweet, and these Ginger Buttercream-stuffed molasses cookies encompass all of that (minus the greenery). There are heaps of ginger in these, but don't let the quantities scare you off—it's just the right amount.

1   cup (227 grams) unsalted butter, softened
1   cup (220 grams) firmly packed dark brown sugar
2   large eggs (100 grams), room temperature
1   large egg yolk (19 grams), room temperature
⅓   cup (113 grams) unsulphured molasses
1½   tablespoons (11 grams) grated fresh ginger
1   tablespoon (13 grams) vanilla extract
2   cups (264 grams) bread flour
1   cup (130 grams) all-purpose flour
1½   tablespoons (9 grams) ground ginger
2   teaspoons (10 grams) baking soda
2   teaspoons (4 grams) ground cinnamon
1   teaspoon (3 grams) sea salt
1   teaspoon (2 grams) ground cloves
Ginger Buttercream (recipe follows)

1. In the bowl of a stand mixer fitted with the paddle attachment, beat butter and brown sugar at medium speed until creamy, 2 to 3 minutes, stopping to scrape sides of bowl. Add eggs and egg yolk, one at a time, beating well after each addition. Add molasses, grated ginger, and vanilla, and beat for 1 minute.
2. In a medium bowl, whisk together flours, ground ginger, baking soda, cinnamon, sea salt, and cloves. With mixer on low speed, gradually add flour mixture to butter mixture, beating just until combined, about 1 minute. Using a spatula, scrape sides and bottom of bowl to ensure everything is incorporated. Shape dough into a disk, and wrap tightly in plastic wrap. Refrigerate until firm, about 1 hour.
3. Preheat oven to 350°F (180°C). Line several baking sheets with parchment paper.
4. Roll dough into 1-tablespoon (14-gram) balls, and place 2 inches apart on prepared pans. If dough is a little sticky, use 2 spoons or a cookie scoop to help.
5. Bake for 9 to 10 minutes. Let cool on pans for 5 minutes. Remove from pans, and let cool completely on wire racks. Smear Ginger Buttercream onto flat side of half of cookies. Place remaining cookies, flat side down, on top of filling. Store in an airtight container for up to 3 days.

GINGER BUTTERCREAM
Makes 2 cups

¼   cup (57 grams) unsalted butter, softened
2   ounces (55 grams) cream cheese, softened
2   cups (240 grams) confectioners' sugar
3   tablespoons (33 grams) finely minced candied ginger
1   tablespoon (15 grams) whole milk

1. In the bowl of a stand mixer fitted with the paddle attachment, beat butter, cream cheese, and confectioners' sugar at low speed until smooth and creamy, about 2 minutes. Add candied ginger and milk, and beat until milk is completely absorbed and small bits of candied ginger are visible throughout, about 1 minute. Use immediately.

Photo by Rebecca Firth

SHORTBREAD LINZER COOKIES WITH RASPBERRY JAM FILLING

Makes about 18 cookies

Recipe by Erin Clarkson

These are a nod to my grandma's shortbread. We went to stay with my grandparents every summer, which is where I first learned to bake. Grandma's shortbread recipe came from her grandma, and it's a Christmas tradition I will pass on to the next generation. I revamped the recipe and turned it into a Linzer-style cookie.

¾   cup (170 grams) unsalted butter, softened
½   cup plus 1 tablespoon (67 grams) confectioners' sugar, sifted
1   teaspoon (6 grams) vanilla bean paste
¼   teaspoon kosher salt
2⅛ cups (265 grams) all-purpose flour
Raspberry Jam Filling (recipe follows)
Garnish: confectioners' sugar

1. In the bowl of a stand mixer fitted with the paddle attachment, beat butter, confectioners' sugar, vanilla bean paste, and salt at medium speed until creamy, 2 to 3 minutes, stopping to scrape sides of bowl. Add flour, and beat at low speed just until combined. Turn out dough, and shape into a disk. Wrap tightly in plastic wrap, and refrigerate for at least 2 hours or overnight.
2. Let dough stand at room temperature until slightly softened, 10 to 15 minutes. Cut 2 (18x13-inch) sheets of parchment paper. Turn out dough onto one sheet of parchment, and flatten into a rough rectangle. Top with second sheet of parchment, smoothing down well. Roll to ¼-inch thickness. (Remove top sheet, and smooth down again if you are getting wrinkles.) Transfer dough between parchment to a half sheet pan. Freeze for 15 to 20 minutes.
3. Preheat oven to 325°F (170°C). Line 2 baking sheets with parchment paper.
4. Remove dough from freezer, and remove top sheet of parchment. Using a 2-inch fluted round cutter, cut dough, and place 2 inches apart on prepared pans. If at any point your dough gets difficult to work with

or gets too soft, place in freezer again for 5 minutes to firm up. Reroll any scraps, refreeze, and cut out more rounds. Freeze for 10 minutes. Using desired small holiday-shaped cutters, cut centers from half of cookies.
5. Bake, one batch at a time, until set and just beginning to turn golden, 11 to 12 minutes. Let cool on pans for 15 minutes. Remove from pans, and let cool completely on wire racks.
6. Pipe or spoon about 1 teaspoon Raspberry Jam Filling onto flat side of all solid cookies. Generously dust cookies with cutouts with confectioners' sugar, if desired. Place cookies with cutouts, flat side down, on top of filling. Store in an airtight container. If you are not planning on eating these on the first or second day, store cookies and filling separately, and sandwich before eating to avoid them getting soggy.

Note: *Freeze dough you are not working with or cookies that are waiting to bake until ready to use.*

RASPBERRY JAM FILLING
Makes about 2 cups

2   cups (342 grams) frozen raspberries
2   cups (400 grams) granulated sugar

1. In a medium heavy-bottomed saucepan, mash raspberries roughly. Bring to a rolling boil; add sugar, and cook for 3 minutes, stirring occasionally. Transfer to a container or sterilized jars, and let cool completely. Refrigerate overnight before using.

Note: *This will make a little more than you need, but it is perfect as the filling for a cake or for your morning toast.*

Photo by Erin Clarkson

JAM-FILLED PECAN SNOWBALLS

Makes 25 cookies

Recipe by Edd Kimber

During the holidays, these classic snowballs are a wonderful thing, especially if you like to entertain or have family visiting. They can be quickly whipped up in a food processor and made in big batches.

- 1   cup (100 grams) pecan halves
- 1   cup (227 grams) unsalted butter, softened
- ⅔   cup (80 grams) confectioners' sugar, plus more for coating
- 1   teaspoon (4 grams) vanilla extract
- 2¼   cups (281 grams) all-purpose flour
- 1   teaspoon (2 grams) ground cinnamon
- ½   teaspoon (2.5 grams) baking soda
- ½   teaspoon (1.5 grams) kosher salt
- ½   cup (160 grams) raspberry jam

1. Preheat oven to 350°F (180°C).
2. Place pecans on a quarter sheet pan, and toast until fragrant and slightly darkened, 8 to 10 minutes. Let cool completely.
3. In the work bowl of a food processor, place toasted pecans; pulse until finely chopped. Transfer to a bowl, and set aside.
4. Place butter, confectioners' sugar, and vanilla in food processor; pulse until well combined and butter is pale and creamy. Add pecans, flour, cinnamon, baking soda, and salt; pulse until a dough forms. Scrape dough into a bowl, and cover with plastic wrap. Refrigerate until firm.
5. Line 2 half sheet pans with parchment paper.

6. Roll dough into 2-tablespoon balls (about 27 grams each). Using a sharp knife, cut each ball in half. Using a finger, make an indentation in center of cut side of each half. Spoon about 1 teaspoon (7 grams) jam into one half. Place second half back on top, and gently smooth seal to join 2 halves back together. Place about 1 inch apart on prepared pans. Refrigerate for 20 minutes.
7. Bake until edges are lightly browned, 15 to 17 minutes. Let cool for a 3 minutes; carefully roll in confectioners' sugar to coat. (This has to be done while warm so sugar sticks to the cookies.) Store in an airtight container for up to 4 days.

Photo by Edd Kimber

EVERYTHING CHOCOLATE
THUMBPRINT COOKIES

Makes 56 cookies

Dear chocolate lovers, you're welcome. To celebrate one of our favorite chocolate companies, Guittard (and their 150th anniversary!), we used a few of our favorite Guittard products to create a sophisticated thumbprint cookie. With cocoa powder in the dough, a pool of melty ganache in the center, and chocolate shavings and a light chocolate drizzle on top, this will be the most indulgent cookie you bake this season.

1	cup (227 grams) unsalted butter, softened
¾	cup (165 grams) firmly packed dark brown sugar
2	large egg yolks (37 grams)
1½	teaspoons (6 grams) vanilla extract
2	cups (250 grams) all-purpose flour
⅓	cup (40 grams) unsweetened cocoa powder*
½	teaspoon (1.5 grams) kosher salt
¼	teaspoon (1.25 grams) baking powder

Ganache (recipe follows)
Garnish: melted bittersweet chocolate, flaked sea salt, bittersweet chocolate shavings (see Note)

1. Preheat oven to 350°F (180°C). Line several baking sheets with parchment paper.
2. In the bowl of a stand mixer fitted with the paddle attachment, beat butter and brown sugar at medium speed until creamy, about 2 minutes, stopping to scrape sides of bowl. Beat in egg yolks and vanilla.
3. In a medium bowl, whisk together flour, cocoa, kosher salt, and baking powder. With mixer on low speed, gradually add flour mixture to butter mixture, beating until combined. Shape dough into 1-inch (13-gram) balls, and place 2 inches apart on prepared pans. Using a ¼ teaspoon, gently make an indentation in center of each ball.
4. Bake for 9 to 11 minutes. Remove from oven, and press down centers again. Let cool on pans for 10 minutes. Remove from pans, and let cool completely on wire racks. Spoon 1 teaspoon Ganache into center of each cookie. Drizzle with melted chocolate, and top with sea salt and chocolate shavings, if desired.

We used Guittard Cocoa Rouge Unsweetened Cocoa Powder.

Note: *Using a vegetable peeler, scrape blade lengthwise across room temperature chocolate to create shavings.*

GANACHE
Makes ¾ cup

⅔	cup (113 grams) chopped bittersweet chocolate*
½	cup (120 grams) heavy whipping cream

1. Place chopped chocolate in a large heatproof bowl.
2. In a small saucepan, bring cream just to a boil over medium heat. Pour hot cream over chocolate. Let stand for 1 minute; whisk until smooth. Refrigerate, stirring occasionally, until slightly thickened, about 30 minutes.

We used Guittard Eureka Works 150th Anniversary Limited Edition 62% Cacao Bar, but Guittard Semisweet Chocolate Baking Bar 64% Cacao will work, too.

PEPPERMINT MERINGUES WITH WHITE CHOCOLATE GANACHE

Makes about 30 meringues

Recipe by Sarah Brunella

These candy cane-inspired meringues impress the eye and please the taste buds. Leaving egg whites at room temperature for an hour before starting the recipe will help them whip better.

1   cup (200 grams) granulated sugar
2   teaspoons (6 grams) cornstarch
4   large egg whites (120 grams), room temperature
½   teaspoon (2 grams) peppermint extract
Red gel paste food coloring
4   ounces (115 grams) white chocolate, chopped
White Chocolate Ganache (recipe follows)
3   large or 6 small candy canes (125 grams), finely crushed

1. Preheat oven to 275°F (140°C). Line a baking sheet with parchment paper. Using a pencil, draw 1-inch circles onto parchment; turn parchment over.
2. In a small bowl, sift together sugar and cornstarch; set aside.
3. In the bowl of a stand mixer fitted with the whisk attachment, beat egg whites at medium-low speed until stiff peaks start to form. With mixer on high speed, gradually add sugar mixture, beating until glossy stiff peaks form. (If you put a dollop of meringue between thumb and forefinger, you should not feel the sugar grains.) Gently fold in peppermint extract.
4. Add rosette tip to a piping bag. Turn bag inside out, and use a wooden pick to apply 4 straight lines of food coloring on bag. Turn back around, and fill piping bag with meringue mixture, twisting end of bag tightly. Pipe rosettes onto drawn circles on prepared pan.
5. Bake until meringues are very dry and peel off parchment easily, 35 to

45 minutes. Turn oven off, and let meringues stand in oven with door closed to let cool completely, about 30 minutes.
6. In a microwave-safe bowl, microwave white chocolate on medium in 30-second intervals, stirring between each, until melted and smooth. Dip flat side of meringues in melted chocolate, and let cool on a parchment-lined baking sheet.
7. Pipe White Chocolate Ganache onto flat side of half of meringues. Place remaining meringues, flat side down, on top of filling. Roll cookies in crushed candy canes. These cookies are better eaten within a few hours, but meringues can be stored in an airtight container or a plastic bag at room temperature.

WHITE CHOCOLATE GANACHE
Makes about 1¼ cups

8   ounces (225 grams) white chocolate, chopped
⅓   cup (80 grams) heavy whipping cream

1. Place white chocolate in a microwave-safe bowl.

2. In a small saucepan, heat cream over medium heat, stirring frequently, just until bubbles form around edges of pan. (Do not boil.) Remove from heat. Pour hot cream over chocolate. Let stand for 1 minute; stir until melted. (If chocolate does not melt completely, microwave on medium in 5-second intervals, stirring between each, until smooth and silky.) Refrigerate for 15 to 20 minutes.
3. Place ganache in the bowl of a stand mixer fitted with the whisk attachment; beat at medium speed until fluffy. Use immediately.

PRO TIP
Always use metal bowls and attachments and be sure they are squeaky clean before making meringue. Scrub them with a slice of lemon. This will ensure there will be no fat in the bowl or on the attachment, which prevents the egg whites from whipping properly, and will guarantee good results.

Photo by Sarah Brunella

HOT CHOCOLATE SANDWICH COOKIES

Makes about 25 cookies

Recipe by Sarah Kieffer

These Hot Chocolate Sandwich Cookies are thin but packed full of chocolate flavor, and the Mint Meringue Filling is reminiscent of a marshmallow. If you are not a fan of mint, the extract can be omitted.

5 tablespoons (70 grams) unsalted butter, softened
8 ounces (225 grams) semisweet chocolate, chopped
3 tablespoons (15 grams) Dutch process cocoa powder
3 large eggs (150 grams)
1¼ cups (250 grams) granulated sugar
½ teaspoon (1.5 grams) fine sea salt
1 tablespoon (14 grams) canola oil
1 teaspoon (4 grams) vanilla extract
½ cup plus 1 tablespoon (71 grams) all-purpose flour
¾ teaspoon (3.75 grams) baking powder
Mint Meringue Filling (recipe follows)
5 large candy canes (210 grams), crushed

1. Preheat oven to 350°F (180°C). Line 3 baking sheets with parchment paper.

2. In a small heavy-bottomed saucepan, heat butter over very low heat. Add chocolate, and melt together, stirring frequently to prevent chocolate from scorching. Cook until mixture is warm to the touch but not hot. Add cocoa, and whisk until combined. Remove from heat, and keep warm. (Alternatively, in a microwave-safe bowl, heat butter and chocolate on high in 30-second intervals, stirring between each, until melted and smooth. Whisk in cocoa.)

3. In the bowl of a stand mixer fitted with the paddle attachment, beat eggs, sugar, and sea salt at medium-high speed until very light and fluffy, 3 to 5 minutes. With mixer on low speed, add oil and vanilla, beating just until combined. Add warm chocolate mixture, beating until combined.

4. In a small bowl, whisk together flour and baking powder. Gradually add flour mixture to egg mixture, beating until combined. Using a spatula, finish stirring batter. Let stand until batter firms to the consistency of a thick brownie batter, about 5 minutes. Drop batter by heaping 2 tablespoonfuls at least 2 inches apart onto prepared pans.

5. Bake, one batch at a time, until puffed and cracked and edges are set, 8 to

12 minutes. Pipe or spoon Mint Meringue Filling onto flat side of half of cookies. Place remaining cookies, flat side down, on top of filling, gently pressing together until filling reaches edges of cookies. Roll cookies in crushed candy canes. Serve warm or at room temperature. Cookies are best the day of baking but will keep in an airtight container at room temperature for up to 3 days.

MINT MERINGUE FILLING
Makes about 5 cups

5 large egg whites (150 grams)
1½ cups (300 grams) granulated sugar
¼ teaspoon fine sea salt
1 tablespoon (15 grams) crème de menthe (optional)
½ teaspoon (2 grams) mint extract, or more if desired
½ teaspoon (2 grams) vanilla extract

1. In the bowl of a stand mixer, stir together egg whites, sugar, and sea salt by hand. Place bowl over a saucepan of simmering water, being careful not to let water touch bottom of bowl. Cook, stirring with a rubber spatula, until sugar is completely dissolved and a candy thermometer registers 160°F (71°C), 4 to 5 minutes. (While stirring, be sure to scrape sides of bowl with spatula—this will ensure no sugar grains are lurking on sides and will also help prevent egg whites from cooking.)

2. Carefully return bowl to stand mixer. Using the whisk attachment, beat mixture at medium-high speed until glossy stiff peaks form and bowl cools to room temperature, 8 to 10 minutes. Add crème de menthe (if using) and extracts, beating until combined. Use immediately.

Photo by Sarah Kieffer

HAZELNUT LINZER COOKIES WITH WINE-INFUSED JAM

Makes 24 cookies

Recipe by Becky Sue Wilberding

Classic Linzer cookies get elevated with a rich hazelnut sandwich cookie base filled with wine-infused jams to toast the spirit of the holiday season.

2	cups (250 grams) plus 2 tablespoons (16 grams) all-purpose flour, divided
1	teaspoon (5 grams) baking powder
1	teaspoon (2 grams) ground cinnamon
½	teaspoon (1.5 grams) kosher salt
½	teaspoon (1 gram) ground ginger
1	cup (142 grams) raw hazelnuts
1	cup (227 grams) unsalted butter, softened
½	cup (100 grams) granulated sugar
1	large egg (50 grams), room temperature
1	teaspoon (4 grams) vanilla extract
½	teaspoon (2 grams) almond extract
¾	cup (240 grams) wine-infused jam*
¼	cup (30 grams) confectioners' sugar

1. Preheat oven to 350°F (180°C).
2. In a medium bowl, whisk together 2 cups (250 grams) flour, baking powder, cinnamon, salt, and ginger. Set aside.
3. Place hazelnuts on a baking sheet, and toast for 8 to 10 minutes. Transfer nuts to a clean towel, and vigorously rub nuts in towel to remove as much of skins as possible. (Don't worry too much about leaving some skin on the nuts—it adds a nice texture and color to the cookies.) Let cool completely.
4. In the work bowl of a food processor, place hazelnuts and remaining 2 tablespoons (16 grams) flour; pulse until nuts are finely ground. (The flour will absorb the oils from the nuts and prevent a nut butter from forming in the food processor.) Add hazelnut mixture to flour mixture, whisking to combine. Set aside.
5. In the bowl of a stand mixer fitted with the paddle attachment, beat butter and granulated sugar at medium speed until creamy, 2 to 3 minutes, stopping to scrape sides of bowl. Add egg and extracts, beating until combined. With mixer on low speed, gradually add flour mixture, beating until combined. Divide dough in half, and shape each half into a disk. Wrap in plastic wrap, and refrigerate for at least 1 hour or overnight.
6. Line 2 baking sheets with parchment paper.
7. On a lightly floured surface, roll half of dough to ¼-inch thickness. Using 2-inch round, fluted round, or fluted square cutters, cut dough, rerolling scraps as necessary. (Refrigerate dough if it becomes too soft to get a clean cut.) Place at least 1 inch apart on prepared pans. Using desired 1-inch or smaller holiday-shaped cutters, cut centers from half of cookies. (Make sure you have the same number of tops to bottoms in each cookie shape.) Reserve some center cutouts for decorative accents. Repeat with remaining dough. Refrigerate for at least 30 minutes or overnight, or freeze until ready to bake.
8. Preheat oven to 350°F (180°C).

9. Bake until edges are golden, 10 to 12 minutes, rotating pans halfway through baking. Let cool completely on wire racks.
10. Spread 1½ teaspoons wine-infused jam on flat side of all solid cookies. Sprinkle cookies with cutouts with confectioners' sugar. Place cookies with cutouts, flat side down, on top of jam. Refrigerate cookies layered between sheets of wax or parchment paper in an airtight container for up to 2 weeks.

*Use various wine-infused jams for variety in taste and color. I used Grapefruit Ginger Rosé Jam, Strawberry & Pinot Noir Jam, and Marionberry Jam with Port from Vintner's Kitchen, available at vintnerskitchen.com. You can also use regular jam.

Note: *You can get creative with sizes and shapes of cookies, but remember to account for the sizes and shapes when baking. If you make varying sizes, be sure to bake the cookies of similar size together as smaller cookies will bake quicker than larger cookies.*

Photo by Becky Sue Wilberding

SAGE, ASIAGO, AND PECAN SAVORY SHORTBREAD COINS

Makes 24 coins

This cheesy, herbaceous take on classic shortbread will be the MVP of your next charcuterie board. Asiago cheese imparts a salty zing that's elevated by the pine-like notes of sage, resulting in a savory coin reminiscent of the flavors of Provence. Pair with a dry white or robust red wine and a few slices of prosciutto, and you're in business.

½   cup (113 grams) unsalted butter, softened
1   cup (99 grams) packed finely shredded Asiago cheese
2   tablespoons (14 grams) finely chopped pecans
1   teaspoon minced fresh sage
½   teaspoon (1.5 grams) kosher salt
½   teaspoon (1 gram) ground black pepper
1¼ cups (156 grams) all-purpose flour
1   large egg white (30 grams)
Garnish: fresh sage leaves, pecan halves

1. In the bowl of a stand mixer fitted with the paddle attachment, beat butter at medium speed until creamy, about 1 minute. Add Asiago, pecans, sage, salt, and pepper, beating until combined. With mixer on low speed, gradually add flour, beating until large clumps form, 2 to 3 minutes. Turn out dough, and gently knead until no longer crumbly. Shape into a 9½-inch-long log. Wrap in plastic wrap, and freeze for 1 hour.
2. Preheat oven to 350°F (180°C). Line a baking sheet with parchment paper.
3. Cut log into 24 (⅜-inch-thick) slices. Place about 1 inch apart on prepared pan. Brush with egg white. Top with sage or pecans, if desired.
4. Bake until very lightly browned on bottom, 18 to 20 minutes. Let cool completely on pan. Store in an airtight container for up to 2 weeks.

SPICED CHINESE ALMOND COOKIES

Makes 30 cookies

Recipe by Rebecca Firth

This is your new favorite holiday cookie that you didn't know you needed. The classic, crisp Chinese takeout almond cookie takes on an updated, soft-batch vibe in these super spiced-up renditions. Be sure to add a thorough coat of the cream-egg wash—it'll give it that über nostalgic, lacquered appearance.

1   cup (227 grams) unsalted butter, softened
1¼ cups (250 grams) granulated sugar
1   large egg (50 grams), room temperature
1   teaspoon (4 grams) almond extract
1¾ cups (219 grams) all-purpose flour
¾   cup (95 grams) bread flour
½   cup (48 grams) blanched almond flour
1   teaspoon (5 grams) baking soda
1   teaspoon (5 grams) baking powder
1   teaspoon (2 grams) ground cinnamon
½   teaspoon (1.5 grams) sea salt
½   teaspoon (1 gram) ground nutmeg
½   teaspoon (1 gram) ground allspice
30   whole raw almonds (34 grams)
1   large egg yolk (19 grams)
2   tablespoons (30 grams) heavy whipping cream

1. Preheat oven to 350°F (180°C). Line several baking sheets with parchment paper.
2. In the bowl of a stand mixer fitted with the paddle attachment, beat butter and sugar at medium speed until fluffy, 2 to 3 minutes, stopping to scrape sides of bowl. Add egg and almond extract, and beat until well combined, about 2 minutes.
3. In a medium bowl, whisk together flours, baking soda, baking powder, cinnamon, sea salt, nutmeg, and allspice. With mixer on low speed, gradually add flour mixture to butter mixture, beating just until combined. Using a spatula, scrape sides and bottom of bowl to ensure everything is incorporated.
4. Using a 1½-tablespoon scoop, scoop dough, and roll into balls. Place 2 inches apart on prepared pans. Press an almond into center of each ball, and gently flatten into a disk.
5. In a small bowl, whisk together egg yolk and cream. Brush egg wash onto top and sides of dough, making sure it is thoroughly covered in wash but not pooling around base of dough.
6. Bake until bronzed, 12 to 13 minutes. Hold pans several inches above counter, and drop to deflate cookies slightly. Let cool on pans for 5 to 10 minutes. Remove from pans, and let cool completely on wire racks.

Photo by Rebecca Firth

CLASSIC SHORTBREAD

Makes 9 cookies

Time to break out your favorite Yuletide cookie molds. Thanks to this dough's wet nature and soft crumb, it holds shape and design better than any other biscuit on the block. Our Classic Shortbread is crumbly, buttery bliss. You'll never go back to store-bought again.

¾   cup (170 grams) unsalted butter, softened
½   cup (60 grams) confectioners' sugar
1   teaspoon (4 grams) vanilla extract*
½   teaspoon (1.5 grams) kosher salt
1½   cups (188 grams) all-purpose flour
Garnish: confectioners' sugar

1. In the bowl of a stand mixer fitted with the paddle attachment, beat butter at medium speed until creamy, about 1 minute. Add confectioners' sugar, vanilla, and salt; beat until smooth, about 1 minute. With mixer on low speed, gradually add flour, beating until combined. Increase mixer speed to medium, and beat until very light and fluffy, about 5 minutes. Turn out dough onto a sheet of parchment paper, and shape into a 6-inch square. Wrap in parchment, and refrigerate for at least 1 hour or up to 3 days.
2. Let dough stand at room temperature for 30 minutes.
3. Preheat oven to 325°F (170°C).
4. Break dough into small pieces, and begin pressing pieces into bottom of an 8-inch square shortbread baking pan*. (The dough should become very soft as you work with it. This is important because it helps when pressing the dough into the small crevices.) Press remaining dough into an even layer in pan; prick dough all over with a fork.

5. Bake until dough looks dry but edges have not yet begun to turn golden, 20 to 25 minutes. Let cool in pan for 15 minutes. Invert pan onto a cutting board. Hit pan with the palm of your hand until shortbread releases. Using a sharp knife, immediately slice into squares following imprinted lines. Let cool completely. Garnish with confectioners' sugar, if desired. Store in an airtight container at room temperature for up to 1 week.

We used Heilala Vanilla Extract and Nordic Ware Snowflake Shortbread Baking Pan.

Note: *Because of how soft this dough is, it works best when baked in a cookie mold rather than using cookie stamps.*

RED VELVET PEPPERMINT SAMMIES

Makes 12 cookies

Recipe by Rebecca Firth

The chocolate flavor is really amped up in these by using both semisweet chocolate and Dutch process cocoa powder. This recipe will work with regular unsweetened cocoa powder as well, but the color won't be as rich and deep. When rolling the dough in the granulated sugar, take care to thickly coat it as this will help the confectioners' sugar adhere and make those high-contrast fissures that are so desirable in a crinkle cookie.

8 ounces (225 grams) semisweet chocolate, finely chopped
½ cup (113 grams) unsalted butter
1 tablespoon (15 grams) whole milk
1 cup (220 grams) firmly packed light brown sugar
1 cup (200 grams) granulated sugar, divided
2 large eggs (100 grams), room temperature
1 tablespoon (23 grams) red gel paste food coloring*
1½ teaspoons (6 grams) vanilla extract
1⅔ cups (226 grams) bread flour
½ cup (43 grams) unsweetened Dutch process cocoa powder
2 teaspoons (10 grams) baking powder
1½ teaspoons (4.5 grams) sea salt
1 teaspoon (5 grams) baking soda
¾ cup (90 grams) confectioners' sugar
Peppermint Buttercream (recipe follows)

1. In the top of a double boiler, combine chocolate, butter, and milk. Cook over simmering water, stirring frequently, until chocolate and butter are melted. Remove from heat; whisk in brown sugar and ¼ cup (50 grams) granulated sugar. Add eggs, one at a time, whisking well after each addition. Add food coloring and vanilla, stirring until combined.
2. In a medium bowl, whisk together flour, cocoa, baking powder, sea salt, and baking soda. Add flour mixture to chocolate mixture, stirring to combine in as few strokes as possible. Let dough stand at room temperature for 15 minutes. If it is still too sticky to roll, refrigerate for 10 to 15 minutes.
3. Preheat oven to 350°F (180°C). Line several baking sheets with parchment paper.
4. Place confectioners' sugar and remaining ¾ cup (150 grams) granulated sugar in separate bowls. Scoop dough by 2 tablespoonfuls (28 grams), and coat heavily in granulated sugar. Roll balls in confectioners' sugar. Don't shake off excess. Make sure dough is covered well in both sugars. Place 2 inches apart on prepared pans.
5. Bake for 11 minutes. Let cool on pans for 15 minutes. Remove from pans, and let cool completely on wire racks. Smear Peppermint Buttercream onto flat side of half of cookies. Place remaining cookies, flat side down, on top of filling. Store in an airtight container for up to 3 days.

*I used Americolor Super Red 420.

PEPPERMINT BUTTERCREAM

Makes 2 cups

¼ cup (57 grams) unsalted butter, softened
2 ounces (55 grams) cream cheese, softened
2 cups (240 grams) confectioners' sugar, sifted
¼ cup (35 grams) peppermint candies, finely crushed
1 tablespoon (15 grams) whole milk
½ teaspoon (2 grams) peppermint extract

1. In the bowl of a stand mixer fitted with the paddle attachment, beat butter, cream cheese, and confectioners' sugar at low speed until smooth and creamy, about 2 minutes. Add crushed peppermint candies, milk, and peppermint extract, and beat for 1 minute. Use immediately.

Photo by Rebecca Firth

PIÑÓN MEXICAN WEDDING COOKIES

Makes about 40 cookies

Recipe by Zoë François

The piñones nuts (a.k.a. pine nuts) make this version of the classic Mexican wedding cookie even more decadent than the traditional. They melt in your mouth and are perfect for your holiday party, ideally served with Champagne.

1   cup (135 grams) pine nuts, toasted
⅔   cup (80 grams) confectioners' sugar, divided
1   cup (227 grams) unsalted butter, softened
1   teaspoon (4 grams) vanilla extract
2   cups (250 grams) all-purpose flour
½   teaspoon (1 gram) ground cinnamon
¼   teaspoon kosher salt
Garnish: confectioners' sugar

1. Preheat oven to 325°F (170°C). Line 2 baking sheets with parchment paper.
2. In the work bowl of a food processor, process pine nuts and ⅓ cup (40 grams) confectioners' sugar until finely ground.
3. In the bowl of a stand mixer fitted with the paddle attachment, beat butter and remaining ⅓ cup (40 grams) confectioners' sugar at medium speed until creamy, 2 to 3 minutes, stopping to scrape sides of bowl. Beat in vanilla.
4. With mixer on low speed, gradually add nut mixture, flour, cinnamon, and salt, beating just until combined. Using a 1-tablespoon scoop, scoop dough, and roll into balls. Place 1 inch apart on prepared pans. Refrigerate for 15 minutes.
5. Bake until golden on bottom but still pale on top, 12 to 15 minutes. Let cool completely on pans. Dust with confectioners' sugar, if desired. Store in an airtight container for up to 5 days.

Photo by Zoë François

APRICOT LINZER COOKIES

Makes 18 cookies

Almond flour makes for a nutty, slightly chewier shortbread, brightened by lemon zest in the dough. The Chambord raspberry liqueur in the filling has a sweet tang that plays up the tartness of the apricot. If you're anything like us, you'll splash what's left of the Loire Valley liqueur in a glass of bubbly to sip as you bake.

1	cup (227 grams) unsalted butter, softened
½	cup (100 grams) granulated sugar
2	cups (250 grams) all-purpose flour
½	cup (48 grams) blanched almond flour
1	teaspoon (1 gram) lemon zest

Apricot Raspberry Filling (recipe follows)
Garnish: confectioners' sugar, lemon zest

1. In the bowl of a stand mixer fitted with the paddle attachment, beat butter at low speed until smooth, 1 to 2 minutes. Add granulated sugar, beating until creamy, 2 to 3 minutes, stopping to scrape sides of bowl. Add flours and zest, beating until combined. Turn out dough, and shape into a disk. Wrap tightly in plastic wrap, and refrigerate for at least 2 hours or up to 5 days.

2. Preheat oven to 300°F (150°C). Line 3 baking sheets with parchment paper.

3. Let dough stand at room temperature until slightly softened, about 15 minutes. On a lightly floured surface, roll dough to ⅛-inch thickness. Using a 2½-inch fluted round cutter dipped in flour, cut dough, rerolling scraps and re-flouring cutter as necessary. Place on prepared pans. Using a 1-inch fluted round cutter, cut centers from half of cookies.

4. Bake until light golden brown around the edges, 20 to 25 minutes, rotating pans halfway through baking. Let cool on pans for 3 minutes. Remove from pans, and let cool completely on wire racks.

5. Spread 2 teaspoons Apricot Raspberry Filling on flat side of all solid cookies. Sprinkle cookies with cutouts with confectioners' sugar, and top with zest, if desired. Place cookies with cutouts, flat side down, on top of filling. Store in an airtight container at room temperature for up to 2 days.

APRICOT RASPBERRY FILLING

Makes 1 cup

1	cup (128 grams) chopped dried apricots
½	cup (120 grams) water
¼	cup (60 grams) raspberry liqueur*
2	tablespoons (24 grams) granulated sugar
1	teaspoon (4 grams) vanilla extract*

1. In a small saucepan, bring all ingredients to a boil over medium heat. Reduce heat to low; simmer for 10 minutes. Using an immersion blender, pulse until smooth. Refrigerate until ready to use.

We used Chambord Black Raspberry Liqueur and Heilala Vanilla Extract.

PRO TIP

It can be a little tricky to check if macarons are done. If you very gently press on the top of one of the shells and it stays stable, then it is likely done. If it is unstable, give it some more time, checking every minute. Baking time varies greatly depending on your oven. If they seem done but will not peel off the parchment paper, pop them in the freezer for 5 to 10 minutes or so to help them release more easily.

SPRINKLE MACARONS WITH VANILLA BEAN BUTTERCREAM

Makes about 40 macarons

Recipe by Erin Clarkson

In Australia and New Zealand, we call sprinkles "hundreds and thousands." It's no surprise that the celebratory jimmies are the secret ingredient to my favorite biscuit: a bright pink cookie adorned in a rainbow assortment of hundreds and thousands. For a twist, I made a cheery red macaron with a snowy white coating of hundreds and thousands.

2½   cups (300 grams) confectioners' sugar
1¾   cups (168 grams) almond meal
5   large egg whites (180 grams), room temperature
¾   cup plus 1 tablespoon (162 grams) granulated sugar
1   teaspoon (5 grams) red gel food coloring
1   teaspoon (6 grams) vanilla bean paste
  White sprinkles
  Vanilla Bean Buttercream (recipe follows)

1. Line baking sheets with parchment paper. Using a pencil, draw 1½-inch circles ¾ inch apart on parchment; turn parchment over.
2. In the work bowl of a food processor, place confectioners' sugar and almond meal; pulse until very finely ground. Sift twice with a fine-mesh sieve, discarding any chunks; set aside. (If there are a large number of chunks, return to the food processor, and pulse again.)
3. In the bowl of a stand mixer fitted with the whisk attachment, beat egg whites at medium speed until foamy. With mixer running, gradually add granulated sugar. Increase mixer speed to high, and beat until meringue starts to firm up. Add food coloring, a few drops at a time, beating until desired color is reached. Add vanilla bean paste, and beat until incorporated. Continue beating until stiff peaks form. Watch this process carefully as you do not want to overwhip.
4. Fold half of almond mixture into meringue. (You want to deflate the meringue just a little at this stage to combine the meringue and almond mixture.) Add remaining almond

mixture, and gently stir to combine. Fold mixture in a series of "turns," deflating batter by spreading it against side of bowl. Turn bowl slightly, and repeat movement, scooping batter from bottom of bowl, and spreading it against the side. Continuously check the consistency of the batter—you want it to flow like lava when you lift the spatula from the bowl, and you should be able to draw a figure 8 without the batter breaking. (This step can take some practice until you know what it should feel and look like. If in doubt, you are better to undermix than overmix. The process of putting the batter into the bag and piping out will help mix the batter further.)
5. Spoon batter into a large pastry bag fitted with a medium round tip, such as an Ateco #805. Holding piping bag at a 90-degree angle to surface, pipe batter onto drawn circles on prepared pans. Finish off each piped circle with a little flick of your wrist to minimize batter forming a point.
6. Holding baking sheet in 2 hands, carefully but firmly bang on counter a few times to release any air bubbles, remove points on top, and help them to spread out slightly. Sprinkle top of macarons with sprinkles. Let stand at room temperature until they form a skin that you can touch without your finger sticking to them, about 30 minutes. (This time will drastically vary depending on the humidity.)
7. Preheat oven to 300°F (150°C). About 15 minutes before you are going to bake, place a sheet pan in oven to preheat. (This is going to be used to place under the pan with the macarons on it to double up, which should help with even baking.) Place baking sheet of macarons onto preheated sheet (so you have double thickness baking sheets).
8. Bake, one batch at a time, for about 18 minutes, rotating pan once, and checking for doneness after 15 minutes. Macarons should develop a foot (the ruffled part on the bottom of the macaron) and bake without browning. To see if they are done, press down lightly on a shell. If the foot gives way, it needs a little longer; if it is stable, then it is close to being done. Test a macaron shell—if you can peel it away cleanly from the paper, they are

done. If they are stable but cannot yet peel away cleanly, give them another minute or so. Again, this part takes a little trial and error depending on your oven. If they seem done but do not peel away cleanly, do not worry—there is a little trick for that. (See next step.)
9. Remove from oven, and let cool on pans for 15 minutes. Remove from pans, and let cool completely on a wire rack. If your macarons do not peel away cleanly, place them on the parchment paper in freezer for 5 to 10 minutes; peel away from paper. Store cooled macarons in an airtight container until ready to use.
10. Place Vanilla Bean Buttercream in a piping bag fitted with a large French star tip, such as an Ateco #866. Pipe buttercream onto flat side of half of macarons. Place remaining macarons, flat side down, on top of buttercream. Refrigerate in an airtight container overnight to let flavors meld. Bring to room temperature before serving.

Note: *Macarons can be a little finicky, so if possible, make this recipe using grams for greatest accuracy.*

VANILLA BEAN BUTTERCREAM
Makes about 2½ cups

¾   cup (170 grams) unsalted butter, softened
1   teaspoon (6 grams) vanilla bean paste
⅛   teaspoon kosher salt
3   cups plus 2 tablespoons (374 grams) confectioners' sugar, sifted
1 to 2 tablespoons (15 to 30 grams) whole milk, as needed

1. In the bowl of a stand mixer fitted with the paddle attachment, beat butter, vanilla bean paste, and salt at high speed until pale and creamy. Sift in confectioners' sugar, and beat at medium speed until well combined. If needed, add milk, 1 tablespoon (15 grams) at a time, until light and fluffy and a pipable consistency is reached.

Photo by Erin Clarkson

HAZELNUT SPICE SPECULAAS

Makes 12 (3-inch-round) cookies (see Note)

Recipe by Zoë François

You can make this recipe using cookie molds, stamps, or both. Speculaas is an Eastern European spiced shortcrust biscuit made on or just before St. Nicholas Day in places like the Netherlands, Belgium, and Germany. Typically, they are more about the pretty stamped decoration, but these are so full of toasted hazelnuts and spices that you'll be admiring them for a whole new reason.

½ cup (113 grams) unsalted butter, softened
¾ cup (165 grams) firmly packed dark brown sugar
1 large egg yolk (19 grams)
1 tablespoon (15 grams) heavy whipping cream
1½ cups (188 grams) all-purpose flour
¼ cup (35 grams) finely ground blanched hazelnuts
¾ teaspoon (1.5 grams) ground cinnamon
½ teaspoon (1 gram) ground nutmeg
½ teaspoon (1 gram) ground cloves
¼ teaspoon (1.25 grams) baking powder
¼ teaspoon kosher salt
Cornstarch, for brushing cookie mold and stamps

1. In the bowl of a stand mixer fitted with the paddle attachment, beat butter and brown sugar at medium speed until fluffy, 2 to 3 minutes, stopping to scrape sides of bowl. Add egg yolk, and beat for 1 minute. Add cream, and beat until combined.
2. In a medium bowl, whisk together flour, hazelnuts, cinnamon, nutmeg, cloves, baking powder, and salt. With mixer on low speed, gradually add flour mixture to butter mixture, beating just until combined. Shape dough into a disk, and wrap in plastic wrap. Refrigerate for at least 2 hours or overnight.
3. Line a baking sheet with parchment paper.
4. For cookie molds*, generously brush mold with cornstarch. Quickly knead a small amount of chilled dough on a lightly floured surface, and roll to ¼-inch thickness. Dust surface with more flour, and press into prepared mold. Work quickly so dough doesn't get warm and sticky. Place on prepared pan.
5. For cookie stamps, roll dough to ¼-inch thickness. Using a round cutter that matches the size of your stamps, cut dough, and place on prepared pan. Brush stamps with cornstarch, and press rounds with stamps. Work quickly so dough doesn't get warm and sticky. Refrigerate dough if it gets too sticky. Refrigerate until well chilled.
6. Preheat oven to 350°F (180°C).
7. Bake until edges are golden, 8 to 12 minutes Let cool on pan for 5 minutes. Remove from pans, and let cool completely on wire racks.

I used Brown Bag Designs cookie molds and stamps, available on brownbagcookiemolds.com or amazon.com. The lamb mold is vintage, and the stamp is the Thistle Cookie Stamp from the British Isle Series.

Note: *Your yield for these cookies will depend on which cookie stamps or molds you use.*

PRO TIP
Dusting the cookie molds and stamps with plenty of cornstarch and keeping your dough chilled is key to getting a clean impression in your cookies.

Photo by Zoë François

TAHINI CHOCOLATE RUGELACH

Makes 24 rugelach

Recipe by Joshua Weissman

This traditional Jewish pastry is essentially a cream cheese-based sweet dough that's rolled with all sorts of fillings. Traditionally, rugelach is crescent-shaped, but I cut these into rounds instead. They are a little easier to make than the classic version, which means you get to enjoy them even sooner.

1 cup (227 grams) unsalted butter, softened
8 ounces (225 grams) cream cheese, softened
3 tablespoons (42 grams) firmly packed dark brown sugar
2 large egg yolks (37 grams)
1 teaspoon (4 grams) vanilla extract
2 cups (250 grams) all-purpose flour*
½ teaspoon (1.5 grams) kosher salt
1 cup (267 grams) tahini*, chilled
6 ounces (175 grams) 50% to 60% cacao chocolate, finely chopped
1 large egg (50 grams), lightly beaten
Sesame seeds, for sprinkling
Garnish: confectioners' sugar

1. In ther bowl of a stand mixer fitted with the paddle attachment, beat butter, cream cheese, and brown sugar at medium speed until creamy, 2 to 3 minutes, stopping to scrape sides of bowl. Add egg yolks, one at a time, beating well after each addition. Beat in vanilla.
2. With mixer on low speed, gradually add flour and salt, beating until combined. Divide dough in half, and shape each half into a disk. Wrap in plastic wrap, and refrigerate for at least 6 hours or overnight.
3. Preheat oven to 350°F (180°C). Line baking sheets with parchment paper or nonstick baking mats.
4. Roll half of dough into an oval, ¼ inch thick. Using a bench scraper or a knife, cut edges to form a clean rectangle. Spread half of tahini onto dough, leaving a ½-inch border on all sides. Sprinkle with half of chocolate. Starting with one long side, roll dough into a tight log. Using a sharp knife, cut log into 1½-inch slices. Place on prepared pans. Repeat with remaining dough, remaining tahini, and remaining chocolate. Brush slices with egg wash, and lightly sprinkle with sesame seeds.
5. Bake until golden brown, 20 to 30 minutes. Let cool on a wire rack. Dust with confectioners' sugar, if desired. Store in an airtight container.

*I used Bob's Red Mill All-Purpose Flour and Ziyad Tahini.

Photo by Joshua Weissman

GINGERBREAD CHAI COOKIES

Makes about 9 cookies

Packing a hit of chai and gingerbread spice, these rustic, aromatic wonders are rolled in a crystal coat of sparkling sugar for a touch of glitter and crunch.

½   cup (113 grams) unsalted butter, softened
¾   cup (150 grams) granulated sugar
1   teaspoon (4 grams) vanilla extract
1   large egg (50 grams)
¼   cup (85 grams) unsulphured molasses
2¼   cups (281 grams) all-purpose flour
1½   teaspoons (3 grams) Chai Spice (recipe follows)
1   teaspoon (5 grams) baking soda
1   teaspoon (2 grams) ground ginger
¼   teaspoon kosher salt
1   cup (200 grams) sparkling sugar

1. Preheat oven to 350°F (180°C). Line baking sheets with parchment paper.
2. In the bowl of a stand mixer fitted with the paddle attachment, beat butter, granulated sugar, and vanilla at medium speed until fluffy, 2 to 3 minutes, stopping to scrape sides of bowl. Beat in egg and molasses.
3. In a medium bowl, whisk together flour, Chai Spice, baking soda, ginger, and salt. With mixer on low speed, gradually add flour mixture to butter mixture, beating until well combined. Using a ¼-cup spring-loaded scoop, scoop dough, and shape into 2-inch balls. Roll balls in sparkling sugar, and place 2½ inches apart on prepared pans.
4. Bake until tops are cracked, 15 to 16 minutes. Let cool completely on wire racks.

CHAI SPICE
Makes about ½ cup

⅓   cup (32 grams) ground cardamom
2½   tablespoons (15 grams) ground cinnamon
4   teaspoons (8 grams) ground ginger
2   teaspoons (4 grams) ground cloves
2   teaspoons (4 grams) ground black pepper

1. In a small bowl, stir together all ingredients.

CIAMBELLINE AL VINO

Makes about 36 cookies

Recipe by Sarah Brunella

These white wine cookies are typical to the Lazio region of Italy. They originated from the concept of making a cookie using only the ingredients that you had on hand. Today, recipes vary, with versions calling for anything between red, white, dry, or sweet wine. The ideal recipe calls for one of the many vinos from Lazio, such as the Moscato di Terracina or the Cannellino. You can substitute anise seeds with 1 to 2 tablespoons (15 to 30 grams) of anise liqueur as most Romans do.

¾   cup (150 grams) granulated sugar, plus
       more for coating
¾   cup (168 grams) extra-virgin olive oil
       (see PRO TIP)
¾   cup (180 grams) white wine
1   teaspoon (5 grams) baking powder
½   teaspoon (1.5 grams) kosher salt
½   teaspoon (5 grams) anise seeds
5   cups (625 grams) all-purpose flour,
       sifted
Wine, to serve

1. Preheat oven to 325°F (170°C). Line 2 baking sheets with parchment paper.
2. In a large bowl, stir together sugar, oil, wine, baking powder, salt, and anise seeds with a wooden spoon. Add flour, stirring until combined. Turn out mixture, and knead until a soft, smooth dough forms (not too dry). Shape dough into a ball, and cover with a bowl. Let rest for 10 to 15 minutes.
3. Place sugar in a small bowl. Shape dough into 6-inch-long logs. Gently curve ends, and pinch together to form a ring. Gently press ring into sugar, coating completely. Place on prepared pans.
4. Bake until pale (not golden brown), about 22 minutes. Let cool on pans for 5 minutes. Remove from pans, and let cool completely on wire racks. Serve with wine, letting cookies

soak in it for a few seconds. Delicious eaten fresh, but they can be stored in an airtight container for up to 2 weeks.

Note: *If you do not like anise seeds, you can flavor the cookies with vanilla (extract or seeds).*

PRO TIP
I suggest using a fresh fruity olive oil. I used Anfosso's Extra Virgin Olive Oil (available online) made with Taggiasca olives from Italy's Liguria region. It has a gentle taste, which works better in desserts. You can also use regular olive oil, in which case I would suggest adding an additional ½ teaspoon (5 grams) anise seed and ½ teaspoon (2 grams) vanilla extract to balance the strong flavor.

Photo by Sarah Brunella

JAMARETTI COOKIES

Makes about 26 cookies

Recipe by Laura Kasavan

These cookies are a hybrid of two classics: Italian amaretti and traditional American thumbprint cookies. The amaretto is an almond-flavored macaron native to Saronno in Northern Italy. Fragrant with almond paste and filled with sweet apricot jam, the Jamaretti Cookies are finished with a drizzle of Cinnamon Cardamom Glaze.

2¼ cups (281 grams) all-purpose flour
1 teaspoon (5 grams) baking powder
½ teaspoon (1.5 grams) kosher salt
½ teaspoon (1 gram) ground cinnamon
4 ounces (118 grams) almond paste, cubed
¾ cup (150 grams) granulated sugar
½ cup (113 grams) unsalted butter, cubed and softened
2 large eggs (100 grams), room temperature
½ teaspoon (2 grams) almond extract
⅔ cup (213 grams) apricot jam
Cinnamon Cardamom Glaze (recipe follows)

1. In a medium bowl, whisk together flour, baking powder, salt, and cinnamon. Set aside.
2. In the work bowl of a food processor, place almond paste and sugar; process until combined. Add butter, eggs, and almond extract, and process until smooth. Add flour mixture, and process just until a soft dough forms, no more than 30 seconds. Using a bench scraper, divide dough in half, and turn out onto 2 pieces of plastic wrap. (Dough will be sticky.) Shape each half into a disk, and wrap in plastic wrap. Refrigerate for at least 1 hour.
3. Preheat oven to 350°F (180°C). Line a rimmed baking sheet with parchment paper.
4. On a lightly floured surface, shape each disk of dough into 2 (14x3-inch) logs; place on prepared pan.
5. Bake just until set, about 15 minutes. Remove from oven, and make an indentation down center of each log using the back of a tablespoon. In a small microwave-safe bowl, microwave jam for 10 seconds. Stir jam to loosen; fill center of each log with jam. Bake until golden, 12 to

14 minutes more. Let cool completely on a wire rack.
6. Drizzle Cinnamon Cardamom Glaze over cooled cookies. Let stand until set, about 30 minutes. Using a serrated knife, cut logs diagonally into slices.

CINNAMON CARDAMOM GLAZE
Makes about ½ cup

¾ cup (90 grams) confectioners' sugar, sifted
2 tablespoons (30 grams) whole milk
½ tablespoon (7 grams) unsalted butter, melted
1 teaspoon (4 grams) vanilla extract
¼ teaspoon ground cinnamon
⅛ teaspoon kosher salt
⅛ teaspoon ground cardamom

1. In a small bowl, whisk together all ingredients until smooth. Use immediately.

Photo by Laura Kasavan

MINCEMEAT RUM CHOCOLATE SANDWICH COOKIES

Makes 15 cookies

Recipe by Edd Kimber

I love Oreo® sandwich cookies and playing around with different flavored homemade versions. This one hearkens back to a British classic, the mince pie. Originally made with meat, they're individual pies filled with a syrupy spiced fruit filling. These cookies follow the same pattern, served alongside a rum-infused buttercream.

¾　cup plus 2 tablespoons (198 grams) unsalted butter, softened
½　cup plus 2 tablespoons (124 grams) granulated sugar
½　cup plus 1 tablespoon (124 grams) firmly packed light brown sugar
1　teaspoon (4 grams) vanilla extract
2　cups plus 2 tablespoons (266 grams) all-purpose flour
½　cup (43 grams) black cocoa powder
½　teaspoon (2.5 grams) baking soda
½　teaspoon (1.5 grams) kosher salt
Rum Buttercream (recipe follows)
Quick Mincemeat Filling (recipe follows)
Garnish: confectioners' sugar

1. In the bowl of a stand mixer fitted with the paddle attachment, beat butter, granulated sugar, and brown sugar at medium speed until fluffy, 2 to 3 minutes, stopping to scrape sides of bowl. Beat in vanilla.
2. In a medium bowl, whisk together flour, black cocoa, baking soda, and salt. With mixer on low speed, gradually add flour mixture to butter mixture, beating just until dough starts to come together. (If you overmix the dough, your cookies will end up chewy rather than crisp.) Turn out dough onto a work surface, and bring together into a uniform dough. Divide dough in half, and shape each half into a disk. Wrap in plastic wrap, and refrigerate for at least 1 hour.
3. Preheat oven to 350°F (180°C). Line 2 half sheet pans with parchment paper.
4. On a lightly floured surface, roll half of dough to ⅛-inch thickness. Using a 2¾-inch fluted round cutter, cut dough, reserving scraps. Place cookies on prepared pans. Using a 1-inch star-shaped cutter, cut centers from half of cookies. Repeat with remaining dough. Gather all scraps, and briefly knead back into a uniform dough. Refrigerate until firm before repeating procedure once. (Don't use the second round of scraps because working the dough further will make tough cookies.) Refrigerate cookies for 20 minutes.
5. Bake until firm, about 9 minutes. Let cool on pans for 10 minutes. Remove from pans, and let cool completely on wire racks.

6. Place Rum Buttercream in a piping bag fitted with a small round piping tip. Pipe a ring of Rum Buttercream on flat side of all solid cookies. Fill centers with Quick Mincemeat Filling. Dust cookies with cutouts with confectioners' sugar, if desired. Place cookies with cutouts, flat side down, on top of filling. Store in an airtight container for up to 3 days.

RUM BUTTERCREAM
Makes 1½ cups

½　cup (113 grams) unsalted butter, softened
2　cups (240 grams) confectioners' sugar
2　tablespoons (30 grams) spiced rum
1　teaspoon (4 grams) vanilla extract
⅛　teaspoon kosher salt

1. In the bowl of a stand mixer fitted with the paddle attachment, beat butter at medium speed until smooth and creamy. Add confectioners' sugar, and beat until fluffy, about 5 minutes. Add rum, vanilla, and salt, and beat until combined, about 1 minute. Use immediately.

QUICK MINCEMEAT FILLING
Makes 1 cup

Zest and juice of 1 orange (131 grams)
½　cup (64 grams) sultanas
½　cup (64 grams) raisins
¼　cup (55 grams) firmly packed light brown sugar
1　teaspoon (2 grams) mixed spice*
2　tablespoons (30 grams) spiced rum

1. In a small saucepan, combine orange zest and juice, sultanas, raisins, brown sugar, and mixed spice. Cook over medium-high heat until sugar is dissolved and liquid has reduced and become syrupy. Remove from heat; stir in rum. Cover with plastic wrap, and refrigerate until ready to use. When fully cooled, mixture should be thick like caramel. If too loose, it needs to cook slightly longer.

*Mixed spice, available on amazon.com, is the most traditional British spice mix used in most classic Christmas fruit dessert recipes. You can substitute with pumpkin pie spice, available at American grocery stores, or make your own mixed spice. Stir together 1 tablespoon (6 grams) ground allspice, 1 tablespoon (6 grams) ground cinnamon, 1 tablespoon (6 grams) ground nutmeg, 2 teaspoons (4 grams) ground ginger, ½ teaspoon (1 gram) ground cloves, and ½ teaspoon (1 gram) ground coriander.

Photo by Edd Kimber

CHOCOLATE COCONUT ALFAJORES

Makes 25 cookies

Recipe by Edd Kimber

A South American holiday favorite, alfajores feature a thick layer of dulce de leche sandwiched between two crumbly butter cookies sprinkled with coconut flakes. A final coat of dark chocolate makes these cookies even more decadent than the classic. Thanks to the cornstarch, these are especially tender and will melt in your mouth.

2   cups (250 grams) all-purpose flour
⅔   cup (80 grams) confectioners' sugar
5   tablespoons (40 grams) cornstarch, plus more for dusting
¼   teaspoon kosher salt
1   cup (227 grams) cold unsalted butter, cubed
2   large egg yolks (37 grams)
1   teaspoon (4 grams) vanilla extract
⅔   cup (200 grams) dulce de leche
7   ounces (200 grams) dark chocolate, roughly chopped
⅔   cup (56 grams) desiccated coconut

1. In the work bowl of a food processor, place flour, confectioners' sugar, cornstarch, and salt; pulse until combined. Add cold butter, and pulse until mixture resembles coarse meal. Add egg yolks and vanilla, and pulse until mixture comes together and a dough forms. Divide dough in half.
2. On a work surface lightly dusted with cornstarch, roll each portion of dough into a 2-inch-wide log. Wrap in plastic wrap, and refrigerate until firm, about 2 hours.
3. Preheat oven to 350°F (180°C). Line 2 half sheet pans with parchment paper.
4. Using a sharp knife, cut logs into ¼-inch-thick slices. Place about 1 inch apart on prepared pans.
5. Bake until lightly browned around the edges, 10 to 11 minutes. Let cool completely on pans.
6. Place dulce de leche in a piping bag fitted with a small round tip. Pipe a small round of dulce de leche onto half of cookies. Place remaining cookies on top of dulce de leche, gently pressing together until dulce de leche just reaches edges of cookie. Refrigerate cookies while preparing chocolate.

7. In a medium microwave-safe bowl, microwave chocolate on high in 15- to 20-second intervals, stirring between each, until almost fully melted but some small pieces remain visible. Remove bowl from microwave, and stir vigorously until fully melted. (This is the simplest method of tempering chocolate and needs no thermometer.)
8. Dip cookies halfway into melted chocolate, letting excess drip off. Place on a sheet of parchment paper, and sprinkle coconut over melted chocolate while still warm. Let stand until chocolate is set. Store in an airtight container for up to 2 days, but cookies will soften over time.

Photo by Edd Kimber

GERMAN ALMOND CRESCENT COOKIES

Makes 24 cookies

This crumbly, almond-scented cookie is a Christmas classic from Germany. We changed the confectioners' sugar dusting to a homemade vanilla sugar, a vanilla bean-speckled coating worth the bit of extra effort.

½ cup (100 grams) superfine castor sugar
1 vanilla bean, split lengthwise, seeds scraped, reserved, and divided
2 cups (250 grams) all-purpose flour
1 cup (227 grams) cold unsalted butter, cubed
¾ cup (90 grams) confectioners' sugar
¾ cup (72 grams) almond flour
½ teaspoon (1.5 grams) kosher salt

1. In the container of a blender, place castor sugar and half of vanilla bean seeds; blend on high until a fine powder is achieved, about 10 seconds. Set aside.

2. In the bowl of a stand mixer fitted with the paddle attachment, beat all-purpose flour, cold butter, confectioners' sugar, almond flour, salt, and remaining vanilla bean seeds at medium-low speed until a crumbly dough forms, 3 to 4 minutes. (Mixture will start out dry and crumbly but will come together.) Shape dough into a disk, and wrap in plastic wrap. Refrigerate for 1 hour.

3. Preheat oven to 350°F (180°C). Line 2 baking sheets with parchment paper.

4. Divide dough into 24 (25-gram) balls. Roll dough balls into 4½-inch logs with tapered ends, and bend each one into a crescent shape. Place about 1 inch apart on prepared pans.

5. Bake, one batch at a time, until edges are just beginning to turn golden (not browned), 12 to 15 minutes. Sift vanilla sugar over hot cookies. Let cool completely; dust with vanilla sugar again. Store in an airtight container for up to 3 weeks.

HAZELNUT BUTTER COOKIES

Makes 20 cookies

Step aside, Nutter Butter cookies. This hazelnut revamp of a classic sandwich cookie comes equipped with our homemade Hazelnut Butter, your new condiment obsession and the perfect homemade holiday gift. A dip in dark chocolate and a roll in even more hazelnuts sends this cookie right over the nutty edge.

1	cup (227 grams) unsalted butter, softened
⅓	cup (87 grams) Hazelnut Butter (recipe follows)
½	cup (110 grams) firmly packed dark brown sugar
1	large egg (50 grams)
1½	teaspoons (9 grams) vanilla bean paste
1⅔	cups (200 grams) all-purpose flour
1	teaspoon (5 grams) baking soda
¾	teaspoon (3.75 grams) baking powder
¼	teaspoon kosher salt
1¼	cups (100 grams) old-fashioned oats
¼	cup (28 grams) chopped dry roasted unsalted hazelnuts

Hazelnut Buttercream (recipe follows)
1   (10-ounce) package (283.5 grams) dark chocolate melting wafers
Garnish: finely chopped roasted hazelnuts

1. In the bowl of a stand mixer fitted with the paddle attachment, beat butter and Hazelnut Butter at medium speed until smooth, about 3 minutes. Add brown sugar, and beat until creamy, 2 to 3 minutes, stopping to scrape sides of bowl. Add egg and vanilla bean paste, and beat at low speed just until combined, about 30 seconds.
2. In a medium bowl, whisk together flour, baking soda, baking powder, and salt. Gradually add flour mixture to butter mixture, beating just until combined. Add oats and hazelnuts, beating just until combined. Shape dough into a disk, and wrap in plastic wrap. Refrigerate until firm, about 2 hours.
3. Preheat oven to 325°F (170°C). Line 2 baking sheets with parchment paper.
4. Between 2 sheets of parchment paper, roll dough to ¼-inch thickness. Transfer dough between parchment to freezer. Freeze until set, about 20 minutes.
5. Using a 2¼-inch round cutter, cut dough, and place 2 inches apart on prepared pans.
6. Bake until golden brown, about 12 minutes, rotating pans halfway through baking. Let cool on pans for 5 minutes. Remove from pans, and let cool completely on wire racks. (While first round of cookies is baking, reroll any scraps between parchment again, freeze until set, and cut out cookies.

Reroll scraps a third time if needed. Keep cut cookies in freezer until ready to bake.)
7. Place Hazelnut Buttercream in a piping bag fitted with an Ateco #855 closed star tip. Pipe Hazelnut Buttercream onto flat side of half of cookies in a spiral starting at center. Place remaining cookies, flat side down, on top of filling. Refrigerate for 15 minutes.
8. In a microwave-safe bowl, heat chocolate melting wafers on high in 30-second intervals, stirring between each, until melted and smooth. Let cool slightly, 3 to 5 minutes. Line a baking sheet with parchment paper. Place chopped hazelnuts on a plate. Dip half of each cookie in melted chocolate, and roll in hazelnuts, if desired. Place on prepared pan. Let stand until chocolate is set, 8 to 10 minutes. Store in an airtight container at room temperature if unfilled, or in refrigerator if filled, for up to 3 days.

HAZELNUT BUTTER
Makes ⅔ cup

1¼	cups (178 grams) dry roasted unsalted hazelnuts
1½	tablespoons (18 grams) granulated sugar
½	teaspoon (1 gram) ground cinnamon
¼	teaspoon kosher salt

1. In the work bowl of a food processor, process hazelnuts until smooth, about 3 minutes. Add sugar, cinnamon, and salt; process until combined, about 30 seconds. Refrigerate in an airtight container for up to 3 weeks.

HAZELNUT BUTTERCREAM
Makes 3½ cups

¾	cup (170 grams) unsalted butter, softened
⅓	cup (87 grams) Hazelnut Butter (recipe precedes)
4½	cups (540 grams) confectioners' sugar
¼	cup (60 grams) heavy whipping cream
¼	teaspoon kosher salt

1. In the bowl of a stand mixer fitted with the paddle attachment, beat butter and Hazelnut Butter at medium speed until smooth, 2 to 3 minutes. With mixer on low speed, gradually add confectioners' sugar alternately with cream, beating until combined. Add salt, and beat until fluffy, about 3 minutes. Use immediately.

BARS

Packed with jam, slathered in frosting, or dense with white
chocolate, our bars are the perfect indulgence for bakers
who like their dessert by the slice.

ZESTY LEMON BARS

Makes about 24 bars

Both sweet and tart, lemon bars are as at home at a ladies' luncheon as they are at a picnic. They're like the little black dress of Southern sweets. This recipe will keep you stocked up all summer long.

1   cup (227 grams) unsalted butter, softened
3½   cups (700 grams) granulated sugar, divided
3   cups (375 grams) all-purpose flour, divided
¼   teaspoon kosher salt
8   large eggs (400 grams), room temperature

2   tablespoons (6 grams) lemon zest
1   cup (240 grams) fresh lemon juice
Confectioners' sugar, for dusting
Garnish: lemon zest

1. Preheat oven to 350°F (180°C). Line a 13x9-inch metal baking pan with parchment paper.
2. In the bowl of a stand mixer fitted with the paddle attachment, beat butter and ½ cup (100 grams) granulated sugar at medium speed until creamy, 3 to 4 minutes, stopping to scrape sides of bowl.
3. In a medium bowl, whisk together 2 cups (250 grams) flour and salt. With mixer on low speed, gradually add flour mixture to butter mixture, beating just until combined.

Gather dough into a ball, and flatten into a disk. Transfer to prepared pan, pressing into bottom.
4. Bake until lightly browned, about 15 minutes. Let cool on a wire rack.
5. In a large bowl, whisk together eggs, lemon zest and juice, and remaining 3 cups (600 grams) granulated sugar. Add remaining 1 cup (125 grams) flour, whisking to combine. Pour filling onto prepared crust.
6. Bake until set, 25 to 30 minutes. Let cool completely. Refrigerate for at least 4 hours or overnight. Cut into bars, and dust with confectioners' sugar. Garnish with zest, if desired. Refrigerate in an airtight container for up to 5 days.

FROSTED CAPPUCCINO COOKIE BARS

Makes 14 bars

Recipe by Thalia Ho

These bars are a dulcet hybrid that's part blondie, part cookie filled with soft pockets of white chocolate and a triple dose of coffee. The thick blanket of Cappuccino Frosting, with its milky coffee undertones, is the real star.

¾ cup plus 3 tablespoons (212 grams) unsalted butter, cubed
¾ cup plus 1 tablespoon (179 grams) firmly packed light brown sugar
¾ cup (150 grams) granulated sugar
1 large egg (50 grams), room temperature
1 tablespoon (13 grams) vanilla extract
1 tablespoon (15 grams) coffee liqueur (optional)
2 cups plus 3 tablespoons (274 grams) all-purpose flour
1 teaspoon (2 grams) coffee powder
¾ teaspoon (3.75 grams) baking soda
¾ teaspoon (2.25 grams) kosher salt
½ teaspoon (1 gram) ground nutmeg
1 cup (170 grams) roughly chopped white chocolate
Cappuccino Frosting (recipe follows)
Garnish: smoked fleur de sel or flaked salt

1. Preheat oven to 350°F (180°C). Grease a 9-inch square baking pan. Line pan with parchment paper, letting excess extend over sides of pan.
2. In a small saucepan, heat butter over medium heat, stirring frequently, until golden and melted. Remove from heat, and pour into a large bowl. Add sugars, whisking until combined. Add egg, vanilla, and coffee liqueur (if using), whisking until smooth and glossy.
3. In a medium bowl, whisk together flour, coffee powder, baking soda, salt, and nutmeg. Add flour mixture to butter mixture, whisking just until combined. (Having some flour chunks throughout batter is OK.) Fold in white chocolate until evenly combined throughout dough. Place dough in prepared pan, and use a rubber spatula to smooth down top and help spread to edges.
4. Bake until golden, just firm and crackled around the edges, and center has begun to set, about 20 minutes. Let cool in pan for 15 minutes. Using excess parchment as handles, remove from pan, and place on a wire rack to let cool completely.
5. Using a large offset spatula or the back of a metal spoon, thickly spread Cappuccino Frosting onto cooled cookie in a swoop-and-swirl motion. Sprinkle with fleur de sel or

flaked salt, if desired. Best on day of baking but can be stored in an airtight container at room temperature for up to 3 days.

Cappuccino Frosting

Makes 2½ cups

2 teaspoons (10 grams) boiling water
1 teaspoon (2 grams) coffee powder
½ cup (113 grams) unsalted butter, softened
2 cups (240 grams) confectioners' sugar
2 tablespoons (30 grams) heavy whipping cream
1 teaspoon (4 grams) vanilla extract

1. In a small bowl, stir together 2 teaspoons (10 grams) boiling water and coffee powder until dissolved. Let cool.
2. In the bowl of a stand mixer fitted with the paddle attachment, beat butter and confectioners' sugar at medium speed until fluffy, 3 to 4 minutes, stopping to scrape sides of bowl. Add coffee mixture, cream, and vanilla, beating until smooth and aerated, about 3 minutes. Use immediately.

Photo by Thalia Ho

CARDAMOM-SPICED COOKIE BARS WITH EGGNOG CREAM CHEESE FROSTING

Makes 18 bars

Recipe by Becky Sue Wilberding

Inspired by a frothy glass of eggnog, these simple cookie bars are warmly spiced with cardamom and slathered in a rich Eggnog Cream Cheese Frosting. Garnishing with freshly grated nutmeg makes them look and taste just like eggnog.

¾ cup (170 grams) unsalted butter, softened
¾ cup (150 grams) granulated sugar
2 large eggs (100 grams)
1 teaspoon (4 grams) almond extract
½ teaspoon (2 grams) vanilla extract
2½ cups (313 grams) all-purpose flour
1 teaspoon (5 grams) baking powder
¾ teaspoon (3 grams) kosher salt
¾ teaspoon (2 grams) ground cardamom
Eggnog Cream Cheese Frosting (recipe follows)
Garnish: grated fresh nutmeg

1. Preheat oven to 350°F (180°C). Line a 13x9-inch baking pan with parchment paper, letting excess extend over sides of pan.
2. In the bowl of a stand mixer fitted with the paddle attachment, beat butter and sugar at medium speed until creamy, 2 to 3 minutes, stopping to scrape sides of bowl. Add eggs, one at a time, beating well after each addition. Beat in extracts.
3. In a medium bowl, whisk together flour, baking powder, salt, and cardamom. With mixer on low speed, gradually add flour mixture to butter mixture, beating until combined. (Dough will be soft and sticky.) Transfer dough to prepared pan, pressing into bottom and up sides.
4. Bake until golden around the edges, 20 to 25 minutes. Let cool completely in pan. Using excess parchment as handles, remove from pan, and set on a flat surface. Using an offset spatula, spread Eggnog Cream Cheese Frosting onto cookie. Garnish with nutmeg, if desired. Cut into bars, and refrigerate until ready to serve.

EGGNOG CREAM CHEESE FROSTING
Makes 2½ cups

4 ounces (115 grams) cream cheese, softened
2 tablespoons (28 grams) unsalted butter, softened
½ teaspoon (2 grams) almond extract
¼ cup (70 grams) prepared eggnog, room temperature
3 cups (360 grams) confectioners' sugar, sifted

1. In the bowl of a stand mixer fitted with the paddle attachment, beat cream cheese, butter, and almond extract at medium speed until creamy. With mixer on low speed, gradually add eggnog, beating until combined. Gradually add confectioners' sugar, beating until smooth. Use immediately.

Photo by Becky Sue Wilberding

LEMON CHESS PIE BARS WITH CORNBREAD-GRAHAM CRUST

Makes 12 to 15 bars

Recipe by Steven Satterfield

The crust to this pie bar is basically a sweetened cornbread that is baked with the flavor profile of a graham cracker and transformed into the crust on the bottom of a lemon chess pie. I mean, what? It works, y'all, and the Sweet Cornbread is amazing on its own!

Sweet Cornbread (recipe follows), cubed and dried
¼ cup (55 grams) firmly packed light brown sugar
6 tablespoons (84 grams) unsalted butter, softened
6 large eggs (300 grams)
1½ cups (300 grams) granulated sugar
¾ cup (180 grams) fresh lemon juice
¼ cup (60 grams) whole buttermilk
1 tablespoon (9 grams) fine cornmeal
½ teaspoon (1.5 grams) kosher salt
6 tablespoons (84 grams) unsalted butter, melted
⅛ teaspoon grated fresh nutmeg

Whipped cream, to serve
Garnish: grated fresh nutmeg

1. Preheat oven to 350°F (180°C).
2. In the work bowl of a food processor, place Sweet Cornbread; pulse until crumbly. Add brown sugar and butter; pulse just until combined. Firmly press mixture to about ¼-inch thickness in a 13x9-inch baking dish with sides no higher than 2 inches. (Crust will only be on bottom of bars, not up sides; there might be slightly more dough than you need. The remainder can be frozen in an airtight container for another use.)
3. Bake until lightly browned and slightly dried and crisp, about 20 minutes. Let cool completely.
4. In a medium bowl, whisk together eggs, granulated sugar, lemon juice, buttermilk, cornmeal, and salt. Add melted butter and nutmeg, stirring until combined. Pour filling into prepared crust.
5. Bake just until set, 25 to 30 minutes. Let cool completely. Serve at room temperature with whipped cream. Garnish with nutmeg, if desired.

Note: *This can be refrigerated after cooling and served the following day.*

SWEET CORNBREAD
Makes 1 (9-inch) skillet

3 tablespoons (42 grams) unsalted butter, melted and divided
1 cup (240 grams) whole buttermilk
½ cup (100 grams) granulated sugar
¼ cup (85 grams) molasses
1 large egg (50 grams)
½ cup (75 grams) fine yellow cornmeal
½ cup (60 grams) graham flour*
1 teaspoon (3 grams) fine sea salt
½ teaspoon (2.5 grams) baking soda

1. Preheat oven to 400°F (200°C). Grease a 9-inch cast-iron skillet or cake pan with 1 tablespoon (14 grams) melted butter.
2. In a medium bowl, whisk together buttermilk, sugar, molasses, and egg. In a small bowl, whisk together cornmeal, flour, sea salt, and baking soda. Add cornmeal mixture to buttermilk mixture, whisking until well combined. Add remaining 2 tablespoons (28 grams) melted butter, whisking until combined. Pour batter into prepared pan.
3. Bake until set and golden brown, about 20 minutes. Let cool for 15 minutes. Remove from pan, and cut into 1-inch cubes. Let stand at room temperature for a few hours to become stale, or bake in a 200°F (93°C) oven for 20 minutes to speed things up. (The goal is to dry out the cornbread a bit so that it makes a nice crust.)

*Graham flour can be found at most health food stores or online. Whole wheat flour can also be substituted for graham flour.

Photo by Angie Mosier

SUMMER BERRY CRUMB BARS

Makes 15 to 20 bars

Recipe by Marian Cooper Cairns

To brighten up these picnic-perfect bars even more, we added fresh lime juice to the batter for a citrusy sweet-tart kick. Customize with your own mix of available farmers' market berries or try pitted fresh cherries, too, for equally delicious results.

3   cups (375 grams) all-purpose flour
1⅓   cups (267 grams) granulated sugar, divided
1   tablespoon (3 grams) lime zest
1   teaspoon (5 grams) baking powder
¾   teaspoon (2.25 grams) kosher salt
1   cup (227 grams) cold unsalted butter, cubed
1   large egg (50 grams), lightly beaten
1½   tablespoons (12 grams) cornstarch
2   cups (260 grams) fresh raspberries
1   cup (170 grams) fresh blackberries
1   cup (170 grams) fresh blueberries
1   cup (147 grams) chopped fresh strawberries
3   tablespoons (15 grams) fresh lime juice
1   teaspoon (4 grams) vanilla extract

1. Preheat oven to 375°F (190°C). Lightly grease a 13x9-inch baking pan. Line pan with parchment paper, letting excess extend over sides of pan.
2. In a large bowl, stir together flour, 1 cup (200 grams) sugar, zest, baking powder, and salt. Using a pastry blender, cut in cold butter until pea-size pieces remain. Using a fork, stir in egg until combined and mixture is crumbly. Reserve 1½ cups dough, and refrigerate. Press remaining 3½ cups dough into bottom of prepared pan.
3. Bake for 30 minutes.
4. In a large bowl, stir together cornstarch and remaining ⅓ cup (67 grams) sugar. Gently fold in berries, lime juice, and vanilla until combined. Scatter berry mixture over prepared crust. Crumble reserved 1½ cups chilled dough over berries, pressing to form small clumps.
5. Bake until top is golden, about 30 minutes. Let cool completely. Refrigerate overnight. Using excess parchment as handles, remove from pan, and cut into bars.

Photo by Matt Armendariz

HUMMINGBIRD COOKIE BARS

Makes 24 bars

These party-perfect bars are creamy, crumbly, and crispy all at once. For the best results, we suggest refrigerating overnight. But if you're in a hurry, you can cut that time down to at least 1 hour before serving.

12 ounces (340 grams) cream cheese, softened
¼ cup (50 grams) granulated sugar
2 large eggs (100 grams)
2 teaspoons (8 grams) vanilla extract
½ cup (114 grams) mashed banana
Spiced Cookie Crust (recipe follows)
2 cups (400 grams) diced fresh pineapple
1⅓ cups (80 grams) sweetened flaked coconut
1 cup (113 grams) chopped pecans
½ cup (44 grams) broken banana chips
¼ cup (57 grams) unsalted butter, melted

1. Preheat oven to 350°F (180°C).
2. In the bowl of a stand mixer fitted with the paddle attachment, beat cream cheese and sugar at medium speed until creamy, 3 to 4 minutes, stopping to scrape sides of bowl. Add eggs and vanilla, beating until well combined. Fold in mashed banana. Spread cream cheese mixture onto prepared Spiced Cookie Crust. Sprinkle with pineapple.
3. In a medium bowl, stir together coconut, pecans, banana chips, and melted butter until well combined. Sprinkle over pineapple.
4. Bake until filling is set, 35 to 40 minutes, covering with foil to prevent excess browning, if necessary. Let cool completely. Refrigerate overnight. Using excess parchment as handles, remove from pan, and cut into bars.

SPICED COOKIE CRUST

Makes 1 (13x9-inch) crust

2 cups (250 grams) all-purpose flour
½ cup (100 grams) granulated sugar
¾ teaspoon (1.5 grams) ground cinnamon
½ teaspoon (1.5 grams) kosher salt
¼ teaspoon ground nutmeg
¾ cup (170 grams) unsalted butter, cubed and softened

1. Preheat oven to 350°F (180°C). Butter a 13x9-inch baking dish. Line pan with parchment paper, letting excess extend over sides of pan.
2. In a medium bowl, whisk together flour, sugar, cinnamon, salt, and nutmeg. Using a pastry blender, cut in butter until mixture is crumbly. Firmly press mixture into bottom of prepared pan.
3. Bake until lightly golden, about 40 minutes. Let cool completely.

Photo by Stephen DeVries

BROWNED BUTTER APRICOT BLONDIES

Makes 9 blondies

The blondie—that golden, caramelized bar that verges on butterscotch bliss—was begging for a tangy-sweet swirl of Apricot Jam. We obliged, stirring in a hefty dose of nutty browned butter for good measure and finishing it off with a light sprinkle of sea salt.

½   cup (113 grams) unsalted butter
1¼ cups (156 grams) all-purpose flour
1   teaspoon (5 grams) baking powder
½   teaspoon (1.5 grams) kosher salt
1   teaspoon (4 grams) vanilla extract
1   cup (220 grams) firmly packed light
    brown sugar
2   large eggs (100 grams)
¼   cup (80 grams) Apricot Jam (recipe
    follows)
Garnish: flaked sea salt

1. Preheat oven to 350°F (180°C). Butter and flour a 9-inch square baking dish.

2. In a medium saucepan, melt butter over medium heat. Cook until butter turns a medium-brown color and has a nutty aroma, about 10 minutes. Remove from heat.
3. In a large bowl, whisk together flour, baking powder, and salt. Whisk in browned butter and vanilla. (Mixture will be thick.)
4. In the bowl of a stand mixer fitted with the whisk attachment, beat brown sugar and eggs at high speed until tripled in size, 4 to 5 minutes. Add one-third of egg mixture to flour mixture, stirring just until combined. Fold in remaining egg mixture in 2 additions until well combined. Pour into prepared pan. Spoon Apricot Jam, 1 to 2 teaspoons at a time, over batter.
5. Bake until a wooden pick inserted in center comes out clean, 20 to 30 minutes, covering with foil 10 minutes into baking for lighter-colored blondies. Let cool completely on a wire rack. Sprinkle with sea salt, if desired. Store in an airtight container at room temperature for up to 4 days.

APRICOT JAM
Makes about 2 cups

3   cups (480 grams) chopped fresh apricots*
1½ cups (300 grams) granulated sugar
1   teaspoon (1 gram) lemon zest
1   tablespoon (15 grams) fresh lemon
    juice
½   teaspoon (1.5 grams) kosher salt
½   teaspoon (1 gram) ground black pepper

1. In a medium saucepan, bring all ingredients to a boil over medium-high heat. Cook for 5 minutes, stirring frequently. Reduce heat to medium; cook, stirring frequently, until mixture thickens, 20 to 45 minutes. Remove from heat, and let cool for 1 hour before transferring to a clean jar. Jam will keep refrigerated for up to 2 weeks.

*Reserve apricot pits for Noyaux Pastry Cream (recipe on page 162). Pits can be frozen for up to 1 month.

OATMEAL CHOCOLATE CHIP COOKIE BARS

Makes 12 bars

These gooey bars are loaded with peanut butter and chocolate chunks. Oats bring a solid note of chew to the base and crispiness to the top.

1 cup (227 grams) unsalted butter, softened
1 cup (220 grams) firmly packed light brown sugar
½ cup (100 grams) granulated sugar
1 cup (256 grams) creamy peanut butter
2 large eggs (100 grams)
2 teaspoons (8 grams) vanilla extract
2 cups (250 grams) all-purpose flour
2¼ cups (251 grams) old-fashioned oats, divided
1 teaspoon (3 grams) kosher salt
1 teaspoon (5 grams) baking soda
1 teaspoon (5 grams) baking powder
8 ounces (230 grams) bittersweet chocolate, chopped and divided

1. Preheat oven to 350°F (180°C). Line a metal 13x9-inch baking pan with parchment paper, letting excess extend over sides of pan.
2. In the bowl of a stand mixer fitted with the paddle attachment, beat butter and sugars at medium speed until fluffy, 3 to 4 minutes, stopping to scrape sides of bowl. Add peanut butter, beating until combined. Add eggs and vanilla, beating until combined.
3. In a medium bowl, whisk together flour, 2 cups (208 grams) oats, salt, baking soda, and baking powder. With mixer on low speed, gradually add flour mixture to butter mixture, beating just until combined. Spread half of batter in prepared pan. Sprinkle with 6 ounces (175 grams) chopped chocolate. Spoon remaining batter over chocolate. Sprinkle with remaining 2 ounces (55 grams) chocolate and remaining ¼ cup (20 grams) oats.
4. Bake until golden brown, 25 to 30 minutes. Let cool completely on a wire rack, about 2 hours. Using excess parchment as handles, remove from pan, and cut into bars. Store in an airtight container for up to 5 days.

CONCORD GRAPE AND PEANUT BUTTER CRUMB BARS

Makes 12 bars

Recipe by Laura Kasavan

With a spiced Concord Grape Jam and peanut butter crumb topping, these jammy bars are a grown-up spin on the nostalgic peanut butter and jelly combo from childhood. Bonus: This is a peanut butter crust you won't want to cut off.

½ cup (128 grams) creamy peanut butter
½ cup (113 grams) unsalted butter
½ cup (100 grams) granulated sugar
½ cup (110 grams) firmly packed light brown sugar
1 teaspoon (4 grams) vanilla extract
2 cups (250 grams) all-purpose flour
¼ teaspoon (1.25 grams) baking soda
¼ teaspoon kosher salt
Concord Grape Jam (recipe follows)

1. Preheat oven to 350°F (180°C). Line an 8-inch square baking pan with parchment paper, letting excess extend over sides of pan.
2. In a small saucepan, heat peanut butter and butter over medium-low heat until melted and smooth. Transfer to a large bowl; add sugars and vanilla, whisking until combined.
3. In a medium bowl, whisk together flour, baking soda, and salt. Add flour mixture to peanut butter mixture, folding until combined. Reserve 1 cup (230 grams) dough for topping; refrigerate until ready to use. Press remaining dough into bottom of prepared pan.
4. Bake until lightly golden brown and set, 14 to 20 minutes. Let cool on a wire rack for 15 minutes.
5. Pour Concord Grape Jam over prepared crust, and spread with an offset spatula. Sprinkle reserved 1 cup (230 grams) dough over filling.
6. Bake until topping is golden and filling is bubbly, 30 to 35 minutes. Let cool completely in pan.
7. Freeze for 15 minutes. Using excess parchment as handles, remove from pan, and cut into bars.

CONCORD GRAPE JAM

Makes about ½ cup

2 cups (300 grams) Concord grapes
½ cup (100 grams) granulated sugar
1½ tablespoons (22.5 grams) water, divided
⅛ teaspoon kosher salt
⅛ teaspoon ground cloves
1½ teaspoons (4.5 grams) cornstarch

1. In a medium saucepan, bring Concord grapes, sugar, 1 tablespoon (15 grams) water, salt, and cloves to a boil over medium heat. Reduce heat to low, and simmer for 10 minutes. Press mixture through a fine-mesh sieve into a bowl; discard solids. Return mixture to saucepan.
2. In a small bowl, stir together cornstarch and remaining ½ tablespoon (7.5 grams) water. Add cornstarch mixture to saucepan. Simmer, stirring constantly, until mixture is slightly thickened, about 3 minutes.

PRO TIP

If fresh Concord grapes are not available, you can substitute high-quality store-bought Concord grape jam for the homemade jam. We suggest using Stonewall Kitchen Concord Grape Jelly, available at *stonewallkitchen.com.*

Photo by Laura Kasavan

BLACK FOREST BROWNIES

Makes 12 brownies

Your favorite German cake, now in a fudgy brownie package. Plump with kirsch-drunk cherries and dark chocolate chips, these decadent bars get pushed over the edge with a tangy Crème Fraîche Glaze.

2⅔ cups (453 grams) 63% cacao dark chocolate chips, divided
1 cup (227 grams) unsalted butter, cubed
1 teaspoon (2 grams) espresso powder
2 cups (400 grams) granulated sugar
4 large eggs (200 grams), lightly beaten
2 tablespoons (30 grams) half-and-half
1 teaspoon (4 grams) vanilla extract
1½ cups (188 grams) all-purpose flour
½ cup (43 grams) Dutch process cocoa powder
1 teaspoon (3 grams) kosher salt
1 cup (250 grams) strained, halved, and packed Drunken Cherries (recipe follows)
Crème Fraîche Glaze (recipe follows)

1. Preheat oven to 350°F (180°C). Butter a 13x9-inch baking pan. Line pan with parchment paper, letting excess extend over sides of pan.
2. In the top of a double boiler, combine 1⅔ cups (283 grams) chocolate chips, butter, and espresso powder. Cook over simmering water, stirring occasionally, until mixture is smooth. Turn off heat, and whisk in sugar. Remove from heat, and let cool slightly.
3. Add half of beaten eggs to chocolate mixture, whisking until combined. Add remaining beaten eggs, and whisk until combined. Whisk in half-and-half and vanilla.
4. In a medium bowl, whisk together flour, cocoa, and salt. Fold flour mixture into chocolate mixture until a few bits of flour remain. Fold in Drunken Cherries and remaining 1 cup (170 grams) chocolate chips. Spread batter in prepared pan.
5. Bake until a wooden pick inserted in center comes out with a few crumbs, 35 to 40 minutes. Let cool completely in pan. Using excess parchment as handles, remove from pan, and cut into squares. Drizzle with Crème Fraîche Glaze.

Drunken Cherries
Makes 3 cups

3 cups (420 grams) frozen pitted dark sweet cherries
⅔ cup (133 grams) granulated sugar
⅔ cup (160 grams) cherry brandy

1. Place cherries in a medium bowl.
2. In a small saucepan, heat sugar and brandy over low heat, stirring constantly, until sugar is dissolved. Pour mixture over cherries. Cover and refrigerate overnight.

Crème Fraîche Glaze
Makes 1 cup

1 cup (120 grams) confectioners' sugar
½ cup (120 grams) crème fraîche
2 teaspoons (10 grams) whole milk
1 teaspoon (5 grams) cherry brandy

1. In a small bowl, whisk together all ingredients until smooth. Use immediately.

CRANBERRY STREUSEL BARS

Makes 12 to 16 bars

Recipe by Laura Kasavan

These crumb bars have the perfect ratio of thick browned butter crust and nutty streusel topping separated by a jammy Cranberry Filling.

14 tablespoons (196 grams) unsalted
    butter
¾   cup (150 grams) granulated sugar
¼   cup (55 grams) firmly packed light
    brown sugar
1   teaspoon (4 grams) almond extract
2   cups (250 grams) all-purpose flour
¼   teaspoon (1.25 grams) baking soda
¼   teaspoon kosher salt
¼   teaspoon ground cinnamon
¼   cup (28 grams) sliced almonds
1   tablespoon (15 grams) ice water
Cranberry Filling (recipe follows)

1. Preheat oven to 350°F (180°C). Line an 8-inch square metal baking pan with parchment paper, letting excess extend over sides of pan.

2. In a medium heavy-bottomed saucepan, melt butter over medium heat. Cook, stirring constantly, until butter turns a medium-brown color and has a nutty aroma, about 5 minutes.

3. In a large bowl, whisk together browned butter, sugars, and almond extract. In a medium bowl, whisk together flour, baking soda, salt, and cinnamon. Add flour mixture to browned butter mixture, and fold in until incorporated.

4. Place ¾ cup dough in a small bowl. Add almonds and 1 tablespoon (15 grams) ice water, stirring to combine. Refrigerate until ready to use. Press remaining dough into bottom of prepared pan.

5. Bake until lightly golden and set, 14 to 16 minutes. Let cool on a wire rack for 15 minutes. Spoon Cranberry Filling over prepared crust, and crumble reserved ¾ cup chilled dough over filling. Bake until top is golden and filling is slightly bubbly, 36 to 40 minutes more. Let cool completely on a wire rack.

6. Freeze for 15 minutes. Using excess parchment as handles, remove from pan, and cut into bars.

CRANBERRY FILLING

Makes about 1⅓ cups

2   cups (220 grams) fresh or frozen
    cranberries*
¾   cup (150 grams) granulated sugar
3   tablespoons (45 grams) amaretto
2   tablespoons (30 grams) water
⅛   teaspoon kosher salt
1   teaspoon (3 grams) arrowroot starch**

1. In a medium heavy-bottomed saucepan, bring cranberries, sugar, amaretto, 2 tablespoons (30 grams) water, and salt to a boil over medium-high heat. Cook, stirring constantly, until cranberries begin to split open. Reduce heat to low, and simmer for 10 minutes, stirring occasionally. Add arrowroot starch, and cook until thickened, 1 to 2 minutes. Use immediately.

*If using frozen cranberries, there's no need to thaw—simply cook as directed.

**Arrowroot starch is a natural thickener. Cornstarch may be used instead.

Photo by Laura Kasavan

BLACK COCOA BROWNIES

Makes 12 brownies

You know the rich, molten brownies that never leave a clean tester? These are those. Decadent but not too sweet, our black cocoa bars are for the adult chocoholics looking for a bittersweet fix.

2⅓ cups (397 grams) 63% cacao chocolate chips*, divided
1 cup (227 grams) unsalted butter, cubed
1½ cups (300 grams) granulated sugar
1 cup (220 grams) firmly packed dark brown sugar
1½ cups (188 grams) all-purpose flour
¾ cup (64 grams) black cocoa powder
2 teaspoons (6 grams) kosher salt
5 large eggs (250 grams)
1 tablespoon (13 grams) vanilla extract

1. Preheat oven to 350°F (180°C). Spray a 13x9-inch baking pan with cooking spray. Line pan with parchment paper, letting excess extend over sides of pan.
2. In the top of a double boiler, combine 1⅓ cups (227 grams) chocolate chips and butter. Cook over simmering water, stirring occasionally, until chocolate is melted and mixture is smooth. Turn off heat, and whisk in sugars. Remove from heat, and let cool slightly.
3. In a medium bowl, whisk together flour, black cocoa, and salt. Set aside.

4. In a small bowl, lightly whisk eggs. Add half of beaten eggs to chocolate mixture, whisking until combined. Add remaining beaten eggs, and whisk until combined. Whisk in vanilla. Fold in flour mixture until a few bits of flour remain. Fold in remaining 1 cup (170 grams) chocolate chips. Spread batter into prepared pan.
5. Bake until a wooden pick inserted in center comes out with a few crumbs, about 25 minutes. Let cool completely in pan. Using excess parchment as handles, remove from pan, and cut into squares.

*We used Guittard Extra Dark Chocolate Baking Chips.

MAKE THEM YOUR OWN

Fold your pick of the following ingredients in with the chocolate chips (added in step 4) to create a more personalized batch of brownies.

Nuts: Walnuts, pecans, and almonds add crunchy texture.
Dried Fruit: Dried apricots, cherries, and even currants introduce a note of concentrated sweetness.
Jam: A swirl of raspberry jam bumps up the fruity flavor.
Toffee Bits/Flavored Chips: Bring a hit of salty, caramel-y goodness with toffee or peanut butter, butterscotch, or caramel chips.

NO-BAKE CHOCOLATE PEPITA FEUILLETINE BARS

Makes about 48 bars

Recipe by Zoë François

Feuilletine are sweet crêpes that have been cooked, cooled, and crisped, then broken into caramelized shards (think fancy, delicate Wheaties). The toasted pepitas and feuilletine give these festive bites of chocolate a candy bar-like crunch.

16   ounces (455 grams) dark chocolate, finely chopped and divided
1   cup (340 grams) chocolate-hazelnut spread
2   cups (180 grams) feuilletine flakes*
2   cups (240 grams) toasted pepita seeds, divided
½   cup (120 grams) heavy whipping cream
Sea salt, for sprinkling
Gold leaf, for decorating

1. Butter a 9-inch square baking pan. Line pan with parchment paper, letting excess extend over sides of pan.
2. In the top of a double boiler, place 12 ounces (340 grams) chocolate. Cook over simmering water, stirring frequently, until melted. Add chocolate-hazelnut spread, stirring until well combined. Remove from heat; add feuilletine and 1½ cups (180 grams) pepitas, stirring to combine. Spread mixture in prepared pan. Cover with a piece of plastic wrap, pressing wrap directly onto surface to flatten. Refrigerate until set, about 1 hour or overnight.
3. In a small saucepan, heat cream just to a simmer. Turn off heat, and add remaining 4 ounces (115 grams) chocolate. Swirl pan so chocolate is submerged. Let stand for 3 minutes; gently whisk until chocolate is smooth. Let cool to nearly room temperature but still pourable.

4. Run a fork over surface of set feuilletine mixture so ganache will stick to surface. Pour ganache over surface, and spread evenly. Bang pan a few times to smooth out surface. Sprinkle with sea salt and remaining ½ cup (60 grams) pepitas. Refrigerate until set, about 30 minutes.
5. Run a hot knife around edges of pan. Using excess parchment as handles, remove from pan, and cut into bars with hot knife. Decorate with gold leaf as desired.

*I used Essential Pantry Feuilletine Flakes, available on amazon.com. You can also substitute finely crushed corn flakes for feuilltine.

Photo by Zoë François

SALTY CARAMELIZED WHITE CHOCOLATE BLONDIES

Makes 16 blondies

Recipe by Jesse Szewcyzk

Can blondies go blonder? We think yes. Starring white chocolate in its hottest new hue, these blondies are even better than the golden bars you know and love. To make slicing them easier, feel free to pop them in the refrigerator for about 20 minutes before cutting.

6   tablespoons (84 grams) unsalted butter, melted and cooled

1   cup (220 grams) firmly packed light brown sugar

1   large egg (50 grams)

2   teaspoons (8 grams) vanilla extract

1   cup (125 grams) all-purpose flour

¼   teaspoon kosher salt

¼   teaspoon ground cinnamon

4   ounces (115 grams) Caramelized White Chocolate (recipe on page 371), coarsely chopped

¾   cup (85 grams) coarsely chopped toasted walnuts

½   teaspoon (1.5 grams) flaked sea salt

1. Preheat oven to 350°F (180°C). Line an 8-inch square baking pan with parchment paper, letting excess extend over sides of pan. Butter and flour parchment.

2. In the bowl of a stand mixer fitted with the paddle attachment, beat melted butter and brown sugar at medium speed until combined. Add egg and vanilla, beating until creamy and smooth, about 2 minutes.

3. In a medium bowl, stir together flour, salt, and cinnamon. With mixer on low speed, gradually add flour mixture to butter mixture, beating just until combined. Fold in Caramelized White Chocolate and toasted walnuts. Spoon batter into prepared pan.

4. Bake until lightly browned and just barely set, 20 to 22 minutes, sprinkling with sea salt halfway through baking. Let cool for at least 1 hour. Using excess parchment as handles, remove from pan, and cut into squares. Store in an airtight container at room temperature for up to 4 days.

Photo by Mark Weinberg

ENGLISH TOFFEE COOKIE BARS

Makes 12 to 16 bars

Recipe by Laura Kasavan

A decadent spin on the classic holiday confection, these chewy cookie bars feature a browned butter-toffee cookie crust and thin layer of chocolate. Topped with crunchy toffee bits and a sprinkling of flaked sea salt, they're sure to become your signature cookie bar.

¾   cup (170 grams) unsalted butter
½   cup (100 grams) granulated sugar
½   cup (110 grams) firmly packed light brown sugar
1   teaspoon (4 grams) vanilla extract
½   teaspoon (2 grams) almond extract
1½   cups (188 grams) all-purpose flour
½   teaspoon (1.5 grams) cornstarch
¼   teaspoon (1.25 grams) baking soda
¼   teaspoon kosher salt
½   cup (75 grams) plus 3 tablespoons (32 grams) toffee bits, divided
1¼   cups (213 grams) semisweet chocolate chips
Garnish: flaked sea salt

1. Preheat oven to 350°F (180°C). Line an 8-inch square metal baking pan with parchment paper, letting excess extend over sides of pan.
2. In a medium heavy-bottomed saucepan, melt butter over medium heat. Cook, stirring constantly, until butter turns a medium-brown color and has a nutty aroma, about 5 minutes.
3. In a large bowl, whisk together browned butter, sugars, and extracts. In a medium bowl, whisk together flour, cornstarch, baking soda, and salt. Add flour mixture to browned butter mixture, and fold in until incorporated. Fold in ½ cup (75 grams) toffee bits. Press dough into bottom of prepared pan.
4. Bake until golden and set, 20 to 22 minutes. Let cool completely on a wire rack.
5. In a microwave-safe bowl, heat chocolate chips on high in 30-second intervals, stirring between each, until melted and smooth. Using an offset spatula, spread melted chocolate onto cooled crust. Top with remaining 3 tablespoons (32 grams) toffee bits. Freeze until chocolate is set, about 30 minutes.
6. Using excess parchment as handles, remove from pan, and cut into triangles. Sprinkle with sea salt, if desired.

Photo by Laura Kasavan

MAGIC LAYER BARS

Makes 12 to 24 bars

Recipe by Sarah Kieffer

These bars have four layers of ingredients, which makes for a rich, decadent layer bar that is perfectly gooey and crunchy at the same time.

1¾ cups (228 grams) graham cracker crumbs
½ cup (113 grams) unsalted butter, melted
1 tablespoon (12 grams) granulated sugar
¾ cup (85 grams) chopped toasted pecans
1 cup (170 grams) semisweet chocolate chips

1 cup (60 grams) sweetened flaked coconut
1 (14-ounce) can (396 grams) sweetened condensed milk

1. Preheat oven to 350°F (180°C). Grease an 8-inch square baking pan. Line pan with parchment paper, letting excess extend over sides of pan.
2. In a small bowl, stir together graham cracker crumbs, melted butter, and sugar. Press mixture into bottom of prepared pan. Add pecans, chocolate chips, and coconut in even, separate layers. Pour condensed milk over top until everything is covered.

3. Bake until edges are golden brown and center is light golden brown, 25 to 30 minutes. Let cool completely on a wire rack. Refrigerate until set and firm. Using excess parchment as handles, remove from pan, and cut into bars. Bars can be refrigerated for up to 3 days but taste best at room temperature.

Photo by Sarah Kieffer

MAPLE CHESTNUT BARS

Makes 12 bars

Fair warning: The maple in this recipe will make your whole house smell like a pancake palace. Because the holidays can be an overwhelmingly busy season, save some time without sacrificing any flavor by using prepackaged roasted chestnuts, commonly found in Asian markets or some grocery stores such as Whole Foods and Trader Joe's.

1   cup (227 grams) unsalted butter, softened
1½ cups (300 grams) granulated sugar, divided
2   cups (250 grams) plus 3 tablespoons (24 grams) all-purpose flour, divided
¾   teaspoon (1.5 grams) kosher salt, divided
1   cup (113 grams) coarsely chopped walnuts
1   cup (113 grams) coarsely chopped roasted chestnuts
1   cup (336 grams) maple syrup
3   large eggs (150 grams)
3   tablespoons (42 grams) unsalted butter, melted
1½ teaspoons (6 grams) vanilla extract

1. Preheat oven to 350°F (180°C). Line a 13x9-inch metal baking pan with parchment paper, letting excess extend over sides of pan.
2. In the bowl of a stand mixer fitted with the paddle attachment, beat butter and ½ cup (100 grams) sugar at medium speed until creamy, 3 to 4 minutes, stopping to scrape sides of bowl.
3. In a medium bowl, whisk together 2 cups (250 grams) flour and ¼ teaspoon salt. With mixer on low speed, gradually add flour mixture to butter mixture, beating just until combined. Using slightly greased hands, press dough into bottom of prepared pan.
4. Bake until lightly browned, about 15 minutes. Let cool on a wire rack.
5. In a medium bowl, whisk together remaining 1 cup (200 grams) sugar, remaining 3 tablespoons (24 grams) flour, and remaining ½ teaspoon (1.5 grams) salt. Whisk in walnuts and all remaining ingredients. Pour filling over prepared crust.
6. Bake until set, 40 to 45 minutes. Let cool completely on a wire rack, about 3 hours. Using excess parchment as handles, remove from pan, and cut into bars. Refrigerate for up to 3 days.

CHOCOLATE CHUNK, TOFFEE, AND POMEGRANATE COOKIE BARS

Makes 16 bars

Chock-full of toffee, chocolate, and pomegranate, these bars are a lesson in balancing rich sweetness with acidic tang. And that blushing Pomegranate Glaze? It's as tasty as it is beautiful.

2¼ cups (281 grams) all-purpose flour
1½ teaspoons (4.5 grams) cornstarch
1 teaspoon (5 grams) baking soda
½ teaspoon (1.5 grams) kosher salt
1 cup (166 grams) pomegranate arils
¾ cup (170 grams) unsalted butter, melted
1 cup (220 grams) firmly packed light brown sugar
¼ cup (50 grams) granulated sugar
1 large egg (50 grams)
1 large egg yolk (19 grams)

2 teaspoons (8 grams) vanilla extract
¾ cup (128 grams) semisweet chocolate chunks
¾ cup (122 grams) toffee bits
Garnish: flaked sea salt
Pomegranate Glaze (recipe follows)

1. Preheat oven to 350°F (180°C). Butter a 9-inch square baking dish; line pan with parchment paper.
2. In a large bowl, whisk together flour, cornstarch, baking soda, and salt. Stir in pomegranate arils.
3. In a medium bowl, whisk together melted butter and sugars. Add egg, egg yolk, and vanilla, whisking to combine. Fold butter mixture into flour mixture until well combined. Add chocolate chunks and toffee bits, stirring to combine. Place dough in prepared pan, smoothing top.

4. Bake until golden brown and set, about 35 minutes. Sprinkle with flaked salt, if desired. Let cool completely in pan. Drizzle with Pomegranate Glaze, and cut into bars.

POMEGRANATE GLAZE
Makes about 1 cup

1 cup (120 grams) confectioners' sugar
2 tablespoons (42 grams) Pomegranate Molasses (recipe on page 131)
1 tablespoon (15 grams) heavy whipping cream

1. In a small bowl, whisk together all ingredients until combined. Use immediately.

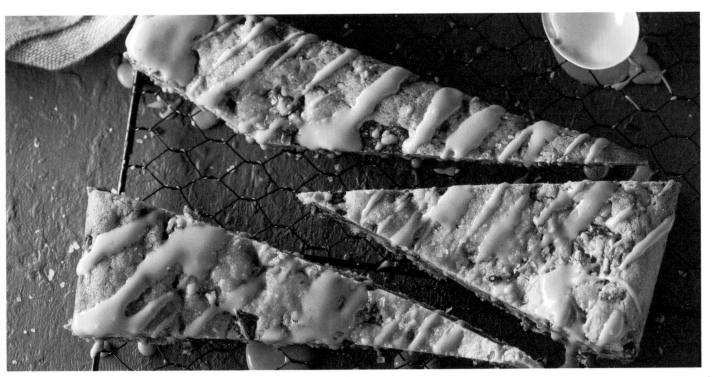

MILLIONAIRE BARS

Makes 25 bars

It doesn't get much richer than Millionaire Bars. Also called millionaire's shortbread, this treat traditionally consists of a shortbread base topped with a layer of gooey caramel filling and chocolate. For a sophisticated holiday spin, we added a homemade Chestnut Praline Paste to the caramel. A final sprinkling of cacao nibs and fleur de sel over the velvety ganache creates an ultra-crunchy topping to offset the sweetness.

2   cups (250 grams) all-purpose flour
⅓   cup (67 grams) granulated sugar
¼   cup (32 grams) cornstarch
1   teaspoon (3 grams) kosher salt
1¼   cups (284 grams) cold unsalted butter, cubed
1   vanilla bean, split lengthwise, seeds scraped and reserved
Chestnut Praline Caramel Filling (recipe follows)
Dark Chocolate Ganache (recipe follows)
Garnish: cacao nibs, fleur de sel

1. Preheat oven to 350°F (180°C). Line a 10-inch square baking dish with parchment paper, letting excess extend over sides of pan.
2. In the bowl of a stand mixer fitted with the paddle attachment, beat flour, sugar, cornstarch, and salt at low speed for 1 minute. Add cold butter and vanilla bean seeds; beat until a ball starts to form, 2 to 3 minutes. Press dough into bottom of prepared pan.
3. Bake until edges are golden brown, about 30 minutes. Let cool completely in pan.
4. Pour warm Chestnut Praline Caramel Filling over prepared crust. Let cool at room temperature for 1 hour. Wrap pan in plastic wrap, and refrigerate overnight.
5. Pour warm Dark Chocolate Ganache over Chestnut Praline Caramel Filling, spreading in an even layer with an offset spatula, if necessary. Let set for 5 minutes. Sprinkle with cacao nibs and fleur de sel, if desired. Refrigerate until firm, about 1 hour.
6. Using excess parchment as handles, remove from pan, and cut into bars. Store in an airtight container at room temperature for up to 3 days or in refrigerator for up to 2 weeks.

CHESTNUT PRALINE CARAMEL FILLING

Makes 3 cups

1   cup (240 grams) heavy whipping cream
¾   cup (255 grams) light corn syrup
½   cup (100 grams) granulated sugar
½   cup (110 grams) firmly packed light brown sugar
½   cup (113 grams) unsalted butter

¼   cup (75 grams) Chestnut Praline Paste (recipe follows)
½   teaspoon (1.5 grams) kosher salt

1. In a 5-quart enamel-coated Dutch oven or large stainless steel saucepan, bring cream, corn syrup, sugars, and butter to a boil over medium heat, stirring frequently. Cook, without stirring, until a candy thermometer registers 248°F (120°C), about 20 minutes. Remove from heat; add Chestnut Praline Paste and salt, stirring to combine. Use immediately.

CHESTNUT PRALINE PASTE

Makes ½ cup

½   cup (80 grams) roasted peeled chestnuts*
¼   cup (60 grams) water
1   tablespoon (12 grams) granulated sugar
¼   teaspoon (1 gram) vanilla extract*

1. In a medium saucepan, bring all ingredients to a boil over medium heat. Reduce heat to low; cover and simmer until chestnuts are softened, about 30 minutes.
2. Transfer to the container of a blender; pulse until smooth. (Alternatively, an immersion blender can be used.) Use immediately, or refrigerate in an airtight container for up to 1 week.

We used Gefen Organic Whole Roasted & Peeled Chestnuts and Heilala Vanilla Extract.

DARK CHOCOLATE GANACHE

Makes 1½ cups

10.5 ounces (315 grams) 70% cacao dark
        chocolate, chopped
¼   cup plus 3 tablespoons (105 grams)
        heavy whipping cream

1. In the top of a double boiler, combine chocolate and cream. Cook over simmering water, whisking constantly, until melted and smooth. Use immediately.

PLAN AHEAD
This recipe is a 2-day process. On day 1, bake the shortbread cookie base, make the Chestnut Praline Caramel Filling, and top the cookie base with the filling. Refrigerate overnight. On day 2, top with the Dark Chocolate Ganache, and refrigerate again before slicing.

DARK CHOCOLATE ROCKY ROAD

Makes about 16 servings

Recipe by Erin Clarkson

The beauty of this recipe: Throw all your favorite things in a bowl, drown them in tempered dark chocolate, and then press the mixture into a tin and leave to set. It's the best way to use up any marshmallows or nuts you may have left over from your holiday baking. Mix up the add-ins with anything you like—this recipe can be whatever you make it!

400 grams* chopped Turkish delight
1½ cups (175 grams) Raspberry Marshmallows (recipe follows) (see Note)
1½ cups (175 grams) Vanilla Bean Marshmallows (recipe follows)
1⅓ cups (162 grams) roasted unsalted pistachios, chopped
5¼ cups (893 grams) chopped dark chocolate
1 tablespoon (9 grams) freeze-dried raspberry powder

1. Grease a 9-inch square baking pan. Line pan with parchment paper, letting excess extend over sides of pan.
2. In a large bowl, place Turkish delight, Raspberry Marshmallows, Vanilla Bean Marshmallows, and pistachios.
3. In the top of a double boiler, place 3¾ cups (670 grams) chocolate. Cook over simmering water, stirring constantly, until melted and a candy thermometer registers 122°F (50°C). Remove from heat; add remaining 1½ cups (223 grams) chocolate, stirring until melted. Continue stirring until candy thermometer registers 84°F (29°C). Return to double boiler, and heat until candy thermometer registers 90°F (32°C). Pour melted chocolate over Turkish delight mixture, stirring until evenly coated.
4. Scrape out mixture into prepared pan, and smooth down slightly. (Due to the marshmallows in the mixture, it will not smooth flat.) Sprinkle with raspberry powder. Lightly cover with plastic wrap, and let stand at room temperature overnight. Using a warm knife, cut into pieces. Store in an airtight container.

Turkish delight can't be put in a cup, so the metric weight must be used.

Note: *If you would like to use store-bought marshmallows, use 1 (340-gram) bag of regular-size marshmallows. Chop each marshmallow in half.*

RASPBERRY MARSHMALLOWS

Makes 144 (¾-inch) marshmallows

¼ cup (32 grams) cornstarch
¼ cup (30 grams) confectioners' sugar
½ cup plus 2 tablespoons (150 grams) cold water, divided
3½ teaspoons (14 grams) unflavored gelatin
2¼ cups plus 1½ tablespoons (468 grams) granulated sugar
¼ cup plus 1 tablespoon (106 grams) light corn syrup
2 tablespoons (18 grams) freeze-dried raspberry powder
1 tablespoon (18 grams) vanilla bean paste or 1 vanilla bean, split lengthwise, seeds scraped and reserved
1 tablespoon (15 grams) liquid red food coloring

1. In a small bowl, sift together cornstarch and confectioners' sugar. Grease a 9-inch square baking pan, and lightly dust with some of the cornstarch mixture.
2. In the bowl of a stand mixer fitted with the whisk attachment, stir together ¼ cup plus 1 tablespoon (75 grams) cold water and gelatin. Let stand until softened, about 5 minutes.
3. In a medium heavy-bottomed saucepan, heat granulated sugar, corn syrup, raspberry powder, vanilla bean paste, and remaining ¼ cup plus 1 tablespoon (75 grams) cold water over medium heat. Cook, stirring occasionally, until a candy thermometer registers 240°F (116°C). Remove from heat, and let cool to 210°F (99°C).
4. With mixer on medium speed, break up gelatin slightly. Add sugar syrup mixture in a slow, steady stream. Increase mixer speed to high; beat until marshmallow is doubled in size, holds a small peak, and is fluffy, 5 to 7 minutes, adding food coloring during last 1 minute. Pour into prepared pan, and spread with a lightly oiled offset spatula to smooth. Dust with more cornstarch mixture, and let stand until set, 3 to 4 hours.
5. Turn out onto a cutting board, and lightly dust with cornstarch mixture. Using a sharp knife, cut marshmallow into ¾-inch squares, dusting knife and marshmallow with cornstarch mixture as needed to prevent sticking. Store in an airtight container for up to 1 month.

Note: *It is especially important to make this marshmallow recipe using grams—with all the sticky ingredients, it is much easier to weigh them all directly into the saucepan and mixing bowl.*

Vanilla Bean Marshmallows

Makes 144 (¾-inch) marshmallows

¼ cup (32 grams) cornstarch
¼ cup (30 grams) confectioners' sugar
½ cup plus 2 tablespoons (150 grams) cold water, divided
3½ teaspoons (14 grams) unflavored gelatin
2¼ cups plus 1½ tablespoons (468 grams) granulated sugar
¼ cup plus 1 tablespoon (106 grams) light corn syrup
1 tablespoon (18 grams) vanilla bean paste or 1 vanilla bean, split lengthwise, seeds scraped and reserved

1. In a small bowl, sift together cornstarch and confectioners' sugar. Grease a 9-inch square baking pan, and lightly dust with some of the cornstarch mixture.

2. In the bowl of a stand mixer fitted with the whisk attachment, stir together ¼ cup plus 1 tablespoon (75 grams) cold water and gelatin. Let stand until softened, about 5 minutes.

3. In a medium heavy-bottomed saucepan, heat granulated sugar, corn syrup, vanilla bean paste, and remaining ¼ cup plus 1 tablespoon (75 grams) cold water over medium heat. Cook,

stirring occasionally, until a candy thermometer registers 240°F (116°C). Remove from heat, and let cool to 210°F (99°C).

4. With mixer on medium speed, break up gelatin slightly. Add sugar syrup mixture in a slow, steady stream. Increase mixer speed to high, and beat until marshmallow is doubled in size, holds a small peak, and is fluffy, 5 to 7 minutes. Pour into prepared pan, and spread with a lightly oiled offset spatula to smooth. Dust with more cornstarch mixture, and let stand until set, 3 to 4 hours.

5. Turn out onto a cutting board, and lightly dust with cornstarch mixture. Using a sharp knife, cut marshmallow into ¾-inch squares, dusting knife and marshmallow with cornstarch mixture as needed to prevent sticking. Store in an airtight container for up to 1 month.

Note: *These are essentially just the Raspberry Marshmallows but without the raspberry powder and food coloring.*

Photo by Erin Clarkson

CRISPY STRAWBERRY TREATS

Makes 12 bars

Embrace your inner child with this throwback treat. Faintly pink with homemade Strawberry Marshmallow and studded with the bright, concentrated sweetness of Oven-Dried Strawberries, these chewy, crunchy squares offer a joyful update on a childhood favorite.

9   cups (270 grams) crisp rice cereal
Oven-Dried Strawberries (recipe follows)
Strawberry Marshmallow (recipe follows)
3   tablespoons (42 grams) unsalted
    butter, cubed and softened

1. Spray a 13x9-inch baking dish with cooking spray.
2. In a large bowl, stir together cereal and Oven-Dried Strawberries.
3. In a medium glass bowl, stir together warm Strawberry Marshmallow and butter until butter is melted and incorporated. (Marshmallow can be reheated by microwaving on high in 30-second intervals, stirring between each, if necessary.)
4. Spoon marshmallow mixture over cereal mixture; fold until cereal is well coated. Press into prepared pan with a greased spatula. Let cool completely. Cut into squares. Store in an airtight container at room temperature for up to 4 days.

OVEN-DRIED STRAWBERRIES
Makes about 1 cup

4   cups (680 grams) (⅛-inch-thick*)
    sliced fresh strawberries
2   tablespoons (30 grams) fresh lemon juice

1. Preheat oven to 200°F (93°C). Line 2 rimmed baking sheets with nonstick baking mats.
2. In a medium bowl, toss together strawberries and lemon juice. Place in a single layer on prepared pans.

3. Bake until dry but tacky, 3 to 3½ hours. Let cool completely. Cover and refrigerate for up to 1 week.

We used a mandoline for thin slices.

STRAWBERRY MARSHMALLOW
Makes 5 cups

⅔   cup (160 grams) water, divided
1   tablespoon plus ½ teaspoon (14 grams)
    unflavored gelatin
1¼ cups (250 grams) granulated sugar
⅔   cup (226 grams) light corn syrup
1½ cups (24 grams) freeze-dried
    strawberries, powdered (see PRO TIP)

1. In the bowl of a stand mixer fitted with the whisk attachment, stir together ⅓ cup (80 grams) water and gelatin; let stand until softened, about 10 minutes.
2. In a large saucepan, combine granulated sugar, corn syrup, and remaining ⅓ cup (80 grams) water. Cook over medium-high heat until sugar is dissolved and a candy thermometer registers 240°F (116°C), about 6 minutes.

3. With mixer on low speed, slowly drizzle hot sugar mixture into gelatin mixture, beating just until combined. Increase mixer speed to medium, and beat until mixture begins to thicken, about 1 minute. Increase mixer speed to high, and beat until mixture turns very thick, white, and fluffy, about 10 minutes. Beat in freeze-dried strawberries.

PRO TIP
To make powdered freeze-dried strawberries, place freeze-dried strawberries in the bowl of a food processor; pulse until reduced to a powder.

GINGERBREAD BLONDIES

Makes about 9 blondies

These Gingerbread Blondies get a spicy boost from grated fresh ginger while chunks of white chocolate add a balancing creamy sweetness. For a note of crunch, consider stirring about 1 cup (113 grams) of chopped pecans, walnuts, or almonds into the batter.

¾   cup (170 grams) unsalted butter, melted
2   cups (440 grams) firmly packed light brown sugar
2   large eggs (100 grams)
1   tablespoon (13 grams) vanilla extract
1   tablespoon (18 grams) finely grated fresh ginger
2¼ cups (281 grams) all-purpose flour

1   tablespoon (6 grams) ground ginger
1   teaspoon (5 grams) baking powder
1   teaspoon (2 grams) ground cinnamon
1   teaspoon (2 grams) ground allspice
½   teaspoon (1.5 grams) kosher salt
½   teaspoon (1 gram) ground cloves
¼   teaspoon (1.25 grams) baking soda
¼   teaspoon ground nutmeg
4   ounces (115 grams) white chocolate, chopped

1. Preheat oven to 350°F (180°C). Line a 10-inch square metal baking pan with parchment paper, letting excess extend over sides of pan.
2. In the bowl of a stand mixer fitted with the whisk attachment, beat melted butter, brown sugar, eggs, and vanilla at high speed until sugar is dissolved and mixture has lightened in color, about 5 minutes. Beat in grated ginger.
3. In a medium bowl, sift together flour, ground ginger, baking powder, cinnamon, allspice, salt, cloves, baking soda, and nutmeg. Fold flour mixture into butter mixture. Fold in half of chopped white chocolate. Spread batter in prepared pan, and top with remaining white chocolate.
4. Bake until a wooden pick inserted in center comes out mostly clean, 35 to 40 minutes. Let cool completely in pan. Using excess parchment as handles, remove from pan. Trim edges, and cut into squares. Store in an airtight container for up to 1 week.

PEPPERMINT NANAIMO BARS

Makes 18 bars

Blending the flavors of a wintry mocha with a Canadian classic, these Nanaimo bars receive a boost from an espresso-spiked ganache, a dose of peppermint extract, and a lightly spiced cinnamon filling. At the base, rich macadamia nuts and sweet coconut flakes add a satisfying element of chew.

½ cup (113 grams) unsalted butter
6 tablespoons (30 grams) unsweetened cocoa powder
⅓ cup (67 grams) granulated sugar
¾ teaspoon (2.25 grams) kosher salt
1 large egg (50 grams), lightly beaten
½ teaspoon (3 grams) vanilla bean paste
¼ teaspoon (1 gram) peppermint extract
1¾ cups (228 grams) shortbread cookie crumbs*
¾ cup (85 grams) sweetened flaked coconut
⅓ cup (38 grams) macadamia nuts, finely chopped
Cinnamon Custard Filling (recipe follows)
Espresso Ganache (recipe follows)
Garnish: crushed peppermints

1. Line an 8-inch square baking pan with parchment paper, letting excess extend over sides of pan. Spray with cooking spray.
2. In the top of a double boiler, combine butter, cocoa, sugar, and salt. Cook over simmering water, stirring constantly, until butter is melted. Add egg, vanilla bean paste, and peppermint extract; cook, stirring constantly, until thickened and smooth, about 1 minute. Remove from heat; stir in cookie crumbs, coconut, and macadamia nuts. Press mixture into bottom of prepared pan.
3. Spread Cinnamon Custard Filling onto prepared crust, smoothing top with an offset spatula. Spread Espresso Ganache onto Cinnamon Custard Filling, smoothing top with an offset spatula. Refrigerate for at least 2 hours.
4. Using excess parchment as handles, remove from pan, and cut into bars. Top with crushed peppermints, if desired. Serve at room temperature.

We used Walkers Pure Butter Shortbread.

CINNAMON CUSTARD FILLING

Makes 1⅔ cups

½ cup plus 2 tablespoons (141 grams) unsalted butter, softened
2 tablespoons (20 grams) vanilla custard powder*
1 teaspoon (4 grams) vanilla extract
¼ teaspoon ground cinnamon
2½ cups (300 grams) confectioners' sugar, sifted
3 tablespoons (45 grams) heavy whipping cream

1. In the bowl of a stand mixer fitted with the paddle attachment, beat butter and custard powder at medium speed until creamy, 2 to 3 minutes, stopping to scrape sides of bowl. Stir in vanilla and cinnamon. Gradually add confectioners' sugar alternately with cream, beating until combined, about 1 minute.

We used Bird's Custard Powder.

ESPRESSO GANACHE

Makes ½ cup

4 ounces (115 grams) 56% cacao semisweet chocolate, chopped
1½ tablespoons (21 grams) unsalted butter
1 teaspoon (2 grams) espresso powder
2 tablespoons (30 grams) heavy whipping cream, warmed

1. In the top of a double boiler, combine chocolate, butter, and espresso powder. Cook over simmering water, stirring constantly, until chocolate is melted and mixture is smooth. Remove from heat; stir in warm cream until combined.

MISCELLANEOUS

PRUNE AND ARMAGNAC CHRISTMAS PUDDING

Makes 8 servings

Recipe by Edd Kimber

On the last Sunday before the season of Advent, a holiday the British call Stir-Up Sunday, bakers across the United Kingdom bring out their mixing bowls and wooden spoons to stir up Christmas pudding. For this pudding, I opted for grated frozen butter in place of the traditional grated suet, a firm fat from beef or mutton. I also added fruity French brandy Armagnac, making this the most luxe pudding you've encountered yet.

2⅓ cups (299 grams) roughly chopped dried prunes
¾ cup (100 grams) fresh bread crumbs
½ cup plus 1 tablespoon (72 grams) roughly chopped dried figs
½ cup plus 1 tablespoon (72 grams) roughly chopped dried dates
⅓ cup (45 grams) whole blanched almonds
⅓ cup (73 grams) firmly packed light brown sugar
2 large eggs (100 grams)
⅓ cup plus 1 tablespoon (95 grams) Armagnac*
⅓ cup (50 grams) grated apple
2 tablespoons (42 grams) honey
1 teaspoon (4 grams) vanilla extract
⅔ cup plus 2 tablespoons (99 grams) all-purpose flour
¼ cup (21 grams) Dutch process cocoa powder**
1 tablespoon (6 grams) mixed spice (see Note)
1 teaspoon (5 grams) baking powder
1 teaspoon (3 grams) kosher salt
½ cup plus 1 tablespoon (127 grams) unsalted butter, frozen
Chocolate Sauce (recipe follows)

1. Lightly grease a 0.95-quart pudding basin** with a little butter, and place a small disk of parchment paper into base.
2. In a large bowl, stir together prunes, bread crumbs, figs, dates, almonds, and brown sugar. Add eggs, Armagnac, apple, honey, and vanilla, stirring until combined. Let stand for 1 hour so the fruit can soak up some of the liquid.
3. In a medium bowl, stir together flour, cocoa, mixed spice, baking powder, and salt. Grate frozen butter into bowl with liquid ingredients, and stir briefly to distribute. Add flour mixture to pudding mixture, and stir until well combined.
4. Firmly press mixture into prepared pudding basin, packing in well so there are no air pockets. Cover pudding with another disk of parchment. Cover basin with a large sheet of parchment paper and a large sheet of foil, both with a pleat across the middle so the pudding has space to expand as it bakes. Secure in place with a piece of kitchen string tied tightly just under lip of basin.

5. To steam, place a small inverted saucer into a large stockpot, and place pudding on top. You don't want the pudding touching the bottom of the pan since you want to steam it, not cook through direct heat. Fill pan with boiling water so that it comes halfway up sides of pudding basin. Place pan over low heat, and simmer for 3 hours. (This is about half the time a regular Christmas pudding steams for because butter has a much lower melting point than suet.) Make sure you check the water level as the pudding steams, and top up with extra boiling water as needed. Remove pudding from heat, and let cool completely.
6. Remove wrappings, and replace with fresh parchment and foil, making sure to secure tightly with string as before. Store in a cool, dry place for the month leading up to Christmas Day or whichever day you wish to enjoy. (Store for at least 12 hours if you do not wish to store for a month.)
7. To serve, repeat steaming process for about 1 hour to heat through. Remove foil and parchment, and carefully turn out pudding onto a plate. Pour Chocolate Sauce over pudding.

Bourbon or spiced rum would also work.

**I used Guittard Cocoa Rouge Unsweetened Cocoa Powder and Mason Cash Steam Bowl (Pudding Basin), available on amazon.com.*

Note: *Mixed spice, also called pudding spice, is a British blend of spices, available on amazon.com. Pumpkin pie spice can be substituted. If you would like to make your own mixed spice, stir together 1 tablespoon (6 grams) allspice, 1 tablespoon (6 grams) cinnamon, 1 tablespoon (6 grams) nutmeg, 2 teaspoons (4 grams) ginger, ½ teaspoon (1 gram) cloves, and ½ teaspoon (1 gram) coriander.*

CHOCOLATE SAUCE

Makes 1 cup

3.5 ounces (100 grams) 63% cacao dark chocolate, chopped
½ cup (120 grams) double cream/heavy whipping cream
1 tablespoon (14 grams) firmly packed light brown sugar
1 teaspoon (4 grams) vanilla extract
2 tablespoons (30 grams) Armagnac

1. Place chocolate in a medium heatproof bowl.
2. In a medium saucepan, bring cream, brown sugar, and vanilla to a simmer. Pour hot cream mixture over chocolate. Let stand for 1 to 2 minutes; stir until melted and smooth. Add Armagnac, stirring to combine. Use immediately.

Photo by Edd Kimber

PRO TIP

Alternatively, you can steam this pudding in the oven using a 6-cup Bundt pan instead of a pudding basin. Preheat oven to 350°F (180°C), and place a deep roasting pan in oven. Follow steps 2 and 3 to prepare pudding batter. Lightly butter and flour Bundt pan, tapping out any excess. Scrape pudding batter into prepared pan, and level out. Wrap pan completely in several layers of parchment paper and one layer of foil. (Because of the hole in the Bundt pan, you need to ensure the entire pan is covered, not just the top as when making in a traditional pudding basin.) Place Bundt inside roasting pan in oven, and fill roasting pan with enough boiling water to reach halfway up sides of Bundt pan. Steam pudding for 3 hours. Remove pudding from heat, and let cool completely. Continue with step 6 as directed.

CARAMELIZED WHITE CHOCOLATE BARK

Makes 8 to 10 servings

Recipe by Jesse Szewcyzk

A small amount of white chocolate is added to give the bark a nice snappiness and prevent it from blooming. Pistachios, tart raspberries, and large flakes of sea salt balance the sweetness and add crunch—but feel free to load it up with whatever toppings you have in your pantry.

2   tablespoons (18 grams) unsalted raw shelled pistachios
6   ounces (175 grams) Caramelized White Chocolate (recipe follows), coarsely chopped
⅔   cup (113 grams) white chocolate chips
2   tablespoons (2 grams) freeze-dried raspberries, lightly crushed
¾   teaspoon (2.25 grams) flaked sea salt

1. Preheat oven to 350°F (180°C).
2. Spread pistachios on a baking sheet, and toast until fragrant, about 6 minutes. Let cool, then coarsely chop. Set aside.
3. Line a 13x9½-inch sheet pan with parchment paper.
4. In the top of a double boiler, place Caramelized White Chocolate. Cook over simmering water, stirring frequently, until melted and a candy thermometer registers 110°F (43°C), about 8 minutes. Remove from heat; slowly add white chocolate chips, stirring until candy thermometer registers 84°F (29°C). (If there are small pieces of unmelted chocolate, place back over heat for a few seconds.)
5. Pour melted chocolate onto prepared pan, and spread in a thin layer. Sprinkle with toasted pistachios, raspberries, and sea salt. Let set for at least 2 hours or overnight. Break into small pieces, and store in an airtight container for up to 1 month.

Photo by Mark Weinberg

CARAMELIZED WHITE CHOCOLATE
Makes about 2 cups

Use high-quality white chocolate with over 30% cocoa butter content for this recipe. Every white chocolate is different and the amount of time (and stirring) it takes to caramelize will vary, so use your senses and treat this recipe as a guideline. Once the chocolate is a deep golden color and smells like toasted marshmallows, it's done.

16   ounces (455 grams) white chocolate baking chips
¼   teaspoon kosher salt

1. Preheat oven to 250°F (130°C). In a completely dry 9-inch round cake pan, combine chocolate and salt.

2. Bake until chocolate is smooth and deep golden and smells like toasted marshmallows, 30 to 60 minutes, stirring every 10 minutes. (At times, the chocolate will look very dry and chalky, but keep stirring until smooth.)

3. Pour chocolate onto a parchment-lined sheet tray, and let set for at least 7 hours or overnight.

4. Break into pieces, and store in an airtight container for up to 4 months.

PRO TIP
For a lighter flavor, roast just until color starts to change, about 30 minutes. This is best for pairing with subtle flavors, such as fresh berries. For a stronger flavor, roast until chocolate resembles peanut butter and has a strong nutty fragrance, about 1 hour. This will produce something slightly less sweet with an assertive caramel flavor.

HAZELNUT MOCHA DACQUOISE

Makes 1 (10x3-inch) cake

To eat a slice of dacquoise is to go on an adventure in texture. This hazelnut and coffee triumph has alternating layers of crispy hazelnut Meringue, silky espresso buttercream, and fudgy ganache.

Meringue (recipe follows)
Ganache Filling (recipe follows)
Espresso French Buttercream (recipe follows)
Ganache Glaze (recipe follows)
Garnish: toasted sliced almonds, chopped toasted hazelnuts

1. Gently peel Meringue off parchment paper. Using a serrated knife, trim edges so they are even and each rectangle is the same size. (Try not to press down on Meringue while trimming edges. If it breaks, you can piece it back together.) Cut a cake round to the size of the Meringue rectangles, and place one Meringue on top. Spoon Ganache Filling into a pastry bag fitted with a ½-inch round tip. Pipe a ½-inch-thick layer of filling on top of Meringue. Gently press a second layer of Meringue on top. Place roughly half (1½ cups) of Espresso French Buttercream in a pastry bag fitted with a ½-inch round tip. Pipe a layer of buttercream onto Meringue. Top buttercream with last layer of Meringue, top down so flat side is facing up. Use remaining Espresso French Buttercream to fill in any gaps, and cover cake with a thin layer of buttercream, making it as smooth as possible. Refrigerate for at least 1 hour.
2. Place chilled cake on a wire rack set over a rimmed sheet pan lined with plastic wrap. Pour warm Ganache Glaze over cake, letting it cover top and sides of cake. Using a large offset spatula, level off top of cake in one swipe. (Do not try to do it more than once or in short strokes—it will leave streaks in the final product. If some of the buttercream is peaking through on the sides, you can smooth it with an offset spatula, but don't worry about it too much since the sides will be decorated.) Decorate sides of cake with almonds and hazelnuts, if desired. Refrigerate in an airtight container until ready to serve, up to 2 days.

Meringue
Makes 3 (10x3-inch) meringues

¾   cup plus 1 tablespoon (78 grams) almond flour
¾   cup (72 grams) hazelnut flour
1½ cups (180 grams) confectioners' sugar
⅛   teaspoon kosher salt
6   large egg whites (180 grams)
⅓   cup (67 grams) granulated sugar
1   teaspoon (4 grams) vanilla extract

1. Preheat oven to 225°F (107°C). Line an 18x13-inch baking sheet with parchment paper. Draw 3 (10x3-inch) rectangles at least 3 inches apart on parchment; turn parchment over, and spray with cooking spray.
2. In a medium bowl, combine nut flours. Add confectioners' sugar and salt, stirring until well combined. Sift.
3. In the bowl of a stand mixer fitted with the whisk attachment, beat egg whites at medium speed until soft peaks form, about 4 minutes. With mixer running, add granulated sugar in three additions, beating well after each addition, about 15 seconds. Increase mixer speed to high, and beat until meringue turns shiny, about 1 minute. Add vanilla, and beat until glossy medium-stiff peaks form, 1 to 2 minutes.
4. Place meringue in a large bowl; fold nut flour mixture in quickly and gently. Gently place meringue in a pastry bag fitted with a ½-inch round tip. Pipe meringue onto drawn rectangles on prepared pan, filling completely.
5. Bake until meringue is firm to the touch, 2 to 2½ hours. Turn oven off, and let meringue stand in oven with door closed for at least 6 hours or overnight.

Ganache Filling
Makes about ¾ cup

⅔   cup (113 grams) chopped bittersweet chocolate
½   cup (120 grams) heavy whipping cream
½   teaspoon (1 gram) espresso powder

1. Place chocolate in a medium heatproof bowl.
2. In a small saucepan, heat cream over medium heat, stirring frequently, just until steaming. (Do not boil.) Whisk in espresso powder. Pour hot cream mixture over chocolate; let stand for 1 minute. Using a silicone spatula, slowly stir small circles in center of bowl until cream and chocolate come together and mixture is shiny and smooth. Let cool completely. Cover and store at room temperature until ready to use or overnight.

Espresso French Buttercream
Makes 3 cups

¾   cup (150 grams) granulated sugar
¼   cup (60 grams) water
2   large eggs (100 grams), room temperature
2   large egg yolks (37 grams), room temperature
1½ cups (340 grams) unsalted butter, softened
1   tablespoon (6 grams) espresso powder
1   teaspoon (6 grams) vanilla bean paste
¼   teaspoon kosher salt

1. In a small saucepan, bring sugar and ¼ cup (60 grams) water to a boil over high heat, without stirring. Cook until mixture registers 240°F (116°C) on an instant-read thermometer.

2. Meanwhile, in the bowl of a stand mixer fitted with the whisk attachment, beat eggs and egg yolks at medium-high speed until pale and light, 4 to 5 minutes. Reduce mixer speed to medium-low. Pour hot sugar syrup into egg mixture in a slow, steady stream, being careful not to hit sides of bowl or whisk attachment. Increase mixer speed to high, and beat until bottom of bowl feels cool to the touch, 4 to 5 minutes. Add butter, 1 tablespoon (14 grams) at a time, letting each piece incorporate before adding the next. (It will look broken, but keep whipping, and it will come back together.) Add espresso powder, vanilla bean paste, and salt, beating until well combined. Use immediately.

GANACHE GLAZE
Makes about 2 cups

2   cups (340 grams) chopped bittersweet chocolate
1½ cups (360 grams) heavy whipping cream

1. Place chocolate in a medium heatproof bowl.
2. In a small saucepan, heat cream over medium heat, stirring frequently, just until steaming. (Do not boil.) Pour hot cream over chocolate; let stand for 1 minute. Using a silicone spatula, slowly stir small circles in center of bowl until cream and chocolate come together and mixture is shiny and smooth. Let cool slightly.

PEACH & BASIL COBBLER

Makes 1 (8-inch) skillet

Slightly sweet basil adds an unexpected herbaceous note to this cobbler's saucy filling while walnuts bring warm crunch to the sugared biscuit topping.

1¼ cups (156 grams) all-purpose flour
½ cup (100 grams) granulated sugar
1 tablespoon (15 grams) baking powder
1 teaspoon (3 grams) kosher salt
6 tablespoons (84 grams) cold unsalted butter, cubed
½ cup (57 grams) chopped walnuts
½ cup (120 grams) heavy whipping cream
2 tablespoons (16 grams) cornstarch
2 tablespoons (30 grams) water
4½ cups (1,012.5 grams) (¼-inch-thick) sliced peeled fresh peaches (about 6 medium peaches)

¾ cup (165 grams) firmly packed light brown sugar
1 teaspoon (6 grams) vanilla bean paste
2 tablespoons (4 grams) chopped fresh basil
1 large egg (50 grams), lightly beaten
1 tablespoon (12 grams) sparkling sugar

1. In a large bowl, stir together flour, granulated sugar, baking powder, and salt. Using a pastry blender, cut in cold butter until mixture is crumbly. Stir in walnuts and cream just until combined. (Dough will be slightly crumbly.) Gently shape dough into a disk. Wrap in plastic wrap, and refrigerate for at least 30 minutes.
2. Preheat oven to 375°F (190°C).
3. On a lightly floured surface, gently roll dough to ½-inch thickness. Using a 2½-inch round cutter, cut 7 rounds. Cover dough

with plastic wrap to prevent a skin from forming. Set aside.
4. In a small bowl, whisk together cornstarch and 2 tablespoons (30 grams) water.
5. In a medium saucepan, bring peaches, brown sugar, and vanilla bean paste to a boil over medium-high heat. Add cornstarch mixture; whisk for 1 minute. Add basil; reduce heat to low, and simmer for 2 minutes. Pour peach mixture into an 8-inch skillet. Top with biscuits. Brush a thin layer of egg wash onto biscuits, and sprinkle with sparkling sugar.
6. Bake until biscuits are deep brown and filling is bubbly, 15 to 20 minutes. Let cool slightly; serve warm.

ENGLISH BREAKFAST ORANGE MARMALADE ROLY POLY

Makes 6 to 8 servings

This British childhood favorite, known cutely as a Roly Poly, is in essence an oven-steamed roulade cake. In our nod to the nostalgic dessert, a generous slather of English breakfast tea-powered orange marmalade runs in the tight spiral of a rolled vanilla cake.

6   cups (1,440 grams) water
¼   cup (57 grams) plus 1 tablespoon (14 grams) cold unsalted butter, cubed and divided
2   cups (250 grams) self-rising flour
½   teaspoon (1.5 grams) kosher salt
⅓   cup (40 grams) shredded vegetable suet*
⅔   cup (160 grams) whole milk
1   teaspoon (4 grams) vanilla extract
¾   cup (240 grams) English Breakfast Orange Marmalade (recipe follows)
Clotted cream and English Breakfast Orange Marmalade, to serve
Garnish: confectioners' sugar

1. Position one oven rack on lowest shelf, and place a deep 3-quart roasting pan on top. Place a second oven rack directly above pan.
2. In a medium saucepan, bring 6 cups (1,440 grams) water to a boil over high heat. Pour boiling water into roasting pan. Preheat oven to 350°F (180°C). Spread 1 tablespoon (14 grams) cold butter onto a 14½-inch square sheet of parchment paper.
3. In the work bowl of a food processor, place flour and salt; pulse until combined. Add remaining ¼ cup (57 grams) cold butter, and pulse until mixture is crumbly. Add shredded suet, and pulse just until combined. With processor running, add milk and vanilla in a slow, steady stream just until dough comes together.
4. Turn out dough onto a heavily floured** surface, and roll into a 10-inch square. Transfer to prepared parchment. Spread English Breakfast Orange Marmalade onto dough, leaving a 1-inch border on one side. Starting with opposite side, roll up dough, jelly roll style; gently pinch seam to seal. Wrap in prepared parchment, and loosely wrap in foil, crushing ends to seal.

5. Bake directly on oven rack above roasting pan for 1 hour. Let cool on a wire rack for 5 minutes. Remove foil and parchment. Cut ends off at a 45-degree angle. Serve with clotted cream and English Breakfast Orange Marmalade. Garnish with confectioners' sugar, if desired.

*We used Atora Shredded Vegetable Suet, available on amazon.com.

**Use plain flour or all-purpose flour for work surface. Self-rising flour can impart a bitter taste with its excess of leavening agents.

ENGLISH BREAKFAST ORANGE MARMALADE
Makes about 4 cups

3   cups (720 grams) water
8   bags (16 grams) English Breakfast tea
2   large navel oranges (690 grams)
2   tablespoons (6 grams) lemon zest
¼   cup (60 grams) fresh lemon juice
1   vanilla bean, split lengthwise, seeds scraped and reserved
3   cups (600 grams) granulated sugar

1. In a medium saucepan, bring 3 cups (720 grams) water and tea bags to a boil over high heat; remove from heat. Cover and let steep for 20 minutes; discard tea bags.
2. Peel oranges, and cut peel into ¼-inch-thick slices. Cut oranges into quarters. Add oranges and peel, lemon zest and juice, and vanilla bean and reserved seeds to tea mixture; bring to a boil over medium heat. Reduce heat to low, and simmer for 10 minutes. Discard vanilla bean.
3. Stir in sugar, and bring to a boil over medium-high heat; cook, stirring occasionally, until mixture is thickened and a candy thermometer registers 222°F (106°C), 15 to 20 minutes. Let cool completely. Cover and refrigerate until set, about 4 hours.

RHUBARB CRUMBLE AND CUSTARD CUPCAKES

Makes 12 cupcakes

Recipe by Jemma Wilson

These cupcakes are a win for me because rhubarb-and-custard boiled sweets were up there in my top five candies of all time as a child. I have always been drawn to the combination of sweet and sour, and this recipe hits both big time!

3	cups (300 grams) washed "field-grown" or "forced" rhubarb
⅔	cup (133 grams) plus 3 tablespoons (36 grams) castor sugar, divided
3	tablespoons (9 grams) orange zest (about 1 orange) (optional)
1	vanilla pod/bean, split lengthwise, seeds scraped and reserved
1	tablespoon (15 grams) water
1	cup (125 grams) self-raising flour/self-rising flour
¼	teaspoon (1.25 grams) bicarbonate of soda/baking soda
½	cup (113 grams) unsalted butter, softened
2	large eggs (100 grams)
1½	tablespoons (22.5 grams) milk
¼	teaspoon (1 gram) vanilla extract

Crème Mousseline (recipe follows)
Crumble Topping (recipe follows)

1. Preheat oven to 325°F (170°C).
2. To prepare the filling, chop your rhubarb into 1- to 1½-inch (3- to 4-centimeter) sticks, and spread evenly over a baking tray (with sides, to catch all the juice!).
3. In a small bowl, mix 3 tablespoons (36 grams) sugar, zest (if using), vanilla pod seeds, and 1 tablespoon (15 grams) water. Sprinkle sugar mixture over rhubarb.
4. Cover whole tray with foil, nice and tight, and bake for 15 to 20 minutes. Once baked, the rhubarb will be very soft and will have released a lot of liquid. Strain fruit, keeping syrup for later. Whizz up pulp in a blender or food processor until thick and smooth. Thicken up rhubarb syrup in a saucepan over low heat until reduced by half, about 10 minutes.
5. Line a 12-cup cupcake tin with paper cases.

6. In the bowl of a stand mixer, sift together flour, bicarbonate of soda, and remaining ⅔ cup (133 grams) sugar. Add butter, which should be squeezable soft, not firm and not sloppy. Add eggs, and get the mixer going at medium speed, and beat for 1 minute, scraping sides down if you need to. Add milk and vanilla extract, and beat at medium-high speed for 30 seconds.
7. To ripple rhubarb filling through batter, drop a couple tablespoons of it into mixing bowl, and poke it around a bit, without stirring. With a spoon, scoop up batter, which should have the odd blob smeared through it, and distribute it evenly among prepared cupcake cases. Add more blobs of rhubarb filling when you look a bit short on ripples, but make sure you hold some back for filling the cupcakes later.
8. Bake until golden and cupcakes spring back to the touch, 19 to 22 minutes. Leave to cool.
9. Remove centers of cupcakes using an apple corer. Fill holes with remaining rhubarb filling. (If you have any left, put it on your granola and yogurt in the morning!)
10. Place Crème Mousseline in a large piping bag fitted with a wide star piping tip. Ice tops of cupcakes. Sprinkle with Crumble Topping, and drizzle with concentrated rhubarb syrup! Bob's your uncle!

CRÈME MOUSSELINE

Makes 2 cups

¾	cup plus 2 tablespoons (210 grams) whole milk
1	teaspoon (4 grams) vanilla extract
⅓	cup (67 grams) castor sugar
1	tablespoon plus 1 teaspoon (11 grams) cornflour/cornstarch
1	large egg (50 grams)
1	large egg yolk (19 grams)

Pinch kosher salt

1	cup (227 grams) very soft unsalted butter

1. Bring milk and vanilla to a boil; set aside to cool a little.

2. In a large bowl, whisk together sugar, cornflour, egg, egg yolk, and salt. Very slowly, pour three-fourths of hot milk mixture into egg mixture, whisking constantly. Pour egg mixture into saucepan with leftover milk mixture.
3. Place over medium-low heat, and heat, whisking constantly to prevent it from "catching" on the bottom, until thickened and bubbly. Once custard has begun to bubble, boil for 1 minute to cook cornflour.
4. Pour into a bowl (strain through a fine-mesh sieve, if necessary), and cover with cling film (plastic wrap). The cling film must touch the custard to prevent a skin from forming. Leave it to cool, then pop it in the fridge to chill.
5. Once cold, put it all into the bowl of a stand mixer fitted with the whisk attachment. Whisk for a few minutes until smooth. Then, with mixer on medium-high speed, drop in very soft butter, 1 teaspoon (5 grams) at a time, until it's all gone! Voila! Custard buttercream!

CRUMBLE TOPPING

Makes ½ cup

⅔	cup (83 grams) plain flour/cake flour
¼	cup (20 grams) porridge oats/oatmeal
3	tablespoons (42 grams) unsalted butter, melted
1	teaspoon (4 grams) castor sugar
1	teaspoon (4 grams) Demerara sugar

Pinch kosher salt

1. Preheat oven to 325°F (170°C).
2. Place all ingredients in a bowl, and stir until they come together. Ditch the spoon, and get your hands in there, rubbing mixture between your fingers lightly for a few minutes, until small little pastry nuggets start to form. Spread these out evenly onto a baking tray.
3. Bake until pastry nuggets are golden in color, 15 to 20 minutes. Toss about once during cooking to ensure nuggets are being cooked evenly. Leave to cool.

Photo by Yuki Sugiura

RASPBERRY PINE NUT PAVLOVA

Makes about 8 servings

Vanilla bean brings warmth to the traditional meringue in this Pavlova topped with Buttermilk Whipped Cream and Raspberry Coulis and toasted pine nuts for another layer of delicate crunch.

4   large egg whites (120 grams), room
     temperature
½   teaspoon (2 grams) vanilla extract
¼   teaspoon cream of tartar
1   cup (200 grams) granulated sugar
1   vanilla bean, split lengthwise, seeds
     scraped and reserved
1   teaspoon (5 grams) distilled white vinegar
1   tablespoon (8 grams) cornstarch
Raspberry Coulis (recipe follows)
Buttermilk Whipped Cream (recipe follows)
Garnish: toasted pine nuts

1. Preheat oven to 180°F (82°C). Line a baking sheet with parchment paper. Using a pencil, draw a 9-inch circle onto parchment; turn parchment over.
2. In the bowl of a stand mixer fitted with the whisk attachment, beat egg whites, vanilla extract, and cream of tartar at medium-low speed until foamy soft peaks form. Increase mixer speed to medium-high. Add sugar, 1 tablespoon (12 grams) at a time, beating until glossy stiff peaks form. Scrape sides of bowl. Increase mixer speed to high. Beat until sugar is dissolved, 5 to 7 minutes. Add vanilla bean seeds and vinegar, beating until combined. Sift cornstarch over meringue mixture, and beat until combined.
3. Spoon meringue onto drawn circle on prepared pan. Using a spoon, loosely shape meringue into a 9-inch round, about 3 inches thick.
4. Bake until set and dry, about 2 hours. Turn oven off, and let meringue stand in oven with door closed for 1 hour.
5. Spoon half of Raspberry Coulis over meringue. Top with Buttermilk Whipped Cream and remaining Raspberry Coulis. Garnish with pine nuts, if desired. Serve immediately.

RASPBERRY COULIS

Makes about 1½ cups

3   cups (390 grams) fresh raspberries,
     divided
3   tablespoons (42 grams) firmly packed
     light brown sugar
2½   tablespoons (37.5 grams) fresh lemon
     juice, divided
1   teaspoon (5 grams) water
½   teaspoon (1.5 grams) cornstarch
1   tablespoon (21 grams) honey

1. In a small saucepan, bring 1½ cups (195 grams) raspberries, brown sugar, and 1½ tablespoons (22.5 grams) lemon juice to a boil over medium heat.
2. In a small bowl, stir together 1 teaspoon (5 grams) water and cornstarch. Add cornstarch mixture to raspberry mixture; cook, stirring constantly, until slightly thickened, about 1 minute.
3. Remove from heat. Stir in honey, remaining 1½ cups (195 grams) raspberries, and remaining 1 tablespoon (15 grams) lemon juice. Let cool completely. Refrigerate in an airtight container for up to 5 days.

BUTTERMILK WHIPPED CREAM

Makes about 1½ cups

½   cup (120 grams) heavy whipping cream
¼   cup (60 grams) whole buttermilk
1   tablespoon (12 grams) granulated sugar
¼   teaspoon kosher salt

1. In the bowl of a stand mixer fitted with the whisk attachment, beat all ingredients at high speed until stiff peaks form. Use immediately.

Photo by Stephen DeVries

SWEET CORN AND GRUYÈRE SOUFFLÉ

Makes 1 (6-cup) soufflé or 12 (6-ounce) soufflés

Recipe by Steven Satterfield

Imagine the lightest, fluffiest corn pudding you have ever tried. This is better than what you just dreamed up. Fresh chopped kernels elevate the texture and bring an earthy sweetness to this classic soufflé technique, made even more indulgent when combined with the undeniable umami of Gruyère cheese. Be careful not to overbake; the soufflé should be barely runny in the center when ready.

¼   cup (57 grams) unsalted butter
¼   cup (31 grams) all-purpose flour
1   cup (240 grams) whole milk
1⅛   teaspoons (3 grams) fine sea salt, divided
½   teaspoon (1 gram) dry mustard
½   teaspoon (1 gram) ground white pepper
⅛   teaspoon ground nutmeg
1½   cups (208 grams) fresh corn kernels, chopped in a food processor

6   large eggs (300 grams), separated
⅛   teaspoon cream of tartar
1½   cups (150 grams) freshly grated Gruyère cheese

1. Preheat oven to 375°F (190°C). Spray a 6-cup soufflé pan or 12 (6-ounce) ramekins with cooking spray.
2. In a small saucepan, melt butter over medium-low heat until foamy. Whisk in flour; cook for 2 to 3 minutes, whisking constantly. Slowly whisk in milk; cook, stirring constantly, until thickened, about 3 minutes. Add 1 teaspoon (3 grams) sea salt, mustard, white pepper, and nutmeg, whisking to combine. Whisk in corn, and cook over low heat until bubbles begin to form. Remove from heat, and add egg yolks, one at a time, whisking well after each addition; set aside.
3. In the bowl of a stand mixer fitted with the whisk attachment, beat egg whites, cream of tartar, and remaining ⅛ teaspoon sea salt at low speed until well combined. Increase mixer speed to high, and beat until

glossy stiff peaks form. (Do not overbeat; it will form dry peaks, which can make a grainy texture.)
4. Carefully fold one-fourth of egg whites into cooled corn sauce, making sure not to deflate air that has been incorporated into whipped whites. Stir in Gruyère; very carefully fold in remaining egg whites in 3 batches with a light but swift touch. Gently spoon mixture into prepared pan or ramekins.
5. Bake until golden brown and soufflé has risen and puffed above rim of pan or ramekins. Bake 6-cup soufflé for about 1 hour, covering with foil halfway through baking to prevent excess browning. Bake 6-ounce soufflés for 25 to 30 minutes. (The goal is to have the soufflé completely set but just barely runny in the very center.) Serve immediately.

Photo by Angie Mosier

SWEET CORN MADELEINES

Makes 24 madeleines

Recipe by Steven Satterfield

These little corn cakes have lots of lift from egg and baking powder but plenty of butter to keep them in touch with Earth's gravity. The secret is the pulverized sweet corn that permeates the batter and naturally sweetens every bite.

3   large eggs (150 grams)
½   cup (100 grams) granulated sugar
1   cup (150 grams) fine yellow cornmeal
1   teaspoon (5 grams) baking powder
1   teaspoon (3 grams) fine sea salt
1½ cups (208 grams) fresh sweet corn
    kernels, roughly chopped in a food
    processor
¾   cup (170 grams) unsalted butter,
    melted and cooled
Garnish: confectioners' sugar

1. Preheat oven to 370°F (188°C). Butter and flour 2 (12-cup) madeleine pans.
2. In a medium bowl, whisk together eggs and granulated sugar. In a small bowl, stir together cornmeal, baking powder, and sea salt. Add cornmeal mixture to egg mixture, whisking until combined. Add chopped corn and melted butter, stirring until well combined. Spoon batter into prepared cups, filling almost to top but not overflowing.
3. Bake until lightly golden and madeleines spring back when lightly pressed in center,

10 to 15 minutes. Tap corner of pan on counter to release madeleines. They should pop right out. If not, gently loosen with the tip of a knife or a wooden pick. Sprinkle with confectioners' sugar, if desired. Serve warm or at room temperature.

Note: *If you don't have madeleine pans, you can use a mini muffin pan instead.*

Photo by Angie Mosier

TROPICAL MERINGUE CLOUDS

Makes 18 to 24 meringue clouds

Recipe by Marian Cooper Cairns

Beautifully light, chewy, and crispy meringues are swirled with the preserves of one of our favorite summer stone fruits: mango. Any kind of preserves will work—just be sure to strain out the large pieces of fruit so it easily flows through the meringue to create artful patterns.

¾   cup (240 grams) mango preserves*
4   large egg whites (120 grams), room
     temperature
¼   teaspoon cream of tartar
⅛   teaspoon kosher salt
1   cup (200 grams) granulated sugar
1   tablespoon (8 grams) cornstarch
¼   teaspoon (1 gram) vanilla extract
¼   teaspoon (1 gram) coconut extract

1. Preheat oven to 225°F (107°C). Line 2 baking sheets with parchment paper.
2. In a small microwave-safe bowl, microwave preserves on high until warmed and melted, 1 to 1½ minutes. Pour through a fine-mesh sieve, discarding solids. Set aside.
3. In the bowl of a stand mixer fitted with the whisk attachment, beat egg whites at medium-high speed for 1 minute. Add cream of tartar and salt, beating until combined.
4. In a small bowl, whisk together sugar and cornstarch. With mixer running, add sugar mixture, 1 tablespoon at a time, beating until glossy stiff peaks form and sugar is dissolved. (Do not overbeat.) Beat in extracts.
5. Scoop 4 to 5 rounded spoonfuls meringue mixture (about 3 tablespoons each), and drop about 1½ inches apart onto prepared pans. Drizzle ½ teaspoon preserves

onto each cookie. Swirl preserves lightly with a wooden pick. Repeat procedure until all meringue is used.
6. Bake until pale golden and outsides have formed a crust, 1 hour and 15 minutes to 1 hour and 25 minutes. Turn oven off, and let meringues stand in oven with door closed and light on for 12 hours. Store in an airtight container for up to 3 days.

We suggest using Goya Mango Jam or Bonne Maman Mango Peach Preserves.

Photo by Matt Armendariz

OVEN-BAKED CONCORD GRAPE DOUGHNUTS

Makes 12 doughnuts

Recipe by Laura Kasavan

Your favorite jelly-filled doughnut, with a homemade, oven-baked twist. To imitate that signature deep-fried crunchy crust, roll these buttery doughnuts in a final coat of sugar.

1¾   cups (219 grams) all-purpose flour
1   cup (200 grams) granulated sugar, divided
1   teaspoon (5 grams) baking powder
½   teaspoon (1 gram) ground nutmeg
¼   teaspoon kosher salt
¾   cup (180 grams) reduced-fat unsweetened plain Greek yogurt
2   tablespoons (30 grams) 2% reduced-fat milk
2   large eggs (100 grams), room temperature
½   teaspoon (2 grams) vanilla extract
½   cup (113 grams) unsalted butter, melted and slightly cooled
Concord Grape Jam* (recipe on page 347)
1   tablespoon (14 grams) unsalted butter, melted

1. Preheat oven to 350°F (180°C). Butter and flour a 12-cup muffin pan.
2. In a large bowl, whisk together flour, ¾ cup (150 grams) sugar, baking powder, nutmeg, and salt. In a medium bowl, whisk together yogurt, milk, eggs, and vanilla. Make a well in center of flour mixture; add yogurt mixture and cooled melted butter, folding until combined.
3. Spoon about 2 tablespoons batter into each prepared muffin cup. Smooth batter, and top with a generous ½ teaspoon Concord Grape Jam. Top with remaining batter, and smooth tops.
4. Bake until tops are set, edges are golden brown, and a wooden pick inserted in center comes out mostly clean, 20 to 25 minutes. Lightly brush tops with melted butter. Let cool in pan for 5 minutes. Remove from pan, and let cool slightly on a wire rack before rolling in remaining ¼ cup (50 grams) sugar to coat. Serve warm or at room temperature.

*When making Concord Grape Jam, omit cloves. At the end of step 2, remove mixture from heat. Pour into a glass bowl, and let cool before using.

PRO TIP
If fresh Concord grapes are not available, you can substitute high-quality store-bought Concord grape jam for the homemade jam. We suggest using Stonewall Kitchen Concord Grape Jelly, available at *stonewallkitchen.com.*

Photo by Laura Kasavan

BEIGNETS

Makes 12 beignets

Freshly fried and dusted in confectioners' sugar, this Creole pastry is like the perfect bite of New Orleans: joyously decadent.

½ cup (113 grams) warm water (105°F/41°C to 110°F/43°C)
1 teaspoon (3 grams) active dry yeast
3 tablespoons (36 grams) plus 1 teaspoon (4 grams) granulated sugar, divided
2 tablespoons (28 grams) all-vegetable shortening
½ teaspoon (1.5 grams) kosher salt
½ cup (113 grams) boiling water
½ cup (128 grams) evaporated milk
1 large egg (50 grams)
4 to 5 cups (500 to 625 grams) all-purpose flour
Cottonseed oil*, for frying
1 cup (120 grams) confectioners' sugar

1. In a small bowl, stir together ½ cup (113 grams) warm water, yeast, and 1 teaspoon (4 grams) granulated sugar. Let stand until mixture is foamy, about 5 minutes.

2. In the bowl of a stand mixer fitted with the paddle attachment, beat shortening, salt, and remaining 3 tablespoons (36 grams) granulated sugar at medium speed until smooth. Add ½ cup (113 grams) boiling water and evaporated milk, beating until combined. Add egg, beating until smooth. Stir in yeast mixture. Gradually add 3 cups (375 grams) flour, beating until smooth. Beat in enough remaining flour to make a soft dough.

3. On a lightly floured surface, turn out dough, and knead until smooth and elastic, 6 to 8 minutes. Spray a large bowl with cooking spray. Place dough in bowl, turning to grease top. Cover and refrigerate for at least 30 minutes or up to 2 hours.

4. On a lightly floured surface, roll dough to ¼-inch thickness. Using a sharp knife, cut dough into 12 (3-inch) squares. (Do not reroll dough.)

5. In a large Dutch oven, pour oil to a depth of 3 inches, and heat over medium-high heat until a deep-fry thermometer registers 370°F (188°C). Working in batches, fry dough, turning frequently, until golden brown, 2 to 3 minutes. Carefully remove from hot oil, and let drain on paper towels. Sift confectioners' sugar over hot beignets. Serve warm.

Available on amazon.com. Vegetable oil can be used instead.

WINTERLAKE LODGE DOG BISCUITS

Makes about 25 treats

Recipe by Mandy Dixon

Very good dog treats for very good dogs. Mandy Dixon, chef of the Alaskan resort Winterlake Lodge, uses Cheddar or provolone cheese, but any semihard or hard cheese is loved and appreciated by the wild (but spoiled) northern sled dogs. If preferred, save your breakfast bacon grease and substitute for the butter.

2½ cups (313 grams) all-purpose flour
1 cup (100 grams) shredded Cheddar or provolone cheese
½ cup (120 grams) beef stock
¼ cup (57 grams) unsalted butter, melted
2 medium eggs (94 grams)

1. Preheat oven to 350°F (180°C). Line a baking sheet with parchment paper, and lightly spray with oil.

2. In a medium bowl, stir together flour, cheese, stock, and melted butter. Stir in eggs, and shape dough into a ball. On a lightly floured surface, knead dough until smooth and shiny. Roll dough to ½-inch thickness. Using a bone-shaped cookie cutter, cut dough. Place on prepared pan.
3. Bake for 15 minutes. Turn, and bake until golden brown, about 10 minutes more. Let cool on a wire rack.

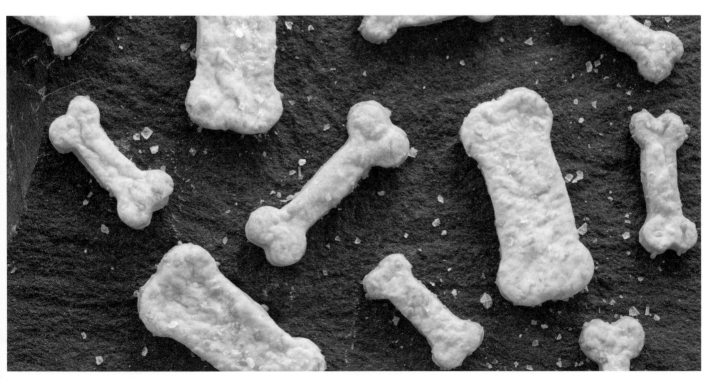

ROASTED TOMATO- AND MARINATED MOZZARELLA-STUFFED DOUGHNUTS

Makes 12 doughnuts

Recipe by Erin Jeanne McDowell

These doughnuts are equal parts soft, melty, and juicy. Roasted tomatoes and marinated mozzarella are stuffed inside a garlicky yeasted dough, which is then fried to golden perfection.

6   cups (750 grams) all-purpose flour
1½ cups (360 grams) whole milk, chilled
⅓   cup (67 grams) granulated sugar
¼   cup (57 grams) unsalted butter, melted
2   large eggs (100 grams)
1   tablespoon (9 grams) instant yeast
1   tablespoon (6 grams) garlic powder
2   teaspoons (6 grams) fine sea salt
Vegetable oil, for frying
Roasted Tomato and Marinated Mozzarella Filling
    (recipe follows)
1¼ cups (172 grams) finely grated Parmesan cheese

1. In the bowl of a stand mixer fitted with the dough hook attachment, beat flour, milk, sugar, melted butter, eggs, yeast, garlic powder, and sea salt at low speed for 3 minutes. Increase mixer speed to medium, and beat for 1 minute. Spray a large bowl with cooking spray. Place dough in bowl, turning to grease top. Cover with plastic wrap, and refrigerate overnight.
2. Remove dough from refrigerator, and let come to room temperature, 1 to 1½ hours.
3. In a medium stockpot, pour oil to a depth of 4 inches, and heat over medium heat until a deep-fry thermometer registers 325°F (170°C). Place a wire rack over a paper towel-lined baking sheet.
4. Divide dough into 12 (106-gram) pieces. Working with one piece of dough at a time, use your hands to press dough into a 4-inch round. Place 2 to 3 tomatoes and 2 mozzarella pearls from Roasted Tomato and Marinated Mozzarella Filling in center of round. Bring edges of dough around filling, and pinch to seal. Roll dough gently on a lightly floured surface to help seal dough and shape it into a round. Repeat with remaining dough and filling.
5. Preheat oven to 350°F (180°C). Place Parmesan in an even layer in a shallow bowl.
6. Working in batches, fry doughnuts until deeply golden brown and an instant-read thermometer inserted in center registers 190°F (88°C) to 200°F (93°C), 5 to 6 minutes. Remove using a slotted spoon, and place on prepared rack. Let drain for 30 seconds; toss in Parmesan to coat. Place on a baking sheet.
7. Bake for 8 to 10 minutes. (This ensures that doughnuts are cooked all the way through without overbrowning in the fryer.) Let cool for at least 5 minutes before serving.

ROASTED TOMATO AND MARINATED MOZZARELLA FILLING
Makes about 2¼ cups

2   cups (280 grams) cherry tomatoes
2   tablespoons (28 grams) extra-virgin
    olive oil
¾   teaspoon (1 gram) dried oregano
½   teaspoon crushed red pepper
Kosher salt and ground black pepper, to taste
24 fresh mozzarella pearls (230 grams)

1. Preheat oven to 300°F (150°C).
2. Place tomatoes in an even layer on a baking sheet. Drizzle with oil, and sprinkle with oregano, red pepper, salt, and black pepper.
3. Roast tomatoes until blistered and very soft, 40 to 45 minutes. Transfer to a medium bowl, and let cool completely.
4. Add mozzarella pearls to tomatoes, tossing to combine.

Photo by Mark Weinberg

RYE PARMESAN PIZZELLES

Makes about 24 pizzelles

Recipe by Erin Jeanne McDowell

These savory pizzelles are more like a cracker—delicious all on their own or as part of an epic cheese plate. The batter comes together as quickly and effortlessly as pancake batter.

1   cup (125 grams) all-purpose flour
½   cup (51 grams) rye flour
1½ cups (115 grams) finely grated Parmesan cheese
¼   cup (50 grams) granulated sugar
1   teaspoon (5 grams) baking powder
¼   teaspoon fine sea salt
¼   teaspoon ground red pepper
4   large eggs (200 grams)
½   cup (113 grams) unsalted butter, melted

1. In a large bowl, whisk together flours, cheese, sugar, baking powder, sea salt, and red pepper. Add eggs and melted butter, whisking until well combined.
2. Preheat a pizzelle iron*, and lightly spray with cooking spray.
3. Scoop 1 tablespoon batter into center of each cavity in iron. Close iron, and cook until golden brown, 1 to 2 minutes. Repeat with remaining batter. Let cool completely before serving.

We used a CucinaPro Non-Stick Electric Pizzelle Baker Press, available on amazon.com.

Photo by Mark Weinberg

PRALINES

Makes 24 pralines

Pecans plunged into buttery sugar is one of the most iconic Southern confections. Pecan pralines (we favor puh-CAWN PRAW-leens over PEE-can PRAY-leens) aren't difficult to make, but they can be tricky. The key is to stir often (at times, constantly) and pay attention. A long-handled spoon and a candy thermometer are your best friends here.

1½ cups (170 grams) pecan halves
2   tablespoons (28 grams) unsalted butter
1   cup (200 grams) granulated sugar
1   cup (220 grams) firmly packed light brown sugar
½   cup (120 grams) heavy whipping cream
2   tablespoons (42 grams) light corn syrup
1   teaspoon (4 grams) vanilla extract
¼   teaspoon kosher salt
⅛   teaspoon ground cinnamon

1. Preheat oven to 350°F (180°C).
2. On a rimmed baking sheet, spread pecans in an even layer. Bake until fragrant and toasted, 6 to 8 minutes. Let cool completely.
3. In a medium saucepan, melt butter over medium heat. Stir in sugars, cream, and corn syrup; bring to a boil. Cook, stirring constantly, until a candy thermometer registers 240°F (116°C). Remove from heat, and let stand until a candy thermometer registers 150°F (65°C), about 25 minutes. (Do not stir.)
4. Line a baking sheet with wax paper.
5. Add toasted pecans, vanilla, salt, and cinnamon to sugar mixture; stir quickly and vigorously until mixture loses some of its shine, about 1 minute. Quickly spoon mixture by heaping tablespoonfuls, and drop onto prepared pan. (If mixture hardens, add hot water, 1 tablespoon [15 grams] at a time, until mixture returns to a spoonable consistency.) Let cool until hardened, about 10 minutes. Store in an airtight container at room temperature for up to 1 week.

SOURDOUGH CHEESE CRACKERS

Makes about 400 snack-size crackers or
100 regular-size crackers

Recipe by Stacey Ballis

*I love a Cheez-It or Cheese Nip snack cracker,
but they are definitely a guilty pleasure. I came
up with a homemade version that was a bit
less guilt-inducing without losing the pleasure
part. This dough freezes beautifully. Double
the recipe and freeze half the dough to have
on hand if you have company coming. If you
want to change the flavor profile, you can use
different spices or herbs, or change the cheese.
I like them with smoked paprika and Manchego
or with herbes de Provence and Parmesan. I
cut them into small squares to mimic those
beloved snack crackers, but cut them any
shape or size you like.*

½ cup (65 grams) white whole wheat
    flour
½ cup (63 grams) all-purpose flour
2 teaspoons (1 gram) finely chopped
    fresh rosemary
¼ teaspoon (1.25 grams) baking soda

¼ teaspoon onion powder
¼ teaspoon dry mustard
¼ teaspoon kosher salt, plus more for
    sprinkling
⅛ teaspoon garlic powder
1 cup (275 grams) sourdough starter
    discard, room temperature
¼ cup (57 grams) salted butter, melted
    and cooled
½ cup (50 grams) freshly grated sharp or
    extra-sharp Cheddar cheese (see Note)

1. In a medium bowl, stir together flours,
rosemary, baking soda, onion powder,
mustard, salt, and garlic powder. In a large
bowl, stir sourdough discard to ensure it is
smooth. Add melted butter, stirring until
well combined. Stir in cheese. Add flour
mixture to discard mixture, and knead until
well combined. (You will get a very pliable
dough that is a bit like the texture of soft
clay. You should not need extra flour to
knead because the butter in the dough will
keep it from sticking.)

2. Place dough in resealable plastic bags, and
refrigerate for at least 8 hours or up to
24 hours. If in a hurry, the crackers will
bake after a 20-minute refrigeration, but
the longer rest period helps the flavor
really develop. (Dough can also be frozen.
Wrap tightly in plastic wrap, and place in
heavy-duty resealable plastic bags. Thaw in
refrigerator overnight before baking.)
3. Let dough stand at room temperature for
30 minutes.
4. Preheat oven to 350°F (180°C).
5. On a sheet of parchment paper, roll
dough to ⅛- to 1⁄16-inch thickness. Cut
dough into crackers. If you want snacking
crackers, cut smaller squares, but if you
want to use them for cheese or other
toppings, make them larger. I use a pizza
wheel cutter for this, but a sharp knife will
do fine. Slide parchment onto baking sheets.
Lightly spray top of crackers with cooking
spray, and very lightly sprinkle with salt.
6. Bake for 14 minutes, rotating and turning
pans halfway through baking. Turn oven off,
and let crackers stand in oven with door
closed for 10 to 15 minutes, watching them
carefully to ensure they don't burn. For
optimal flavor and texture, you want them
pretty golden brown but not too dark, and
you want them stiff and crispy. Let cool
completely on pans. Store in an airtight
container for up to 2 weeks, or freeze in
heavy-duty resealable plastic bags for up to
6 months.

Note: *Preshredded cheese contains starches
that are used to prevent it from clumping, but
the starches can inhibit melting and mixing.
You want a cracker with good cheese flavor,
but without being able to see the shreds of
cheese in the cracker. It's worth the extra
couple of minutes to shred cheese by hand on
the fine side of a box grater.*

Photo by Art Meripol

DIPLOMAT PUDDING

Makes 8 servings

Recipe by Szonja Márk

Reminiscent of the layered Italian dessert zuppa inglese, the custard-based Diplomat Pudding was a staple at Budapest's circa 1858 café Gerbeaud, served in individual metal molds and garnished with brandy-flavored, pink-tinged crème anglaise. Szonja Márk, owner and head baker of Budapest bakery Édesem, puts a homier riff on the classic. She prepares it in jars and swaps out the usual ladyfingers for miniature madeleines.

Miniature Madeleines (recipe follows)
Rum Syrup (recipe follows)
Diplomat Cream (recipe follows)
Garnish: whipped cream

1. Dip Miniature Madeleines in Rum Syrup. In each of 8 (4.7-ounce) jars, place 4 madeleines along sides. Place Diplomat Cream in a pastry bag, and pipe into jars to fill. Garnish with whipped cream, if desired.

MINIATURE MADELEINES

Makes about 48

2   large eggs (100 grams)
¼   cup plus 2½ tablespoons (80 grams) granulated sugar
2¼   teaspoons (16 grams) honey
⅔   cup plus 2 teaspoons (89 grams) all-purpose flour
1   teaspoon (5 grams) baking powder
1   teaspoon (1 gram) finely grated lemon zest
⅛   teaspoon kosher salt
⅓   cup plus 1 tablespoon (90 grams) unsalted butter, melted

1. In the bowl of a stand mixer fitted with the paddle attachment, beat eggs, sugar, and honey at medium speed until pale and tripled in volume.
2. In a medium bowl, whisk together flour, baking powder, zest, and salt. Fold flour mixture and melted butter into egg mixture. Cover and refrigerate for 2 hours.
3. Preheat oven to 375°F (190°C). Butter 2 (24-well) miniature madeleine pans. (See Note.)
4. Place batter in a piping bag, and pipe batter into prepared wells.
5. Bake for 5 to 6 minutes. Tap pans lightly to release cookies, and let cool completely on a wire rack.

Note: *You can also make the Diplomat Pudding with standard-size madeleines. Bake standard madeleines for 8 minutes, and place 2 madeleines in each jar.*

RUM SYRUP

Makes 1⅓ cups

½   cup (100 grams) granulated sugar
⅓   cup plus 1½ tablespoons (97 grams) water
½   cup (120 grams) fresh orange juice, strained
2   tablespoons (30 grams) dark rum

1. In a small saucepan, bring sugar and ⅓ cup plus 1½ tablespoons (97 grams) water to a boil over medium heat. Pour into a small bowl; add orange juice and rum. Let cool to room temperature.

DIPLOMAT CREAM

Makes 5 cups

2   cups (480 grams) whole milk
½   cup (100 grams) granulated sugar, divided
1   vanilla bean, split lengthwise, seeds scraped and reserved
5   large egg yolks (93 grams)
¼   cup plus 1 tablespoon (40 grams) cornstarch
⅛   teaspoon kosher salt
2   tablespoons (30 grams) dark rum
1   tablespoon (15 grams) diced candied orange peel*
1   tablespoon (14 grams) diced candied lemon peel*
1   tablespoon (13 grams) chopped candied maraschino cherries*
1¼   cups (300 grams) heavy whipping cream

1. In a large saucepan, combine milk, ¼ cup (50 grams) sugar, and vanilla bean and reserved seeds. Bring to a boil over medium-low heat.
2. In a large bowl, whisk together egg yolks, cornstarch, salt, and remaining ¼ cup (50 grams) sugar. Slowly add hot milk mixture to egg mixture, whisking constantly. Return mixture to pan, and cook until thickened. Immediately transfer to a medium bowl. Stir in rum, candied citrus peels, and candied cherries. Cover with a piece of plastic wrap, pressing wrap directly onto surface of pastry cream to prevent a skin from forming. Refrigerate until chilled, at least 4 hours or overnight.
3. In the bowl of a stand mixer fitted with the whisk attachment, beat cream at medium speed until stiff peaks form. Fold whipped cream into chilled pastry cream. Use immediately.

We used Paradise Diced Orange Peel, Paradise Diced Lemon Peel, and Paradise Red Cherries, available at amazon.com.

RHUBARB AND GINGER CRUMBLE

Makes 6 servings

Recipe by Edd Kimber

Crumble is one of those dishes that we Brits grow up with. Apple crumble made almost a weekly appearance in my childhood home, generally after my mum would cook us a traditional Sunday roast. Rhubarb is something I didn't really appreciate as a kid, its sharpness off-putting and unusual to me. Thankfully, as an adult, I have grown to absolutely love it, and it has become one of my favourite ingredients to use. The benefit of a crumble is its ease, and this one is the work of just minutes.

6   cups (600 grams) (1-inch) pieces rhubarb
⅓ to ⅔ cup (67 to 133 grams) castor sugar*
2   tablespoons (16 grams) cornflour/cornstarch
2   teaspoons (12 grams) vanilla bean paste
¼   teaspoon ground cardamom
Ginger Crumble (recipe follows)
Vanilla Custard (recipe on page 62), to serve

1. Preheat oven to 350°F (180°C).
2. In a large bowl, toss together rhubarb, castor sugar, cornflour, vanilla bean paste, and cardamom. Pour into a 9-inch square roasting or cake pan. Top with Ginger Crumble.
3. Bake until crumble is golden and filling is bubbly, 50 to 60 minutes. Let cool for 5 to 10 minutes. Serve with Vanilla Custard.

Use ⅓ cup (67 grams) castor sugar for sharper rhubarb flavor.

GINGER CRUMBLE
Makes about 3 cups

1¼   cups (156 grams) plain/cake flour
½   cup (100 grams) castor sugar
2   teaspoons (4 grams) ground ginger
½   cup plus 1 tablespoon (127 grams) cold unsalted butter, cubed
1   cup (80 grams) jumbo old-fashioned oats

1. In a small bowl, stir together flour, sugar, and ginger. Add cold butter, tossing to coat. Using a pastry blender, cut in butter until mixture is crumbly. Stir in oats.

PRO TIPS
The exact size of your pan doesn't matter. Depending on what you have available, you can have a crumble with thicker or thinner layers. I often divide my crumble into two large pie plates and freeze one of the crumbles assembled, ready to bake.

Crumble can be made ahead of time and frozen in a heavy-duty resealable plastic bag. Use straight from the freezer to make dessert incredibly quick and simple.

Photo by Yuki Sugiura

QUEEN OF PUDDINGS

Makes 6 servings

Recipe by Edd Kimber

The roots for this pudding can be traced as far back as the 17th century, but in this form, it is thought to be named for Queen Victoria, who was said to be a fan of this very traditional, even old-fashioned, British pudding. My version is fairly traditional, although I prefer a Swiss meringue to the more classic French, but feel free to use whichever you prefer. If you want to put a little twist on this pudding, add a teaspoon or two of rose water to the raspberry mixture, a flavour combo I am crazy about.

1¼ cups (300 grams) whole milk
¾ cup (180 grams) heavy whipping cream
¼ cup (57 grams) unsalted butter
2 teaspoons (8 grams) vanilla extract
Peel of 1 lemon (30 grams)
3 large egg yolks (56 grams)

⅔ cup (133 grams) plus 2 tablespoons (24 grams) castor sugar, divided
2 cups (75 grams) stale bread crumbs
¼ cup (80 grams) raspberry jam
2 tablespoons (30 grams) water
¾ cup (98 grams) fresh raspberries
2 large egg whites (60 grams)

1. Preheat oven to 275°F (140°C).
2. In a medium saucepan, bring milk, cream, butter, vanilla, and lemon peel to a simmer over medium-low heat.
3. In a medium bowl, whisk together egg yolks and 2 tablespoons (24 grams) sugar. Whisking constantly, pour hot milk mixture over yolk mixture. Remove lemon peel, and stir in bread crumbs. Pour mixture into an 8-inch oval-shaped ovenproof baking dish.
4. Bake until custard is set, 20 to 30 minutes.
5. In a small saucepan, heat jam and 2 tablespoons (30 grams) water over

medium-low heat. Pour warm jam over raspberries, and fold together to coat. Set aside.
6. In the top of a double boiler, whisk together egg whites and remaining ⅔ cup (133 grams) sugar. Cook over simmering water until sugar is dissolved. Transfer mixture to the bowl of a stand mixer fitted with the whisk attachment, and beat at high speed until stiff peaks form, about 7 minutes.
7. Carefully spread raspberry mixture onto custard. Place meringue in a piping bag fitted with a round tip, and pipe peaks over raspberry mixture. Using a kitchen torch, brown meringue. Serve warm.

Photo by Yuki Sugiura

CHESTNUT AND HONEY MADELEINES

Makes about 24 madeleines

Recipe by Zoë François

Roasted chestnuts offer a rich yet subtle flavor and seasonal flare to this French treat from the Lorraine region in northeastern France. I paired the chestnut with bold honey and a touch of dark chocolate. Use chestnut honey if you can find it (available online), but any strong honey will do nicely.

13	tablespoons (182 grams) unsalted butter
⅔	cup (128 grams) roasted peeled chestnuts*
1⅓	cups (200 grams) confectioners' sugar, divided
6	large egg whites (180 grams)
1	tablespoon plus 1 teaspoon (28 grams) strong-flavored honey
½	cup plus 1 tablespoon (71 grams) all-purpose flour
¼	teaspoon kosher salt
4	ounces (115 grams) dark chocolate, melted

1. In a medium saucepan, melt butter over medium heat. Cook until butter turns a medium-brown color and has a nutty aroma, about 8 minutes. Remove from heat, and let cool slightly.

2. In a nut grinder, grind chestnuts and 1 tablespoon (7 grams) confectioners' sugar until a smooth paste forms.

3. In the bowl of a stand mixer fitted with the whisk attachment, beat egg whites at medium speed until foamy. With mixer on low speed, add honey and remaining 193 grams confectioners' sugar, beating to combine. Beat in browned butter and chestnut paste. Add flour and salt, beating until combined. Refrigerate until well chilled, at least 1 hour or overnight.

4. Preheat oven to 350°F (180°C). Generously butter and flour a madeleine pan.

5. Spoon batter into prepared wells, filling three-fourths full. Smooth batter, and freeze for 5 minutes.

6. Bake until edges are caramel colored, about 12 minutes. Let cool in pan for 1 minute. Remove from pan, and let cool completely on a wire rack. Drizzle with melted chocolate. Cookies are best eaten the day they are baked.

*I used prepackaged roasted peeled chestnuts, commonly found online or in Asian markets or some grocery stores such as Whole Foods and Trader Joe's.

Photo by Zoë François

RECIPE INDEX

index

CREDITS

Cover photography by Jim Bathie

Bake from Scratch Photographers: Jim Bathie, William Dickey, Marcy Black Simpson, Stephanie Welbourne Steele

Bake from Scratch Food Stylists/Recipe Developers: Laura Crandall, Nancy Hughes, Ashley Jones, Elizabeth Stringer

Bake from Scratch Stylists: Sidney Bragiel, Mary Beth Jones, Beth K. Seeley

Contributing Photographers: Matt Armendariz **6, 11, 205, 206** Stephen DeVries **13, 366** (bottom right photo) Yuki Sugiura **61** Mark Weinberg **238** (top left photo), **366** (top right and bottom left photos)

Contributing Food Stylists/Recipe Developers: Marian Cooper Cairns **6, 11, 205, 206** Erin Jeanne McDowell **336** (top right photo) Jesse Szewcyk **238** (top left photo), **366** (bottom left photo)

Contributing Food Stylists/Recipe Developers & Photographers: Erin Clarkson **257** Rebecca Firth **256** (bottom right photo) Laura Kasavan **336** (top left photo) Kelsey Siemens **223** Cenk Sönmezsoy **238** (bottom right photo) Joshua Weissman **256** (bottom left photo)